Atelier Ryza 3
Alchemist of the End & the Secret Key

OFFICIAL VISUAL COLLECTION

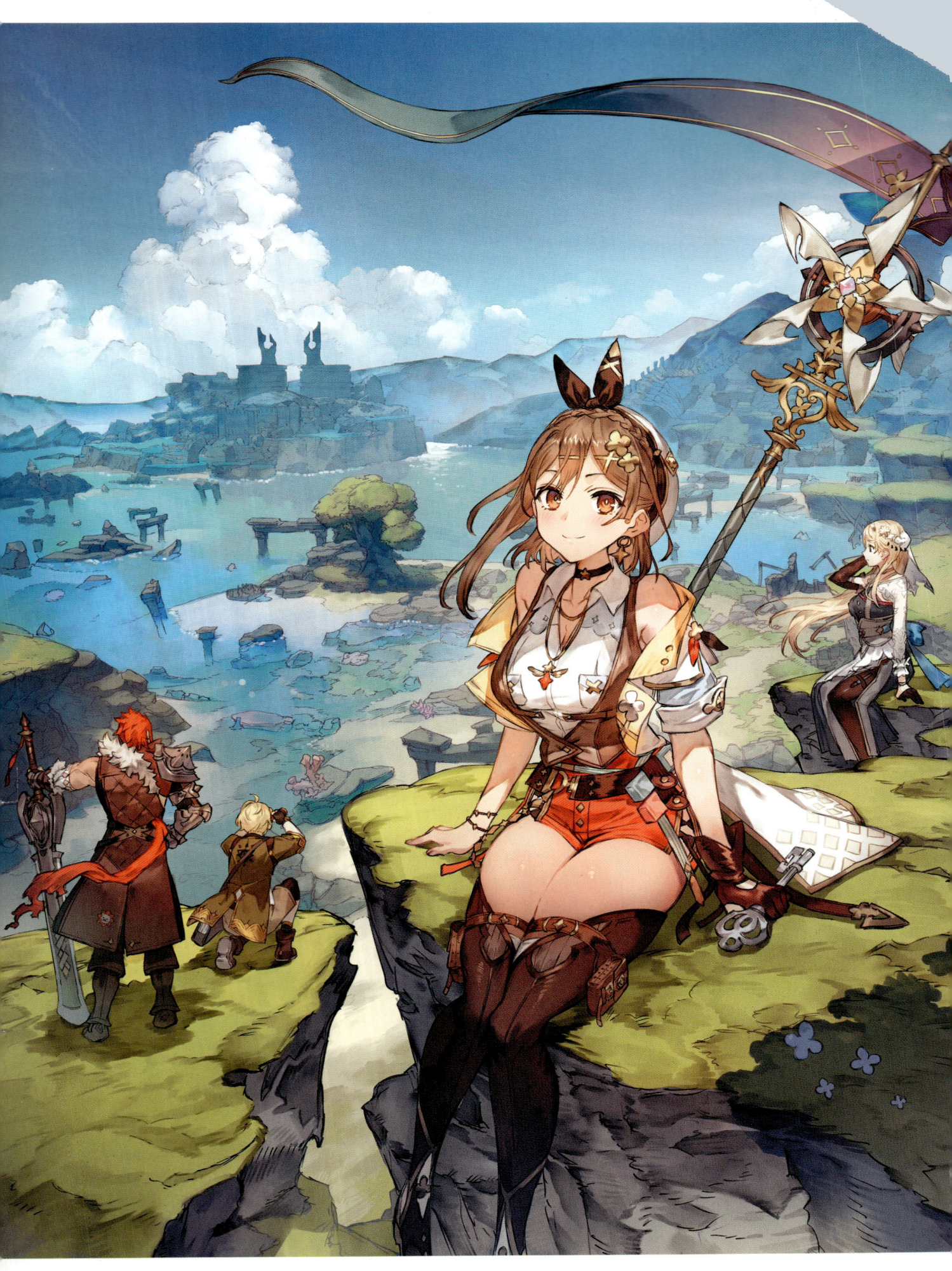

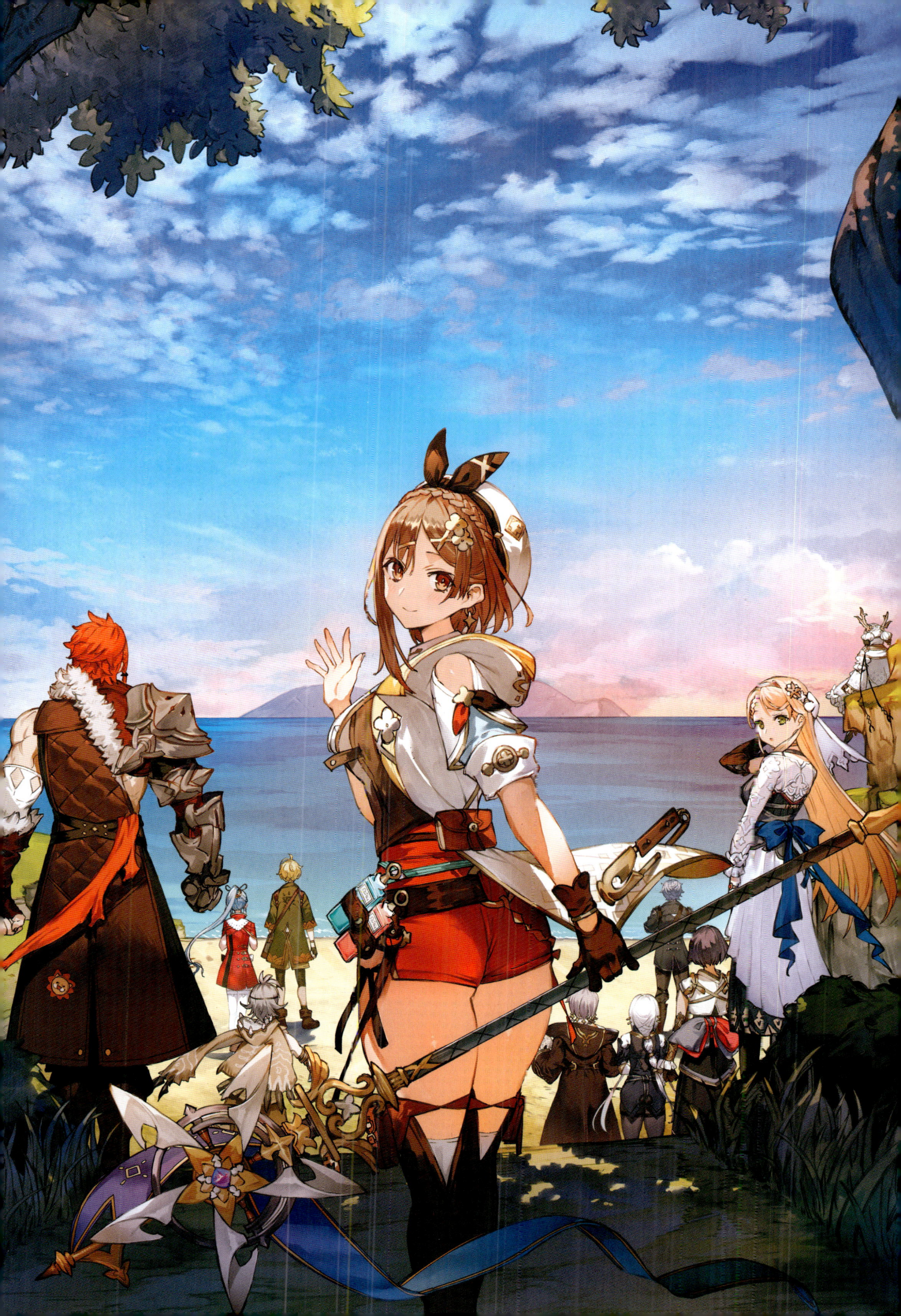

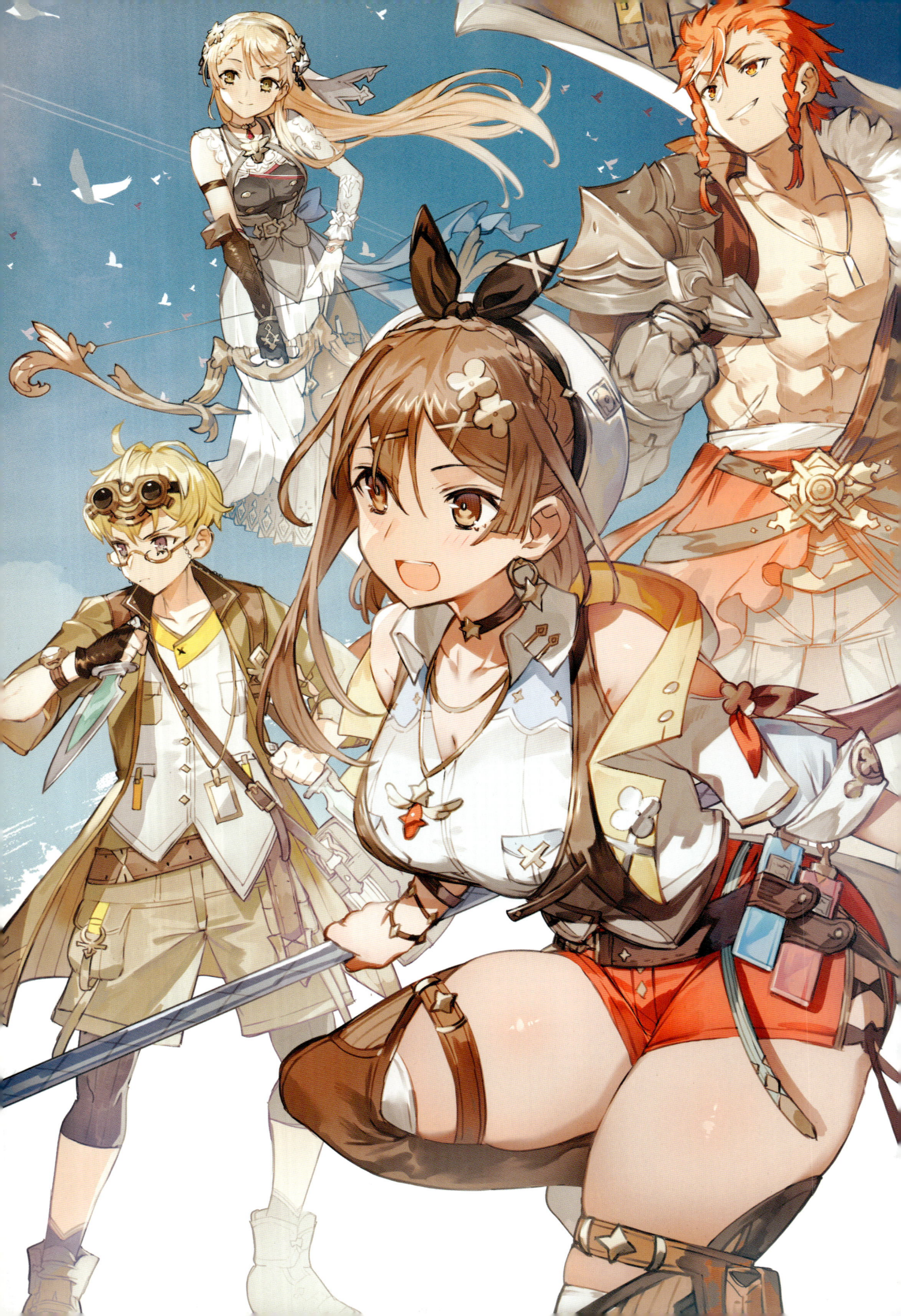

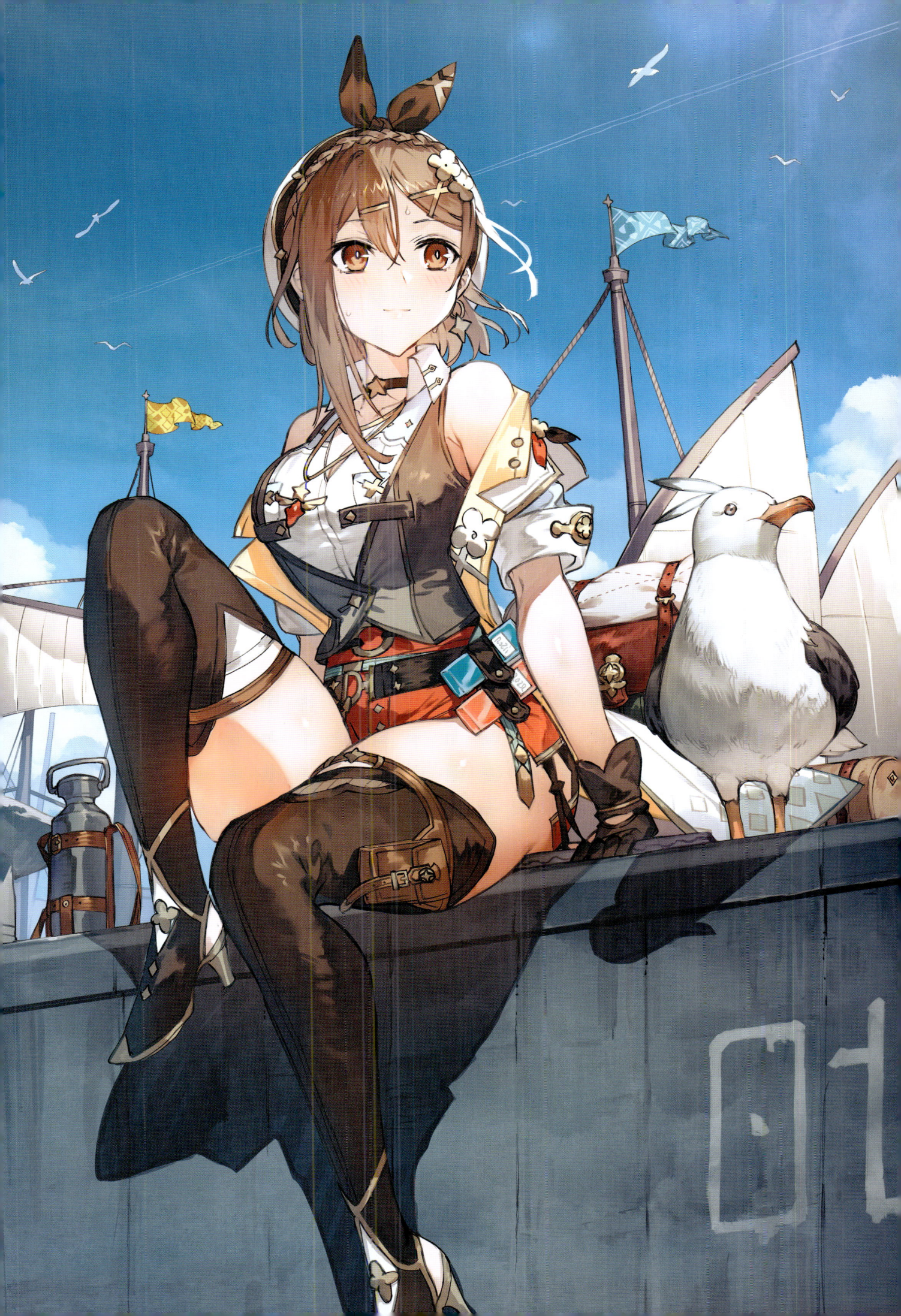

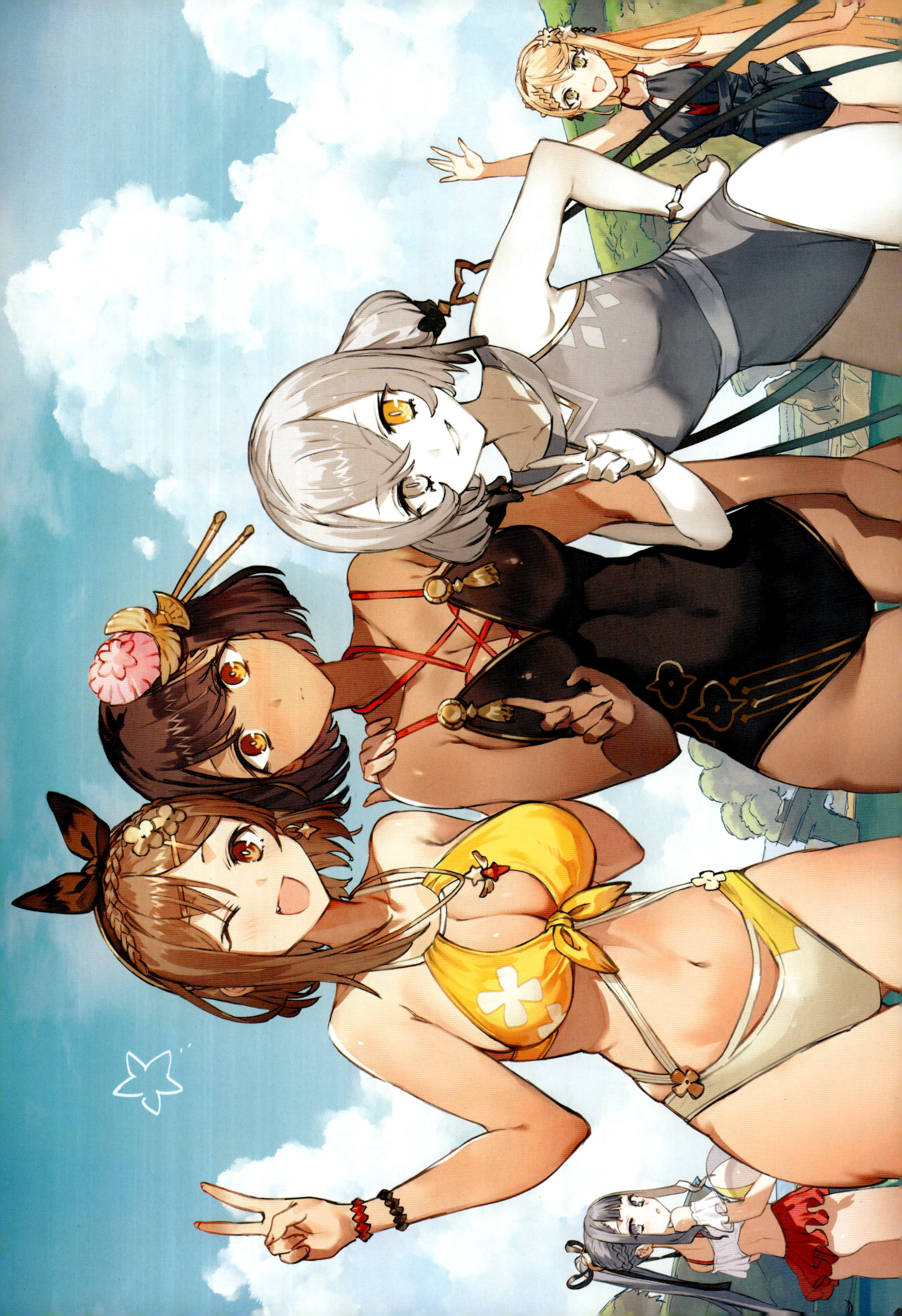

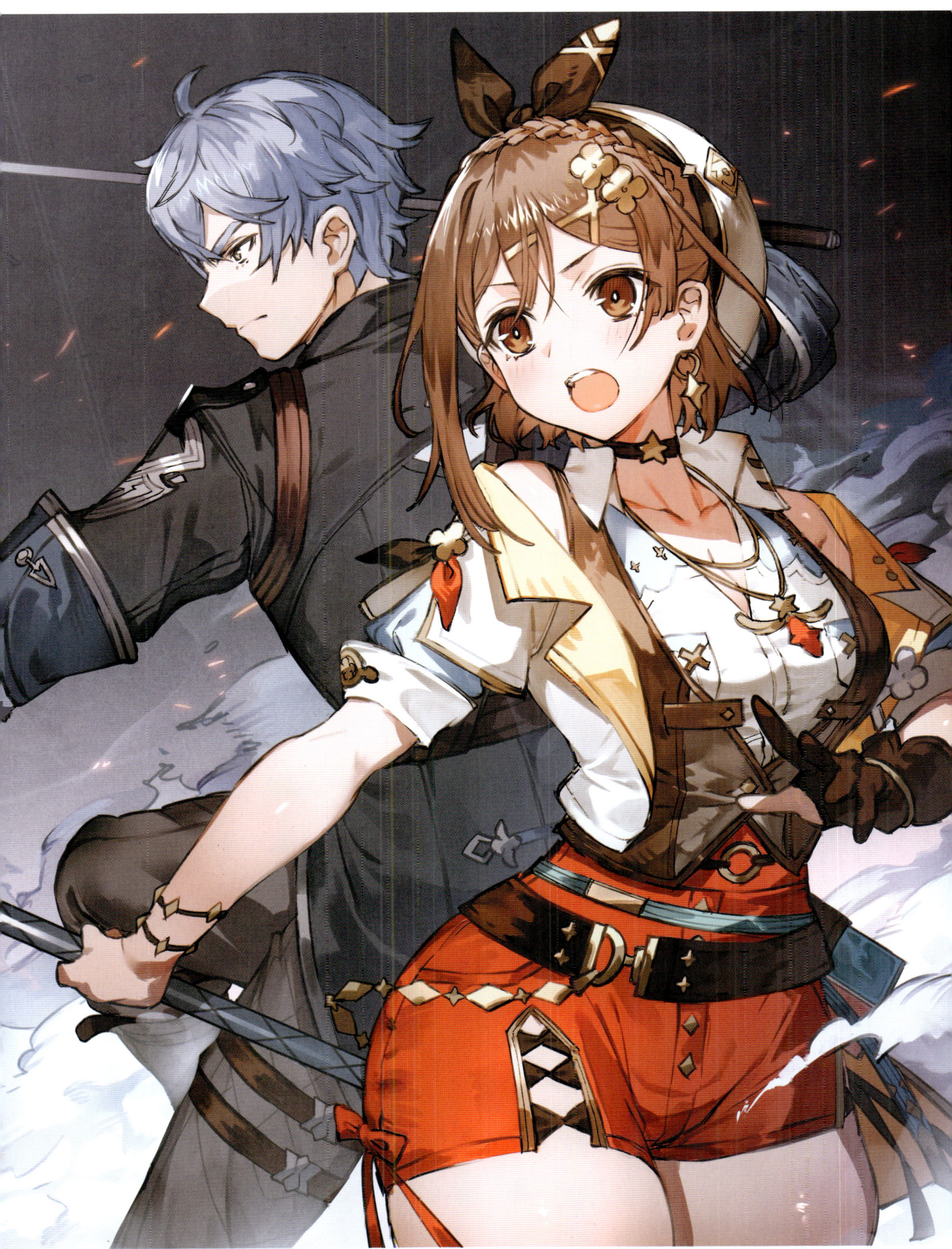

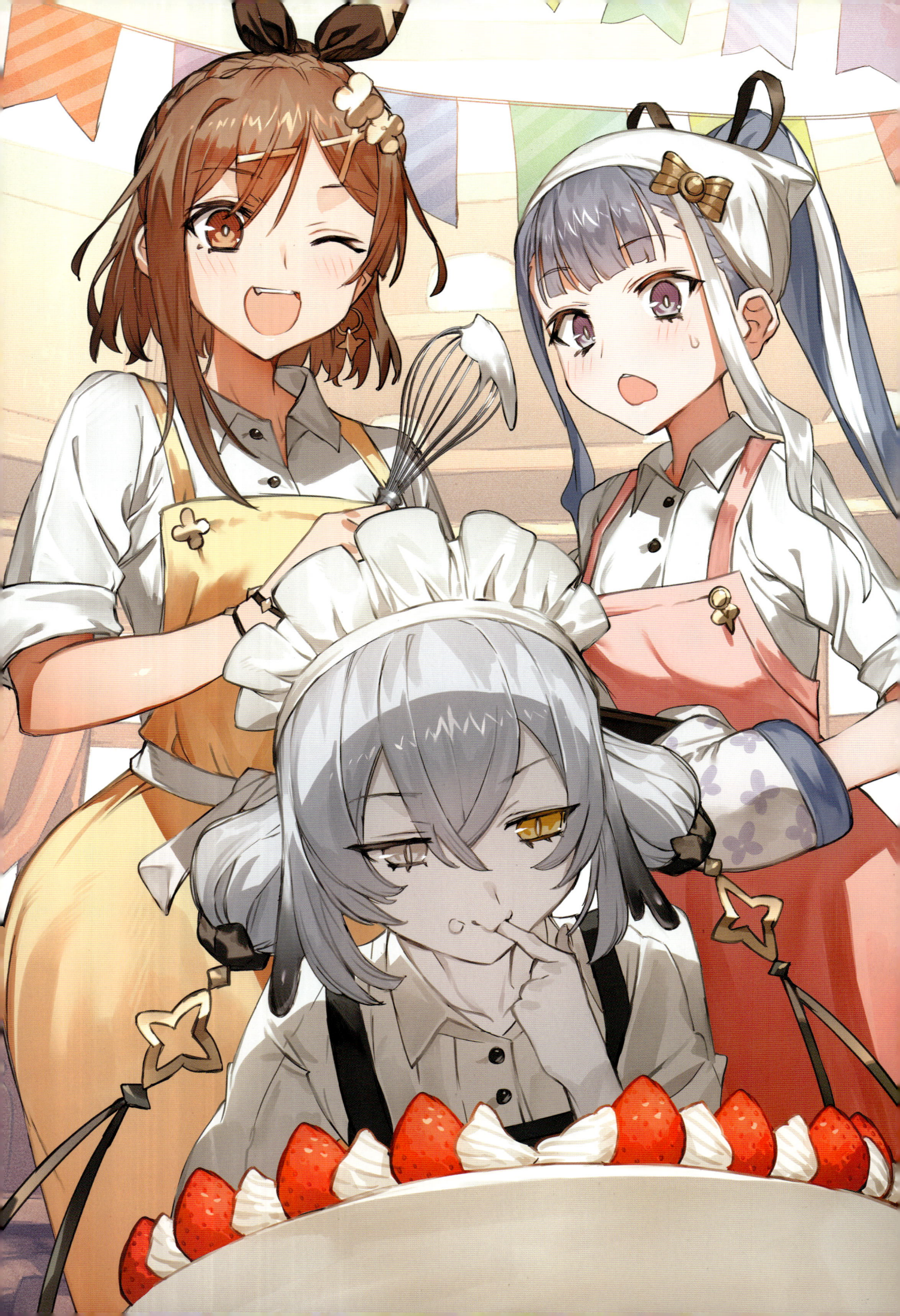

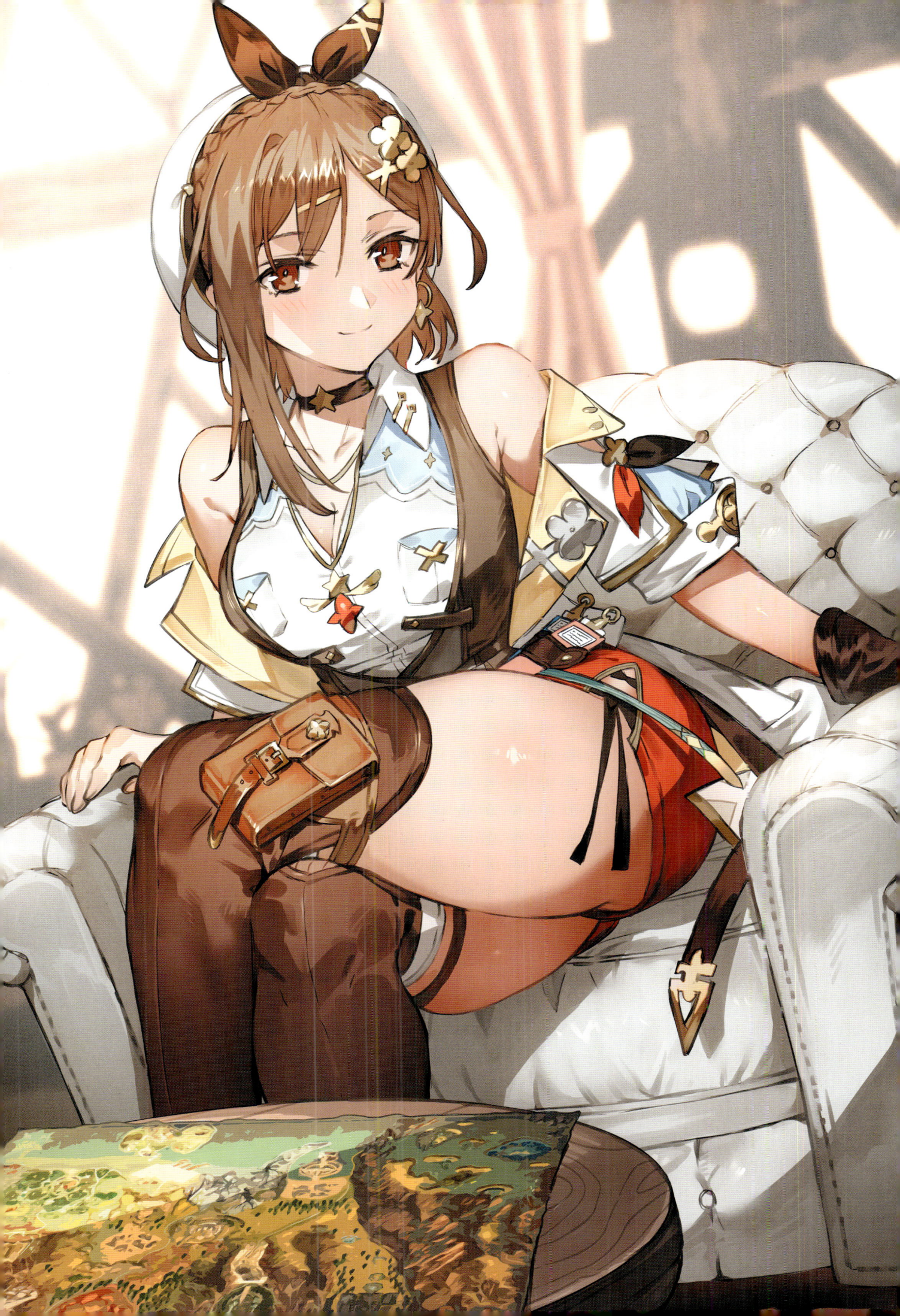

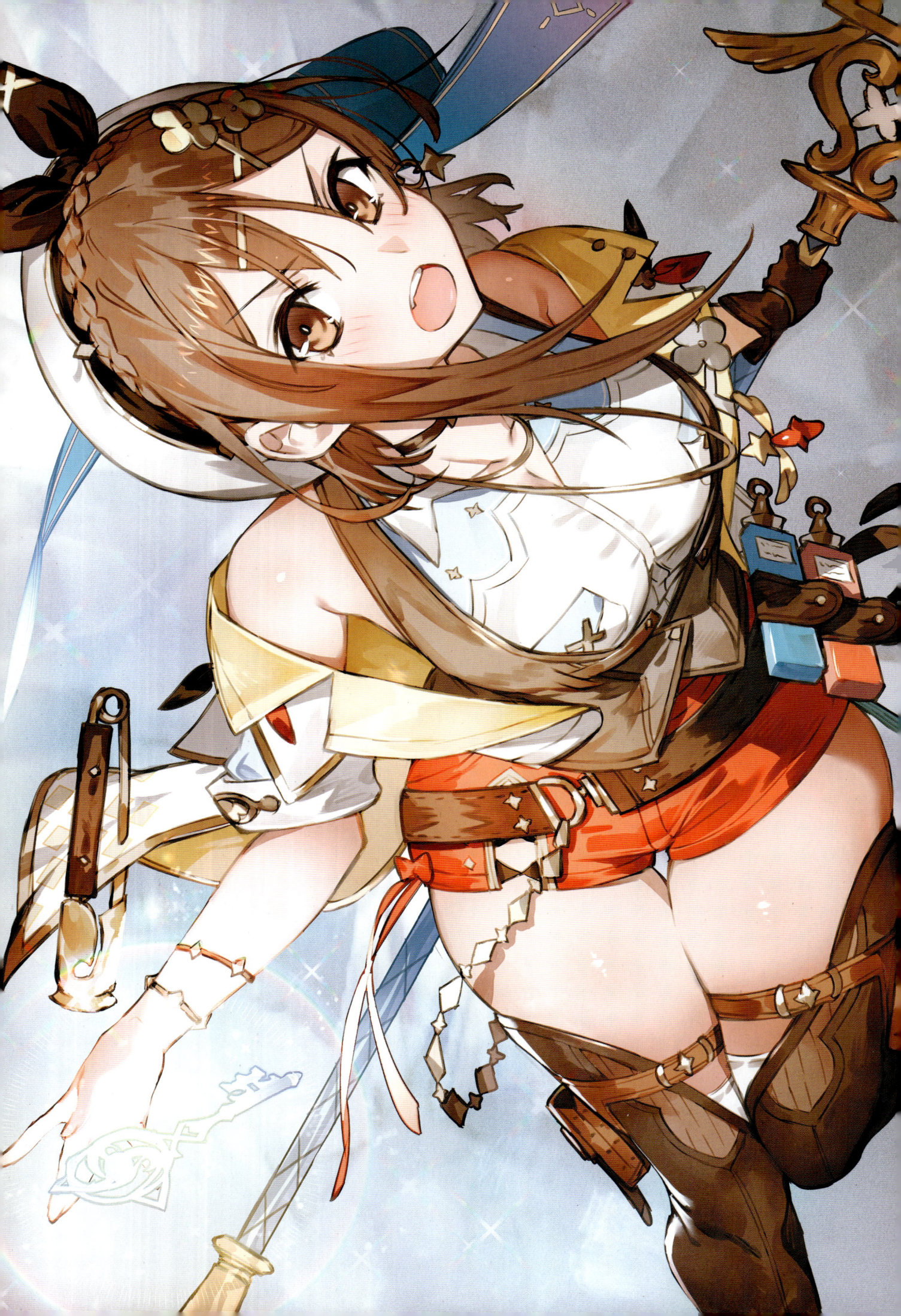

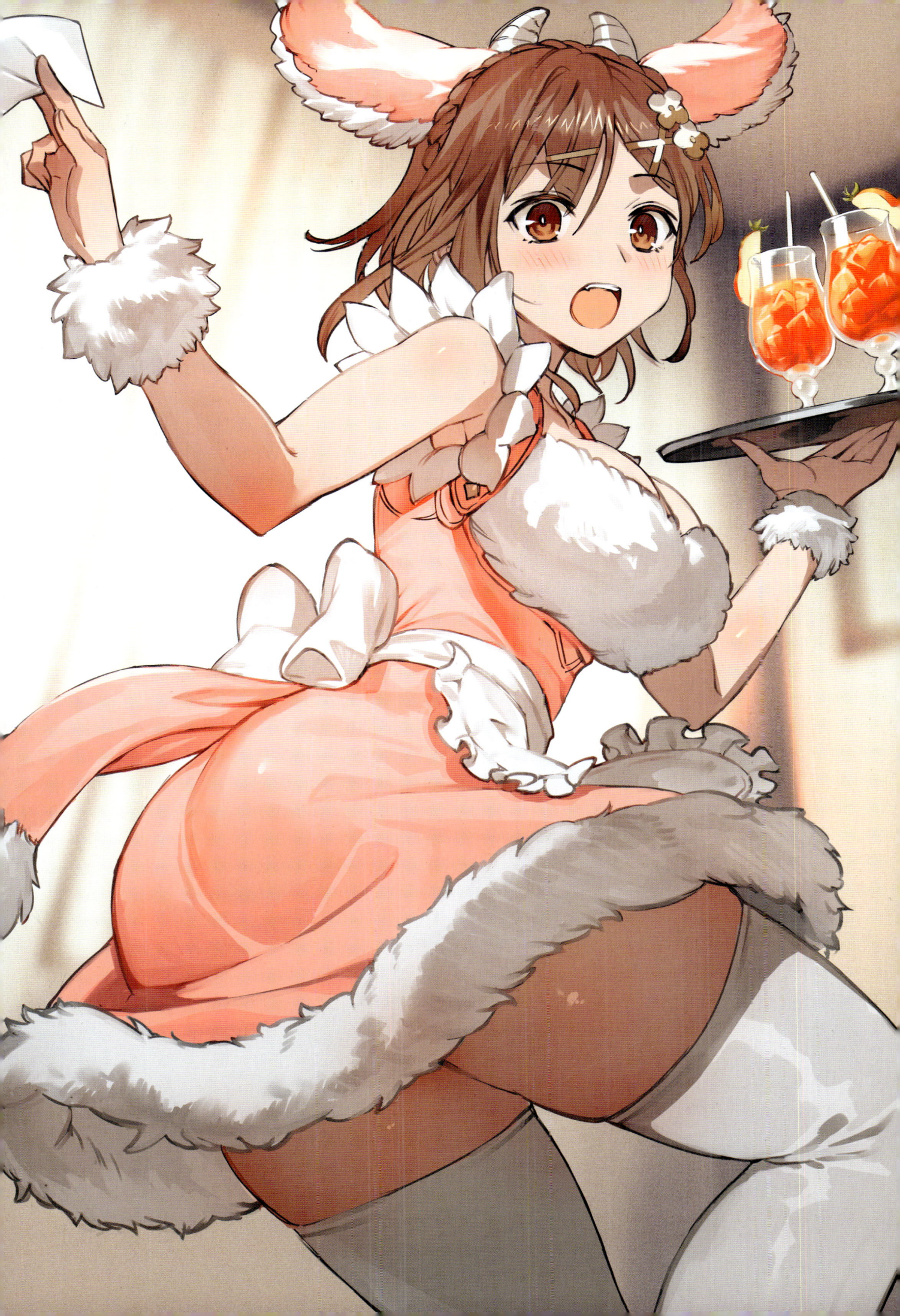

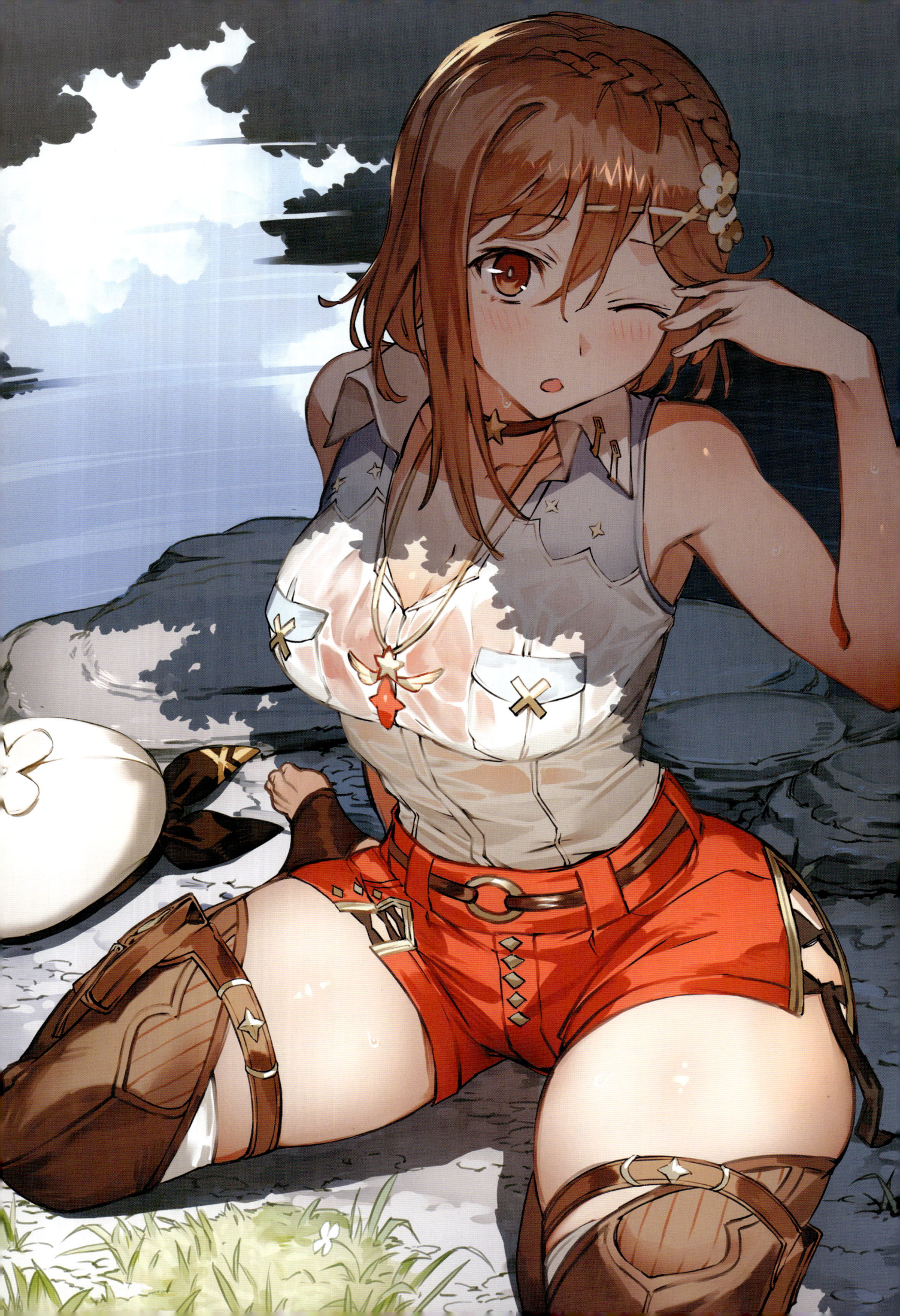

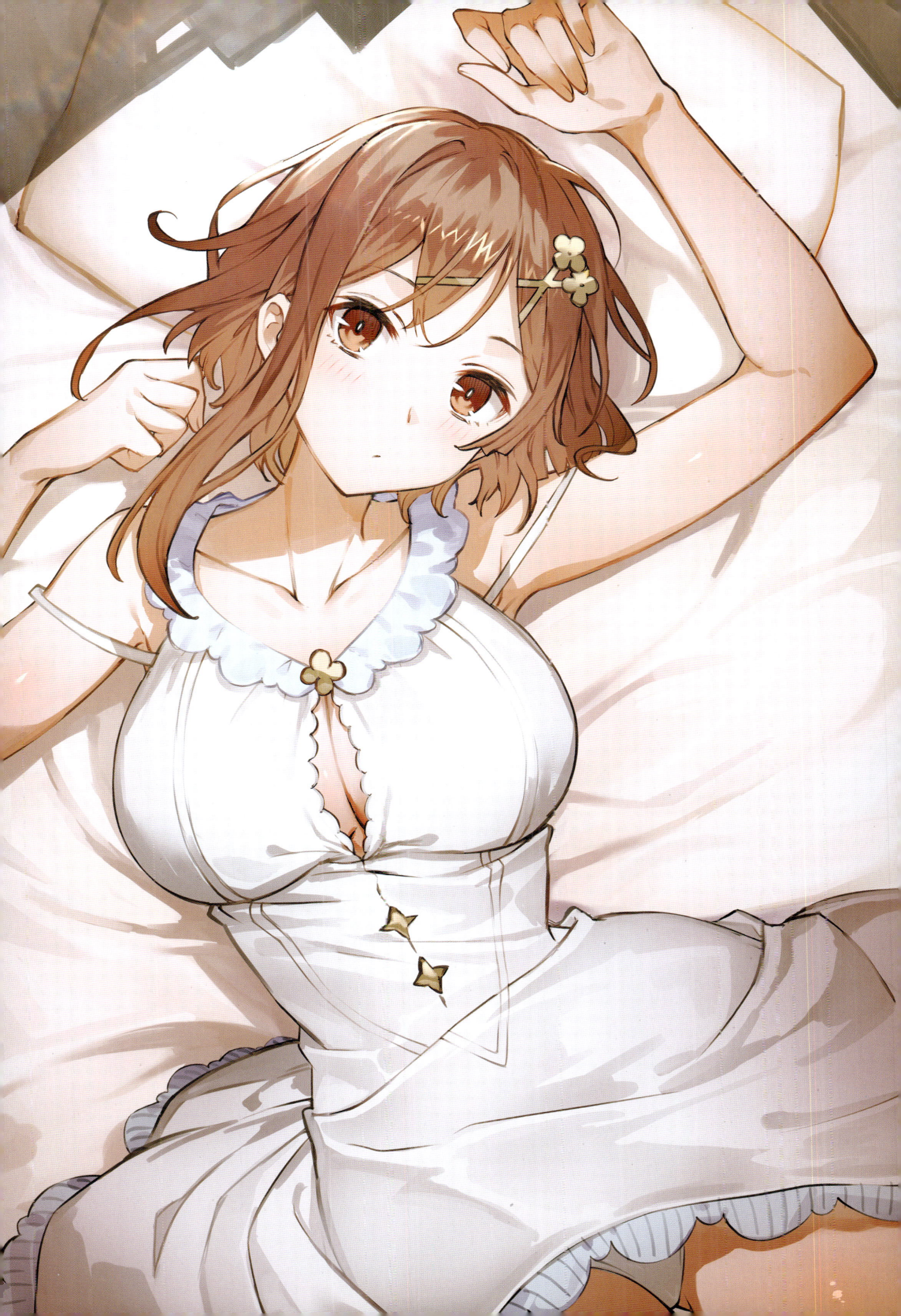

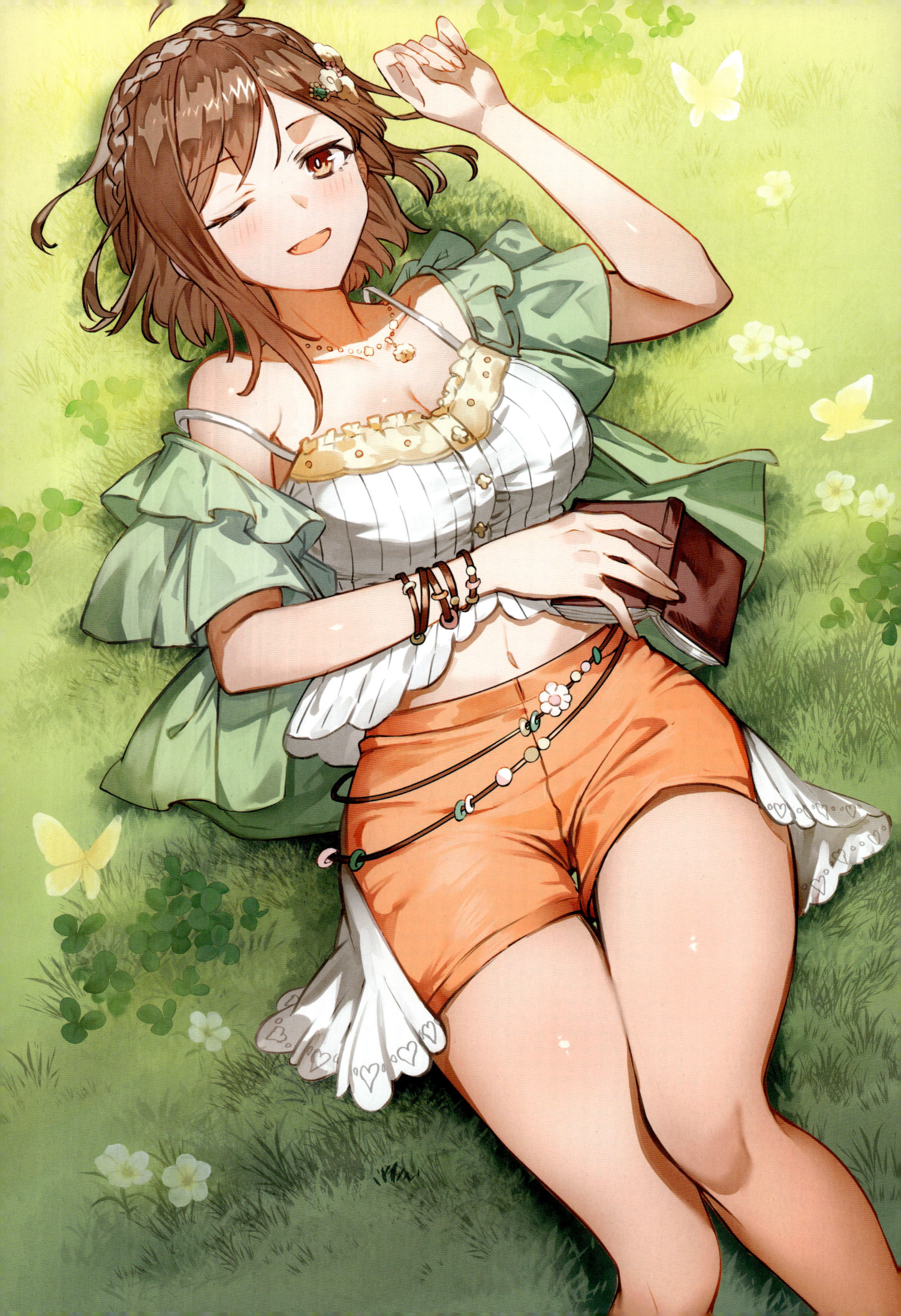

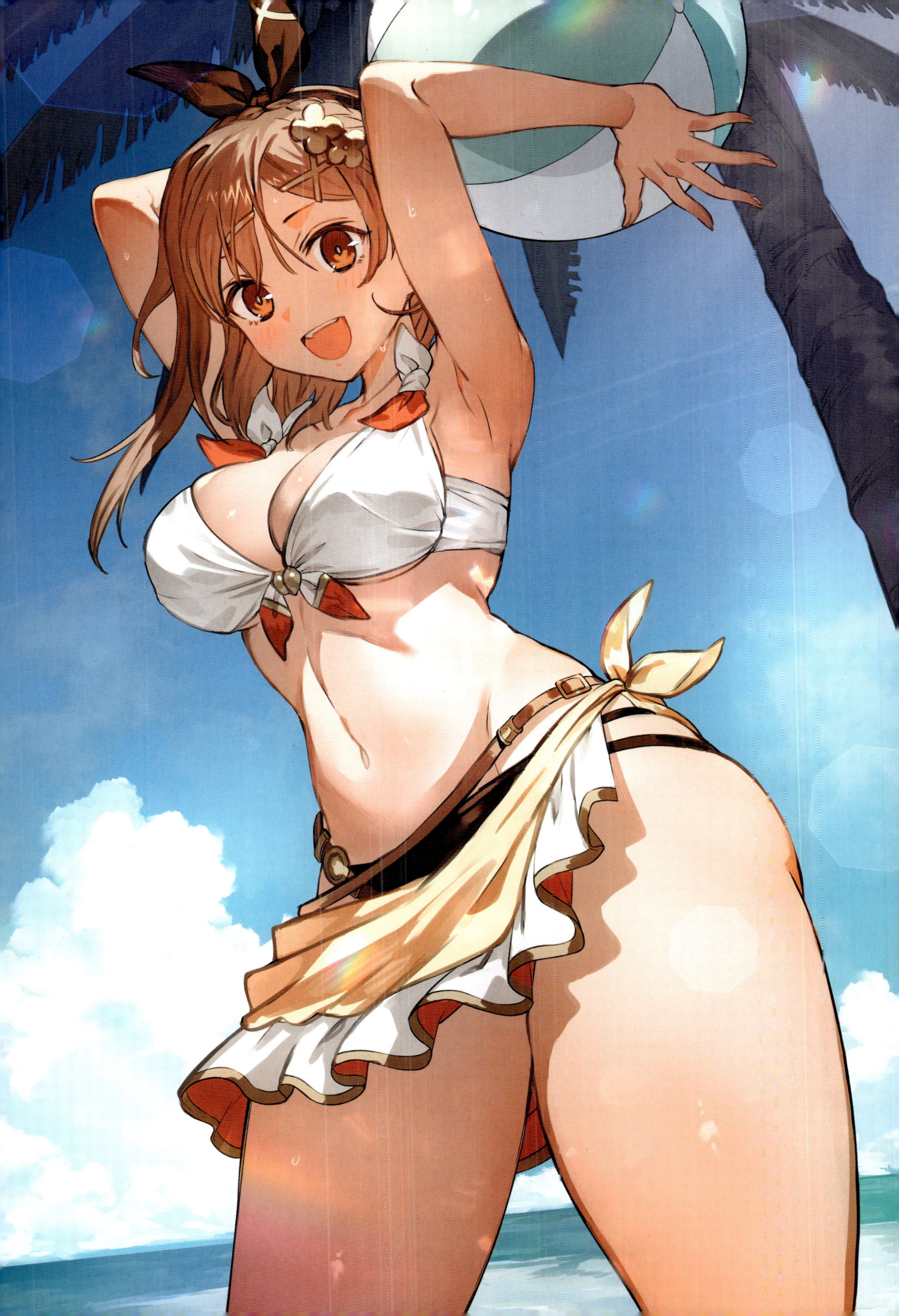

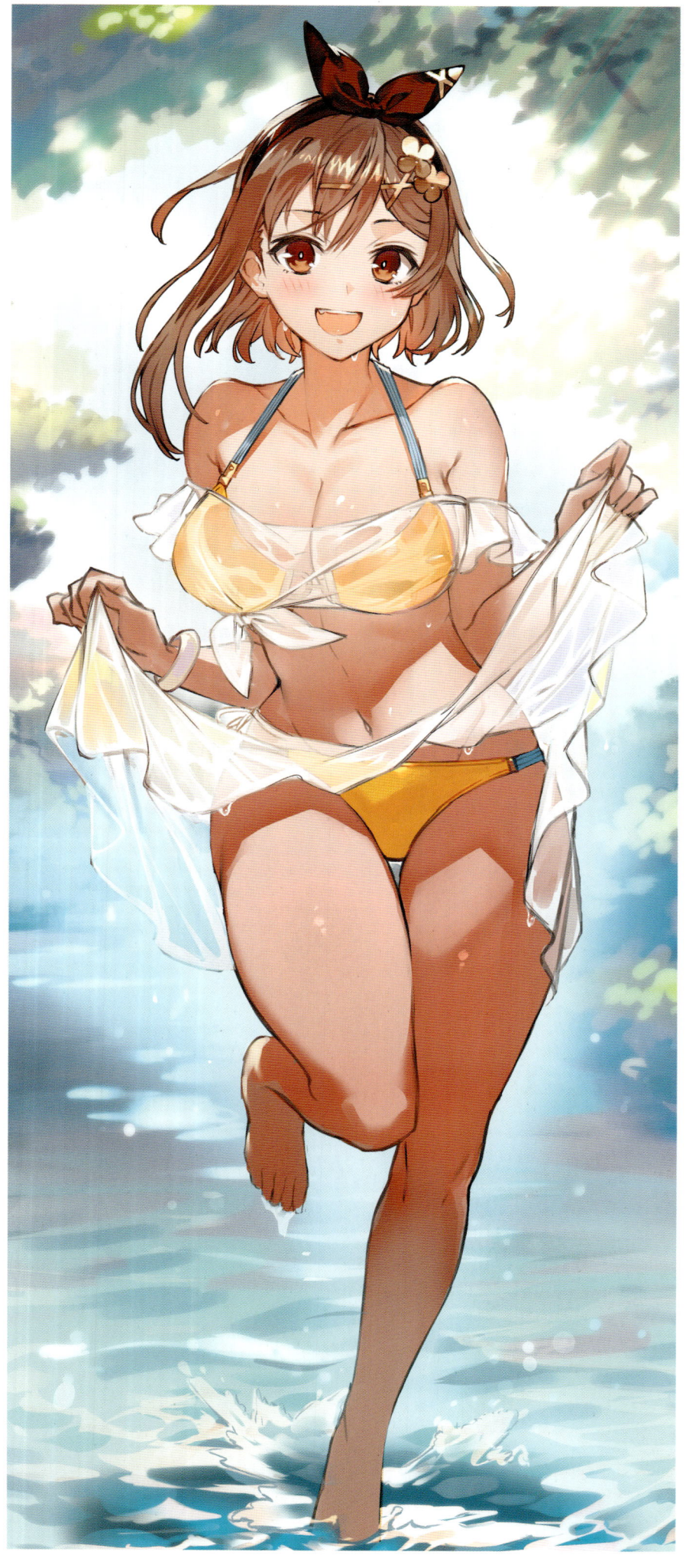

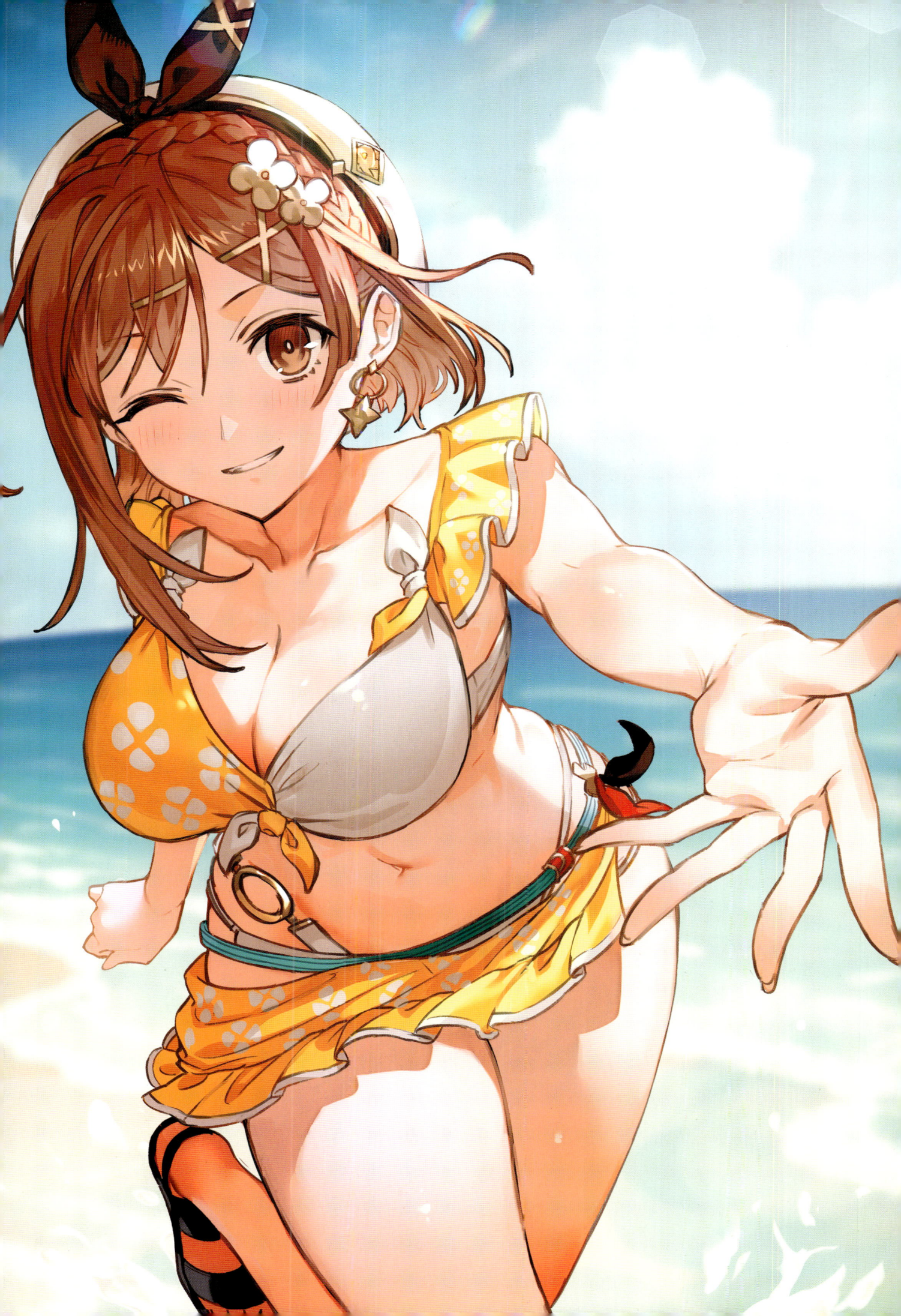

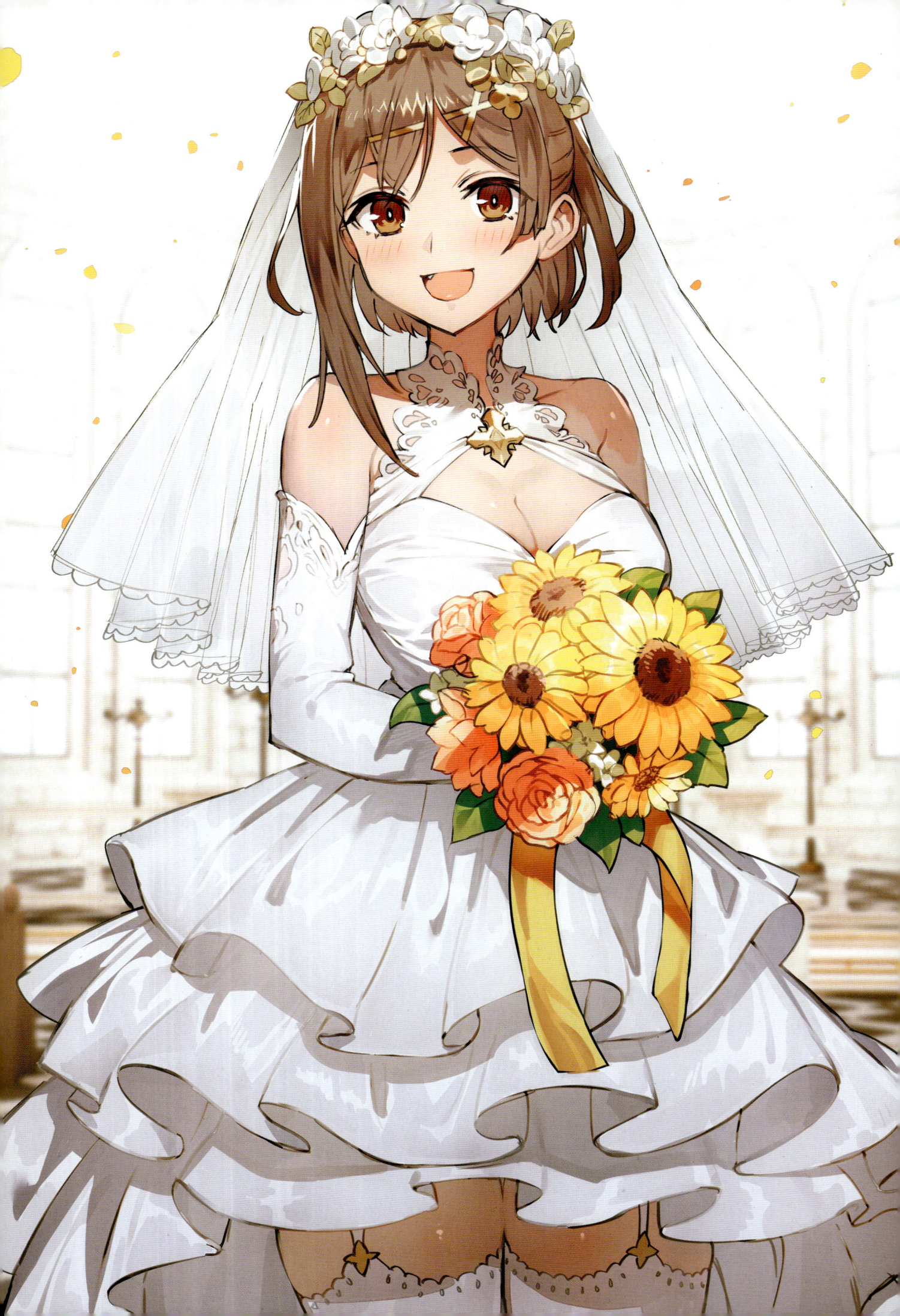

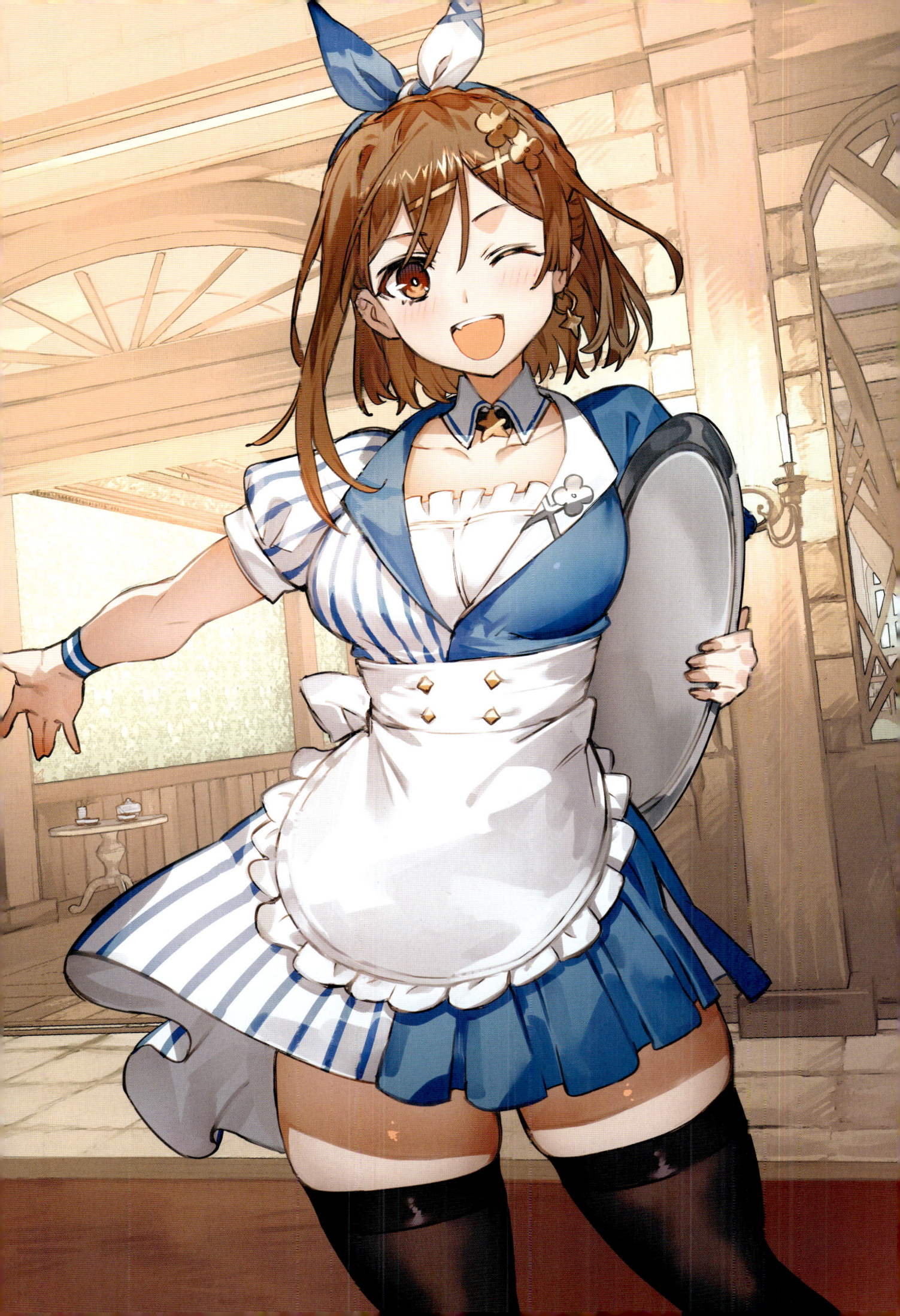

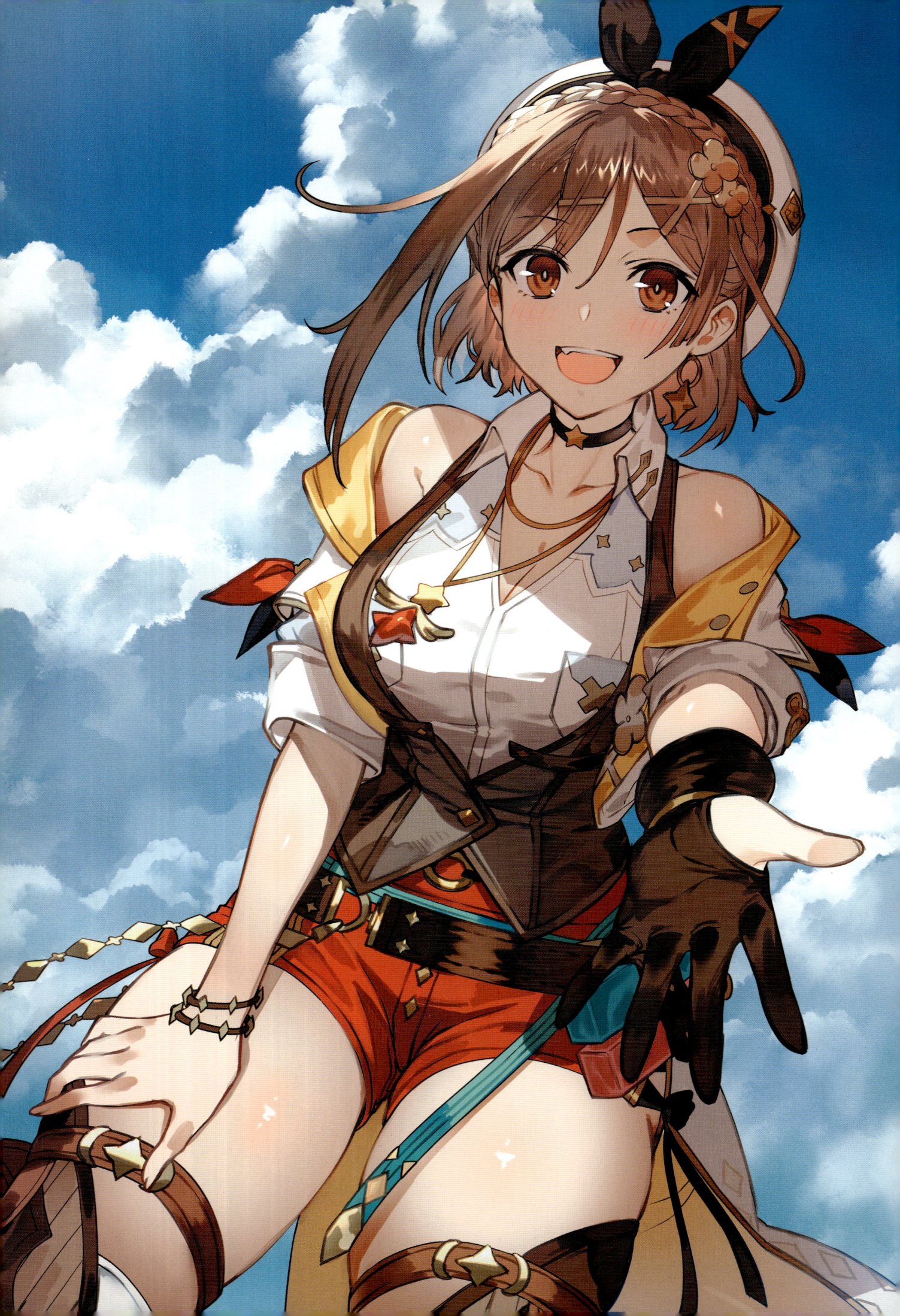

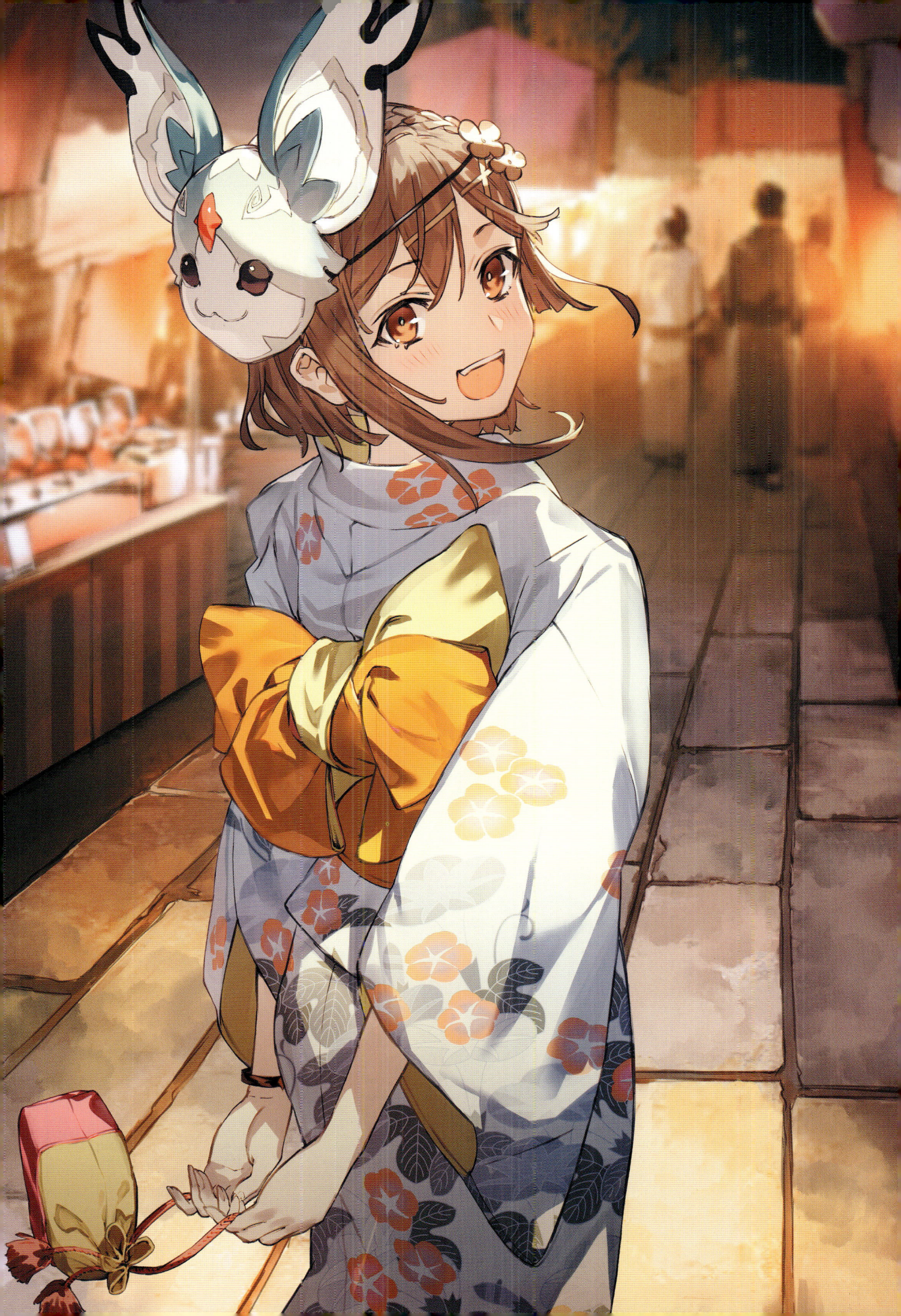

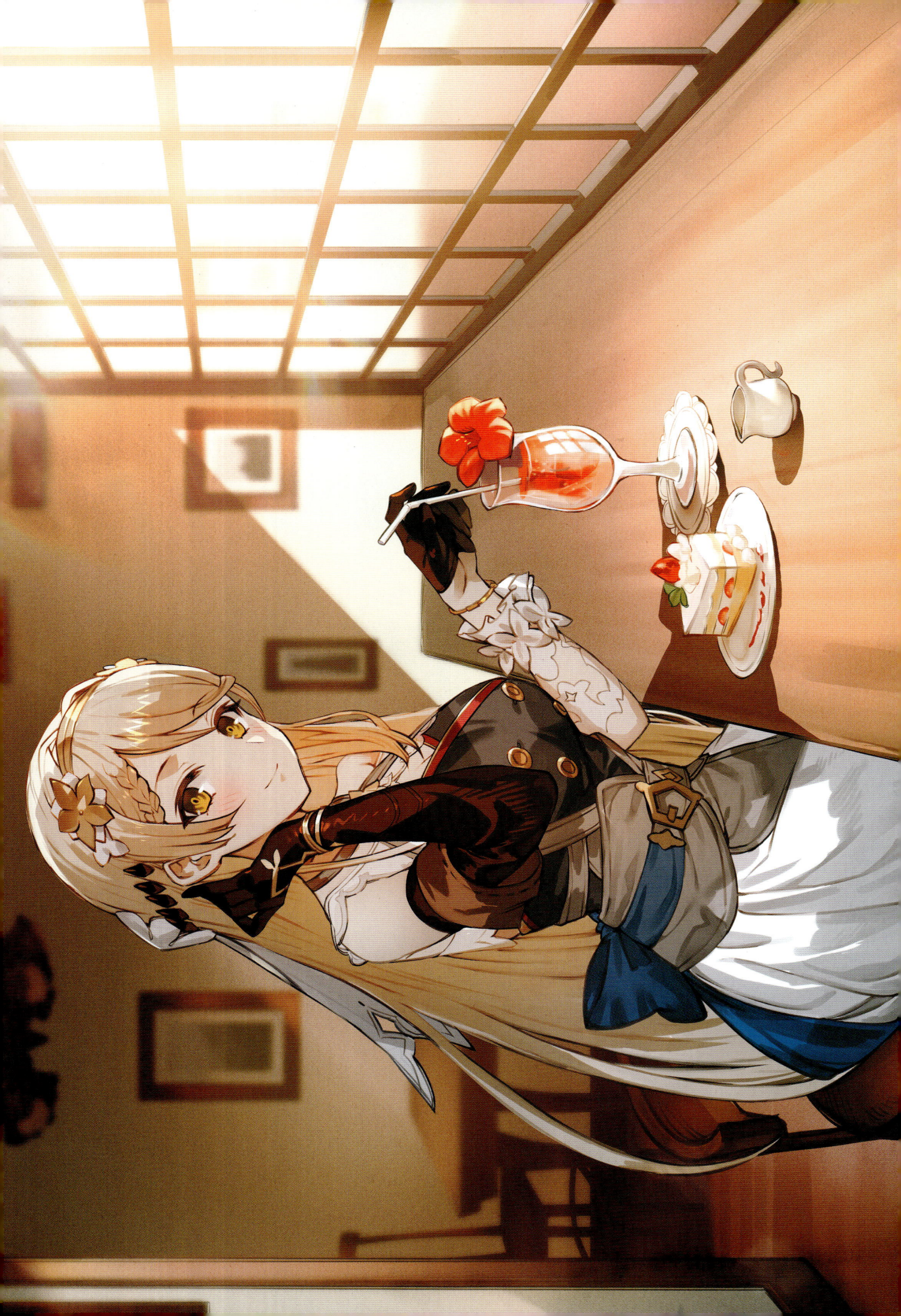

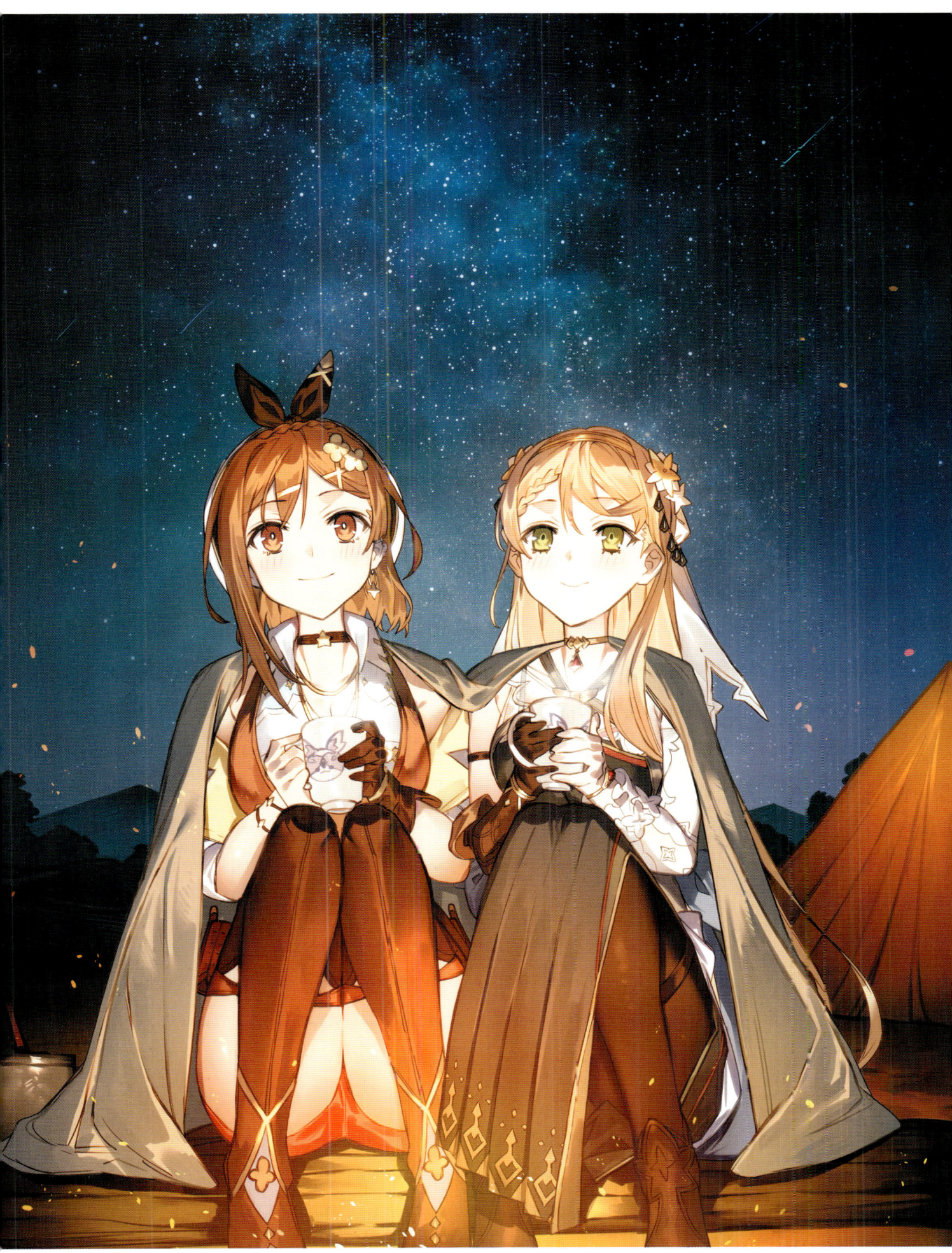

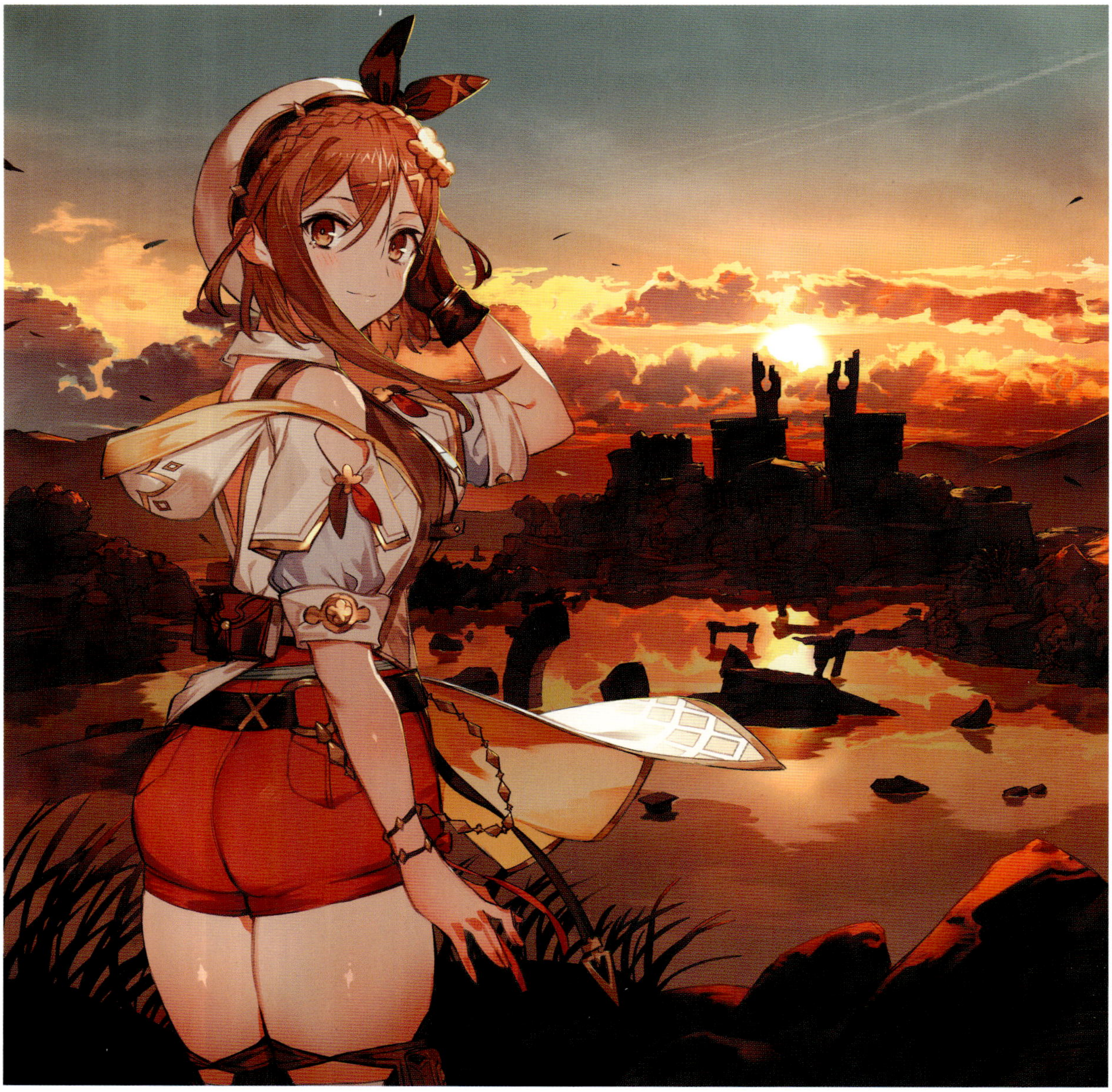

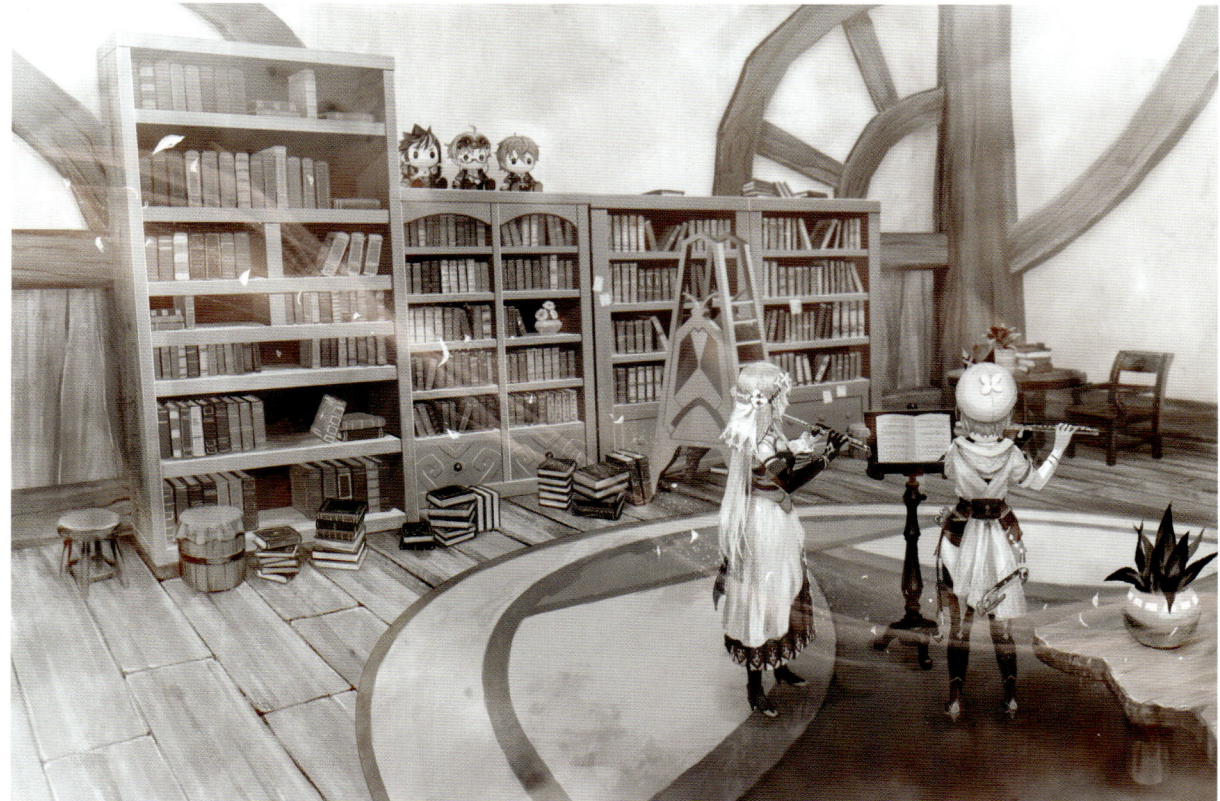

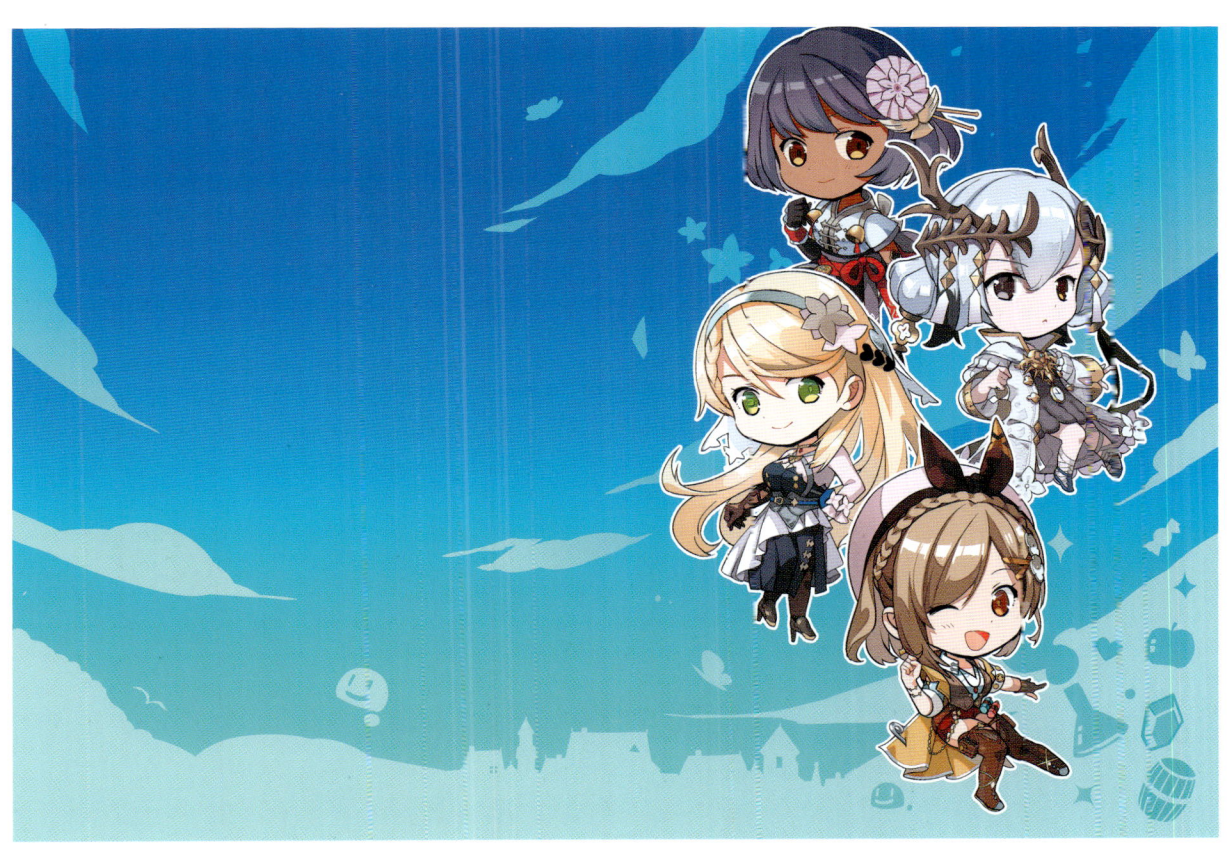
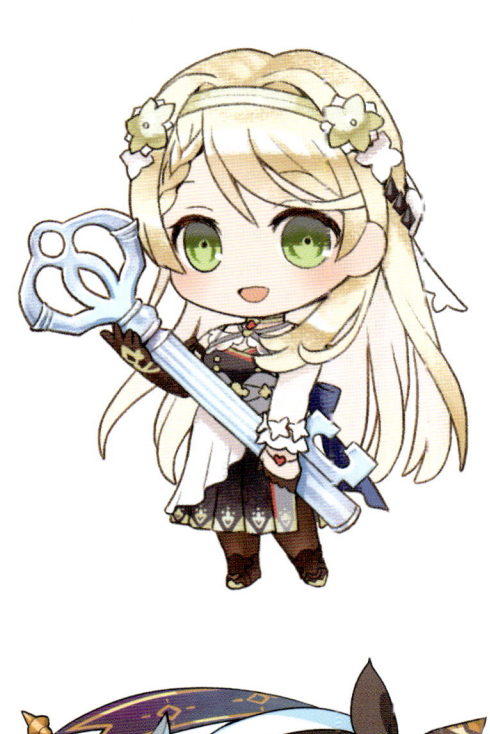
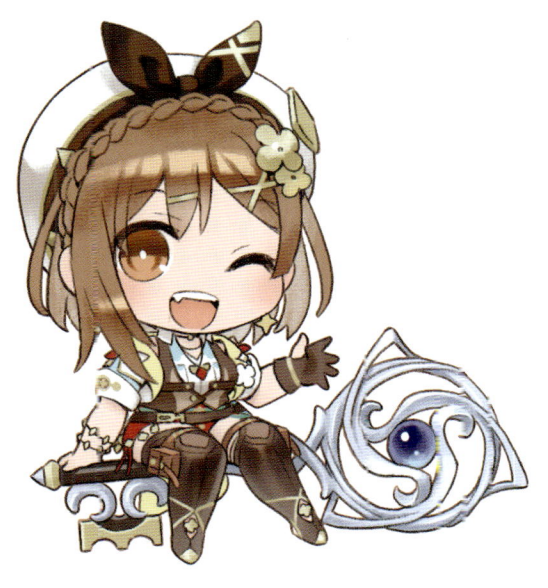
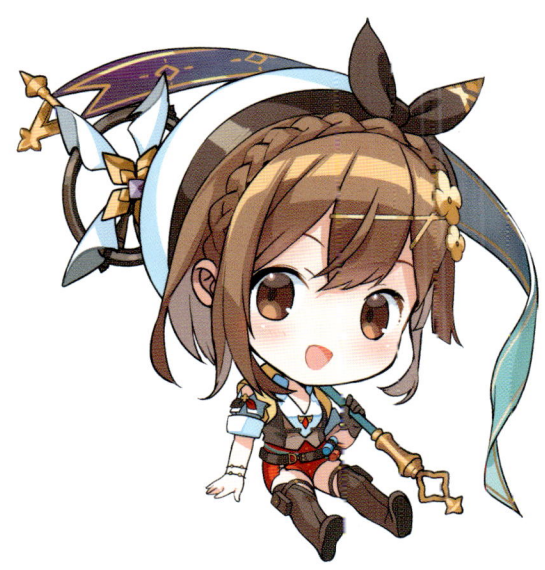
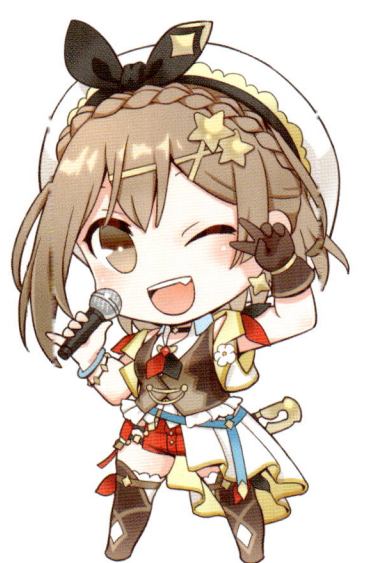

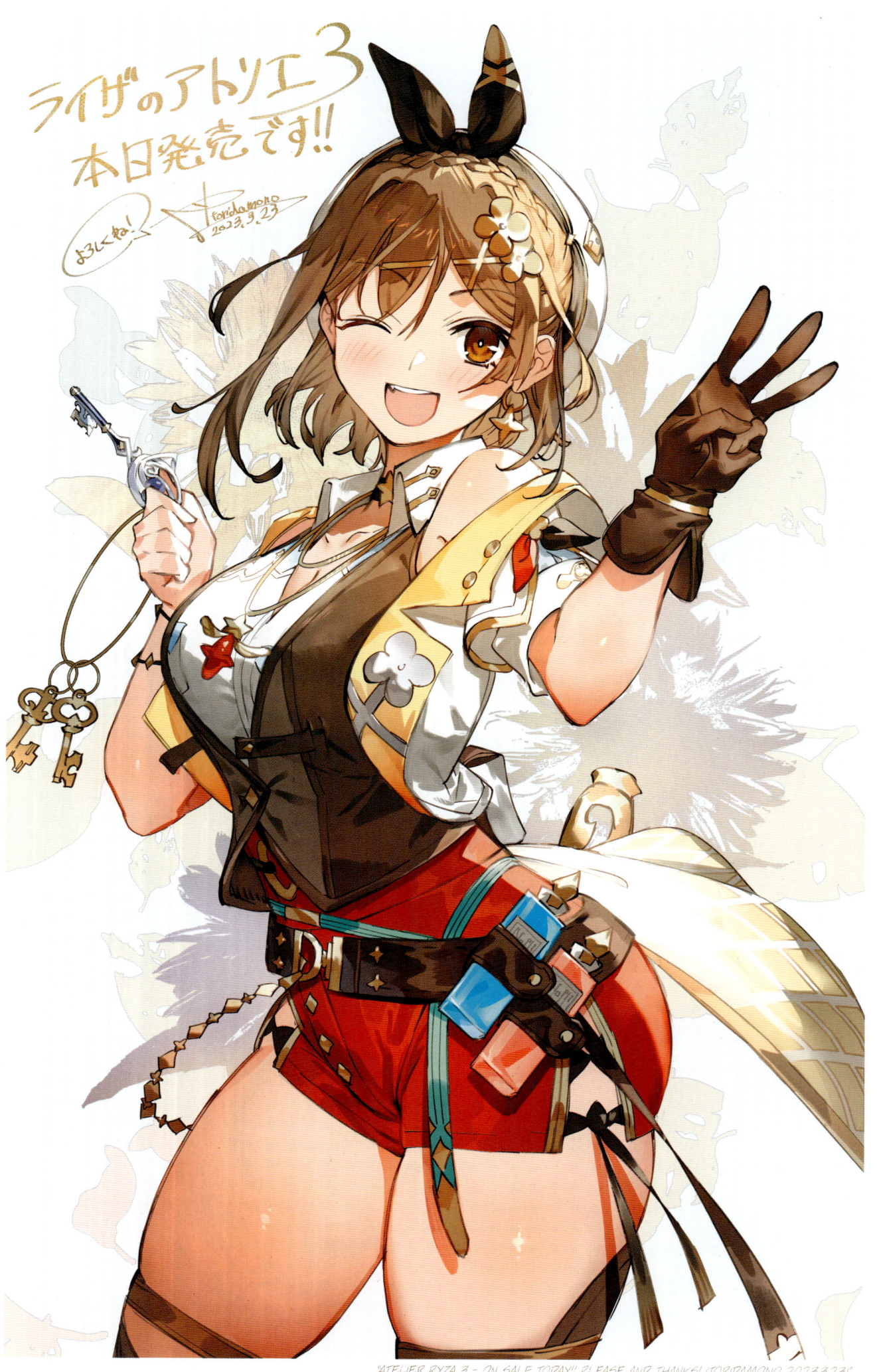

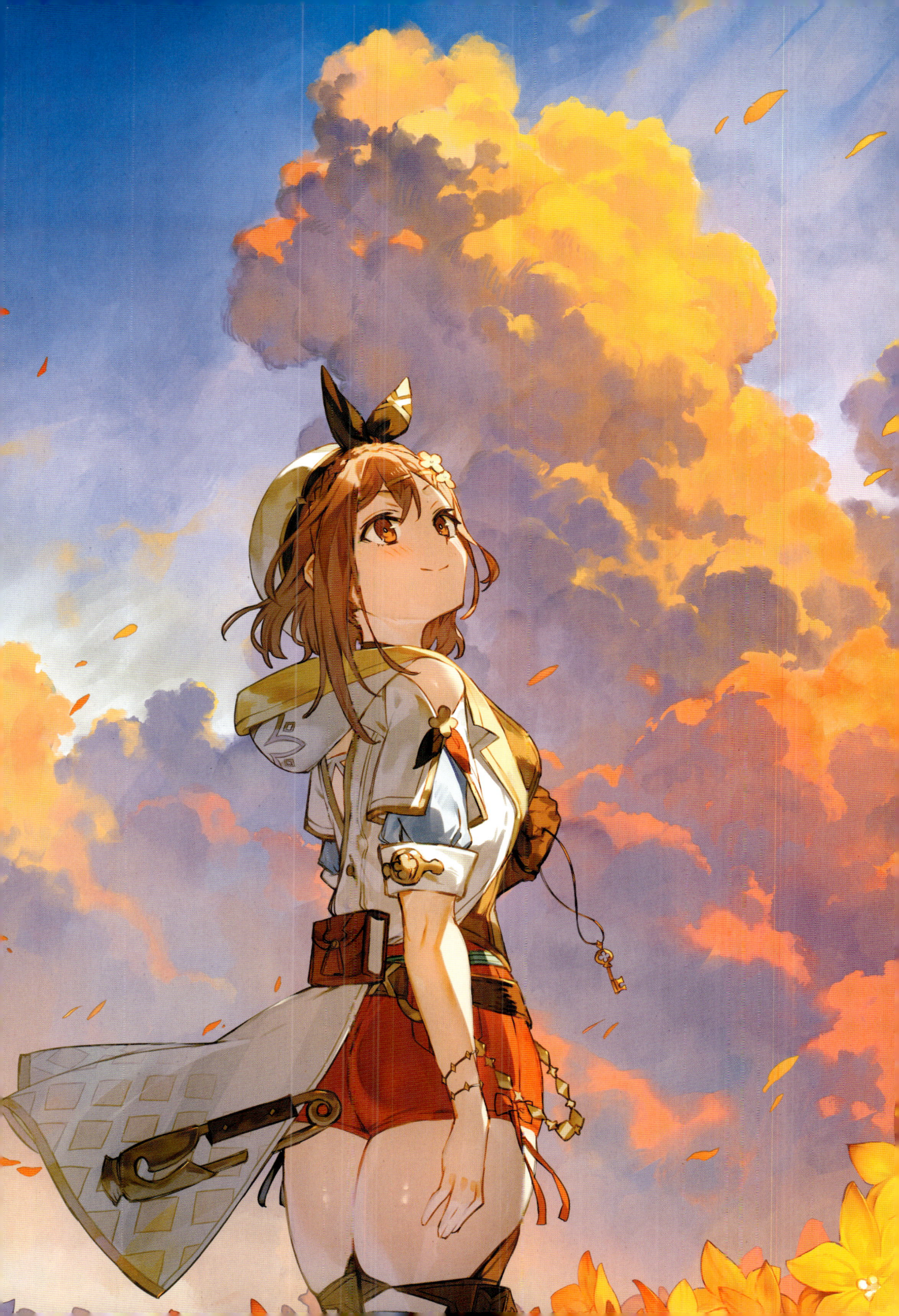

❖ OFFICIAL ILLUSTRATION ARCHIVES
COMMENTS: TORIDAMONO

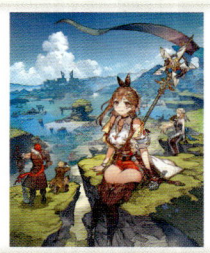

p.002
PLAYSTATION 4 / PLAYSTATION 5 / NINTENDO SWITCH EDITIONS STANDARD EDITION PACKAGE VISUAL
Illustration by Toridamono

Wide open fields were one of the attractions in this game, so I decided on a composition in which you could see a panoramic view of the vast expanse of the world. I wanted to maintain the same composition for all the packages in the "Secrets" series, but I changed it this time because it didn't work well with the concept.

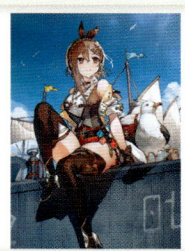

p.005
PREMIUM BOX SPECIAL BONUS B2 CLOTH POSTER
Illustration by Toridamono

The theme is the same as in "2", and Ryza is preparing to set off. She's waiting for a ship. It would be lonely for her to wait alone, so I added seagulls. Animals like Ryza too.

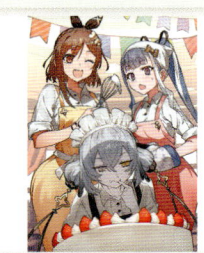

p.008
ASIA BONUS ILLUSTRATION
Illustration by Toridamono

The theme is preparing for a party. Here, too, the characters' personalities are expressed through facial expressions and mannerisms. As I was drawing it I imagined things like: since Kala is mischievous she'd be snatching a taste, and that since Patricia is serious, she would make a strange face when she saw it.

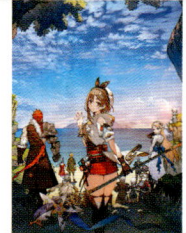

p.003
PROMOTIONAL VISUAL
Illustration by Toridamono

Summer is ending. The theme is the pain of things like Ryza and her friends saying goodbye. Those feelings were close to my own, so I was putting emotion into it as I drew it. I really like this one. Actually, this was the very first illustration I drew, but it was released just before it went on sale in line with the promotional deployment.

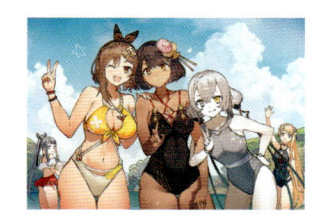

p.006
SPECIAL COLLECTION BOX SPECIAL BONUS A1 TAPESTRY
Illustration by Toridamono

The timid Federica, sandwiched between the assertive Ryza and the philosophical Kala. It expresses the characters' personalities and relationships. The mannerisms of the two people behind them are also key points. Once again, I drew swimsuits that matched my sense of each character.

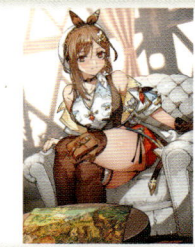

p.009
CHINESE LANGUAGE VERSION PACKAGE SPECIAL BONUS ILLUSTRATION
Illustration by Toridamono

This was a collaboration with authorized cosplayer Miss Iori Moe, so I drew this with on a shot taken by Miss Iori as reference. I was impressed when the white chair Ryza is sitting on was faithfully reproduced at an event in Taiwan.

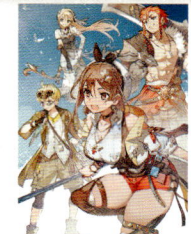

p.004
PROMOTIONAL VISUAL
Illustration by Toridamono

I never drew any energetic combat scenes for the "Secret" series, so I gave it a shot. It was fun, but it demanded a lot of calories, and the deadline was tight, so I was drawing it with a bit of regret. (LOL)

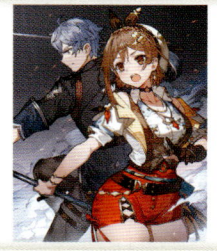

p.007
WEEKLY FAMITSU DENGEKI SPECIAL PACK B2 TAPESTRY ILLUSTRATION
Illustration by Toridamono

This was drawn to coincide with the release of information about Bos's joining the battle. It pleased me to have these two, who used to have such a contentious relationship, now fighting back-to-back in a relationship of trust... Congratulations on joining the team, Bos.

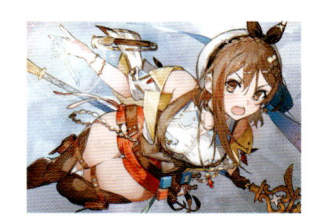

p.010
ENGLISH LANGUAGE VERSION PACKAGE SPECIAL BONUS ILLUSTRATION
Illustration by Toridamono

I was asked to produce an illustration with some flashiness. So I drew a lively Ryza using a key and filling the entire image. To create a flashy effect, I also added jewel-like sparkles in the background.

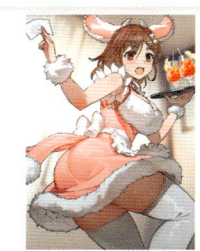

p.011
IN-STORE PURCHASE BONUS
B2 TAPESTRY ILLUSTRATION

Illustration by Toridamono

I draw the in-store special bonuses based on requests regarding composition, etc. Each time, many of these have fan service mindset, but I enjoy drawing them because they are fresh and new. This is Ryza as a waitress-like figure with bunny ears and a maid outfit.

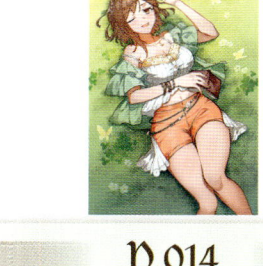

p.014
IN-STORE PURCHASE BONUS
B2 TAPESTRY ILLUSTRATION

Illustration by Toridamono

The request was for Ryza to be resting in a field and soaking up the sun. I was asked to make her clothes casual, so this is a different outfit than usual.

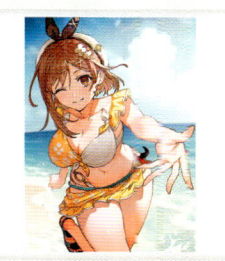

p.017
IN-STORE PURCHASE BONUS
B2 TAPESTRY ILLUSTRATION

Illustration by Toridamono

The impression is of Ryza in a bathing suit reaching out her hand toward us. Her expression is a little grown-up.

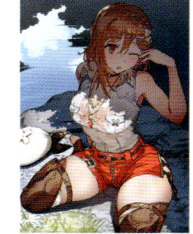

p.012
IN-STORE PURCHASE BONUS
A2 CLEAR POSTER ILLUSTRATION

Illustration by Toridamono

Similar illustrations for "2" were well received, so there was a desire for an illustration of a wet situation. I enjoyed making decisions about the transparency and lighting.

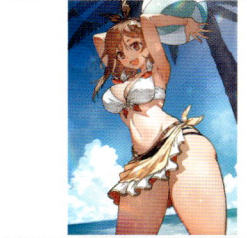

p.015
IN-STORE PURCHASE BONUS
A4 CLEAR FILE ILLUSTRATION

Illustration by Toridamono

"The outfit is a swimsuit!" And the rest was left up to me. A gracious graceful request (LOL). I tried to give it a dynamic feel by choosing a low angle.

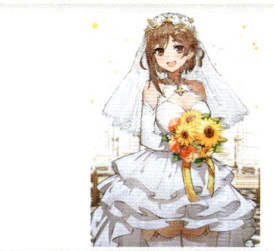

p.018
IN-STORE PURCHASE BONUS
B2 TAPESTRY ILLUSTRATION

Illustration by Toridamono

The request was for a wedding dress. I have a strong mental image of Ryza being boyish and active, so as I drew this I wondered if it would actually suit her, but in the end it did. She looks sweet. But I'm not good at drawing frills, so this was a struggle.

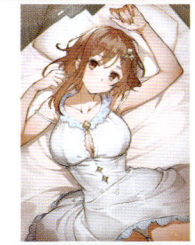

p.013
IN-STORE PURCHASE BONUS
B2 TAPESTRY ILLUSTRATION

Illustration by Toridamono

The request was for Ryza to be dressed in her sleepwear and lying on a bed. This time, I tried to get a closer angle.

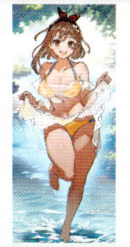

p.016
IN-STORE PURCHASE BONUS
EXTRA-LARGE TAPESTRY

Illustration by Toridamono

Ryza frolicking in a forest waterfront. It helps me in my work if the clothing and composition is specified in detail. I'm usually crazy busy when I'm working on in-store special bonus illustrations, so I don't have a lot of time to spend fretting...

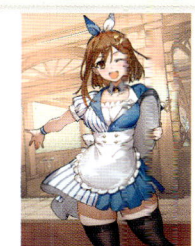

p.019
IN-STORE PURCHASE BONUS
A3 PUB MIRROR ILLUSTRATION

Illustration by Toridamono

This was drawn especially for a collaboration with a certain store. I think I was able to draw her looking cute! It feels like she's always wearing yellow, so the blue clothes were rare and refreshing.

❖ OFFICIAL ILLUSTRATION ARCHIVES
COMMENTS: TORIDAMONO

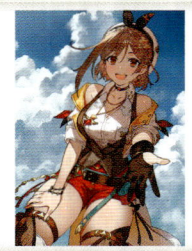

p.020
IN-STORE PURCHASE BONUS
ORIGINAL ILLUSTRATION REPRODUCTION

Illustration by Toridamono

The request was for a composition in which she's reaching out her hand toward the viewer. Since the swimsuit illustration had a similar composition, I changed the angle and pose a little.

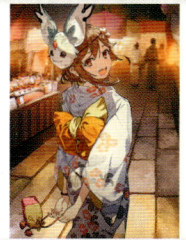

p.021
TOKYO GAME SHOW 2022 COMMEMORATIVE PRODUCT
B2 TAPESTRY ILLUSTRATION

Illustration by Toridamono

The setting is Ryza, who has come to an autumn festival in a yukata. The expression on her face as she looks back over her shoulder is sweet. The obi is yellow and orange, the colors you associate with Ryza. The Fi mask is also a key point!

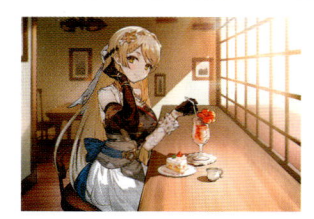

p.022
IN-STORE PURCHASE BONUS
PC WALLPAPER ILLUSTRATION

Illustration by Toridamono

Klaudia sitting next to you at the counter of a cafe. I draw Ryza a lot, so it's refreshing to be able to draw other characters too. I think I was able to draw a good expression on her face.

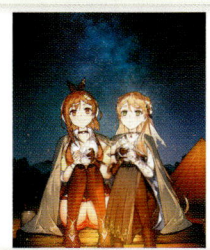

p.023
PROMOTIONAL VISUAL

Illustration by Toridamono

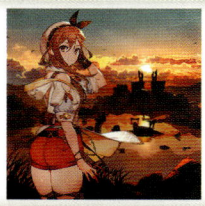

p.024
ORIGINAL SOUNDTRACK
JACKET ILLUSTRATION

Illustration by Toridamono

I was asked to illustrate a scene set in the evening to create a sense of unity among the jackets of the original soundtracks of the "Secret" series. I was given clear ideas about the composition and location, so I created it exactly as asked. I enjoyed creating the reflections on the water, and also the clouds.

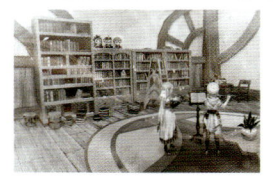

p.024
FINAL SUMMER ENSEMBLE
~ ATELIER RYZA 3 SPECIAL ARRANGE CD ~
JACKET ILLUSTRATION

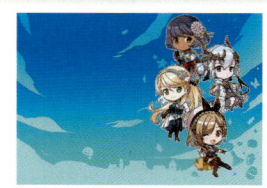

p.025
IN-STORE PURCHASE BONUS
SPECIALLY-MADE CLEAR FILE ILLUSTRATION

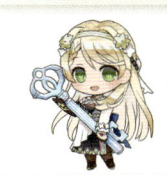 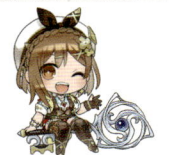

p.025
IN-STORE PURCHASE BONUS / PREMIUM BOX SPECIAL BONUS
ACRYLIC MINI CHARACTER CHARMS ILLUSTRATIONS

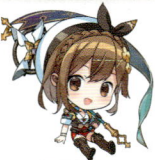

p.025
ATELIER 25TH ANNIVERSARY COMMEMORATION
GUST PREMIUM LIVE USE GOODS
ACRYLIC STAND KEYHOLDER ILLUSTRATION

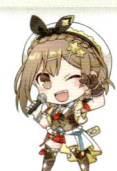

p.025
ATELIER 25TH ANNIVERSARY COMMEMORATION
GUST PREMIUM LIVE
SALES MERCH & GUST LOTTERY PURCHASE BONUS USE
TIN BADGE ILLUSTRATION

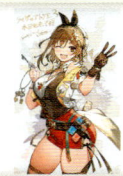

p.026
"ATELIER" SERIES OFFICIAL ACCOUNTS
ON-SALE COMMEMORATION ILLUSTRATION

Illustration by Toridamono

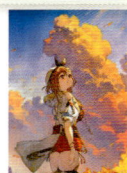

p.027
THIS BOOK'S COVER

Illustration by Toridamono

This is the last official illustration I've done for the "Secret" series. As in the visuals book for "1", I drew this illustration with the image in mind of the scene after her adventures. The key points are the facial expression and the gesture of the left hand. I wonder what Ryza is thinking now after her adventures.

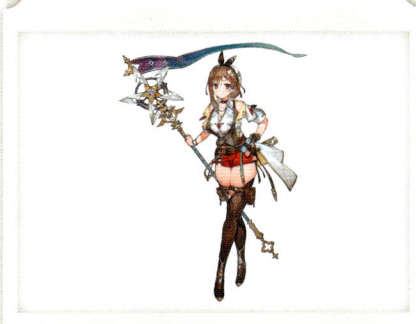

p.034
CHARACTER FULL-LENGTH PORTRAIT
RYZA

Illustration by Toridamono

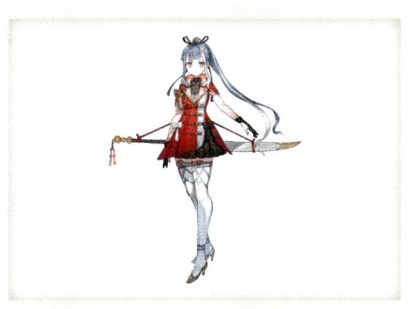

p.038
CHARACTER FULL-LENGTH PORTRAIT
PATRICIA

Illustration by Toridamono

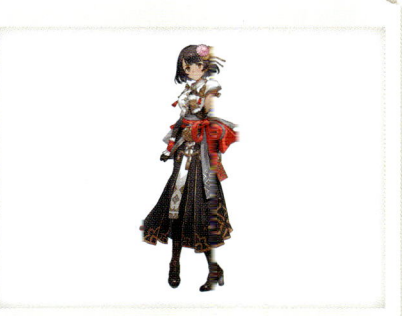

p.042
CHARACTER FULL-LENGTH PORTRAIT
FEDERICA

Illustration by Toridamono

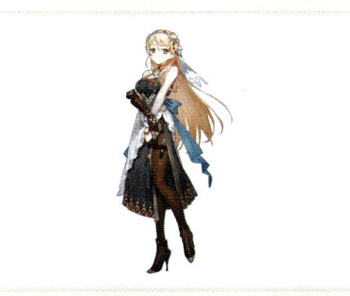

p.035
CHARACTER FULL-LENGTH PORTRAIT
KLAUDIA

Illustration by Toridamono

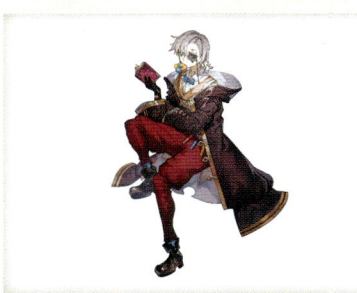

p.039
CHARACTER FULL-LENGTH PORTRAIT
EMPEL

Illustration by Toridamono

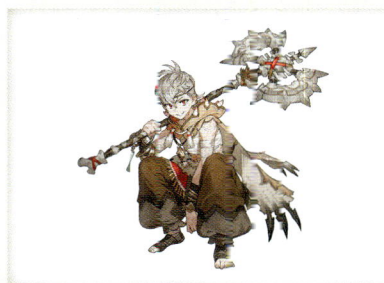

p.043
CHARACTER FULL-LENGTH PORTRAIT
DIAN

Illustration by Toridamono

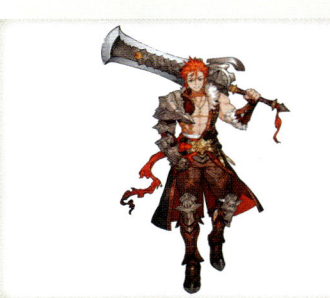

p.036
CHARACTER FULL-LENGTH PORTRAIT
LENT

Illustration by Toridamono

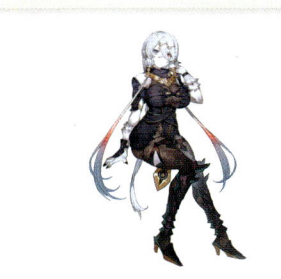

p.040
CHARACTER FULL-LENGTH PORTRAIT
LILA

Illustration by Toridamono

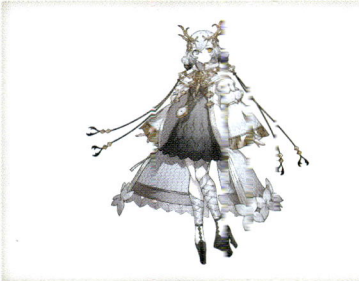

p.044
CHARACTER FULL-LENGTH PORTRAIT
KALA

Illustration by Toridamono

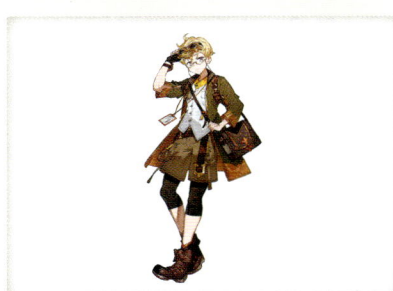

p.037
CHARACTER FULL-LENGTH PORTRAIT
TAO

Illustration by Toridamono

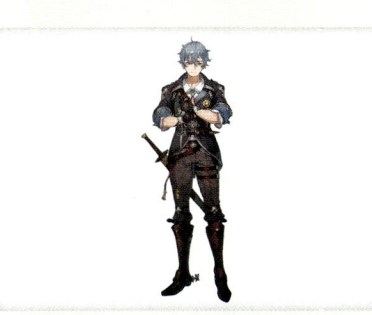

p.041
CHARACTER FULL-LENGTH PORTRAIT
BOS

Illustration by Toridamono

Atelier Ryza 3
Alchemist of the End & the Secret Key
OFFICIAL VISUAL COLLECTION

CONTENTS

ILLUSTRATION GALLERY
002

Official Illustration Commentary 028

CHARACTER ILLUSTRATIONS
033

Reisalin Stout (Ryza) 034	Karl Stout 047
Klaudia Valentz 035	Mio Stout 048
Lent Marslink 036	Samuel Marslink 048
Tao Mogarten 037	Moritz Brunnen 049
Patricia Abelheim 038	Lumbar Dorn 049
Empel Vollmer 039	Agatha Harmon 050
Lila Decyrus 040	Kilo Shiness 050
Bos Brunnen 041	Fi 051
Federica Lamberti 042	Romy Vogel 051
Dian Farrell 043	Elder 052
Kala Ideas 044	Emil 052
Alberta Rose 045	Lubart Valentz 053
Saverio Grante 045	Serri Glaus 053
Anna Miranda 046	Volker Abelheim 054
Dolto Curtis 046	Clifford Diswell 054
Deirdre Northfill 047	Costume Variations 055

EVENT STILLS
071

Event Stills 072

DESIGN WORKS CHARACTERS
087

Character Design Drawings, Rough Sketches 088

DESIGN WORKS MONSTERS & ANIMALS
127

Monster & General Animal Designs 128

DESIGN WORKS WEAPONS & GADGETS
147

Weapon & Gadget Designs 148

DESIGN WORKS SETTINGS & STORY BOARDS
163

Settings 164
Storyboards 171

EXTRAS
177

Toridamono Bonus Illustrations
   Rough Sketch Gallery 178
Special Interview
   Junzo Hosoi X Yasuaki Suzuki X Toridamono 186

* Screen images in this book are from the PlayStation 4 version.
* This book includes design illustrations and content from downloadable material which does not appear in the actual game.
* The data presented in this book is based on materials independently verified by the production staff of this book.
* In sections of this book, "Atelier Ryza: Ever Darkness & the Secret Hideout" is referred to as "1", "Atelier Ryza 2: Lost Legends & the Secret Fairy" as "2", and "Atelier Ryza 3: Alchemist of the End & the Secret Key" as "3".

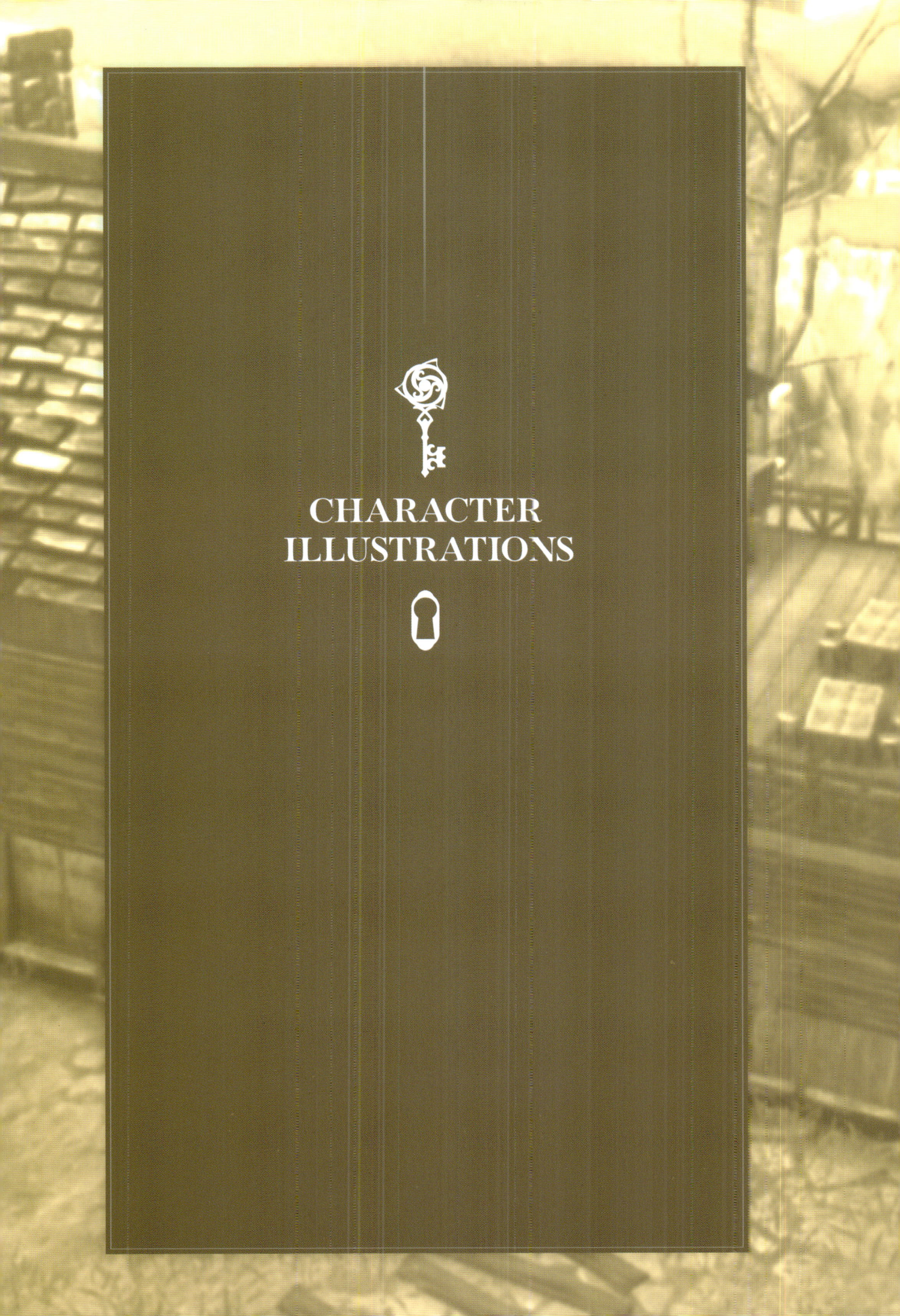
CHARACTER ILLUSTRATIONS

Reisalin Stout [Ryza]

ライザリン・シュタウト (ライザ)

CV Yuri Noguchi

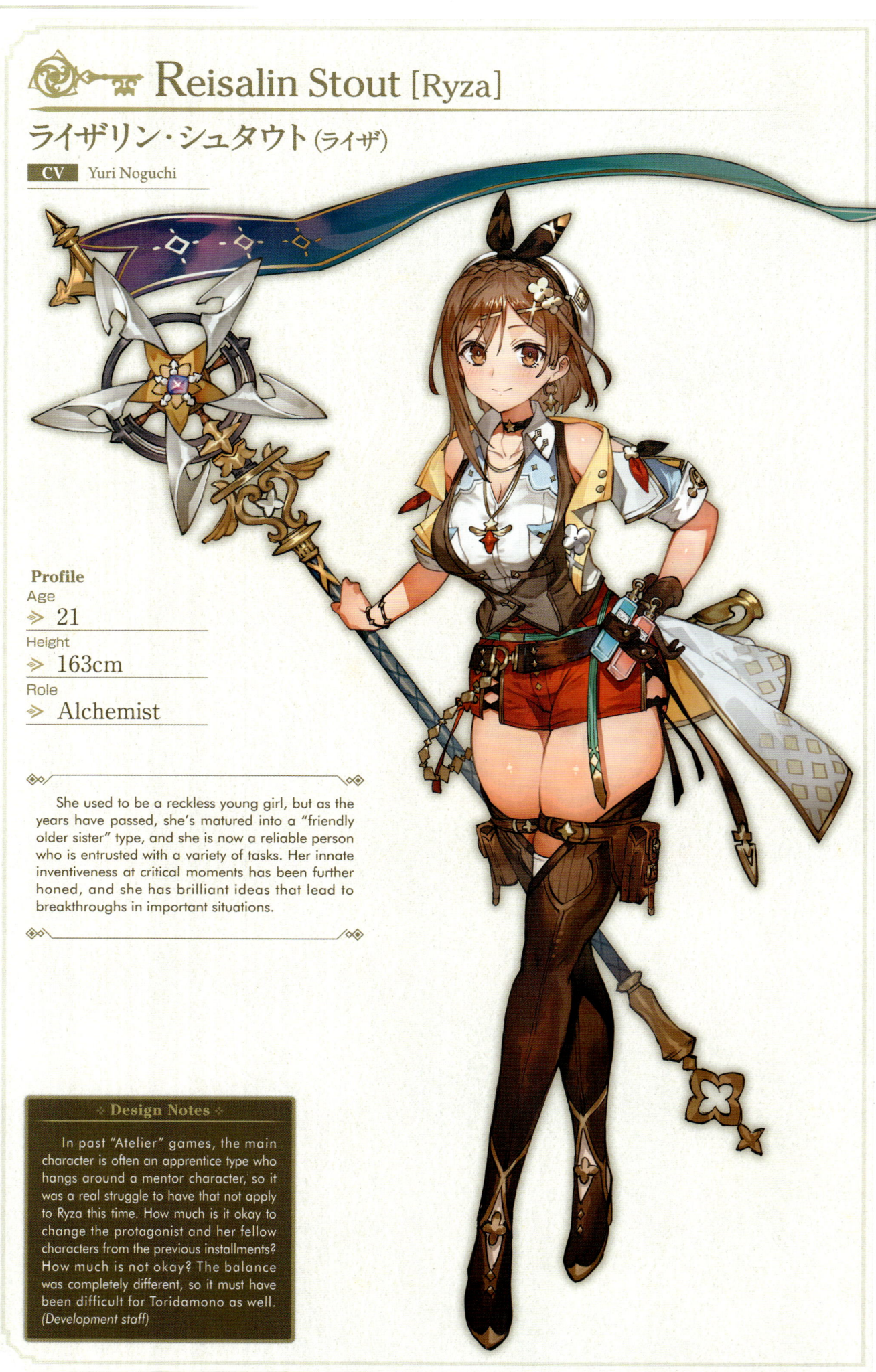

Profile

Age
» 21

Height
» 163cm

Role
» Alchemist

She used to be a reckless young girl, but as the years have passed, she's matured into a "friendly older sister" type, and she is now a reliable person who is entrusted with a variety of tasks. Her innate inventiveness at critical moments has been further honed, and she has brilliant ideas that lead to breakthroughs in important situations.

◆ Design Notes ◆

In past "Atelier" games, the main character is often an apprentice type who hangs around a mentor character, so it was a real struggle to have that not apply to Ryza this time. How much is it okay to change the protagonist and her fellow characters from the previous installments? How much is not okay? The balance was completely different, so it must have been difficult for Toridamono as well. *(Development staff)*

Klaudia Valentz

クラウディア・バレンツ

CV Hitomi Ohwada

Profile

Age
≫ 21

Height
≫ 164cm

Role
≫ Daughter of Merchant

She is a bright and capable professional, and the only daughter of a merchant. She has now solidified her position within the company, and has even been entrusted with a growing department. She has been away from the royal capital, but when she's summoned by Ryza, she once again sets off on a summer adventure.

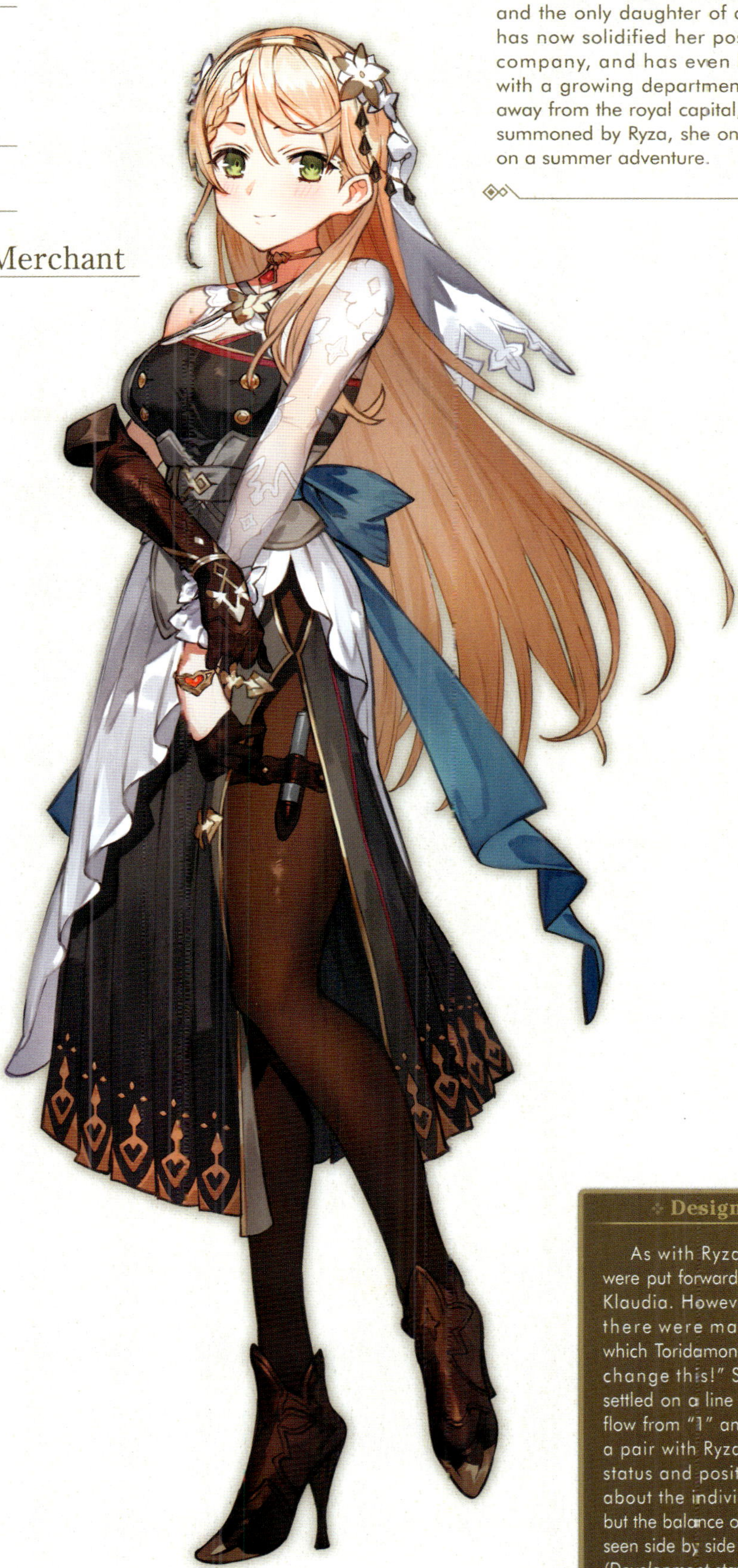

Design Notes

As with Ryza, various ideas were put forward for alterations to Klaudia. However, as with Ryza, there were many parts about which Toridamono said, "We can't change this!" So basically, we settled on a line that takes up the flow from "1" and "2". She forms a pair with Ryza in terms of her status and position. It's not just about the individual characters, but the balance of characters when seen side by side is also important. (Development staff)

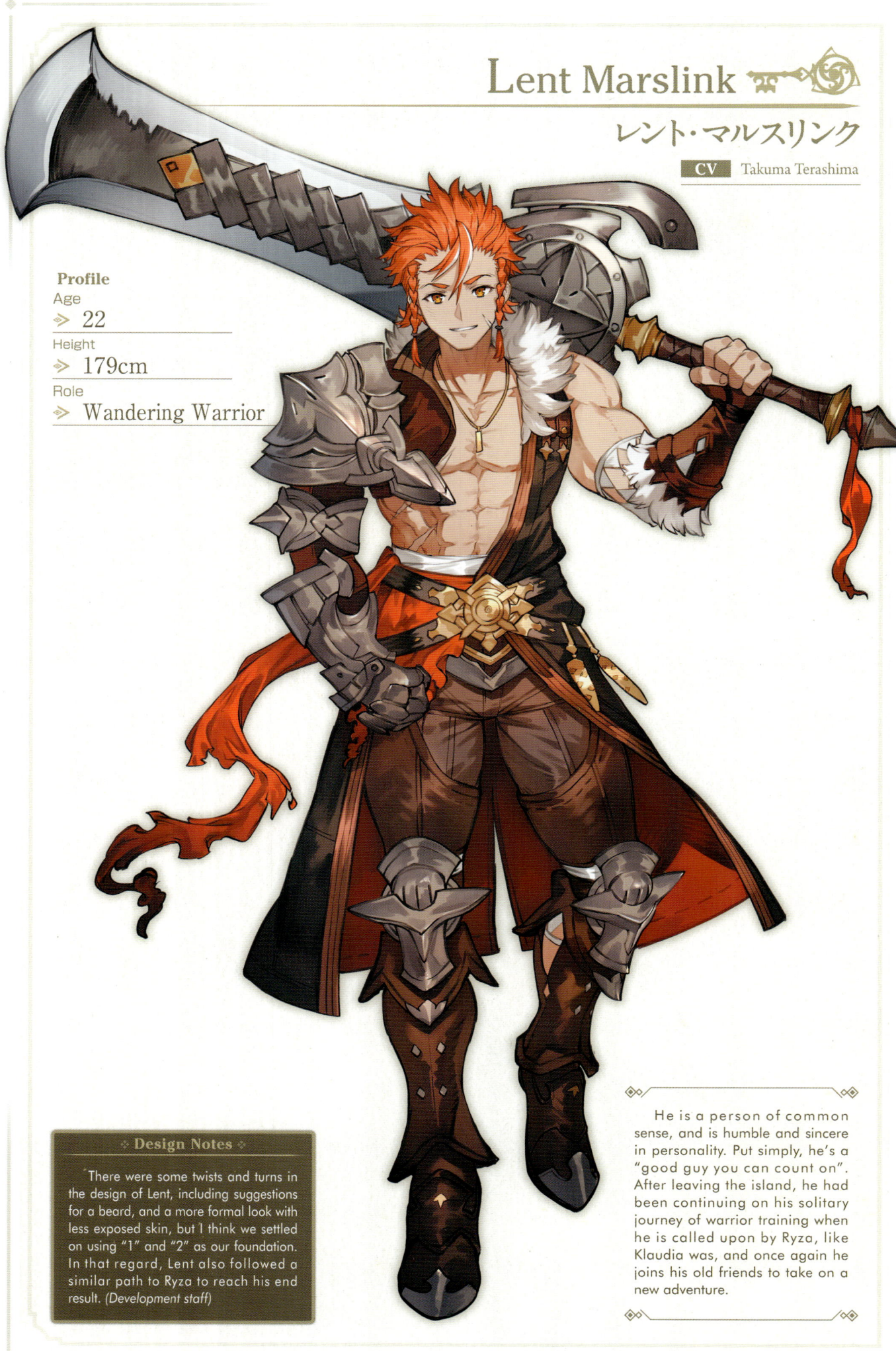

Lent Marslink
レント・マルスリンク

CV Takuma Terashima

Profile

Age
≫ 22

Height
≫ 179cm

Role
≫ Wandering Warrior

❖ Design Notes ❖

"There were some twists and turns in the design of Lent, including suggestions for a beard, and a more formal look with less exposed skin, but I think we settled on using "1" and "2" as our foundation. In that regard, Lent also followed a similar path to Ryza to reach his end result. (Development staff)

He is a person of common sense, and is humble and sincere in personality. Put simply, he's a "good guy you can count on". After leaving the island, he had been continuing on his solitary journey of warrior training when he is called upon by Ryza, like Klaudia was, and once again he joins his old friends to take on a new adventure.

Tao Mongarten

タオ・モンガルテン

CV Junta Terashima

While he continues to be a student at the royal capital, Tao is still as always devoted to the study of ruins. His appearance and mannerisms are more grown up, and he has acquired the ability to explore ruins casually, but at his core he's still the bookworm boy he always was. He seems to be deeply interested in the ruins he encountered in the Kurk Archipelago, and he demonstrates his knowledge to the fullest.

Profile

Age
- 19

Height
- 170cm

Role
- Novice Archaeologist

◆ Design Notes ◆

For both "2" and "3", when we started work on the designs, we asked for a shirt and vest with a strong formal orientation. In the end, the design wasn't complete with only these elements, but had additional idiosyncratic accessories and other attire. These must have been essential elements of Tao's design in Toridamono's mind.
(Development staff)

Patricia Abelheim

パトリツィア・アーベルハイム

CV Naomi Ohzora

Profile

Age
» 17

Height
» 157cm

Role
» Young Lady of the City

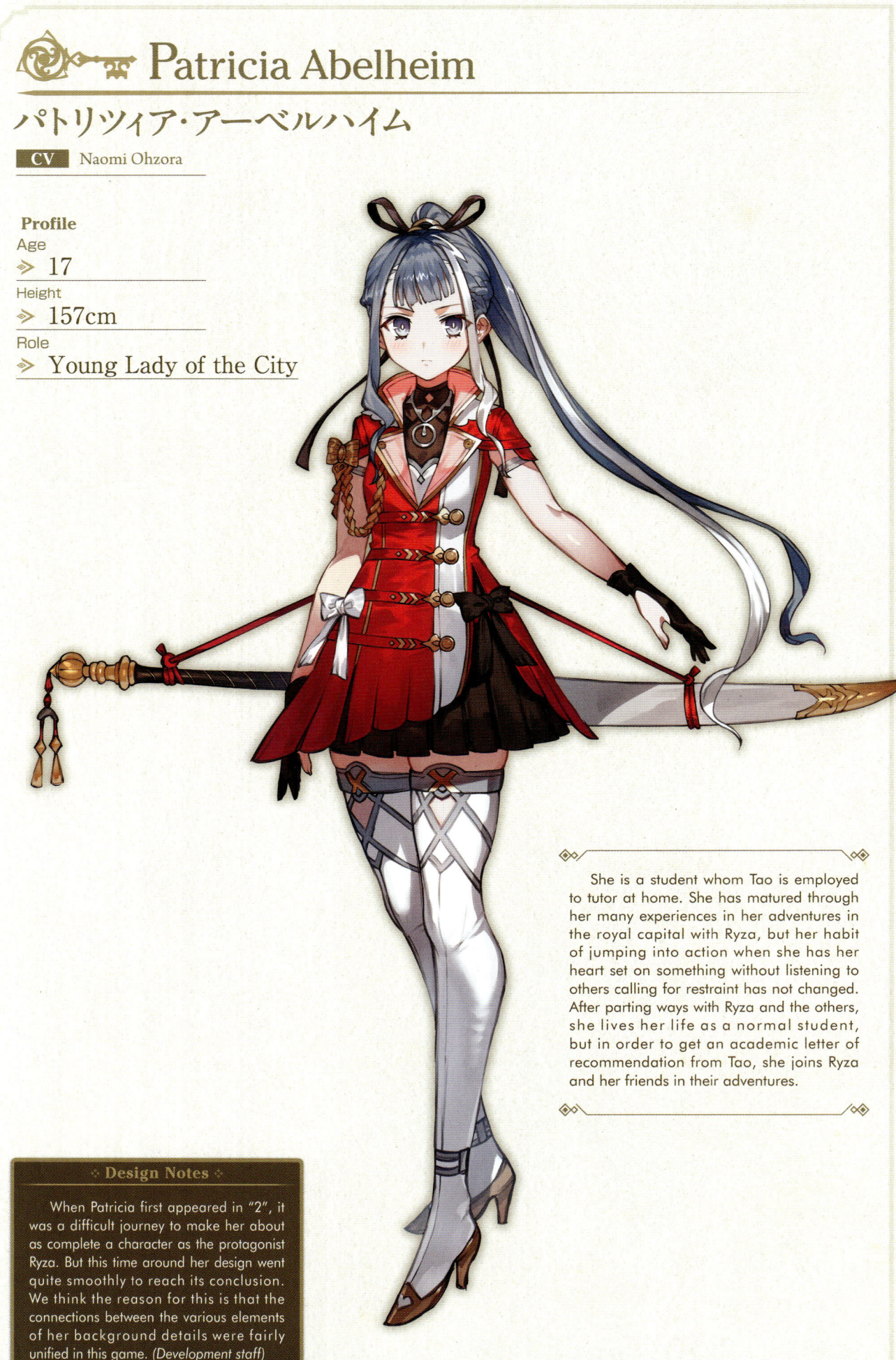

She is a student whom Tao is employed to tutor at home. She has matured through her many experiences in her adventures in the royal capital with Ryza, but her habit of jumping into action when she has her heart set on something without listening to others calling for restraint has not changed. After parting ways with Ryza and the others, she lives her life as a normal student, but in order to get an academic letter of recommendation from Tao, she joins Ryza and her friends in their adventures.

◈ Design Notes ◈

When Patricia first appeared in "2", it was a difficult journey to make her about as complete a character as the protagonist Ryza. But this time around her design went quite smoothly to reach its conclusion. We think the reason for this is that the connections between the various elements of her background details were fairly unified in this game. *(Development staff)*

パトリツィア・アーベルハイム

Empel Vollmer

アンペル・フォルマー

CV Hirofumi Nojima

> Empel is a former alchemist of the royal court who taught alchemy to Ryza. He travels around the world closing gates to the Underworld which were left behind by alchemists of the past. He is friendly in a detached way, but also has a calm personality. While traveling around the world for his own purposes, he joined up with Ryza and her group. Now, once again, he embarks on a journey of adventure along with them.

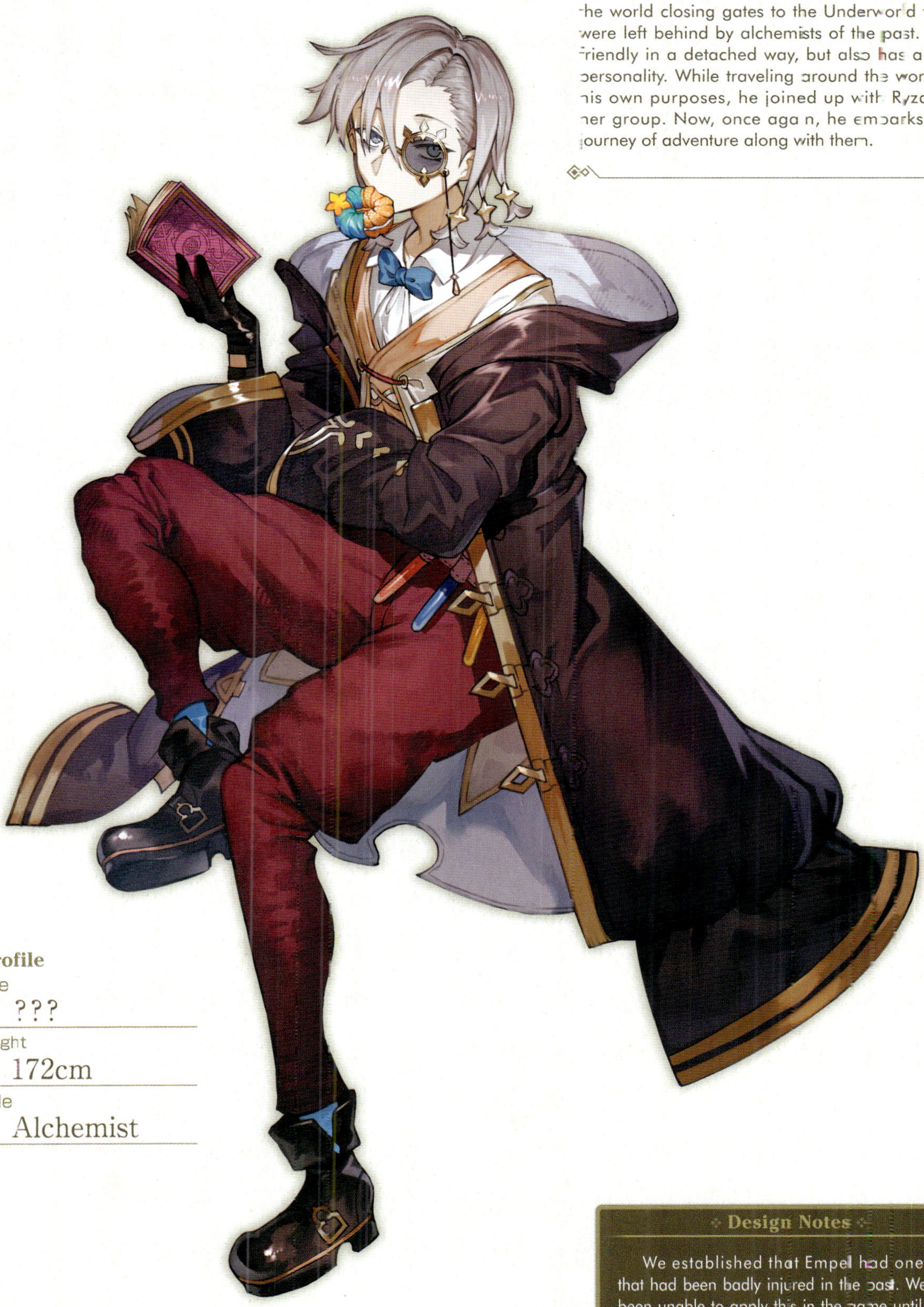

Profile

Age
» ???

Height
» 172cm

Role
» Alchemist

Design Notes

We established that Empel had one arm that had been badly injured in the past. We had been unable to apply this in the game until now, but this time we were finally able to apply "the artificial arm given to him by Ryza and Lila". *(Development staff)*

Lila Decyrus

リラ・ディザイアス

CV Haruka Terui

Profile

Age
⇒ ???

Height
⇒ 164cm

Role
⇒ Underworld Warrior

> She traveled to various places with Empel, and once, when they stopped at Kurken Island, she taught Ryza and her friends how to fight. She is cool, collected, and blunt, but stoic and courageous in battle, and she is a good bodyguard for Empel, who often travels to dangerous places. Like Empel, she joined Ryza and her group when they were traveling the land.

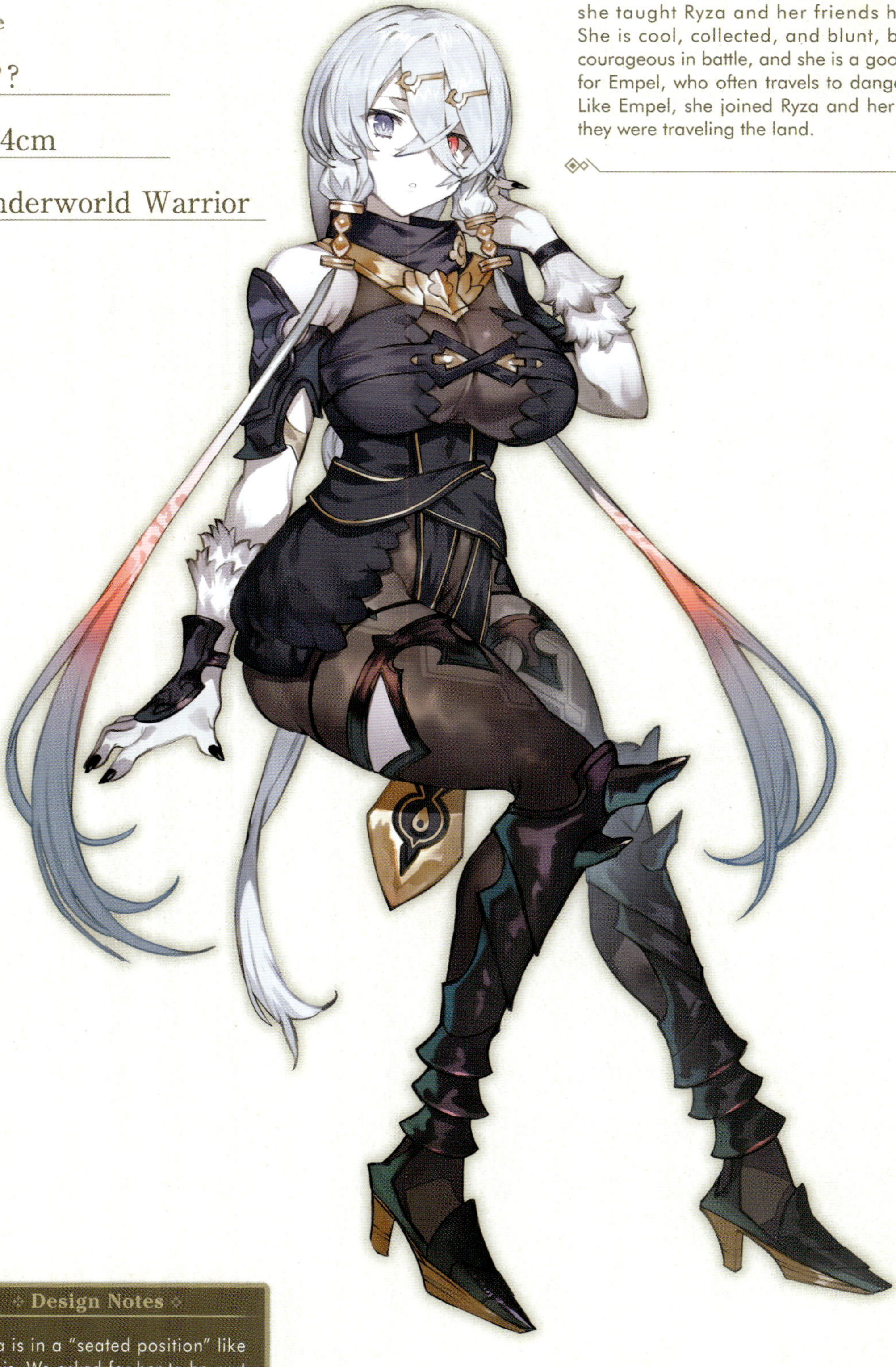

◆ Design Notes ◆

Lila is in a "seated position" like Empel is. We asked for her to be part of a pair with Empel, and this is how she was drawn. In this game, the relationship between the two is explored in depth. *(Development staff)*

Bos Brunnen

ボオス・ブルネン

CV Yohei Azakami

Profile

Age
⇨ 22

Height
⇨ 174cm

Role
⇨ Son of an Influential Family

Bos is the heir of the Brunen family, a powerful family in Ryza's hometown. He used to have a contentious relationship with Ryza and her friends due to a minor misunderstanding, but he has patched things up with them and is returning to being a serious person. However, his habit of speaking about Ryza and the others in a negative way is still alive and well. Going on adventures with his childhood friends is one of his secret longings.

◆ Design Notes ◆

For "1" and "2", our in-house designers handled Bos, but in this game he became a player character, and we got Toridamono to draw him. So he's become a very rare kind of character in the "Atelier" series. Players had big expectations too, so we put a lot of energy into aspects related to the publicity of Bos as well.

Federica Lamberti

フェデリーカ・ランベルティ

CV Sumire Morohoshi

Profile

Age
» 18

Height
» 162cm

Role
» Deputy Head of the Artisans Union

She is the deputy head of the artisans union in the crafting city of Sardonica. She is a graceful woman who always keeps her back straight and behaves politely. She is strong at her core, and is methodical and tenacious. However, she can also be somewhat standoffish. In order to reconcile two opposing factions, she decides to travel with Ryza and her friends and grow as a person.

Design Notes

Many of the female characters in the "Secret" series have been strong-willed and independent, so with Federica we focused on making her a graceful and seemingly timid woman. At one time, we had idea of making her Ryza's cousin. As the story development progressed, we settled on her current details, and her personality gradually changed quite a lot too. *(Development staff)*

Dian Farrell

ディアン・ファレル

CV Yudai Mino

Profile

Age
» 15

Height
» 166cm

Role
» Seed-collecting Warrior

◆ Design Notes ◆

In one of our meetings, Mr. Toridamono wisely said, "A character is a mixture of symbols", and I think Dian is a character that fits that exactly. In the specifications, Dian was a feral child of a tribe living in a secluded region, but that alone was weak as a hook, so we gave him a regent-style haircut to give him a "delinquent" image and added pants that gave him a loose look, and then he was complete. *(Development staff)*

Dian is a warrior from the remote village of Faurre. He is tired of the actions of the "Gleaner" organization, which collects seeds by digging through ruins, and so he has always wished to leave his village. Then, he meets Ryza and her friends, and they set off on adventures together. He's a natural-born hunter, and he tends to give the impression of being rough, but he's actually a good listener and frank.

Kala Ideas

カラ・イデアス

CV Hina Yomiya

Profile

Age
⇒ ???

Height
⇒ 152cm

Role
⇒ Head of the Wave Tuner Clan

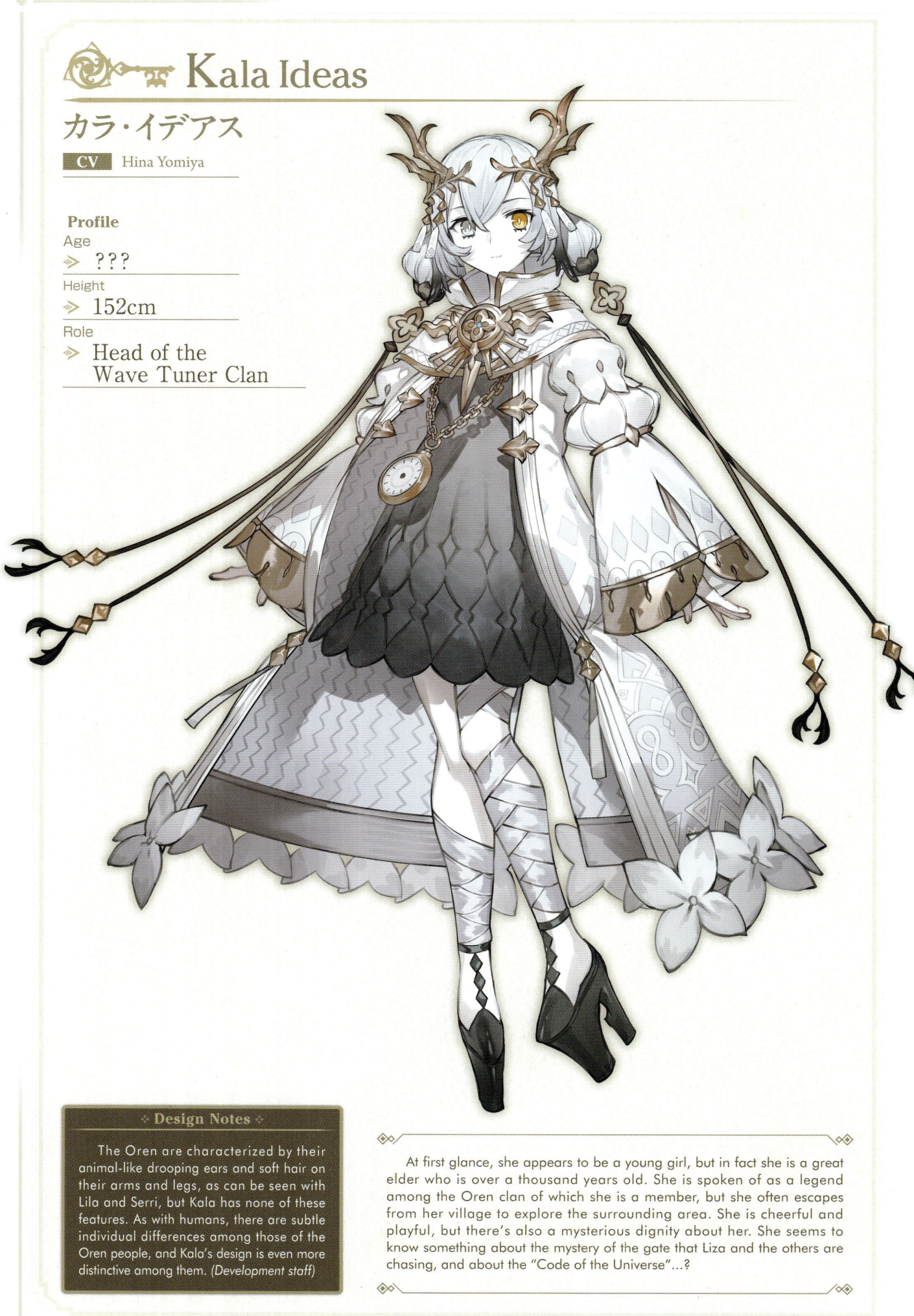

◇ Design Notes ◇

The Oren are characterized by their animal-like drooping ears and soft hair on their arms and legs, as can be seen with Lila and Serri, but Kala has none of these features. As with humans, there are subtle individual differences among those of the Oren people, and Kala's design is even more distinctive among them. *(Development staff)*

At first glance, she appears to be a young girl, but in fact she is a great elder who is over a thousand years old. She is spoken of as a legend among the Oren clan of which she is a member, but she often escapes from her village to explore the surrounding area. She is cheerful and playful, but there's also a mysterious dignity about her. She seems to know something about the mystery of the gate that Liza and the others are chasing, and about the "Code of the Universe"...?

Alberta Rose

アルベルタ・ローズ

CV Yoko Soumi

Profile

Age
⇒ 35

Height
⇒ 164cm

Role
⇒ Fairystone-Crafting Artisan

She is a shrewd woman who governs the Fairystones-crafting faction in Sardonica. Due in part to the traditional and refined quality of her faction, she is proud and confident in her skills. She has strong nerves that allow her to go toe-to-toe with even difficult craftsmen on equal terms.

◇ Design Notes ◇

Since Alberta is a character whose faction is in opposition to Saverio's, we considered the overall color scheme as the starting point. The artisans of Sardonica are dressed in Japanese clothing, which makes the focus of attention different from that of Ryza and her friends in terms of regional characteristics and occupationals. *(Development staff)*

A young man who leads the glasswork faction of Sardonica. He has a progressive and flexible factional temperament, he tackles everything with positive approach, and he has a free inventiveness. Perhaps due to his youth, getting carried away somewhat easily is another of his aspects.

◇ Design Notes ◇

We decided early on that since Saverio would be a counterpart to Alberta, he would be a character with a white and blue costume. The hairstyle was loosely based on advice from Toridamono, but as a result, the overall design feels unique for a male character in "Atelier". *(Development staff)*

Saverio Grante

サヴェリオ・グランテ

CV Hiroki Takahashi

Profile

Age
⇒ 28

Height
⇒ 171cm

Role
⇒ Glasswork Artisan

Anna Miranda

アンナ・ミランダ

CV Hiromi Konno

Profile
Age
≫ 25
Height
≫ 159cm
Role
≫ Union Receptionist

A young woman who works as a receptionist at the headquarters of the Sardonica artisans union. She is shy and always lacks self-confidence, but her work is fast and accurate. She is always eager to support the even younger and inexperienced deputy union head from the shadows.

◆ Design Notes ◆

Unlike Alberta and Saverio, Anna comes from outside Sardonica, so the elements of her costume have less of a Japanese feel compared to theirs. Because of her background role, both professionally and as a character, her design feels more mature at a glance.
(Development staff)

He is the leader and engineer of the village of Faurre. He manufactures special tools which are circulated around the village, and also acts as the village's troubleshooter and mediator. He is aloof, but always acts with the village's best interests in mind.

◆ Design Notes ◆

The conception of Dolto started with a relatively typical collection of fantasy-type ethnic symbols. In the middle stages, his characteristics were quite weak, so we got advice from Toridamono again mainly about his face, and then we made adjustments to the modeling to give him more distinctive features. *(Development staff)*

Dolto Curtis

ドルト・カーティス

CV Ryotaro Okiayu

Profile
Age
≫ 51
Height
≫ 179cm
Role
≫ Ascetic

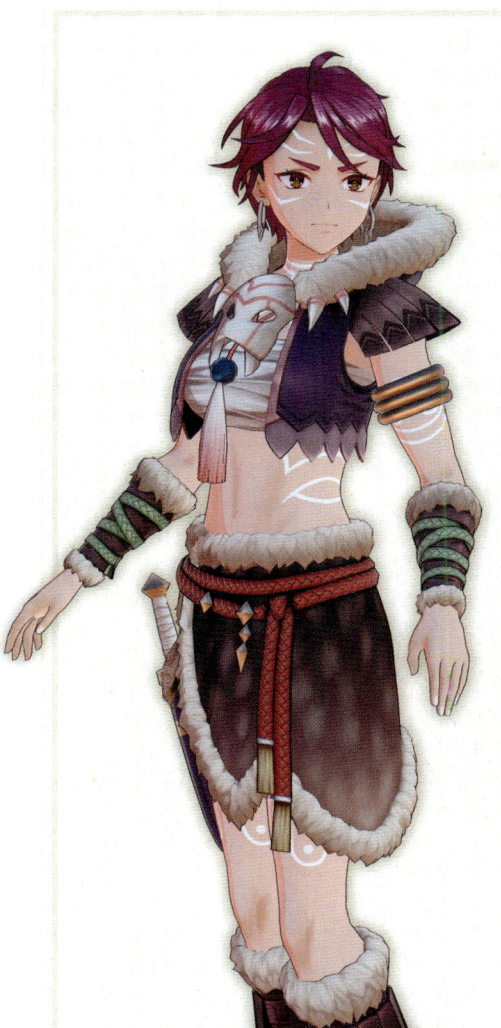

Deirdre Northfill

デアドラ・ノースフィル

CV Houko Kuwashima

Profile
Age
≫ 26
Height
≫ 166cm
Role
≫ Head of Gleaner

Despite her young age, she is a warrior who is also the head of "Gleaner", a vigilante-corps-like organization in the village of Faurre. She raised Dian, who had been orphaned, like a family member, and taught him how to live as a warrior. She has quite a nervous temperament, and is always concerned about Dian.

◆ Design Notes ◆

The starting point for Deirdre is that she has absorbed one element of her younger brother Dian, the "delinquent" part of him. This is why her hair is cut short on the sides, et cetera. Because of things like that, her wild elements are strong, which is rare and has a wild element to it, which is rare for an "Atelier" character. *(Development staff)*

Ryza's father. He attentively runs a small general farm. He is peaceful and kind, and he is somewhat subservient to Mio.

◆ Design Notes ◆

Ryza was described as being an ordinary girl in "1", and in line with that we maintained the point of her parents being extremely ordinary parents in their design. The voice of Karl, performed by Midorikawa, also helped to create a feeling that he was seemingly simple, but also something more. *(Development staff)*

Karl Stout

カール・シュタウト

CV Hikaru Midorikawa

Profile
Age
≫ 46
Height
≫ 176cm
Role
≫ Farmer

Mio Stout

ミオ・シュタウト

CV Yuko Nagashima

Ryza's mother. She has married into the family of Karl, who is a farmer. She is very protective of Ryza, and has a habit of thinking of Ryza as still and always being the child she once was.

Profile
Age
≫ 44
Height
≫ 162cm
Role
≫ Homemaker

◈ Design Notes ◈

As with Karl, the concept of her being very ordinary remains unchanged. In order to make the protagonist stand out, we saw it as important to keep in check the individuality of the supporting characters around her in their designs. *(Development staff)*

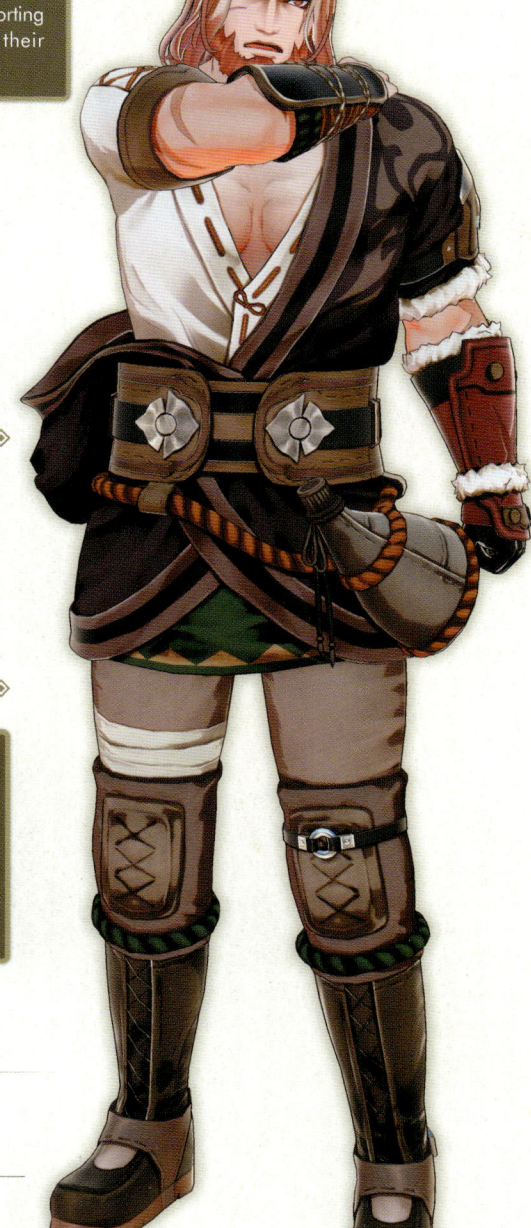

Lent's father. He is skilled in combat, and was once a well-known mercenary. However, he has a violent nature, and since his retirement hre has become a drunkard and fallen on hard times. He is currently separated from his wife.

◈ Design Notes ◈

When it came to Samuel's design, there were plenty of easily understood requirements, such as "he's Lent's father, he's a former mercenary, he's become a drunk". So it was easy enough to complete his design. *(Development staff)*

Samuel Marslink

ザムエル・マルスリンク

CV Takashi Matsuyama

Profile
Age
≫ 51
Height
≫ 184cm
Role
≫ Former Mercenary

Moritz Brunnen

モリッツ・ブルネン

CV Ryota Takeuchi

Profile
Age
≫ 54
Height
≫ 175cm
Role
≫ Man of Wealth

He is the wealthiest man in the village of Rasenboden, and Bos's father. Although he displays a high-handed personality, he is on brilliant person by nature, and he still serves as the face of the village even after the loss of the water source. He is currently busy trying to calm the confusion caused by the appearance of the Kurk Archipelago.

Design Notes

As with Samuel, Moritz's elements in themselves were a collection of fairly straightforward symbols, so the progress itself was smooth. Toridamono also commented that the character was a good match for his background details. *(Development staff)*

A young man who takes up a sword and works for the village. He used to be just a hanger-on who followed Bos around, but, perhaps influenced by Bos's growth, he has reexamined his own life.

Design Notes

In "3," Lumbar has grown up and is making a contribution to Kurken Island. To create an impression of his independence, we made his hair a little longer, giving him a more mature look. The colors of his clothes are similar to those of Bos in the past, as an indication of his respect for Bos. *(Development staff)*

Lumbar Dorn

ランバー・ドルン

CV Fukushi Ochiai

Profile
Age
≫ 22
Height
≫ 168cm
Role
≫ Bos's Former Henchman

Agatha Harmon

アガーテ・ハーマン

CV Masumi Asano

Profile
Age
» 26

Height
» 174cm

Role
» Village Guardian

A warrior of Rasenboden Village, called a Guardian. She's watched over Ryza and the others growing up since they were little. She is frantically doing her job, trying to quell the the chaos that came with the appearance of the Kurk Archipelago.

◆ Design Notes ◆

We think the design of this character strikes just the right balance in the game considering her role on Kurken Island, but seeing that her details do not compete with the main characters. She is also a character that appears frequently in other media. *(Development staff)*

A woman of the Soulspeaker clan, skilled in the spiritual arts. She had a mission to protect a precious water source called Sanctuary in the Underworld.

◆ Design Notes ◆

Kilo is an Oren and ages slowly, so there are no major changes in her appearance, but we focused on different aspects than in "1". Therefore, to make it easier to understand her expressions, we lifted her hood and showed her hidden eyes, which had been hidden. *(Development staff)*

Kilo Shiness

キロ・シャイナス

CV Shiori Mikami

Profile
Age
» ???

Height
» 159cm

Role
» Spirit User

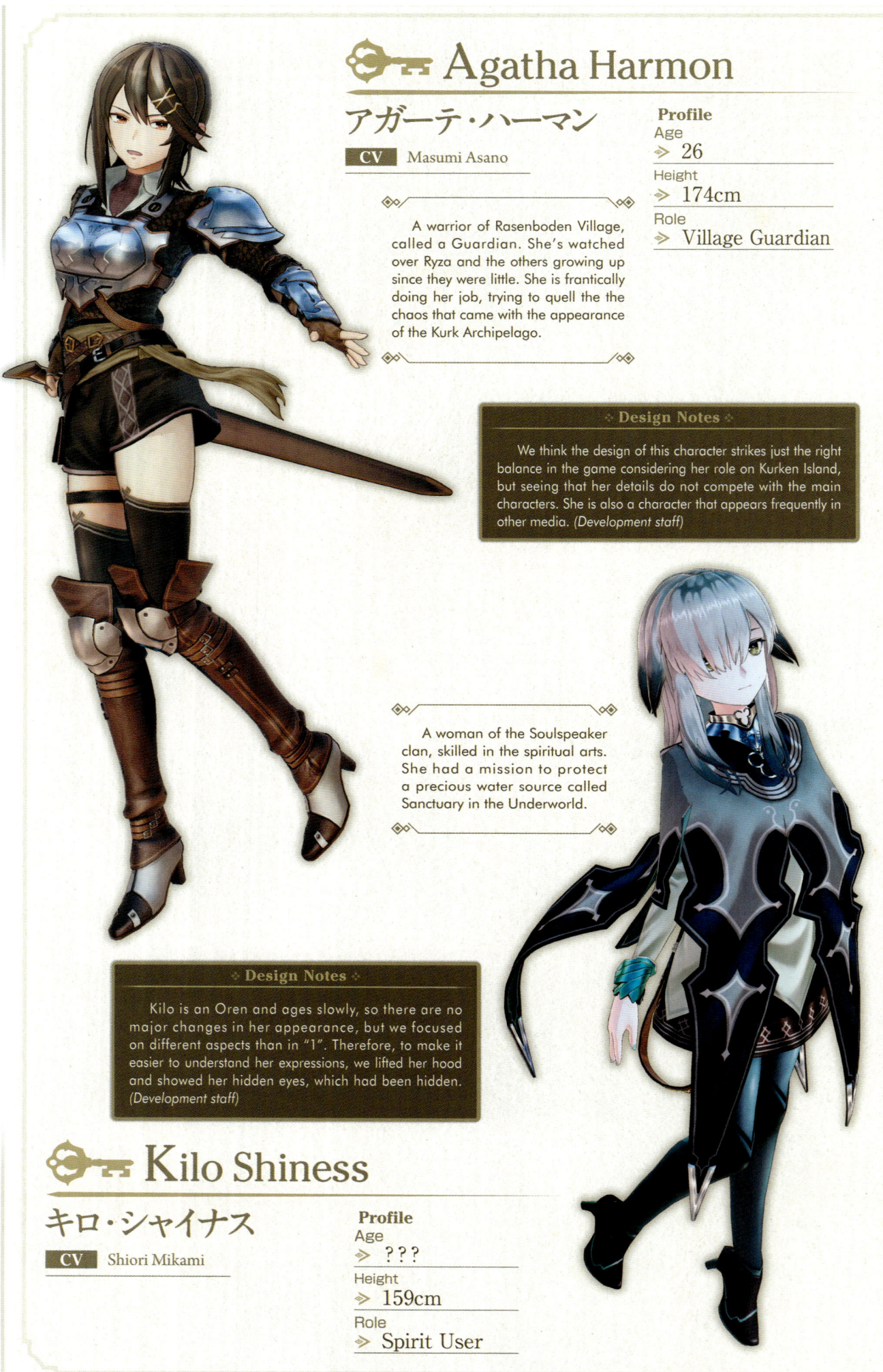

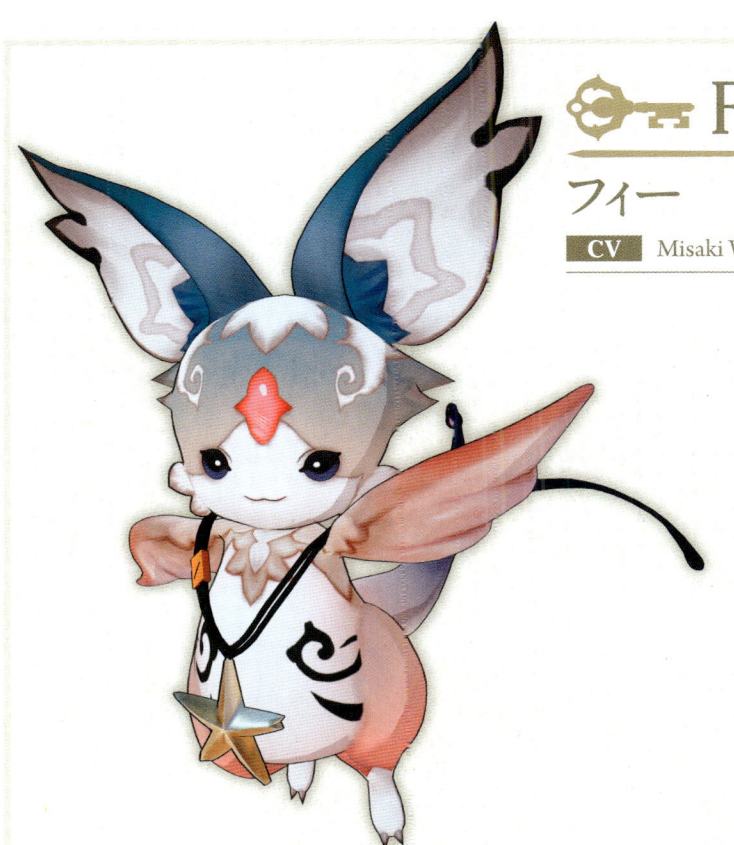

Fi

フィー

CV Misaki Watada

Profile

Age
» 1

Height
» 50cm

Role
» Soothing Sprite

A small creature hatched from a shiny stone-like egg during an adventure in the royal capital. Originally from a race that lives in the Underworld, it cannot survive without magical energy from the demon world. No matter how far apart they are, the bond it shares with Ryza never fades.

Design Notes

We created the base design in-house and refined it from there. It's animal-like, with marine creature aspects, and bird-like parts, and it has a strangeness while also being definitely cute. You can really feels that the design was indeed by Toridamono. *(Development staff)*

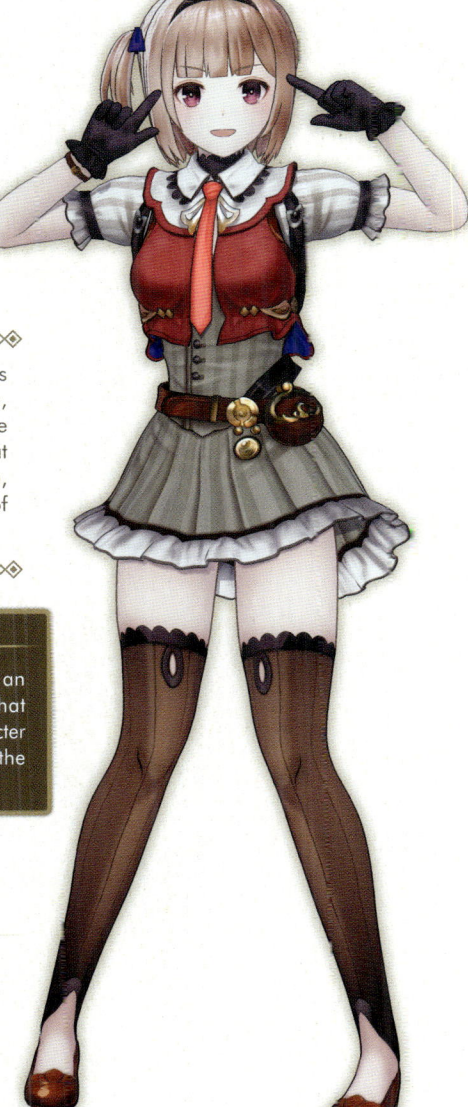

A woman who travels to various regions as a peddler. For a time, she tried setting up a store in the royal capital, but she realized that being a peddler is in her nature, and so she has returned to a life of traveling from place to place.

Design Notes

Romy is one of those rare characters who went from being an utter background character to a named character at a level that needed design refinement (as did Mio and Karl). She is a character that's typical of the old "Atelier" style, and she is loved within the development team as well. *(Development staff)*

Romy Vogel

ロミィ・フォーゲル

CV Yuki Nagaku

Profile

Age
» 27

Height
» 154cm

Role
» Peddler

Elder

古老

CV Takumu Miyazono

One of the major figures of Rasenboden Village. As a member of the village council, he often goes on about various village policies. Although he is not as severe as he used to be, as ever he has not gotten past his rigid ways of thinking.

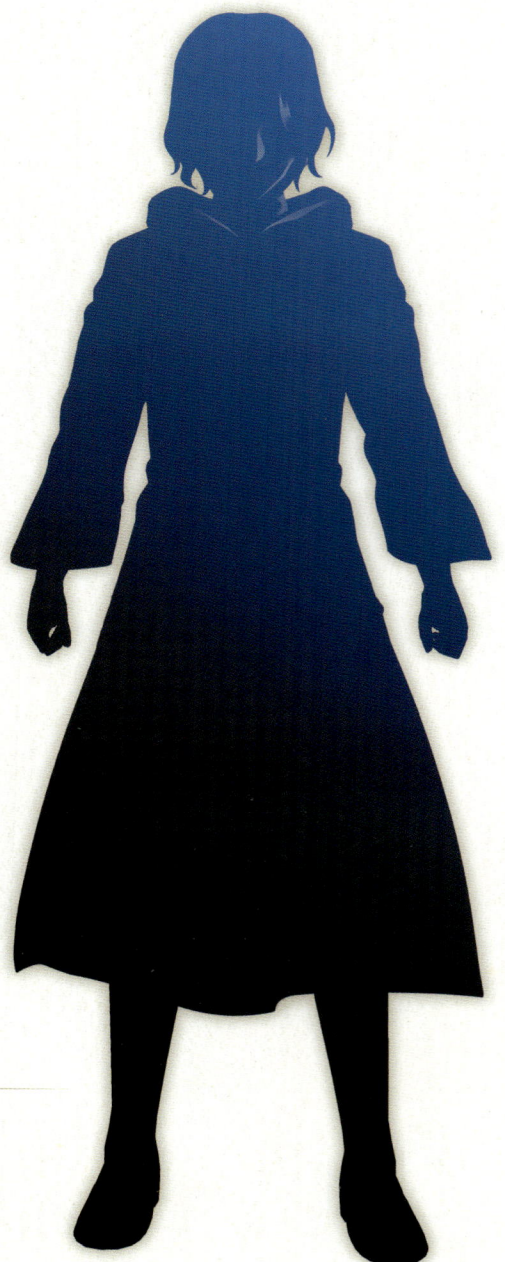

As an alchemist in the employ of the royal court, he was a former colleague and friend of Empel. When Empel would not abide by the will of the court and earned their displeasure, Emil led the plot in which Empel's right arm was injured. Since Empel flew from the palace crushed, his whereabouts and activities have remained unknown.

Emil

エミル

CV ---

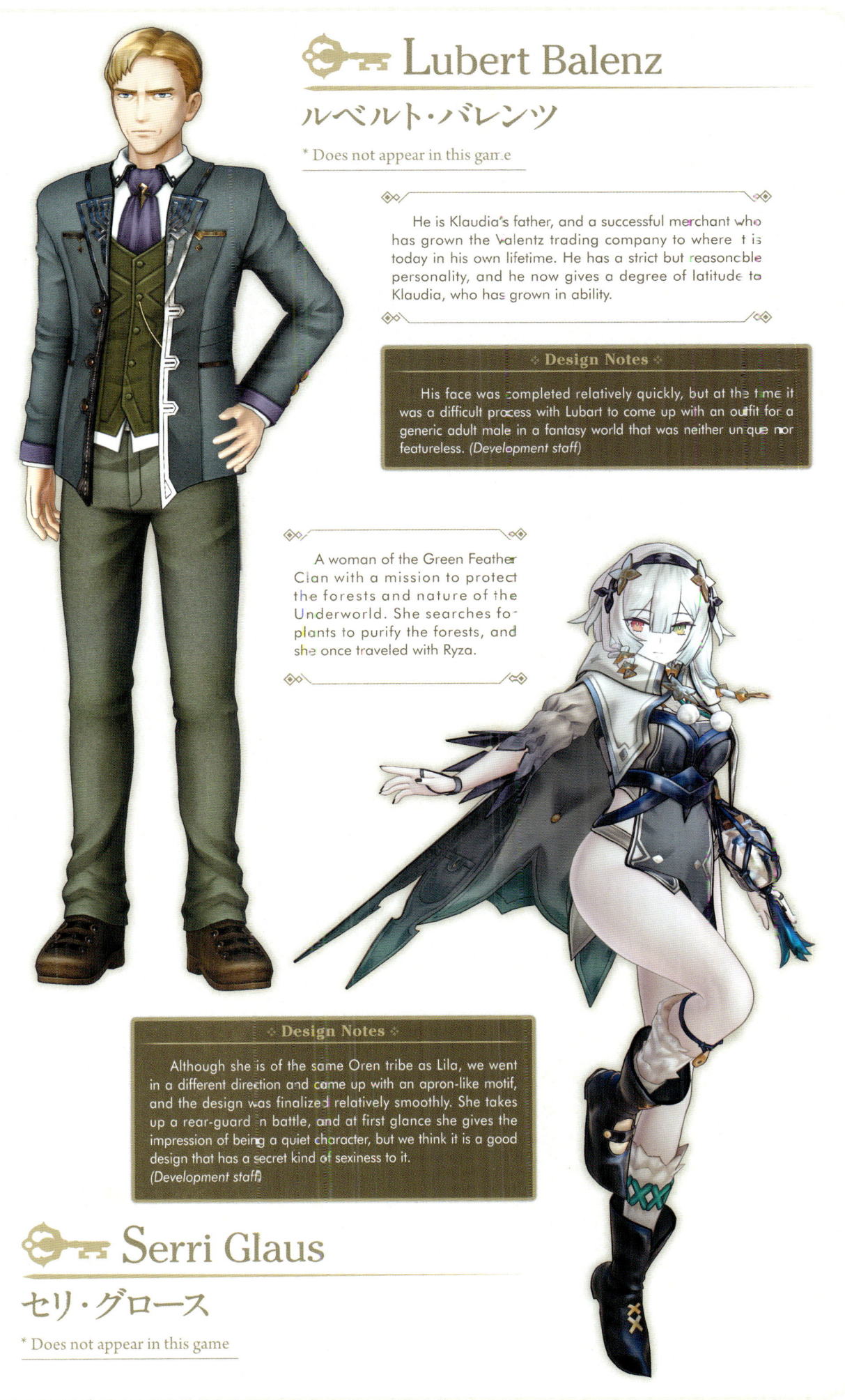

Lubert Balenz
ルベルト・バレンツ

*Does not appear in this game

He is Klaudia's father, and a successful merchant who has grown the Valentz trading company to where it is today in his own lifetime. He has a strict but reasonable personality, and he now gives a degree of latitude to Klaudia, who has grown in ability.

Design Notes

His face was completed relatively quickly, but at the time it was a difficult process with Lubart to come up with an outfit for a generic adult male in a fantasy world that was neither unique nor featureless. *(Development staff)*

A woman of the Green Feather Clan with a mission to protect the forests and nature of the Underworld. She searches for plants to purify the forests, and she once traveled with Ryza.

Design Notes

Although she is of the same Oren tribe as Lila, we went in a different direction and came up with an apron-like motif, and the design was finalized relatively smoothly. She takes up a rear-guard in battle, and at first glance she gives the impression of being a quiet character, but we think it is a good design that has a secret kind of sexiness to it. *(Development staff)*

Serri Glaus
セリ・グロース

*Does not appear in this game

Volker Abelheim
ヴォルカー・アーベルハイム
*Does not appear in this game

Patricia's father, and an aristocrat in the royal capital. Partly because of his background as a knight who made a name for himself and earned his title, he taught swordsmanship to Patricia as well.

◆ Design Notes ◆
Volker was designed with his high status as a nobleman in mind, as well as his physical strength, being the one who teaches martial arts to Patricia. He does not wear a sword, as he basically only appears around town, but he does carry a sword belt as a vestige of that side of him. *(Development staff)*

A treasure hunter who once traveled with Ryza. He is a cheerful young man in pursuit of heroic adventure. Even now he is off adventuring somewhere in search of treasure.

◆ Design Notes ◆
Our initial request was for Clifford to be a traditionally handsome man, but at Toridamono's insistence, he gradually became a character with stronger quirks. He has a mask, hat, and many other accessories, and he became a character with many elements even in "Atelier" as a whole. *(Development staff)*

Clifford Diswell
クリフォード・ディズウェル
*Does not appear in this game

Costume Variations

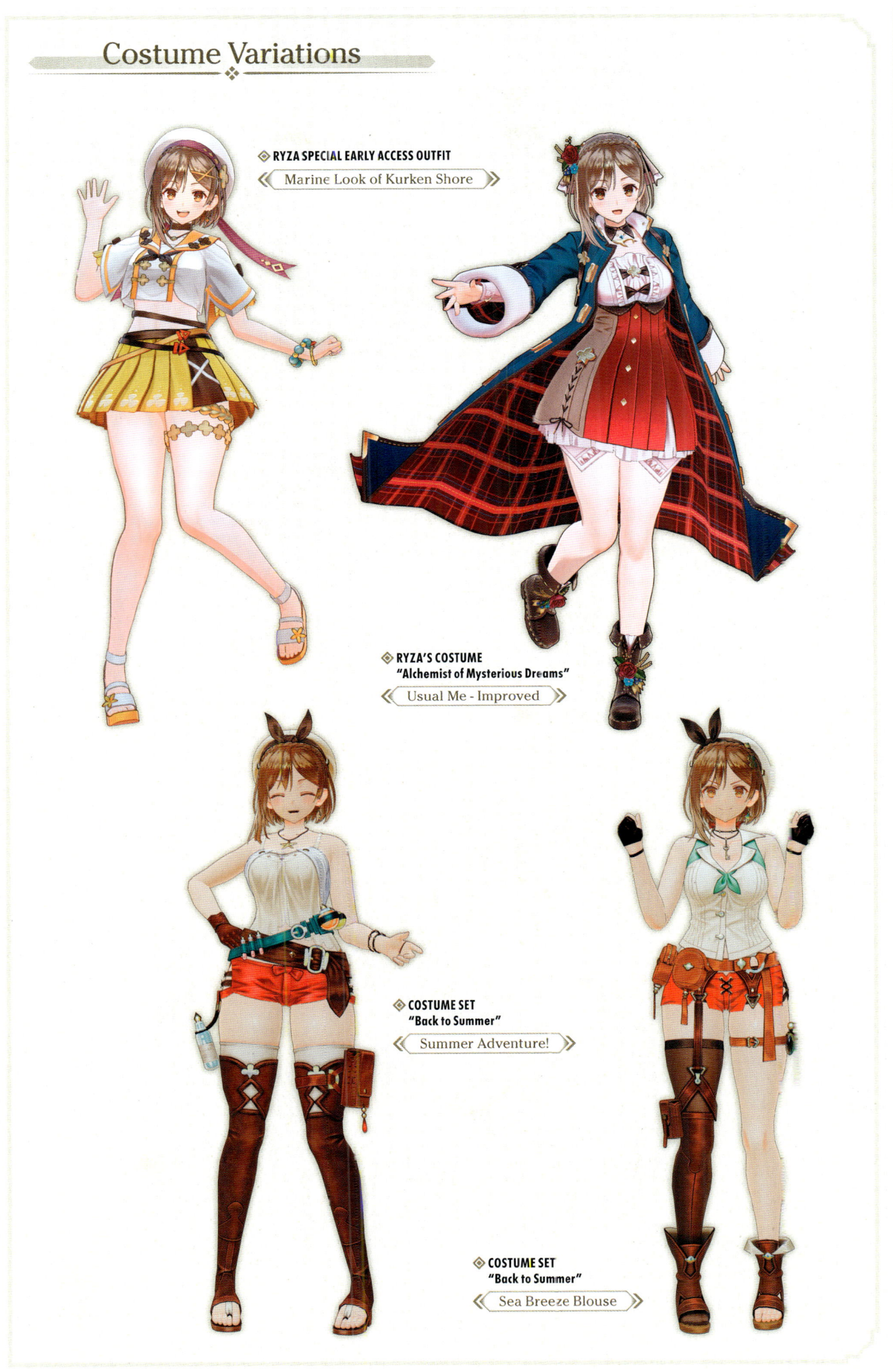

◆ RYZA SPECIAL EARLY ACCESS OUTFIT
《 Marine Look of Kurken Shore 》

◆ RYZA'S COSTUME
"Alchemist of Mysterious Dreams"
《 Usual Me - Improved 》

◆ COSTUME SET
"Back to Summer"
《 Summer Adventure! 》

◆ COSTUME SET
"Back to Summer"
《 Sea Breeze Blouse 》

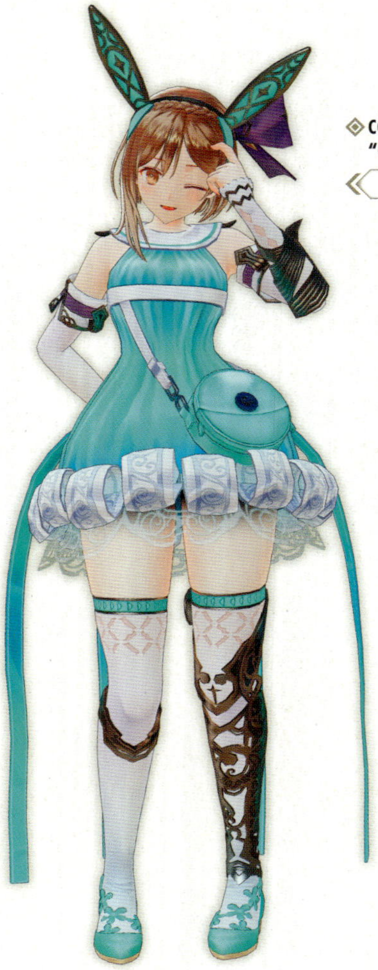

◆ COSTUME SET
"Gust Collaboration"
《 All Grown Up 》

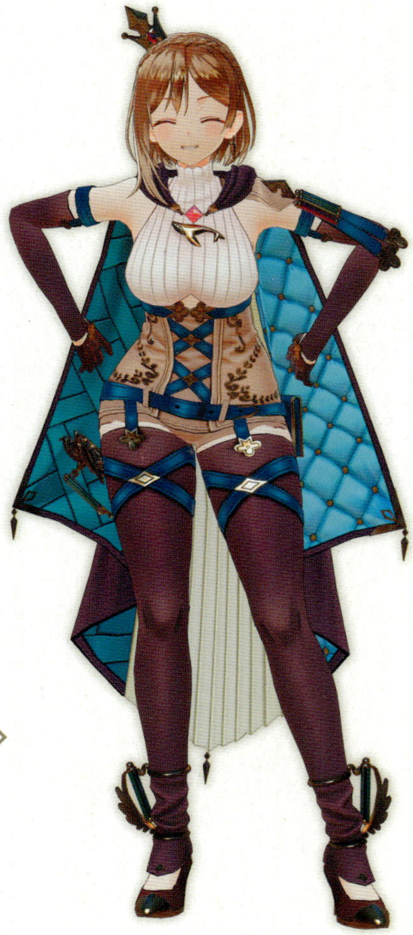

◆ COSTUME SET
"Gust Collaboration"
《 The Usual Me! 》

◆ PRE-ORDER BONUS (3 accessories for Ryza)
《 Straw Hat / Summer Flower Crown / Great Alchemist's Staff 》

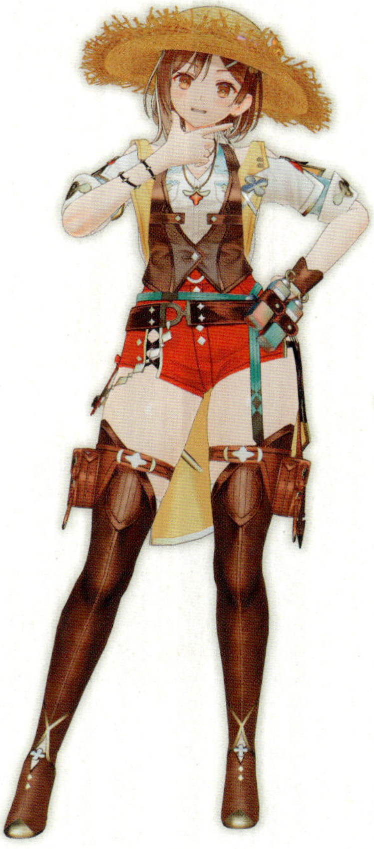

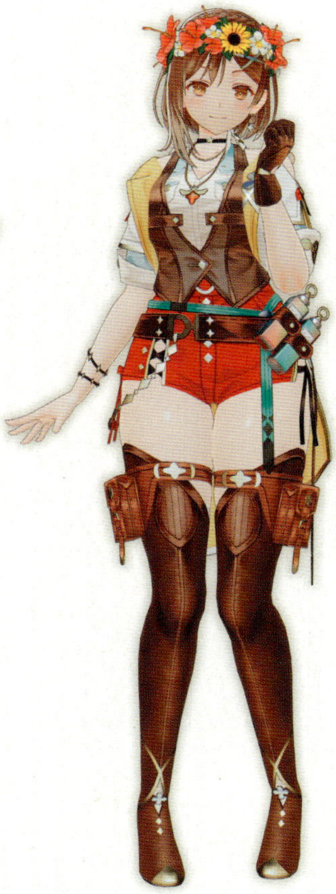

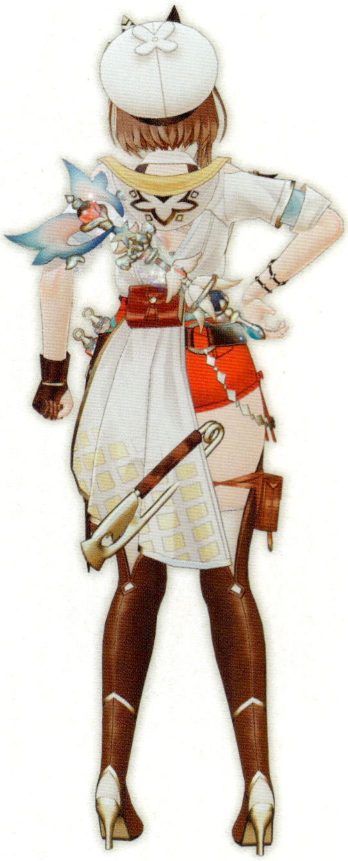

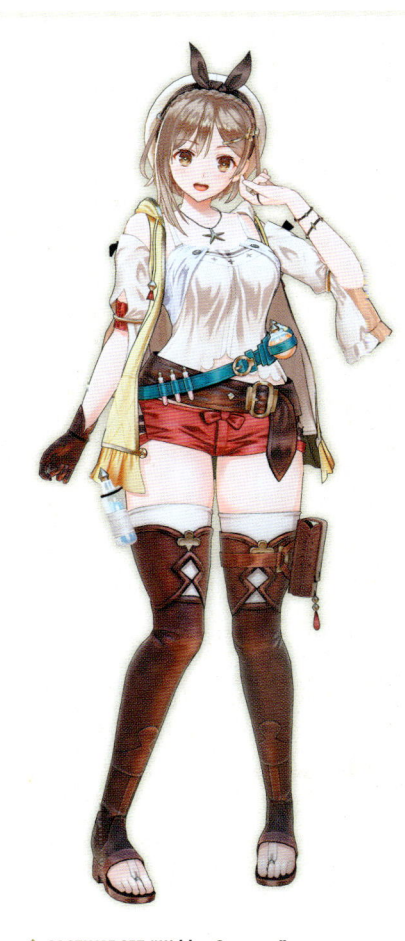

◆ COSTUME SET "Hidden Summer"
《 Ryza: Favorite Outfit 》

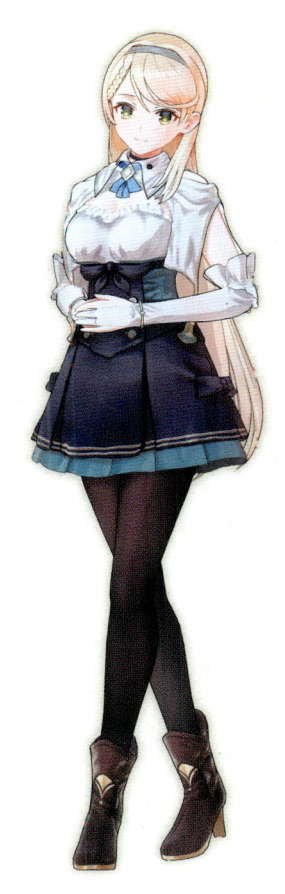

◆ COSTUME SET "Hidden Summer"
《 Klaudia: Lovely Nocturnal Eyes 》

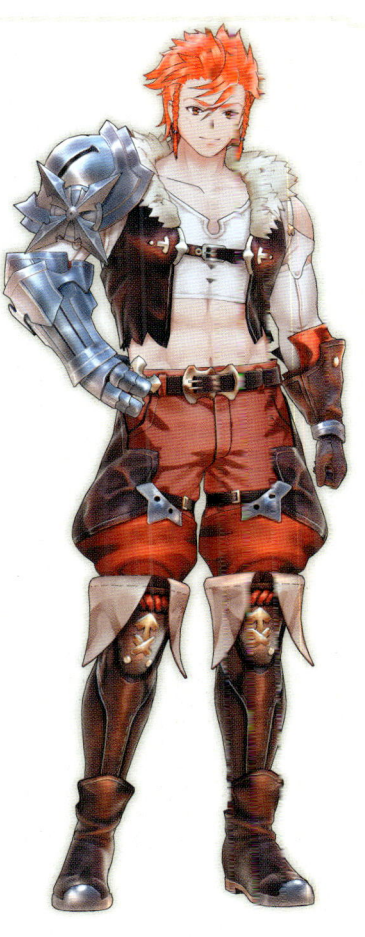

◆ COSTUME SET "Hidden Summer"
《 Lent: Beginner Warrior 》

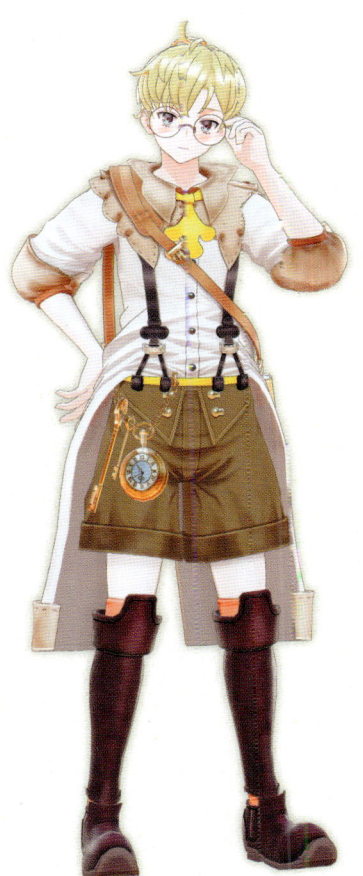

◆ COSTUME SET "Hidden Summer"
《 Tao: Fledgling Researcher 》

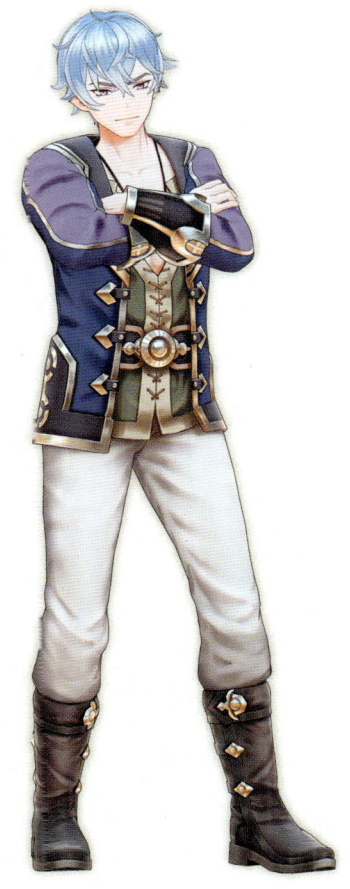

◆ COSTUME SET "Hidden Summer"
《 Bos: Village Bad Boy 》

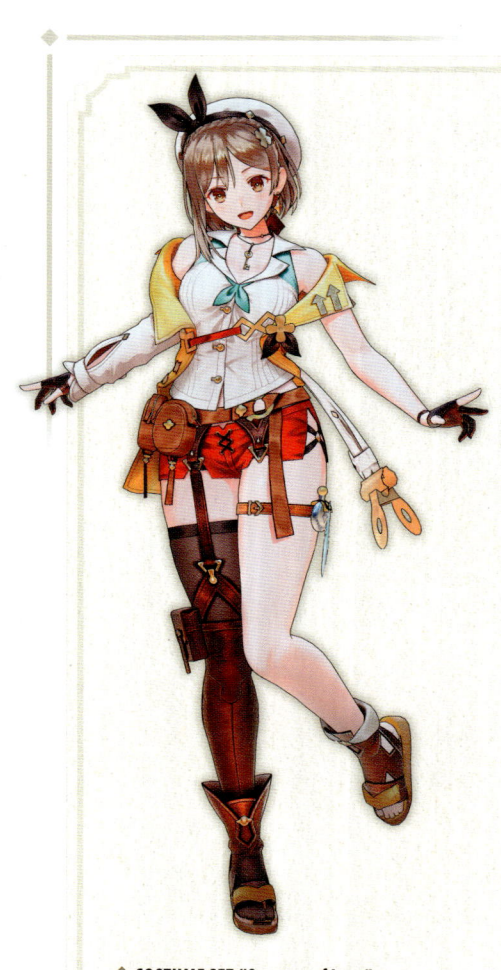
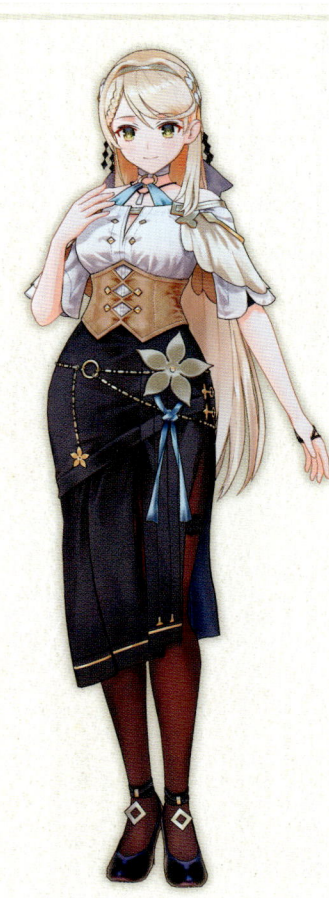
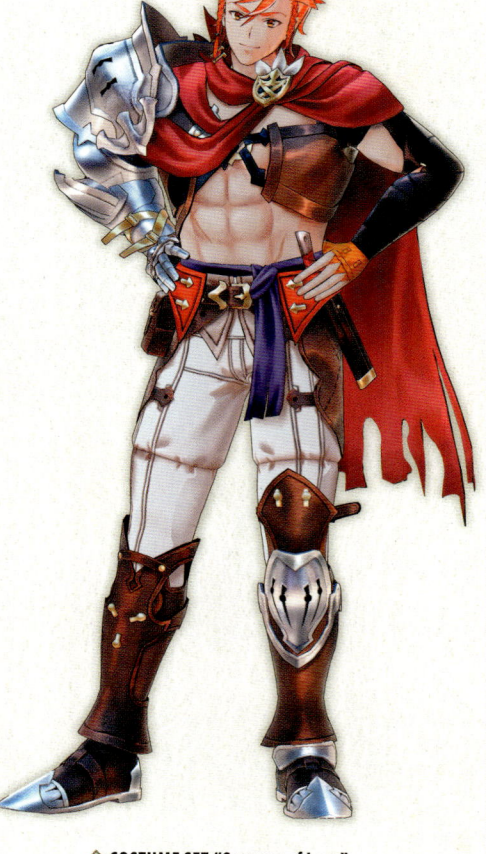

◆ COSTUME SET "Summer of Lore"
《 Ryza: Country Alchemist 》

◆ COSTUME SET "Summer of Lore"
《 Klaudia: Day-to-Day Young Miss 》

◆ COSTUME SET "Summer of Lore"
《 Lent: Wandering Warrior Youth 》

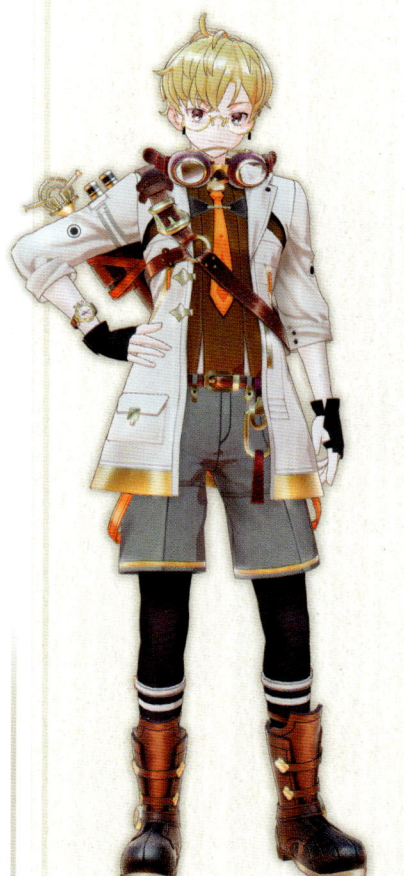
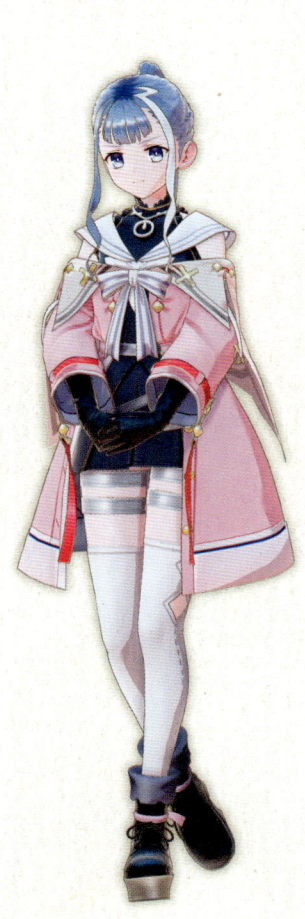
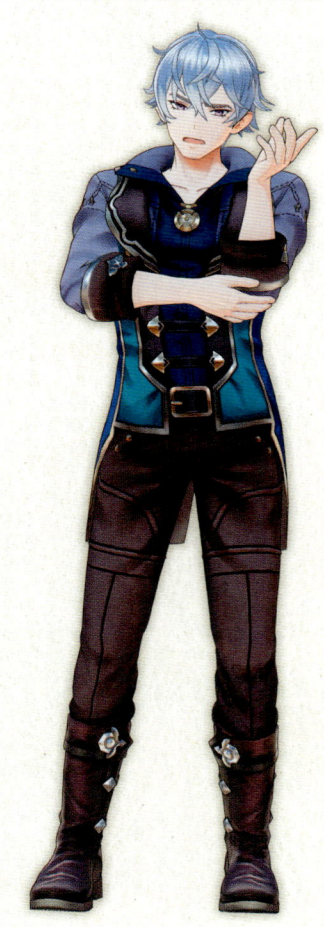

◆ COSTUME SET "Summer of Lore"
《 Tao: Up-and-Coming Archaeologist 》

◆ COSTUME SET "Summer of Lore"
《 Patricia: City Knight's Daughter 》

◆ COSTUME SET "Summer of Lore"
《 Bos: Hardworking Foreign Student 》

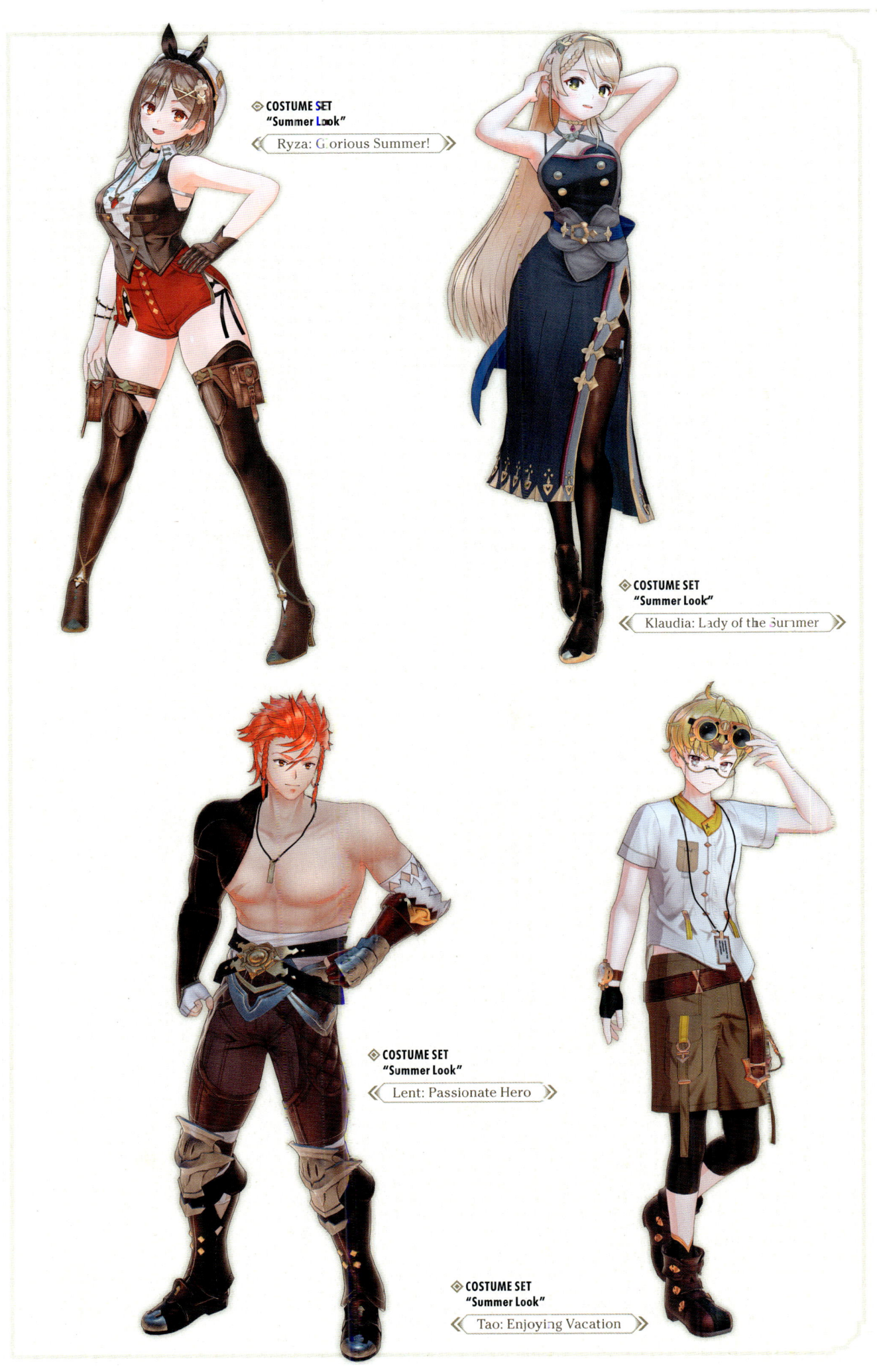

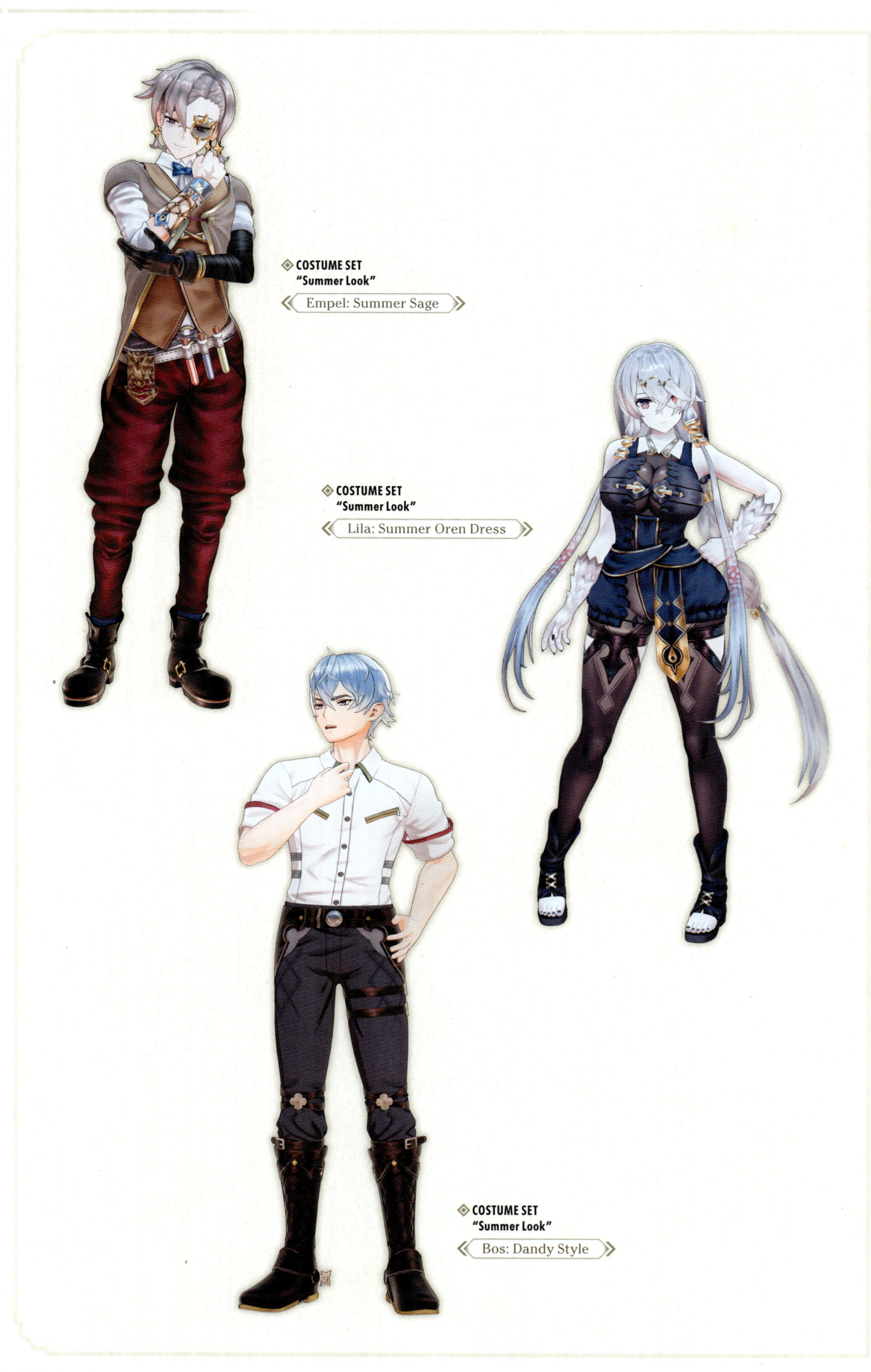

◆ COSTUME SET
"Summer Look"
《 Empel: Summer Sage 》

◆ COSTUME SET
"Summer Look"
《 Lila: Summer Oren Dress 》

◆ COSTUME SET
"Summer Look"
《 Bos: Dandy Style 》

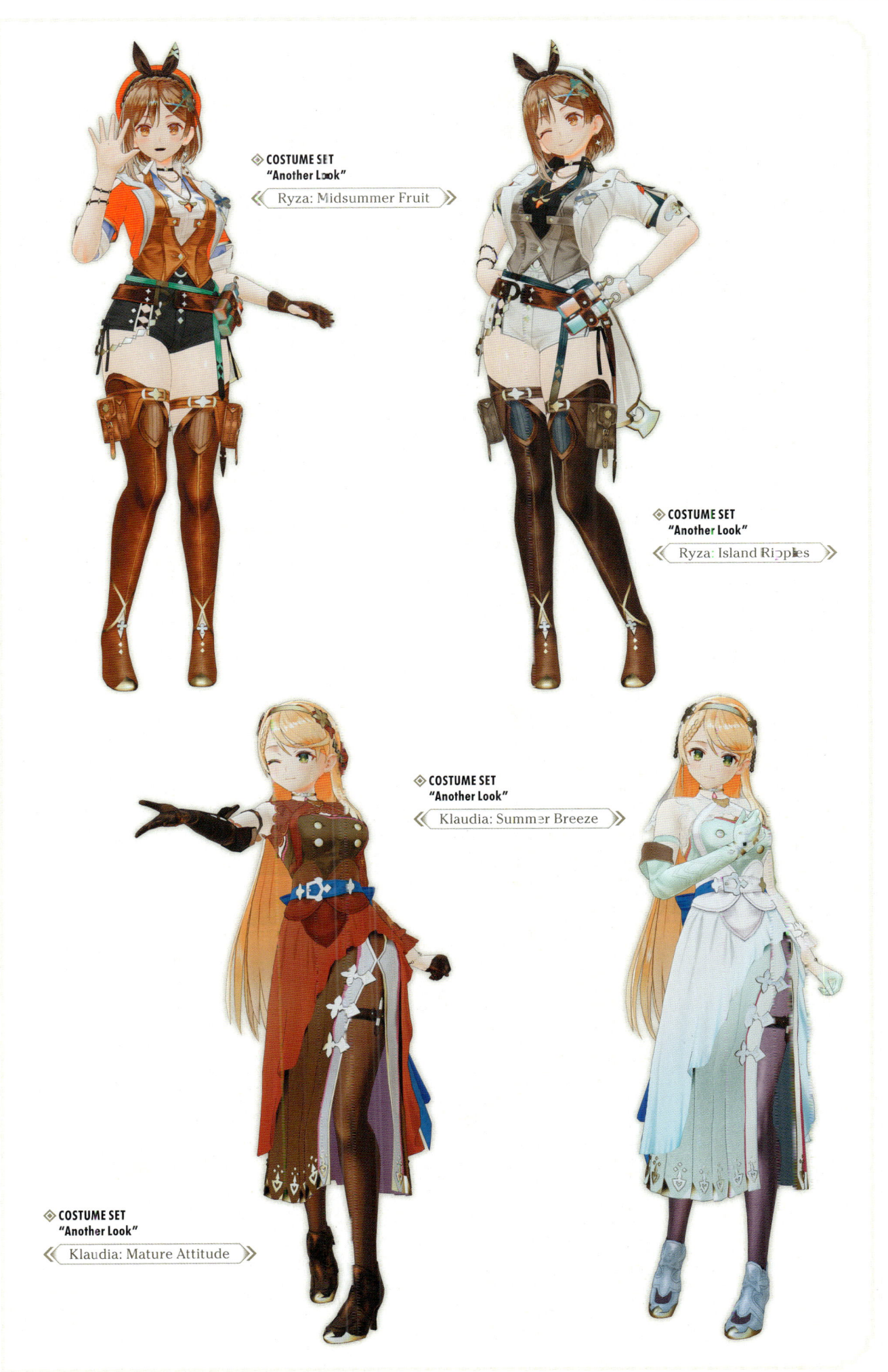

◆ COSTUME SET
"Another Look"
《 Ryza: Midsummer Fruit 》

◆ COSTUME SET
"Another Look"
《 Ryza: Island Ripples 》

◆ COSTUME SET
"Another Look"
《 Klaudia: Summer Breeze 》

◆ COSTUME SET
"Another Look"
《 Klaudia: Mature Attitude 》

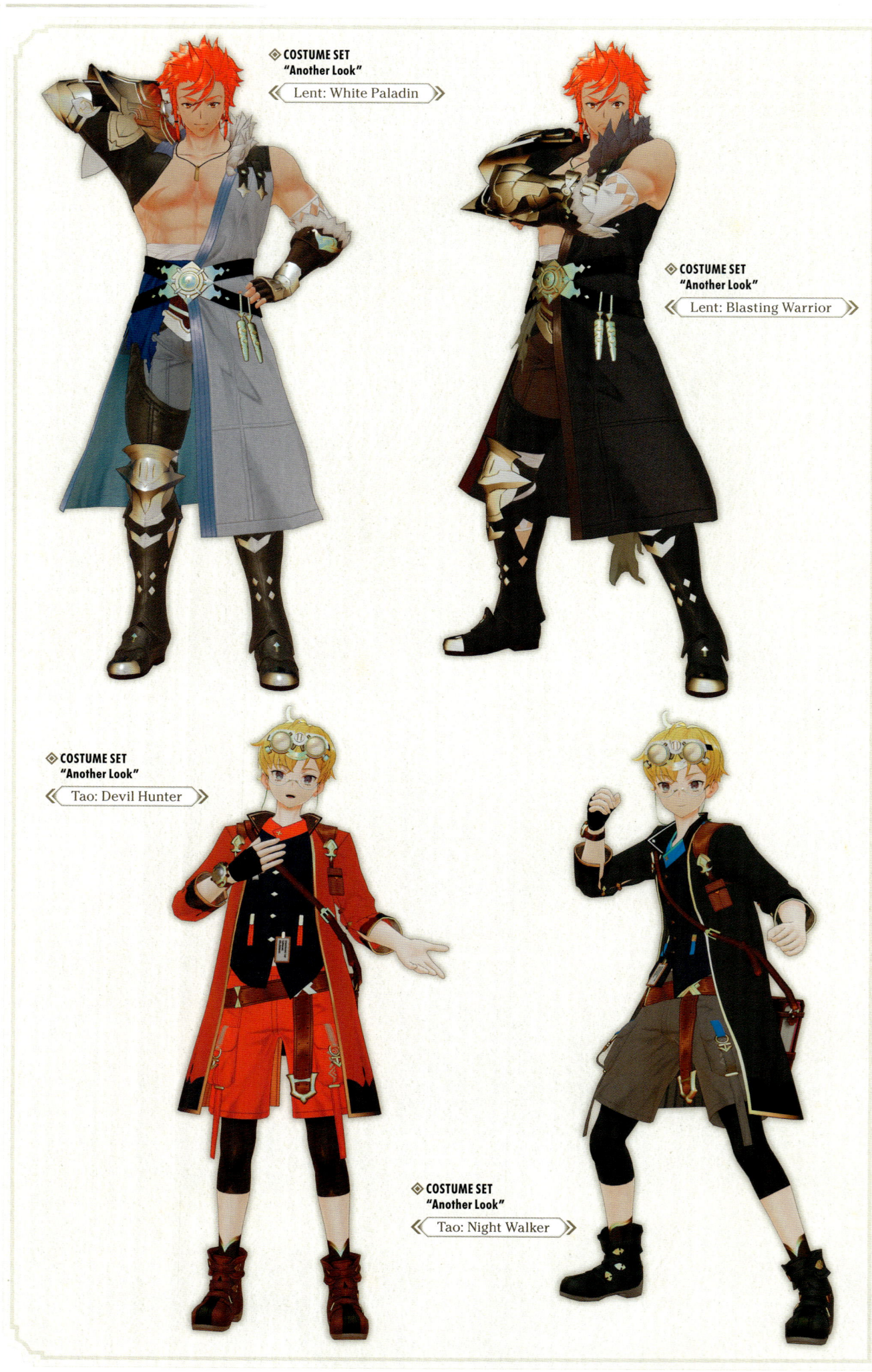

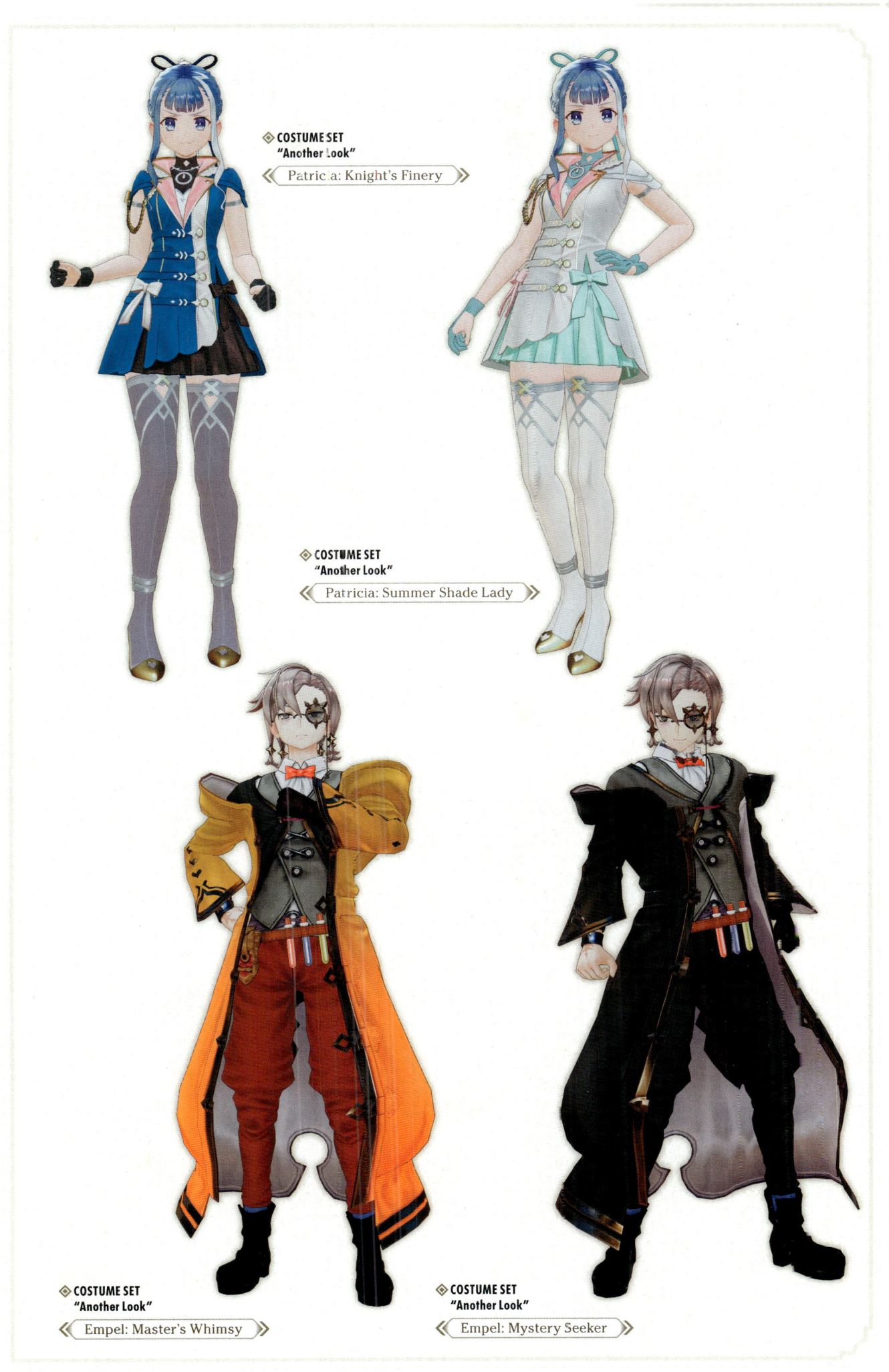

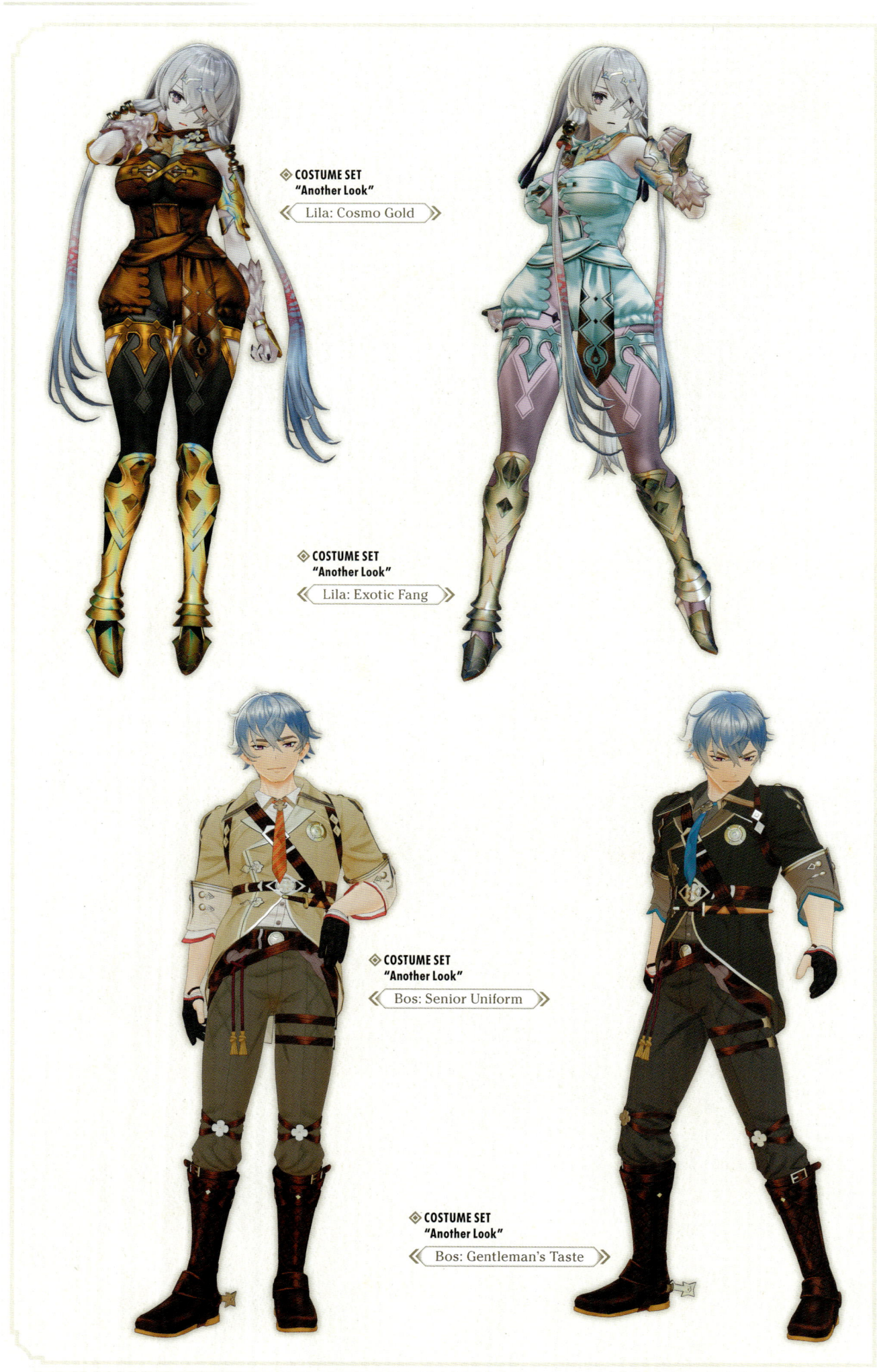

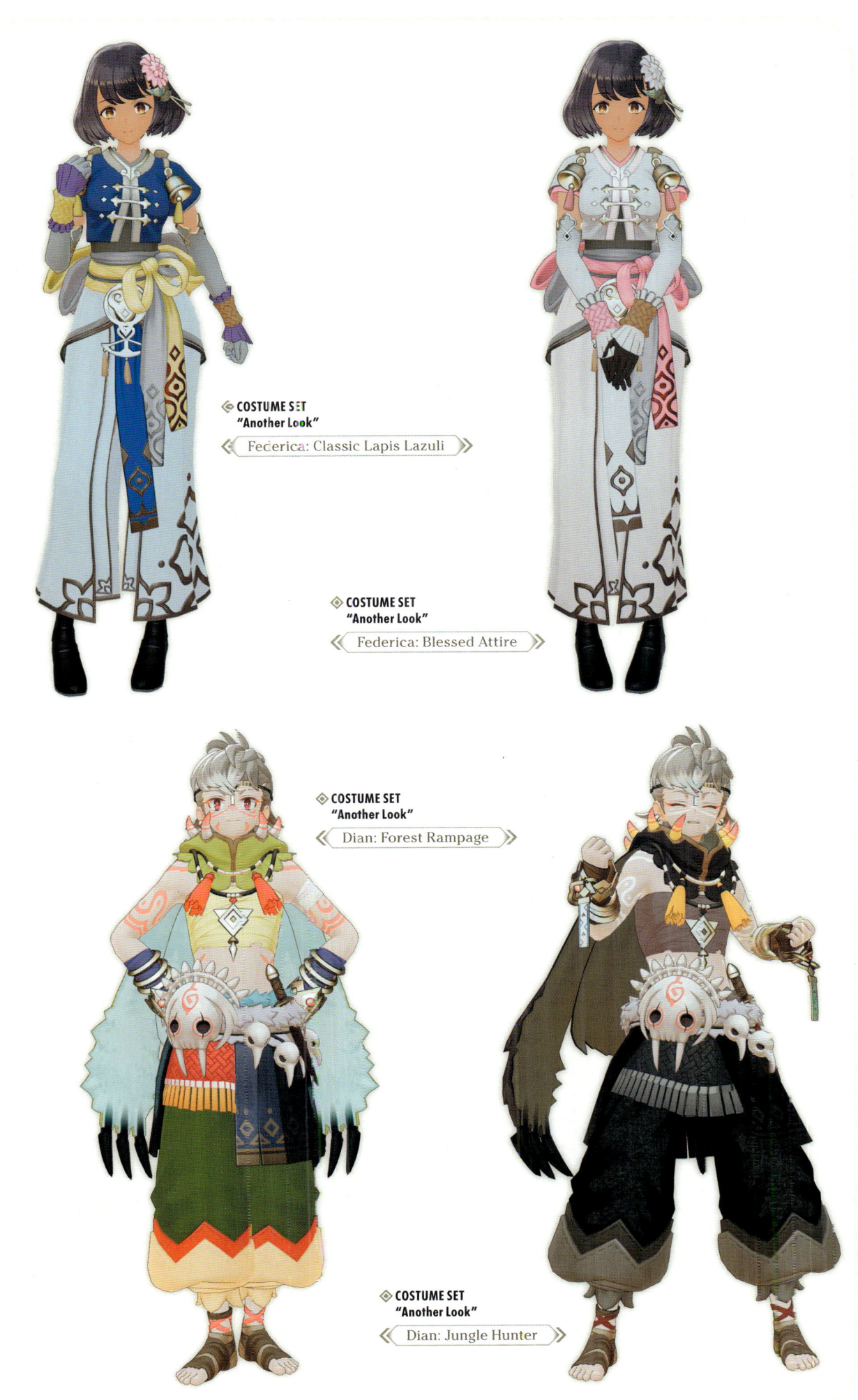

◆ COSTUME SET
"Another Look"
《 Federica: Classic Lapis Lazuli 》

◆ COSTUME SET
"Another Look"
《 Federica: Blessed Attire 》

◆ COSTUME SET
"Another Look"
《 Dian: Forest Rampage 》

◆ COSTUME SET
"Another Look"
《 Dian: Jungle Hunter 》

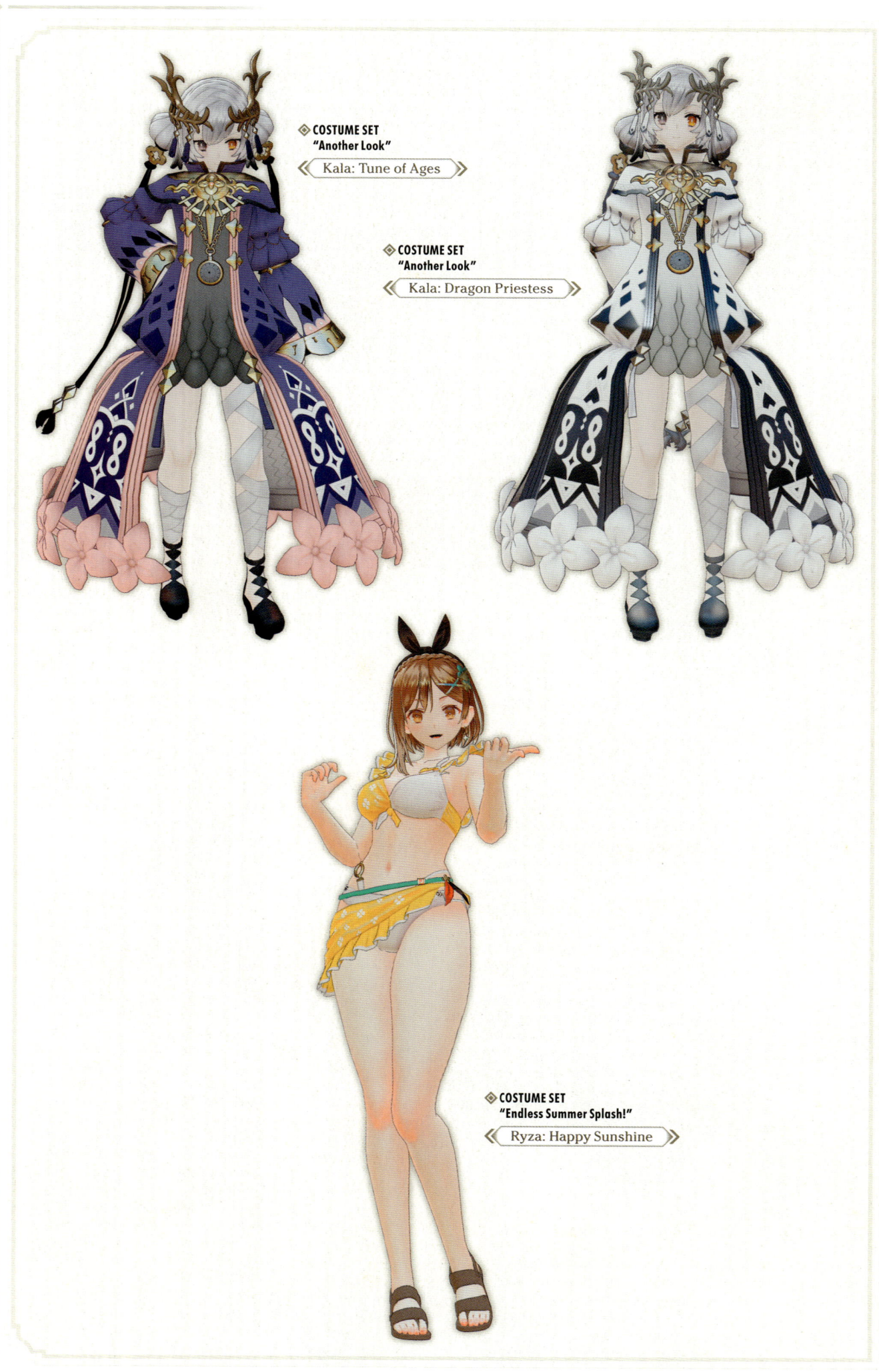

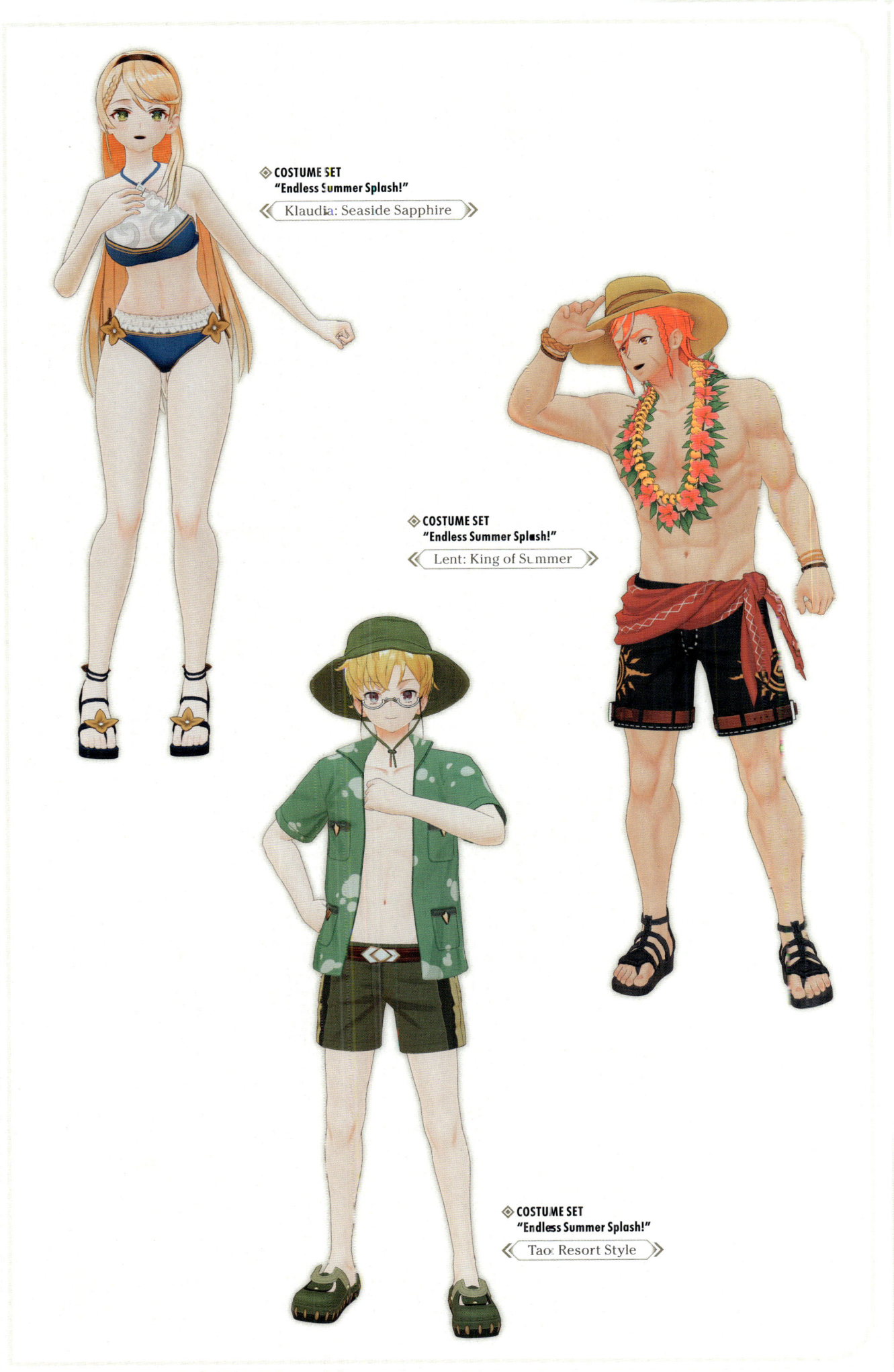

◆ COSTUME SET
"Endless Summer Splash!"
《 Klaudia: Seaside Sapphire 》

◆ COSTUME SET
"Endless Summer Splash!"
《 Lent: King of Summer 》

◆ COSTUME SET
"Endless Summer Splash!"
《 Tao: Resort Style 》

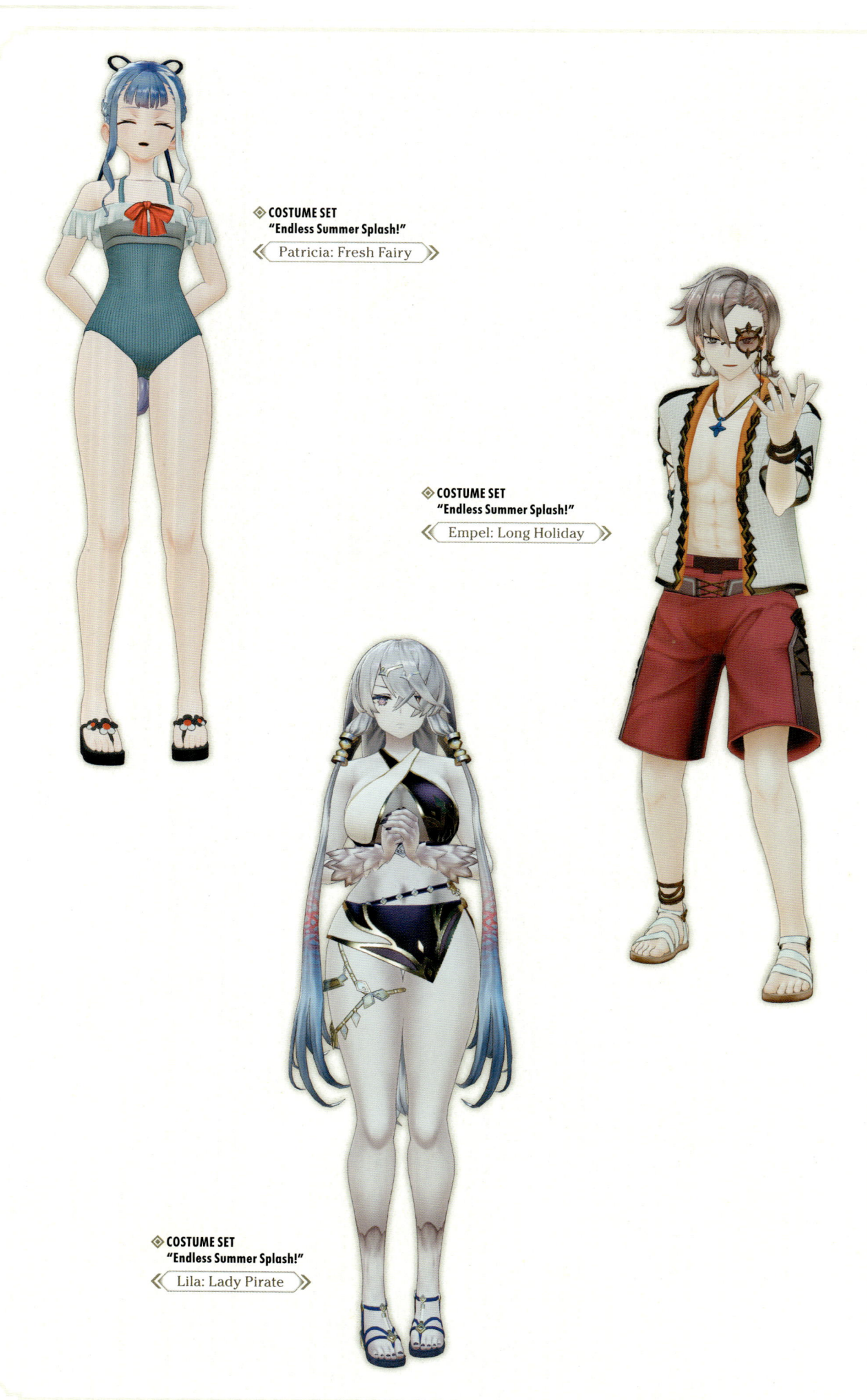

◆ COSTUME SET
"Endless Summer Splash!"
《 Patricia: Fresh Fairy 》

◆ COSTUME SET
"Endless Summer Splash!"
《 Empel: Long Holiday 》

◆ COSTUME SET
"Endless Summer Splash!"
《 Lila: Lady Pirate 》

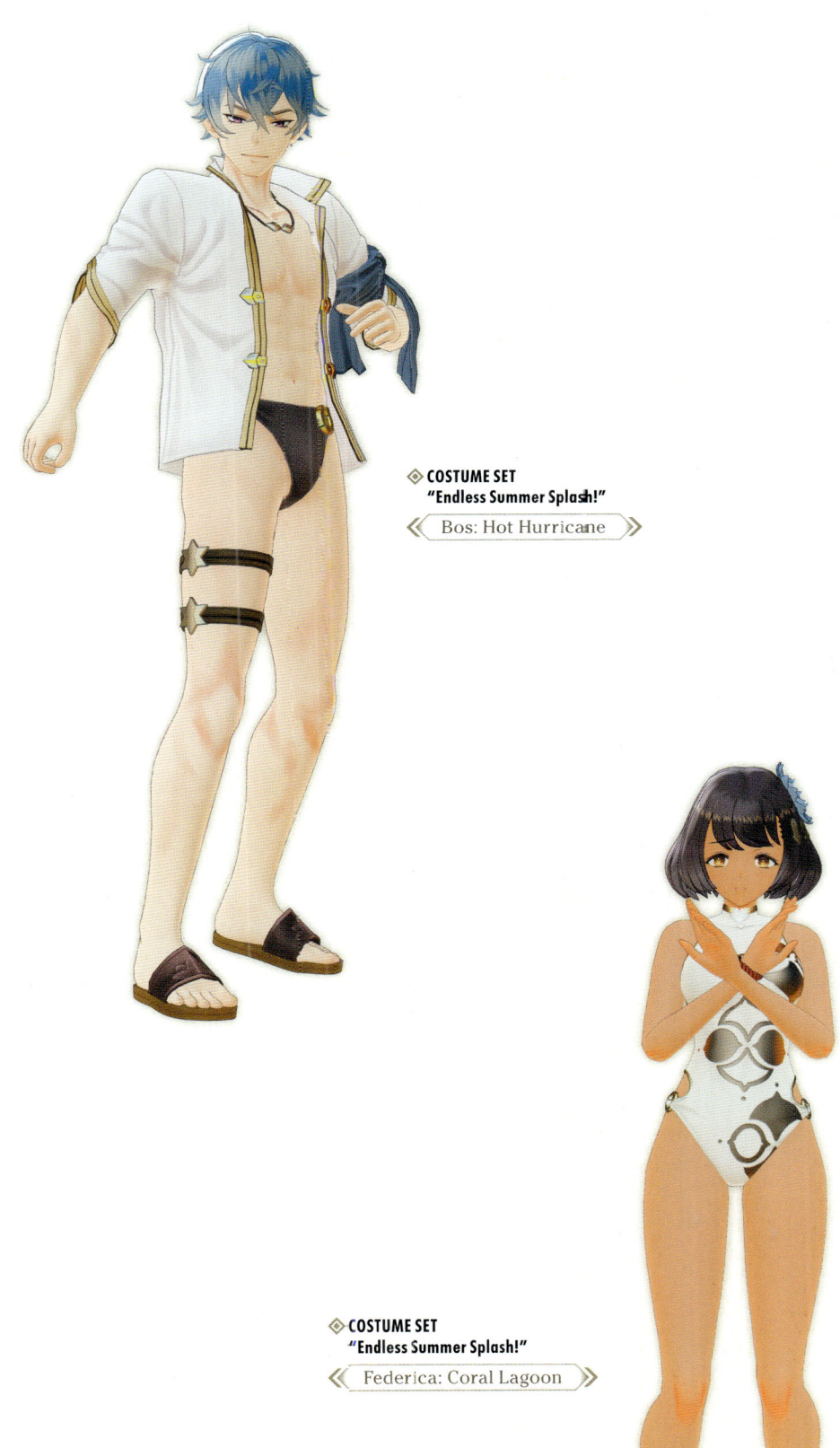

◆ COSTUME SET
"Endless Summer Splash!"
《 Bos: Hot Hurricane 》

◆ COSTUME SET
"Endless Summer Splash!"
《 Federica: Coral Lagoon 》

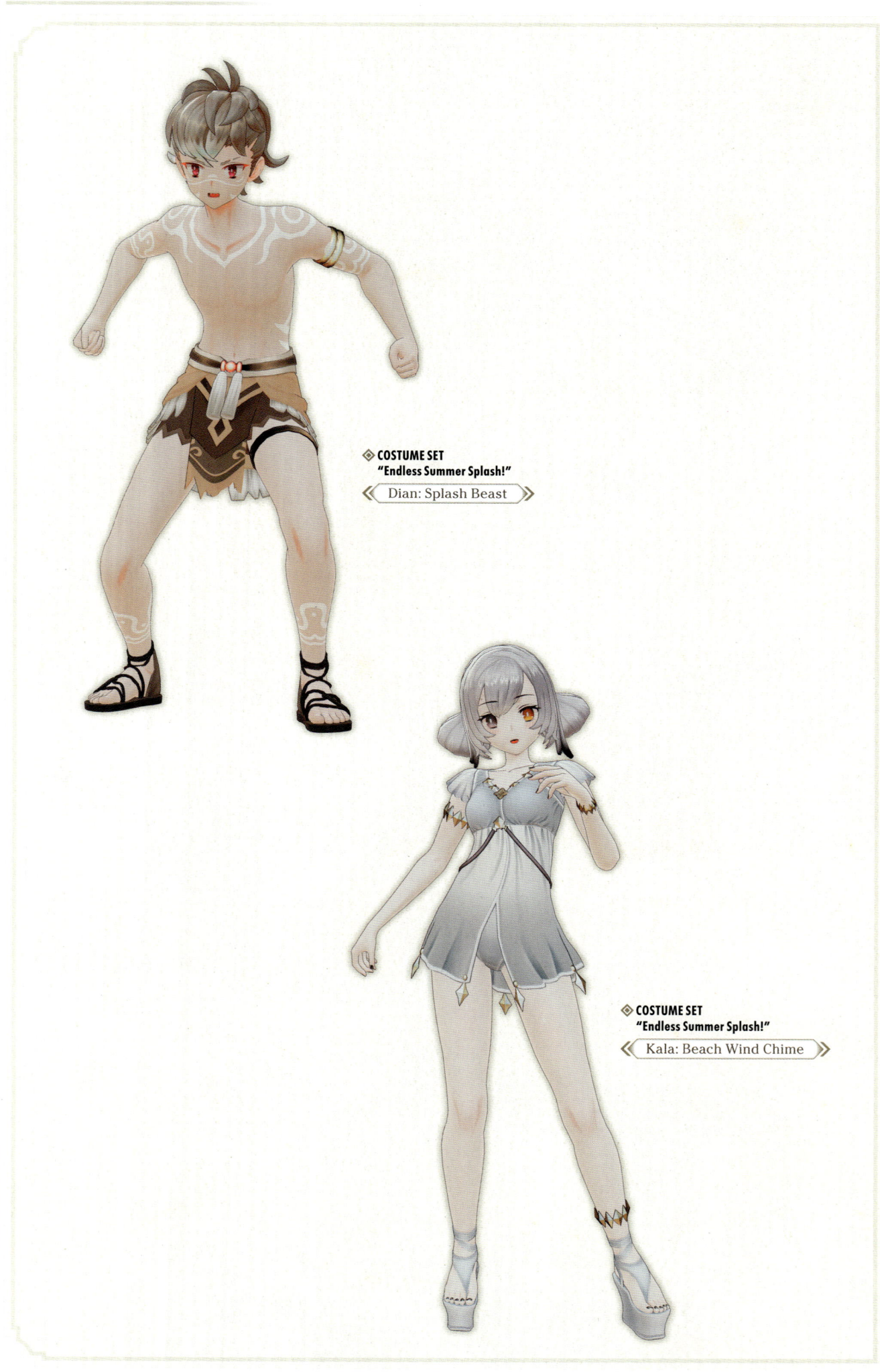

◆ COSTUME SET
"Endless Summer Splash!"
《 Dian: Splash Beast 》

◆ COSTUME SET
"Endless Summer Splash!"
《 Kala: Beach Wind Chime 》

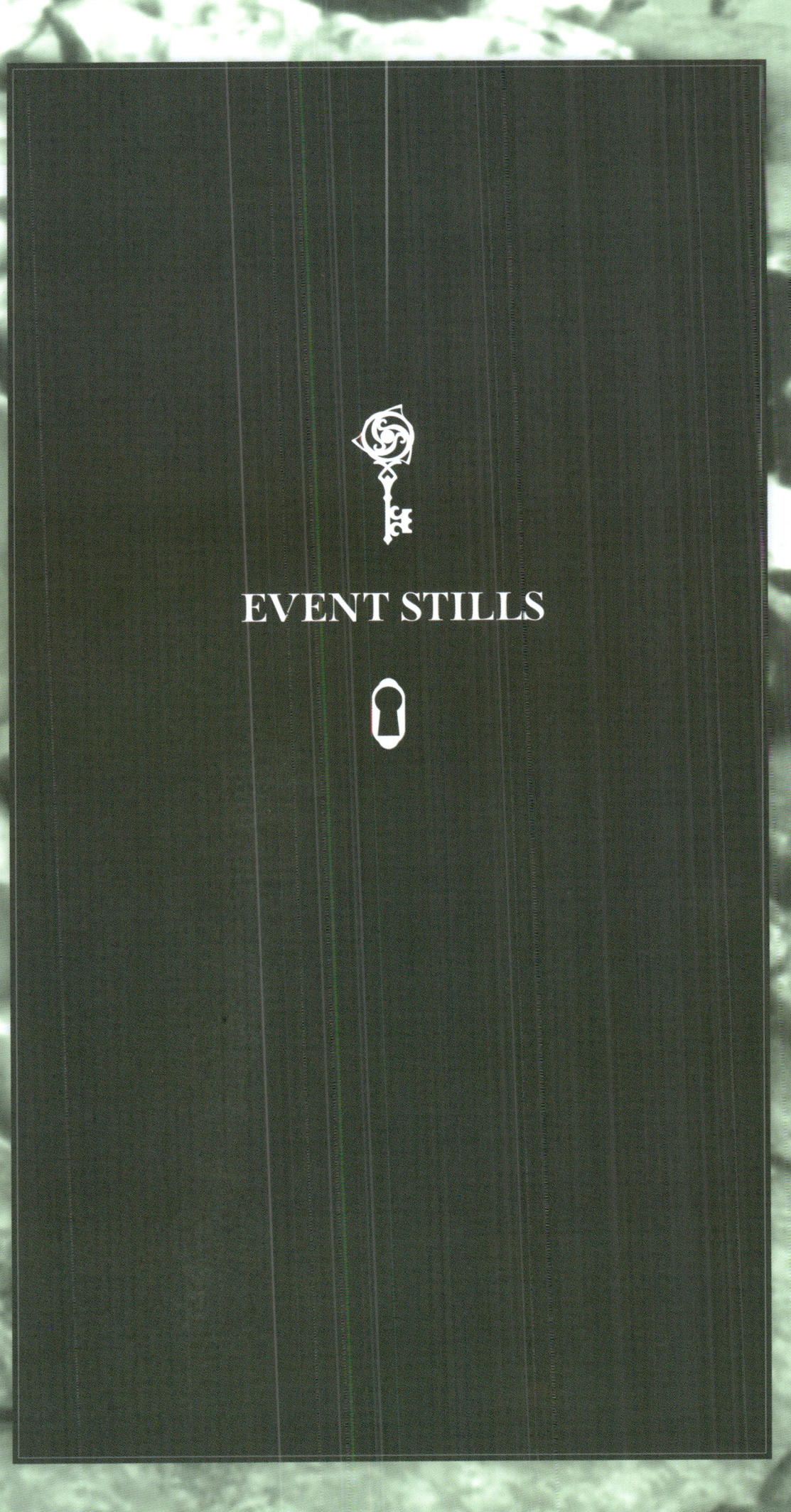

EVENT STILLS

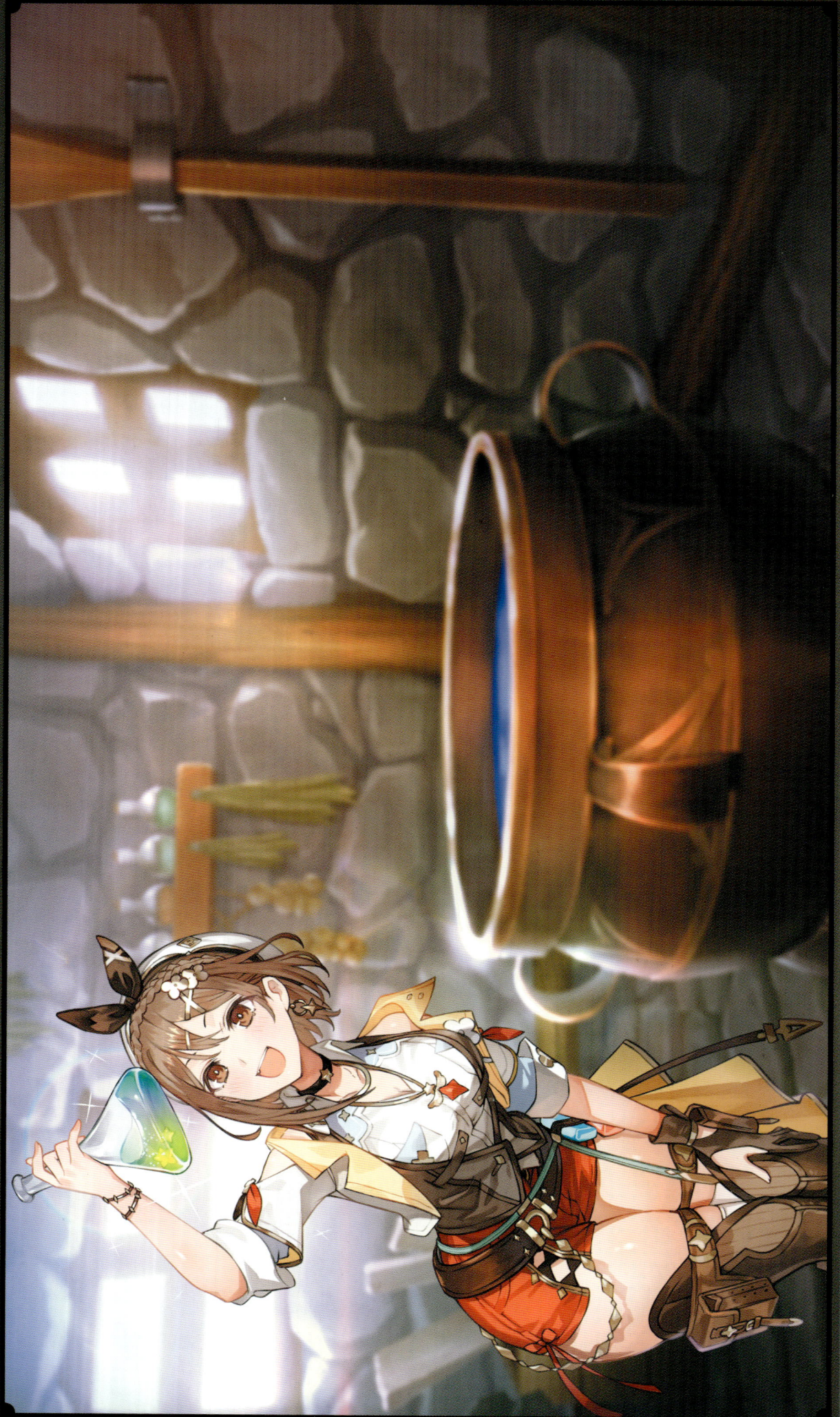

EVENT STILL ▷ 01 Synthesis Complete

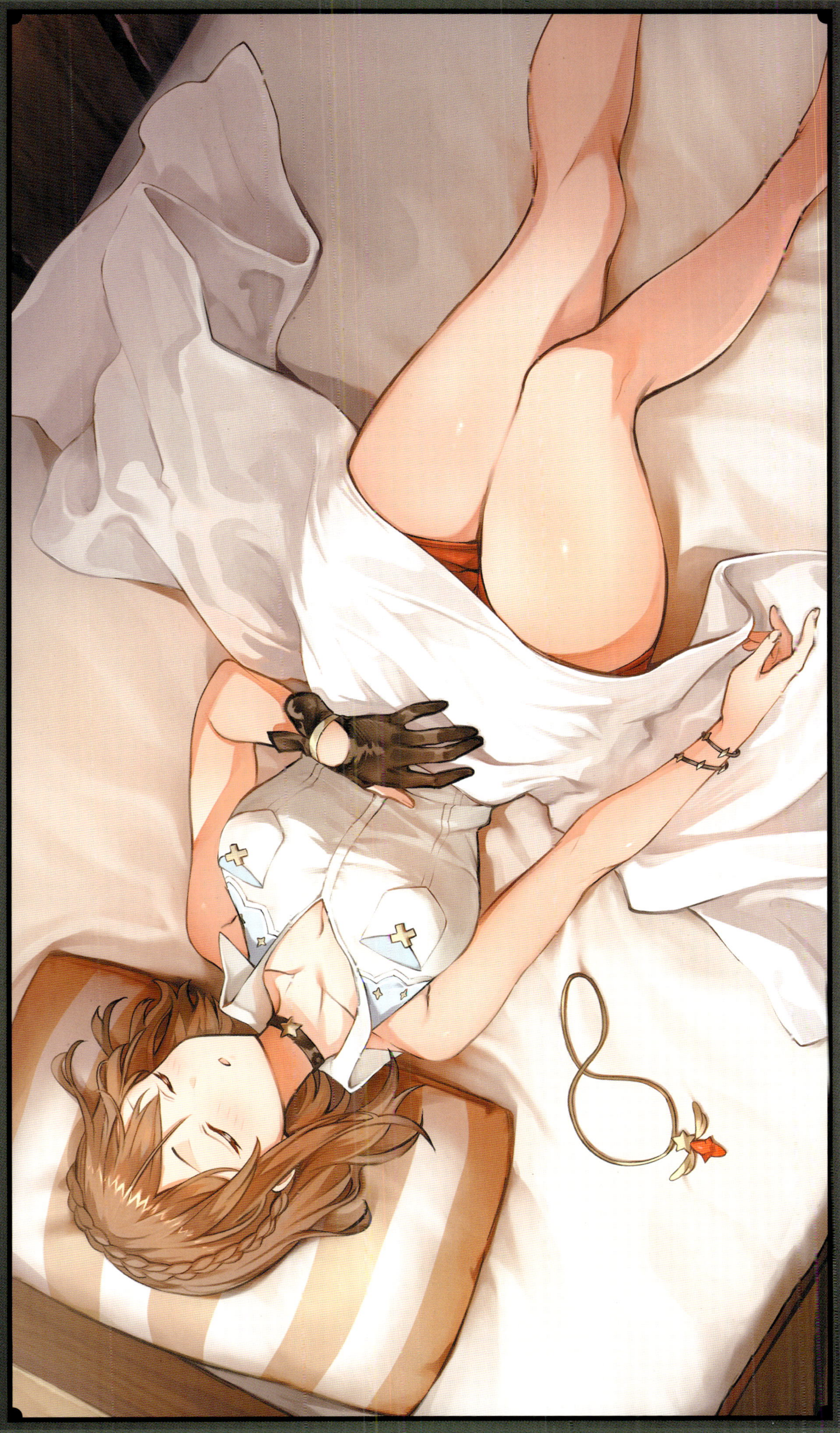

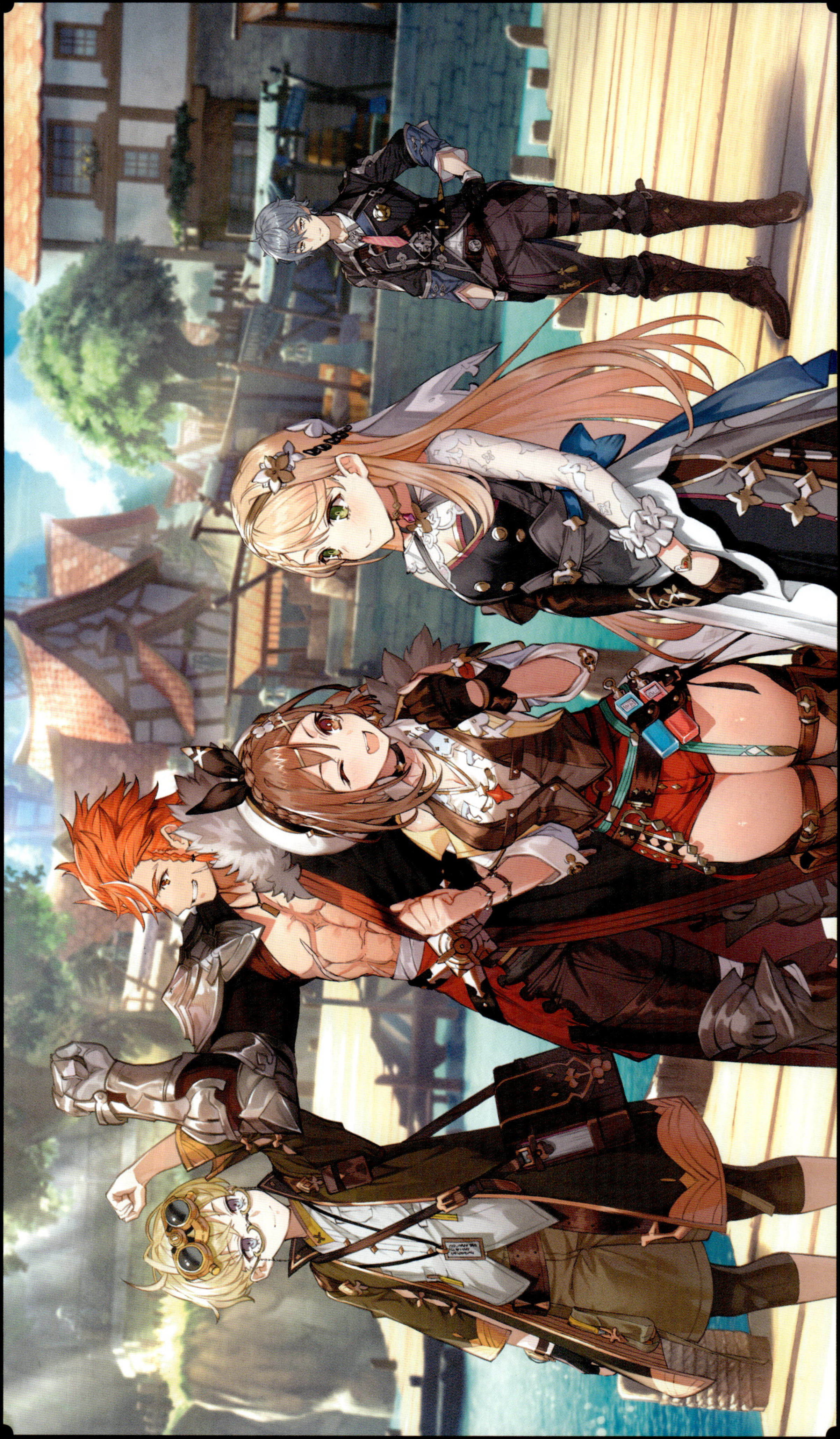

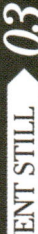

EVENT STILL 03 Setting off on Adventure

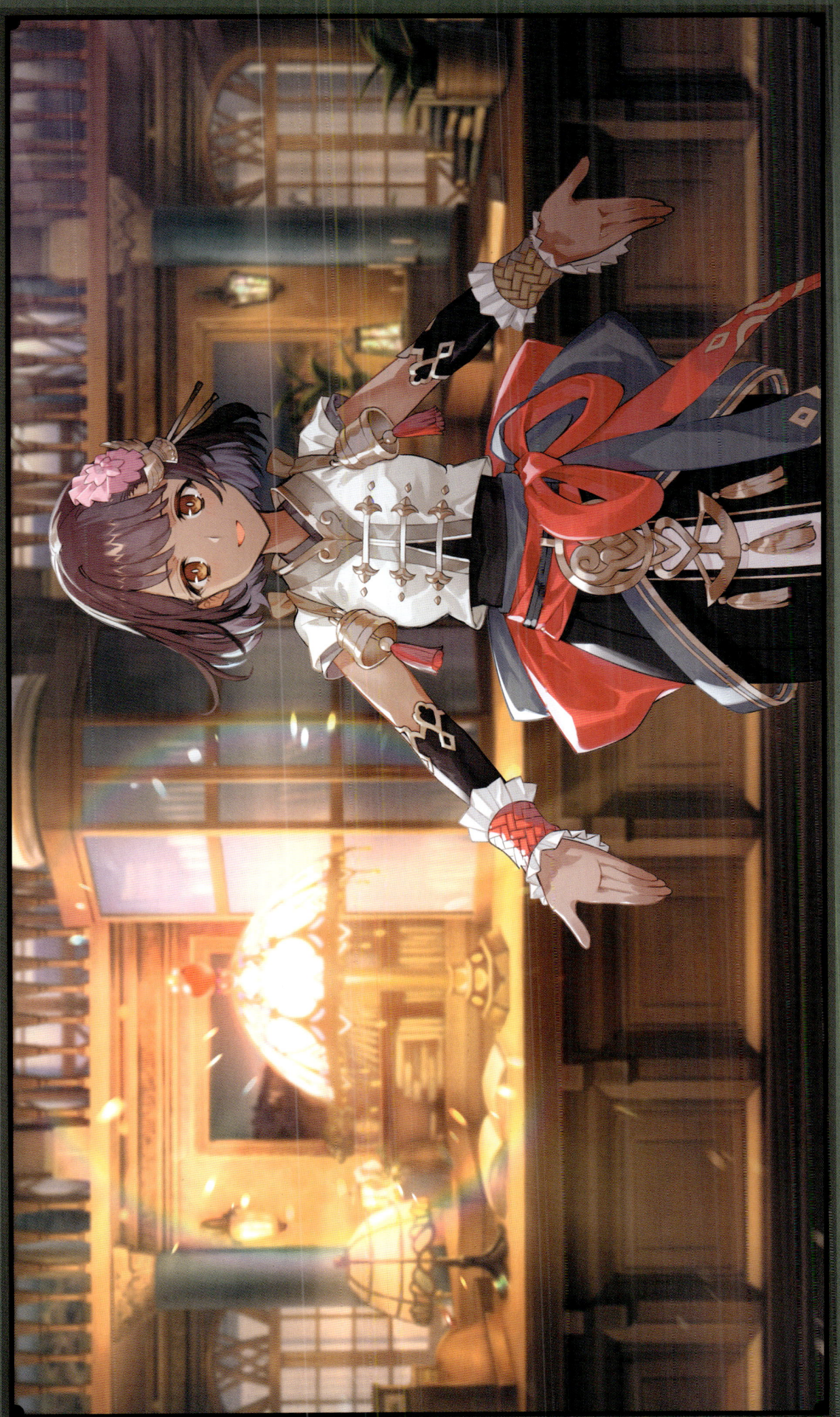

EVENT STILL 04 What My Father and I Envision

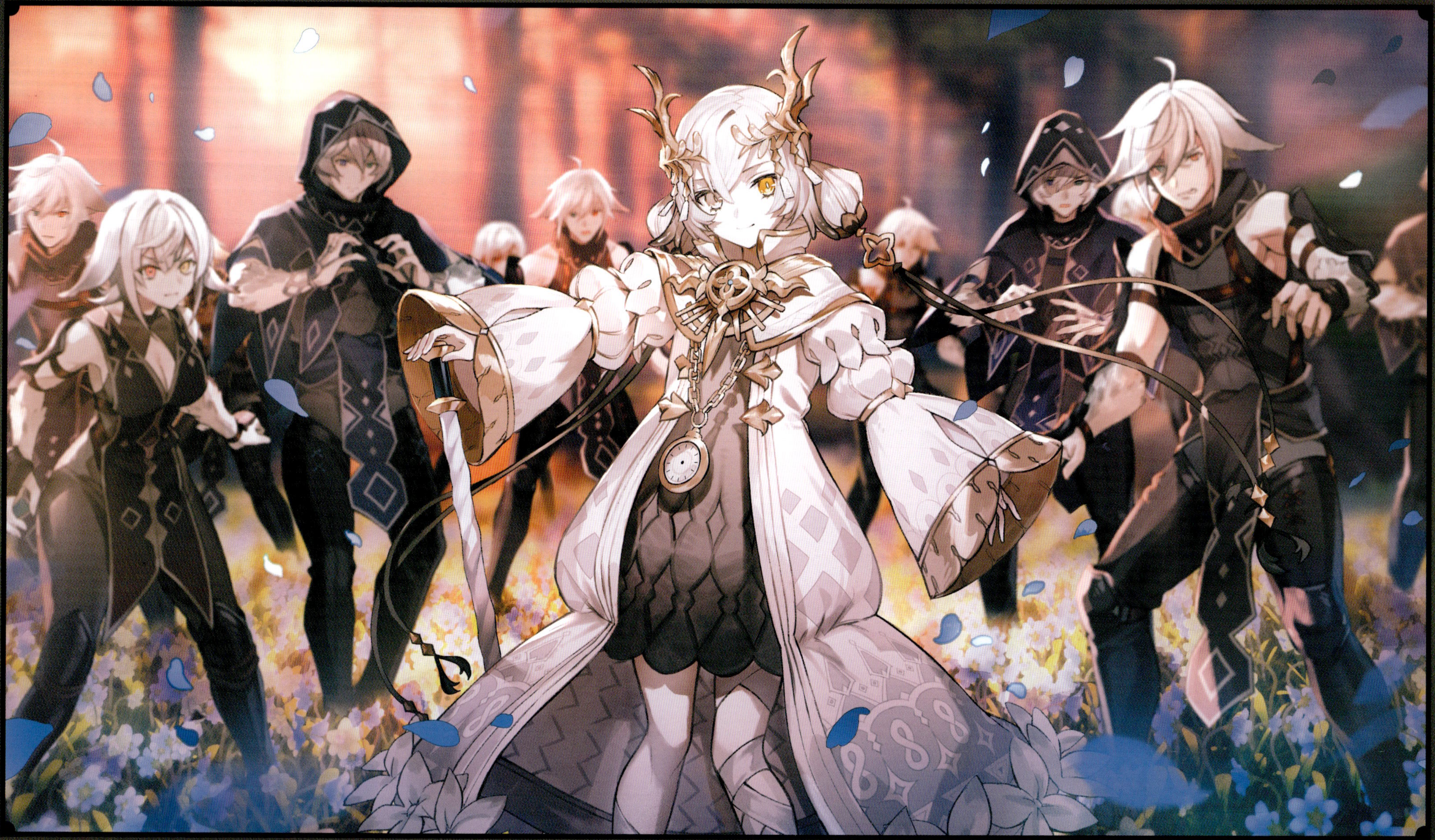

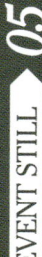

EVENT STILL 05 Orim Elder

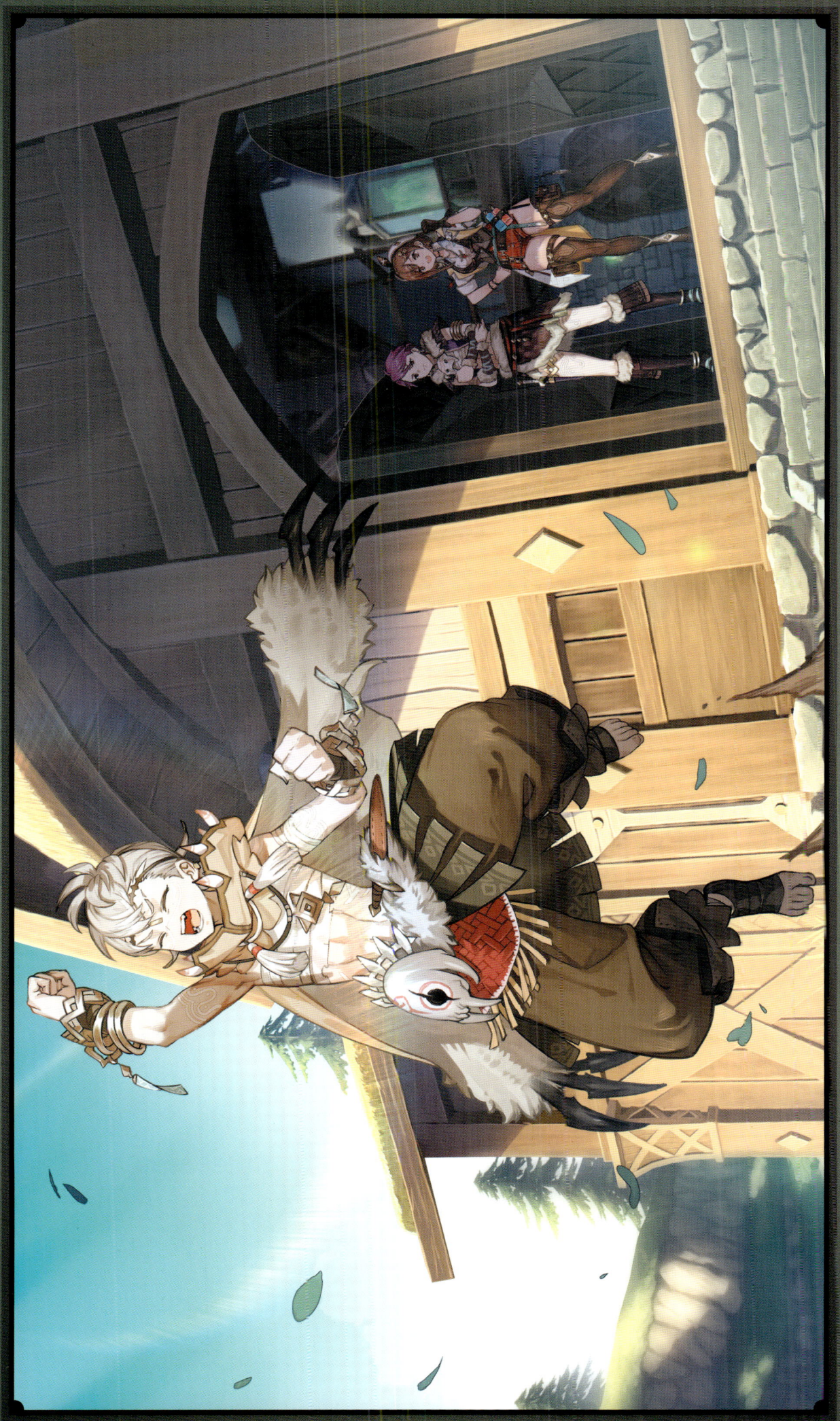

EVENT STILL 06 First Blade

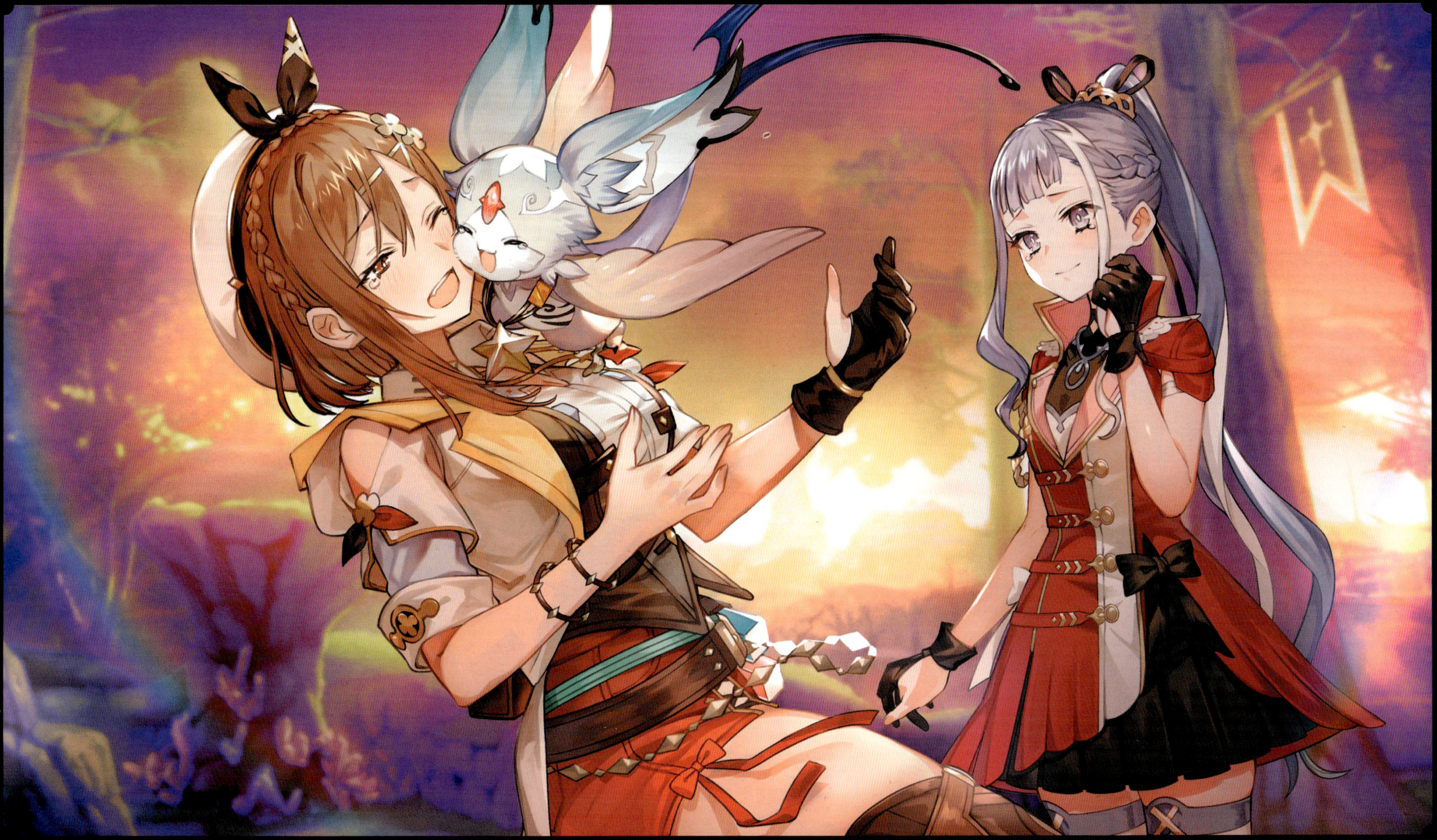

EVENT STILL 07 Reunited

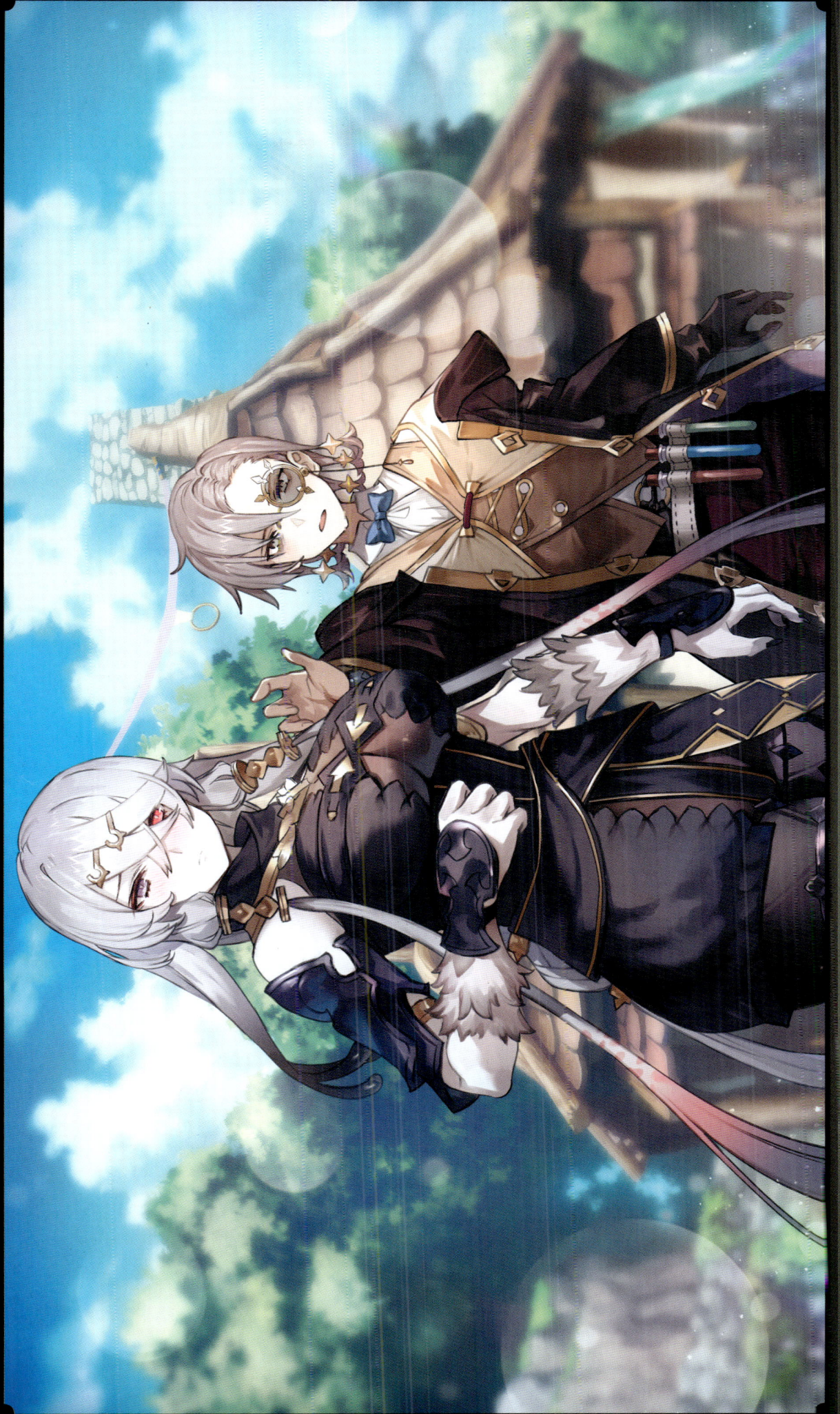

EVENT STILL 08 Flying into a Dream

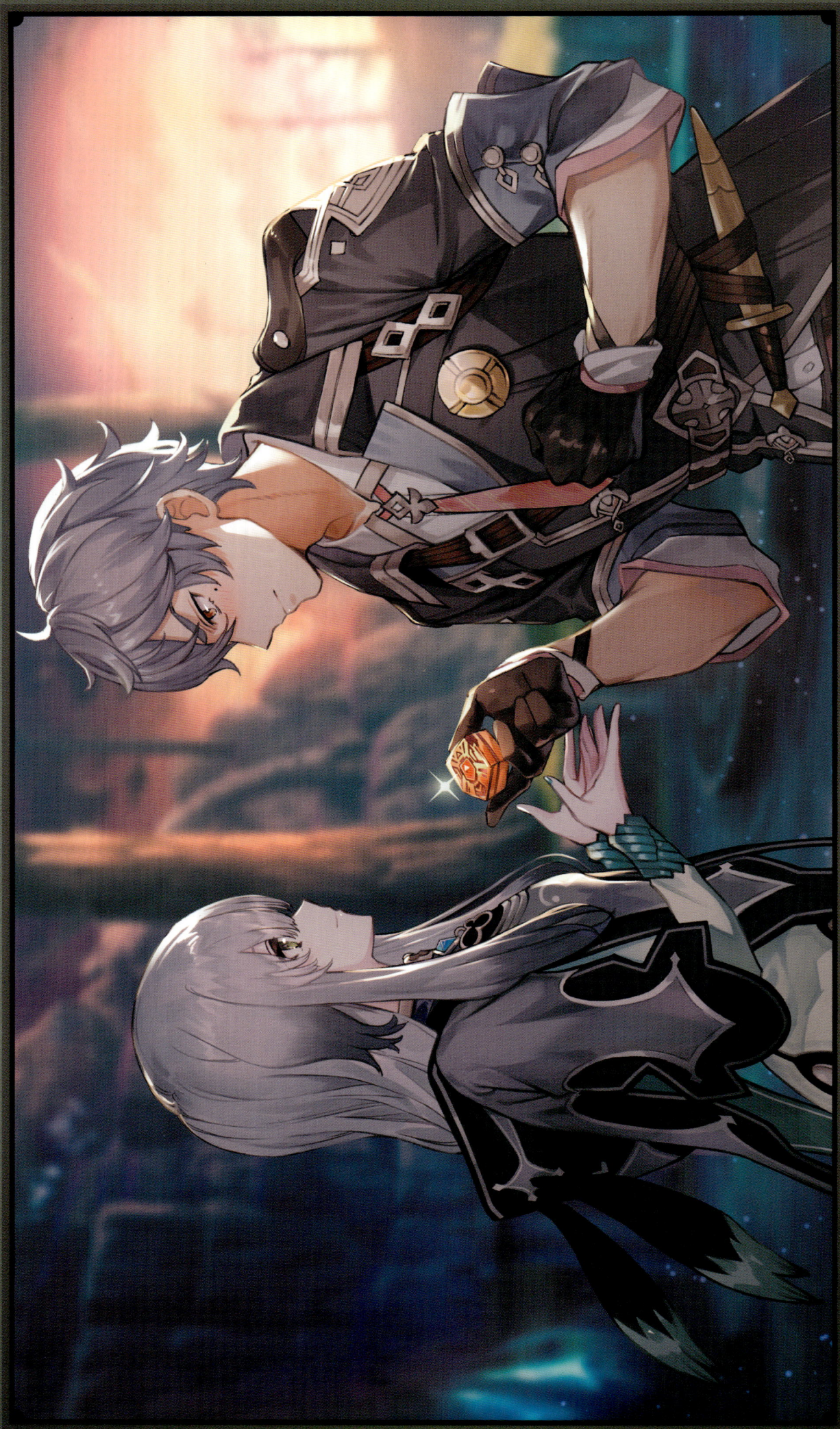

EVENT STILL ▶ 09 Someday I'll Go Home

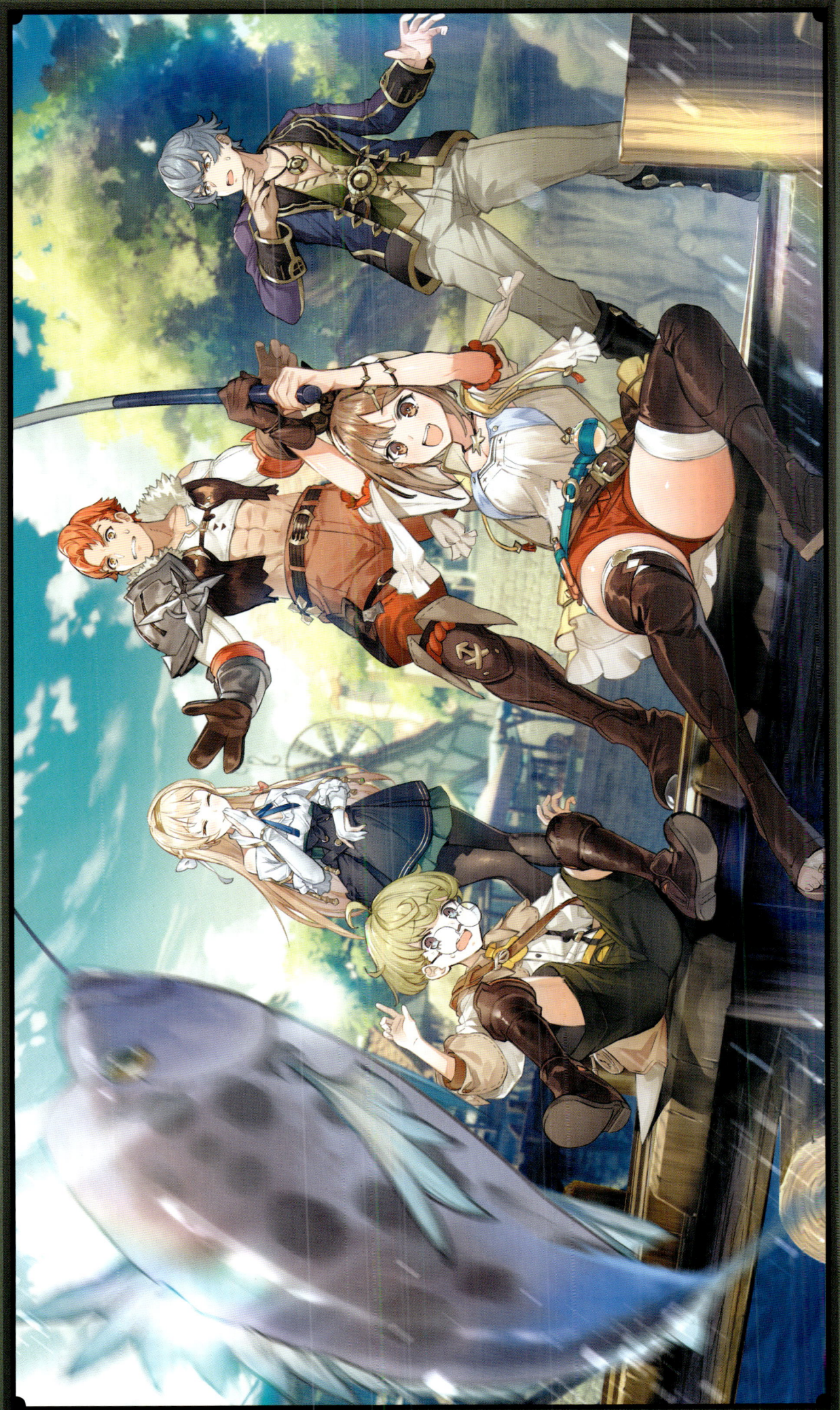

EVENT STILL 10 Memories of That Summer

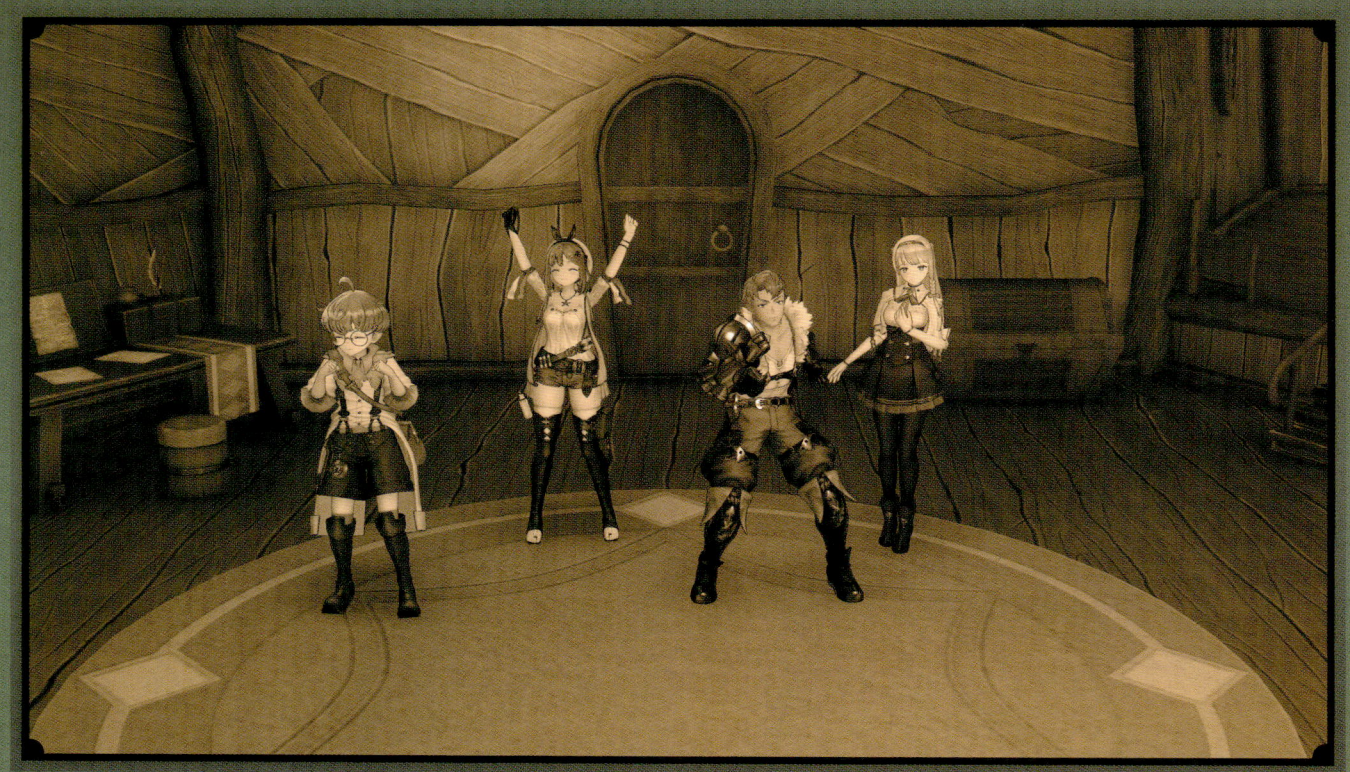
RECOLLECTION EVENT STILL 01

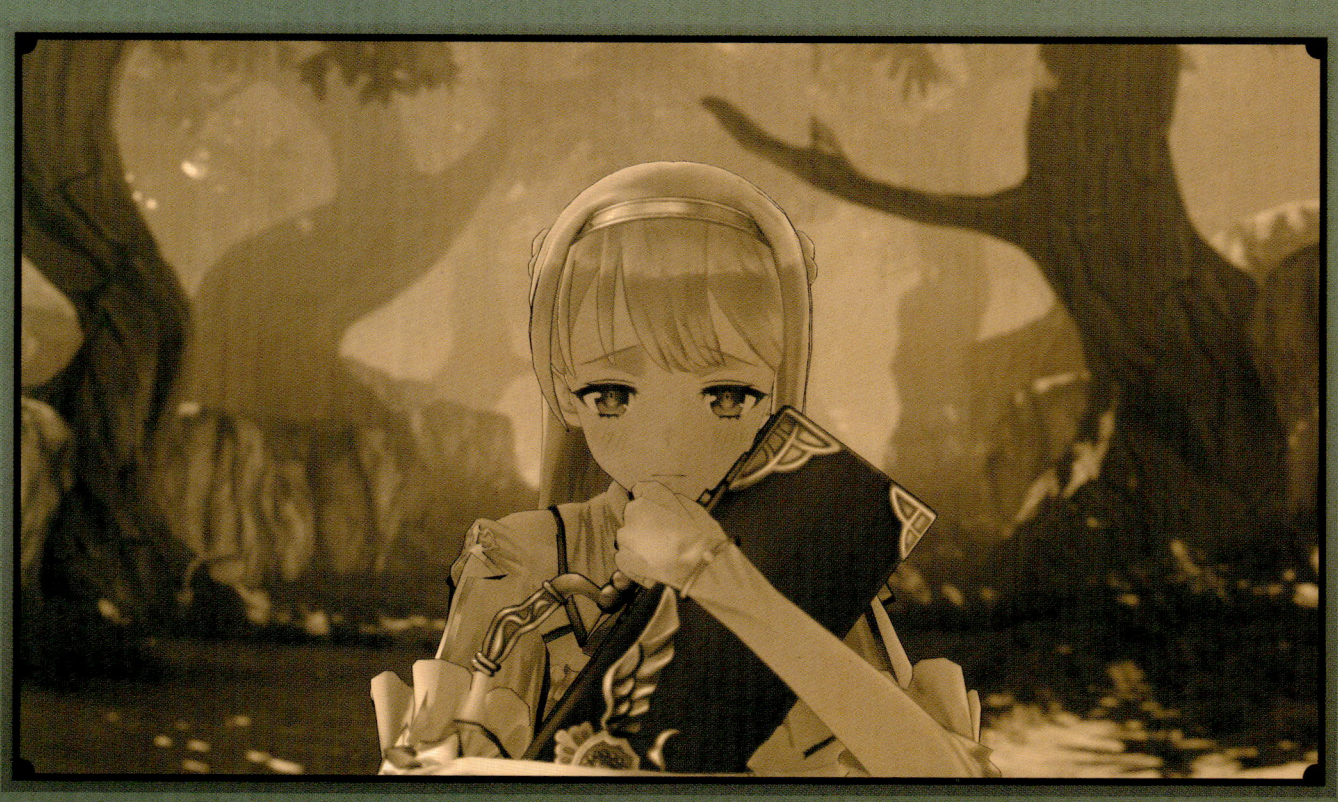
RECOLLECTION EVENT STILL 02

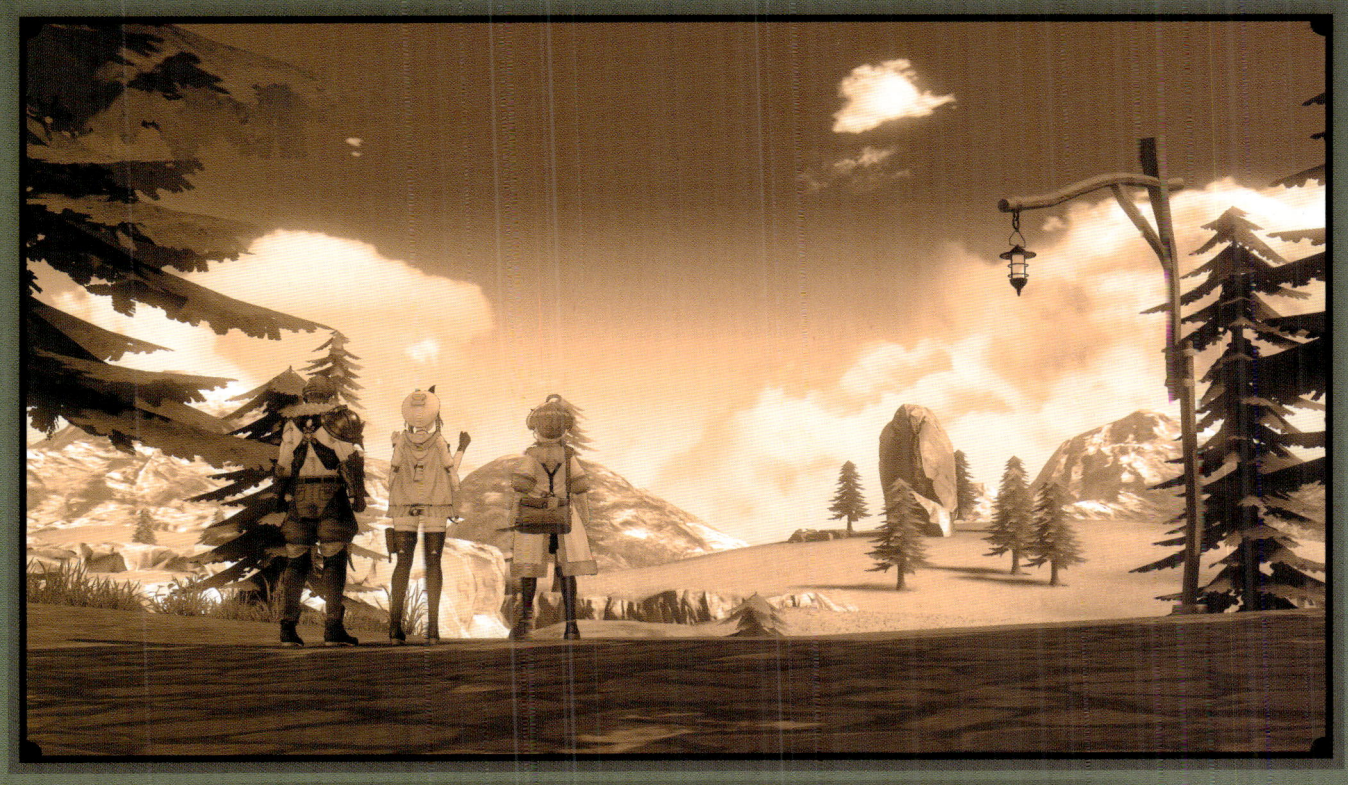
RECOLLECTION EVENT STILL 03

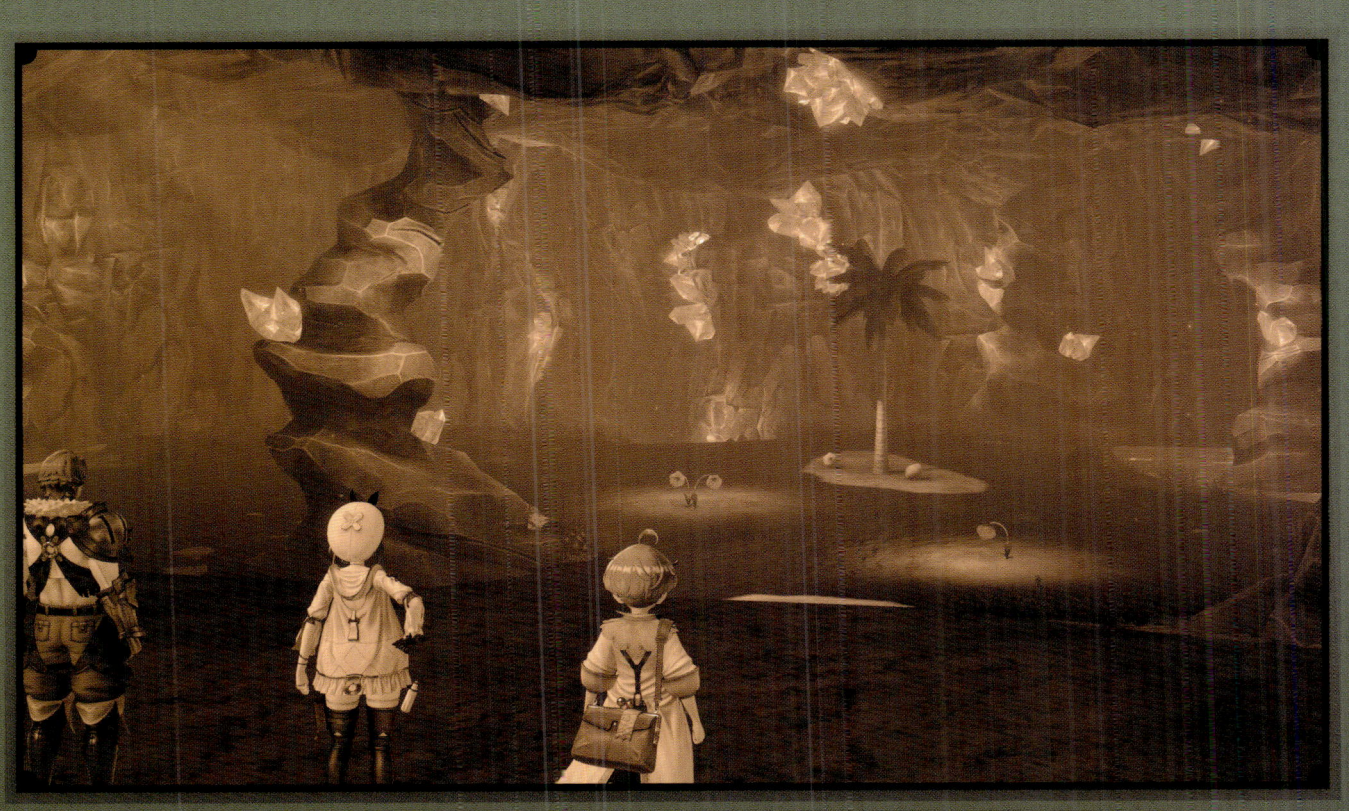
RECOLLECTION EVENT STILL 04

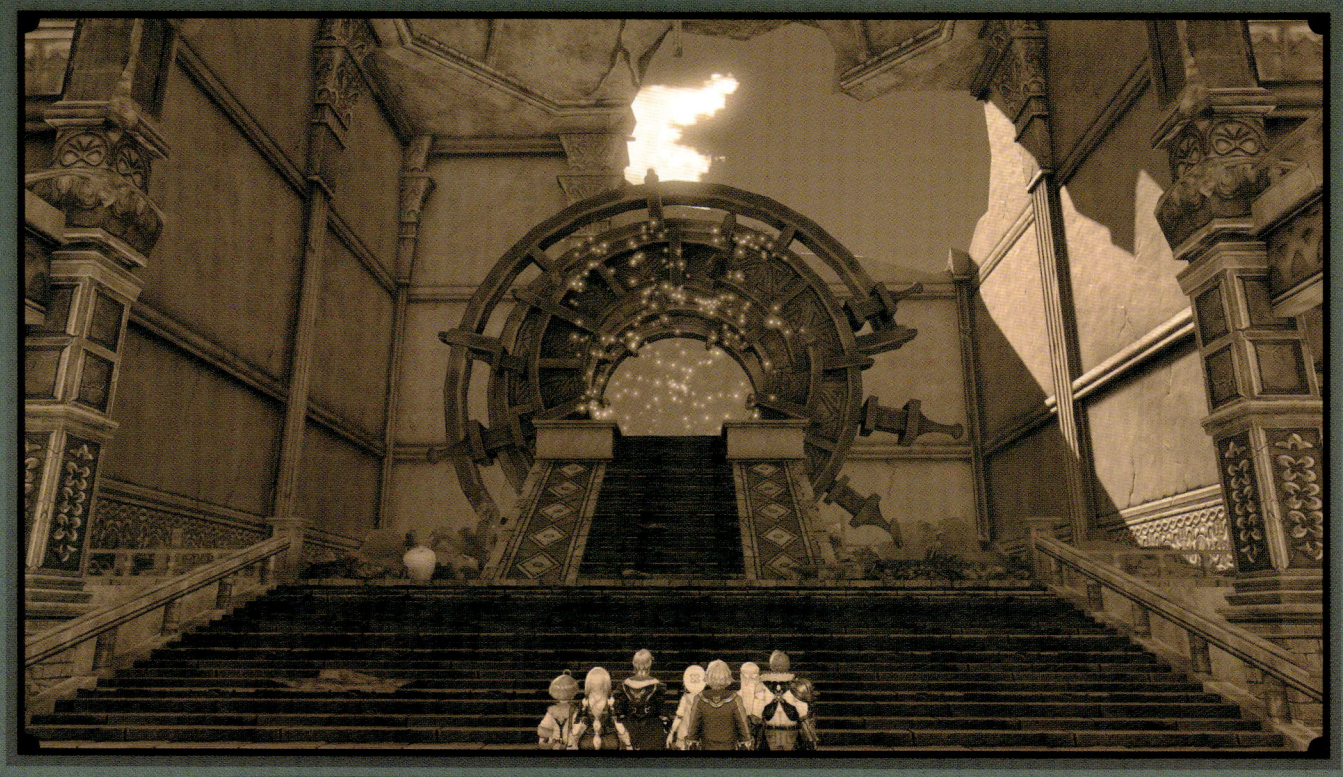

RECOLLECTION EVENT STILL 05

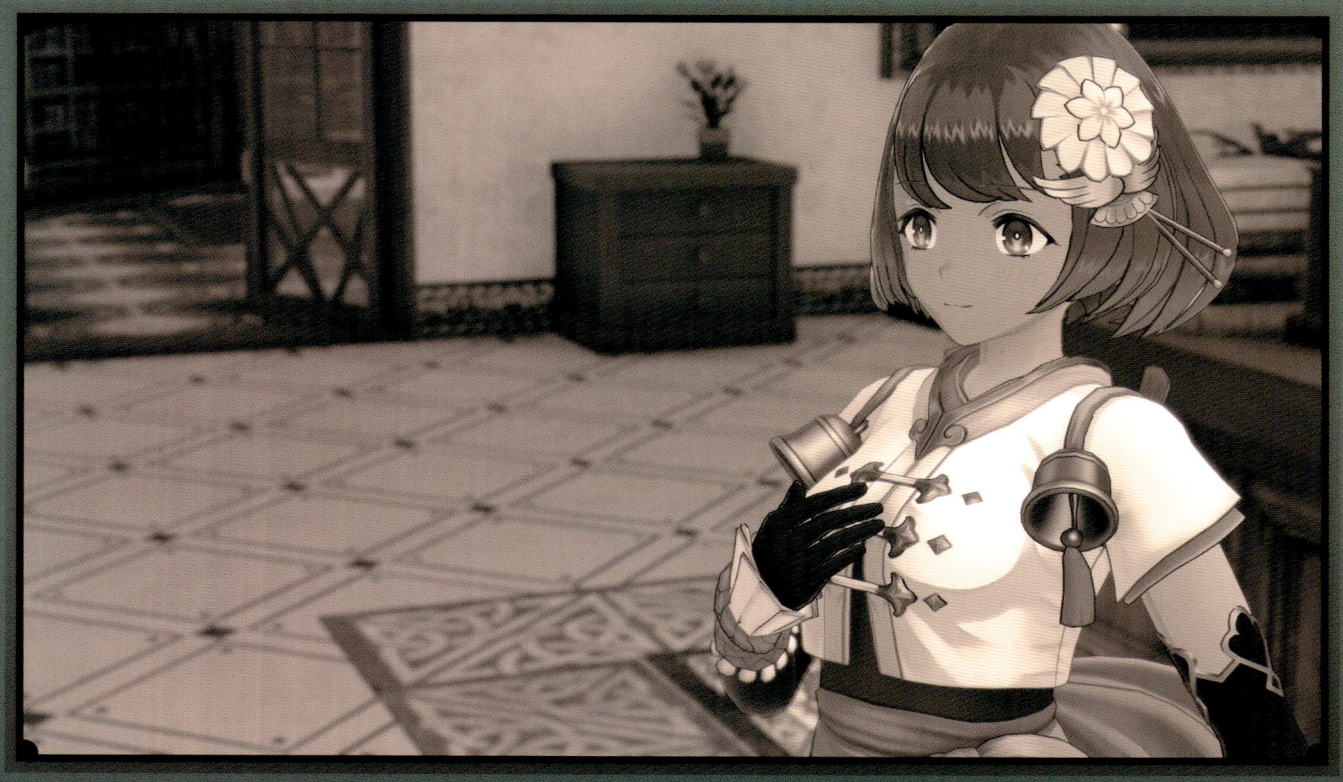

RECOLLECTION EVENT STILL 06

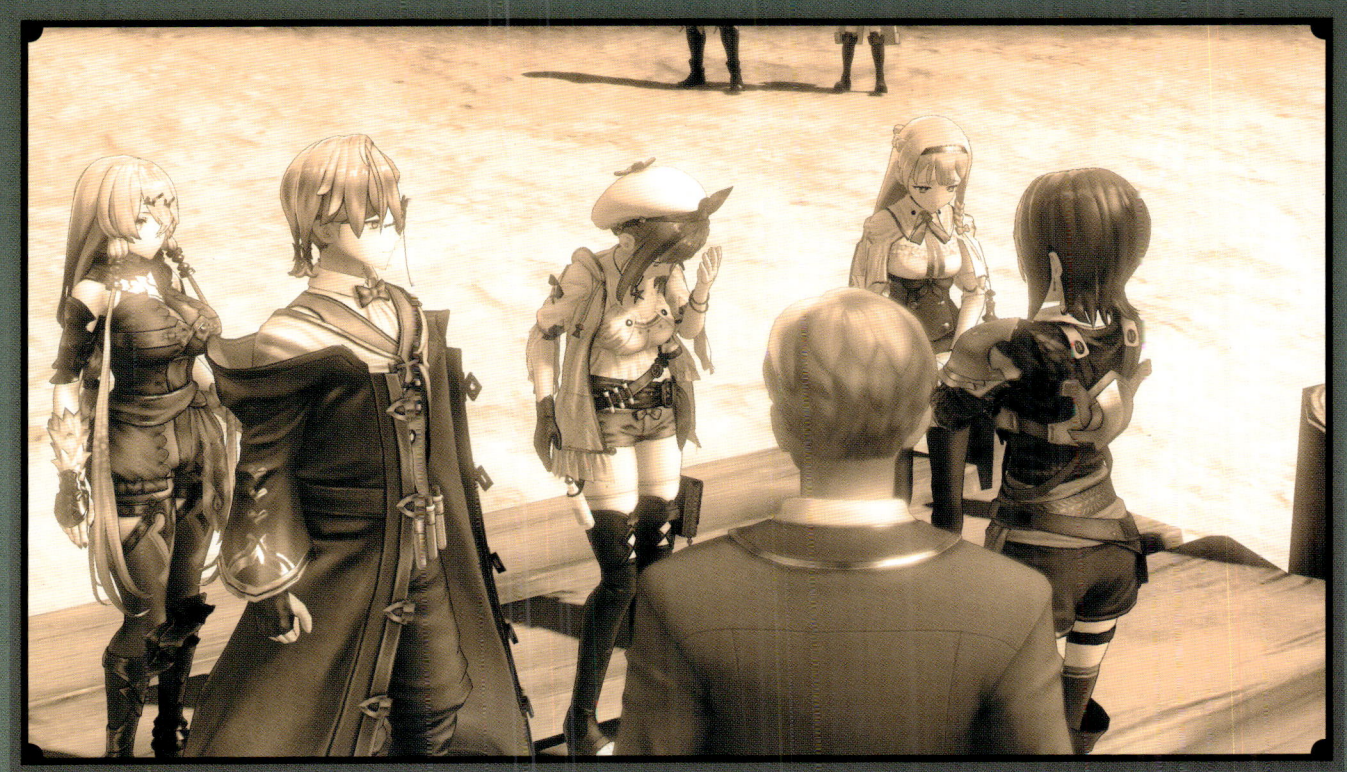

RECOLLECTION EVENT STILL 07

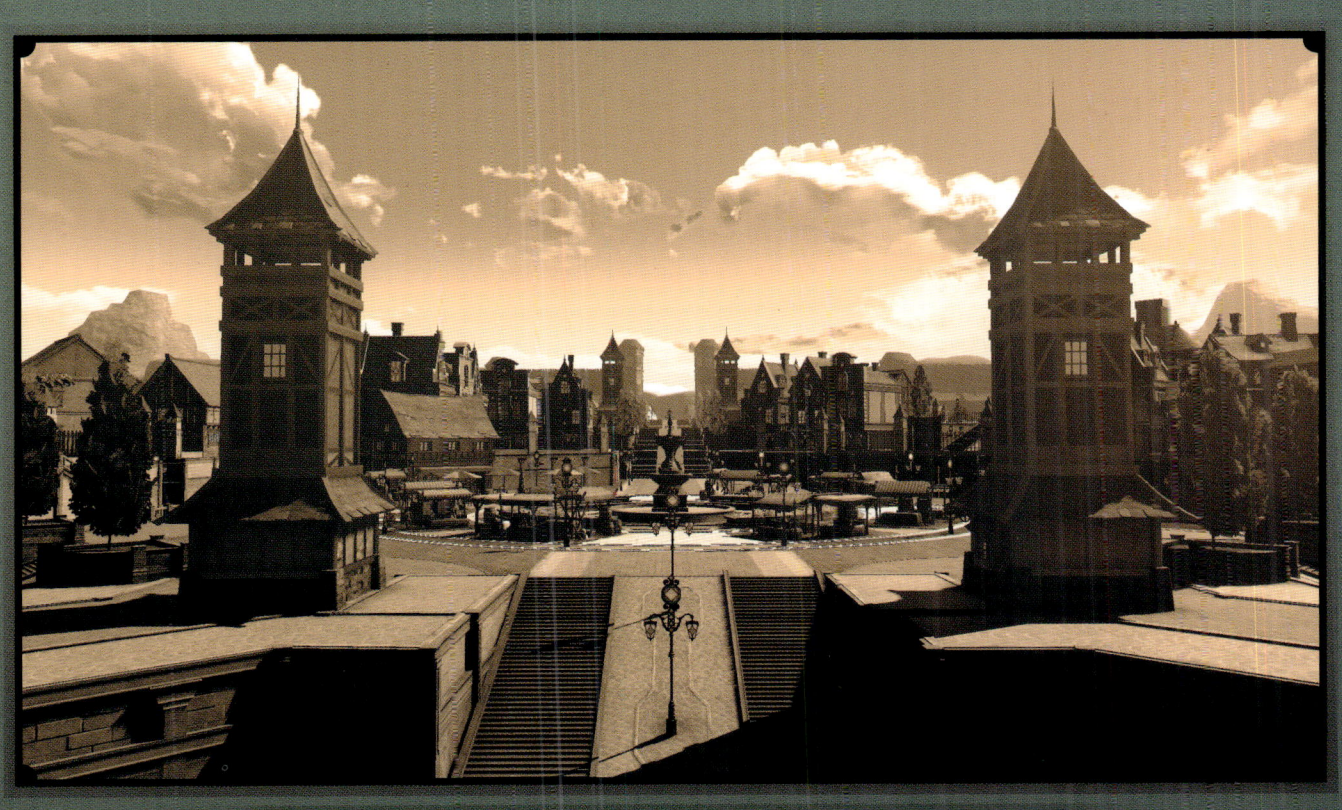

RECOLLECTION EVENT STILL 08

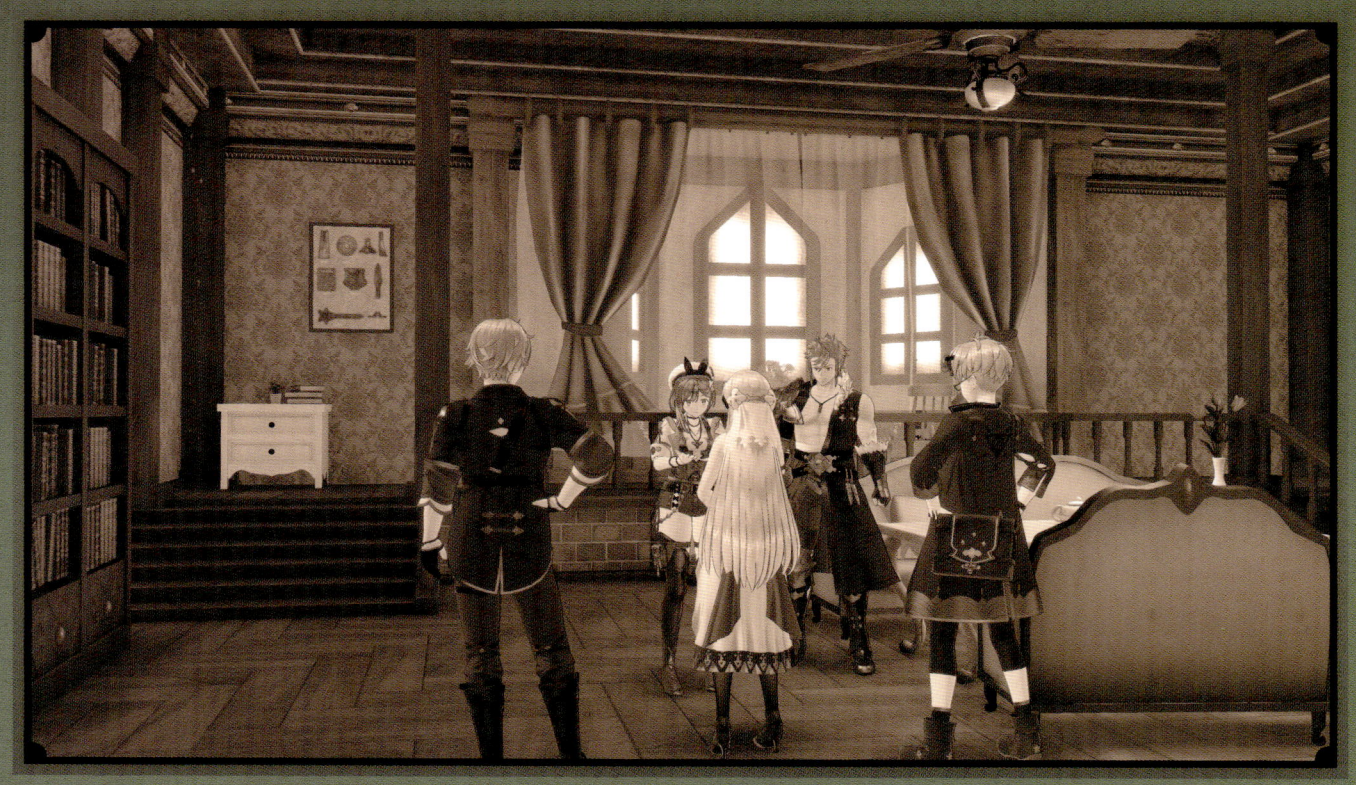

RECOLLECTION EVENT STILL 09

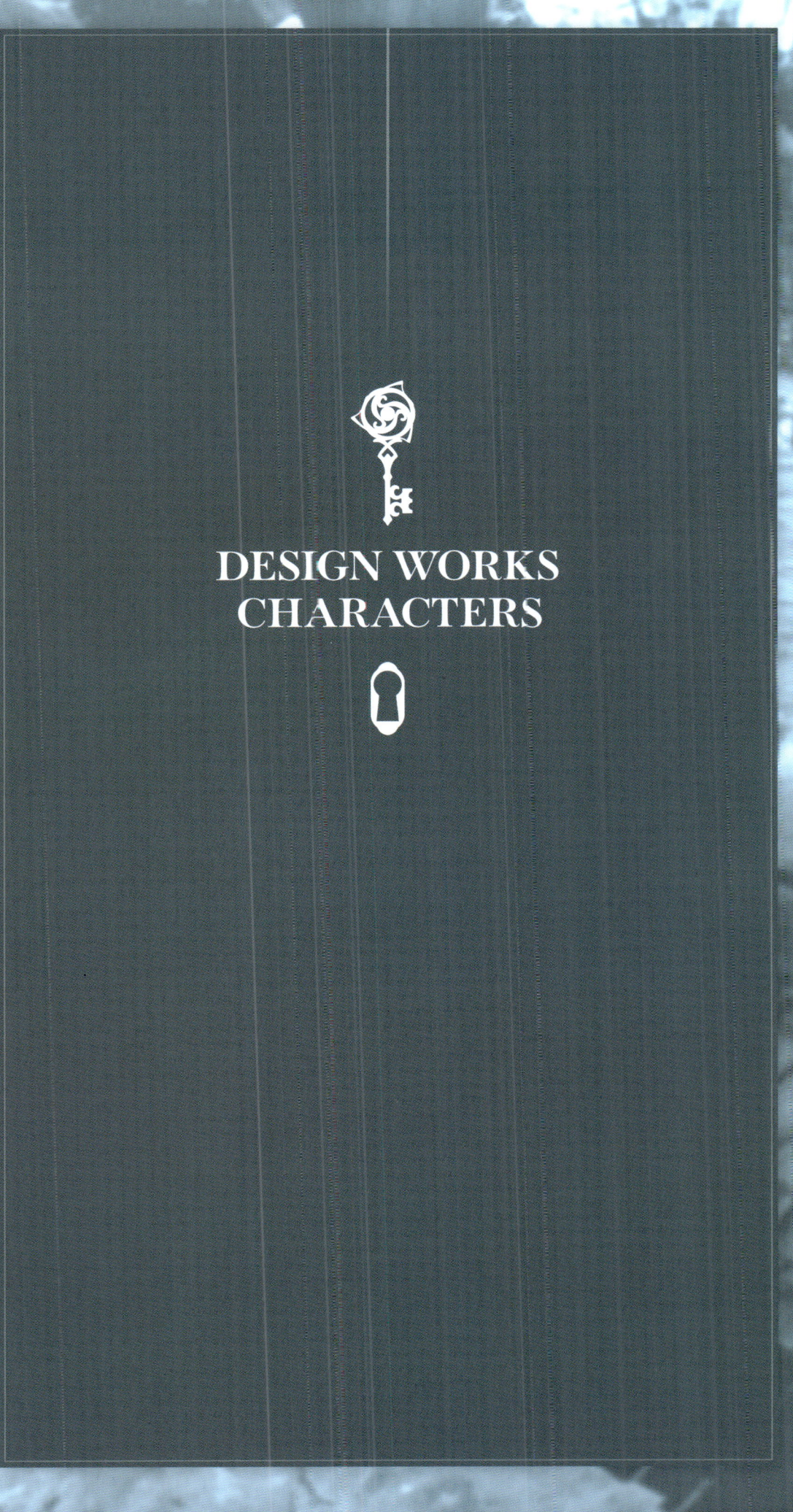
DESIGN WORKS
CHARACTERS

Ryza Design Sketches

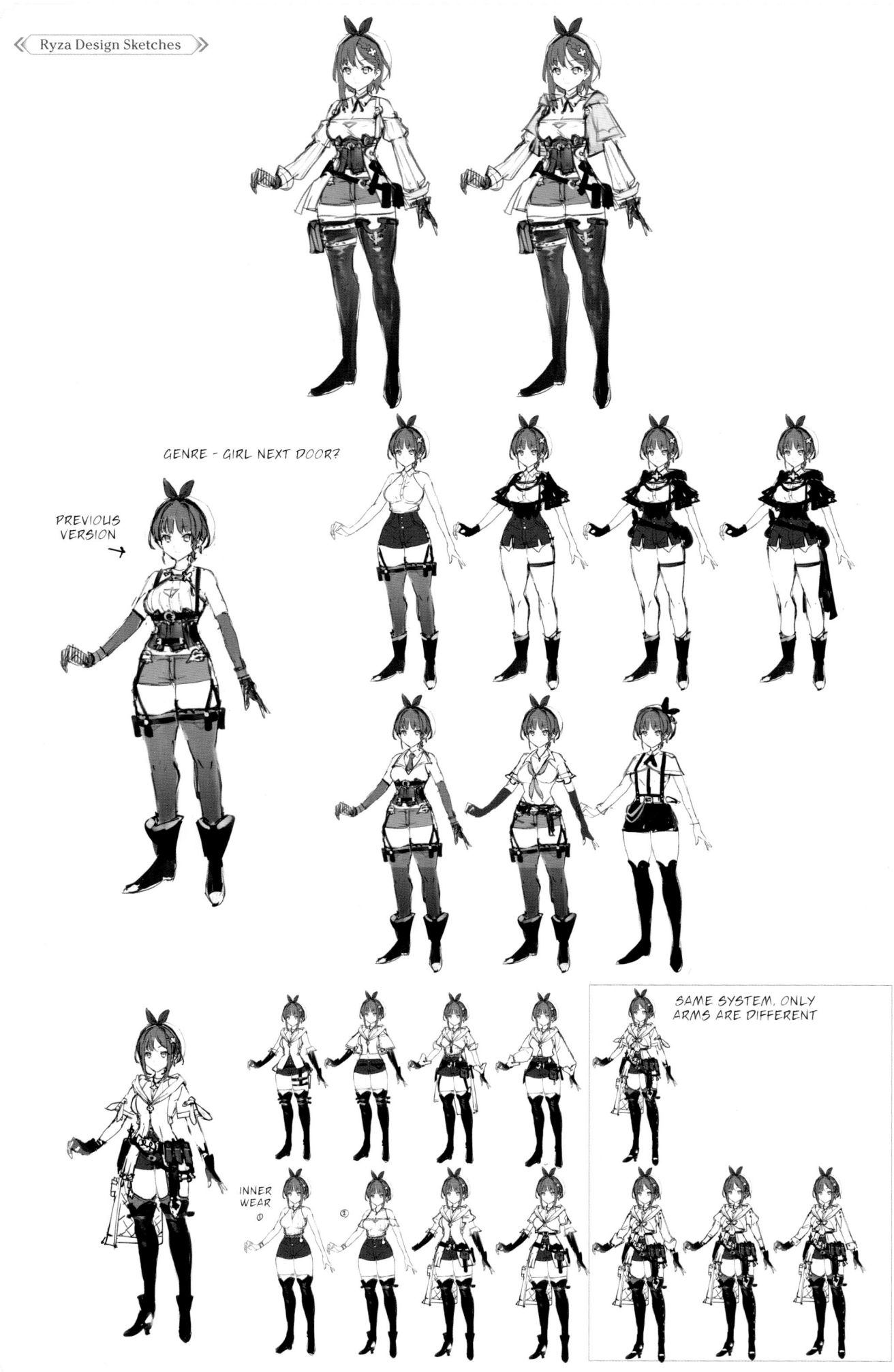

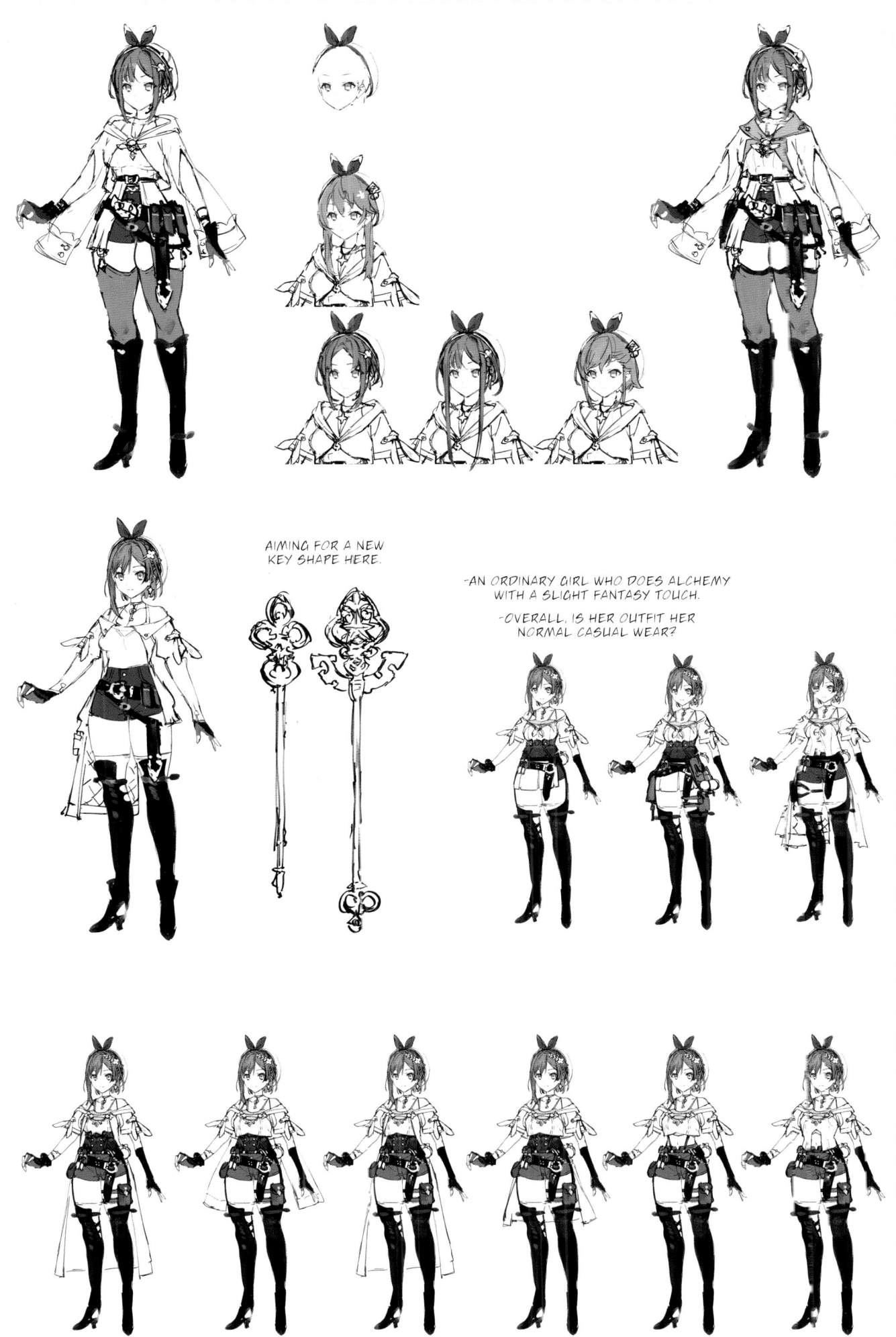

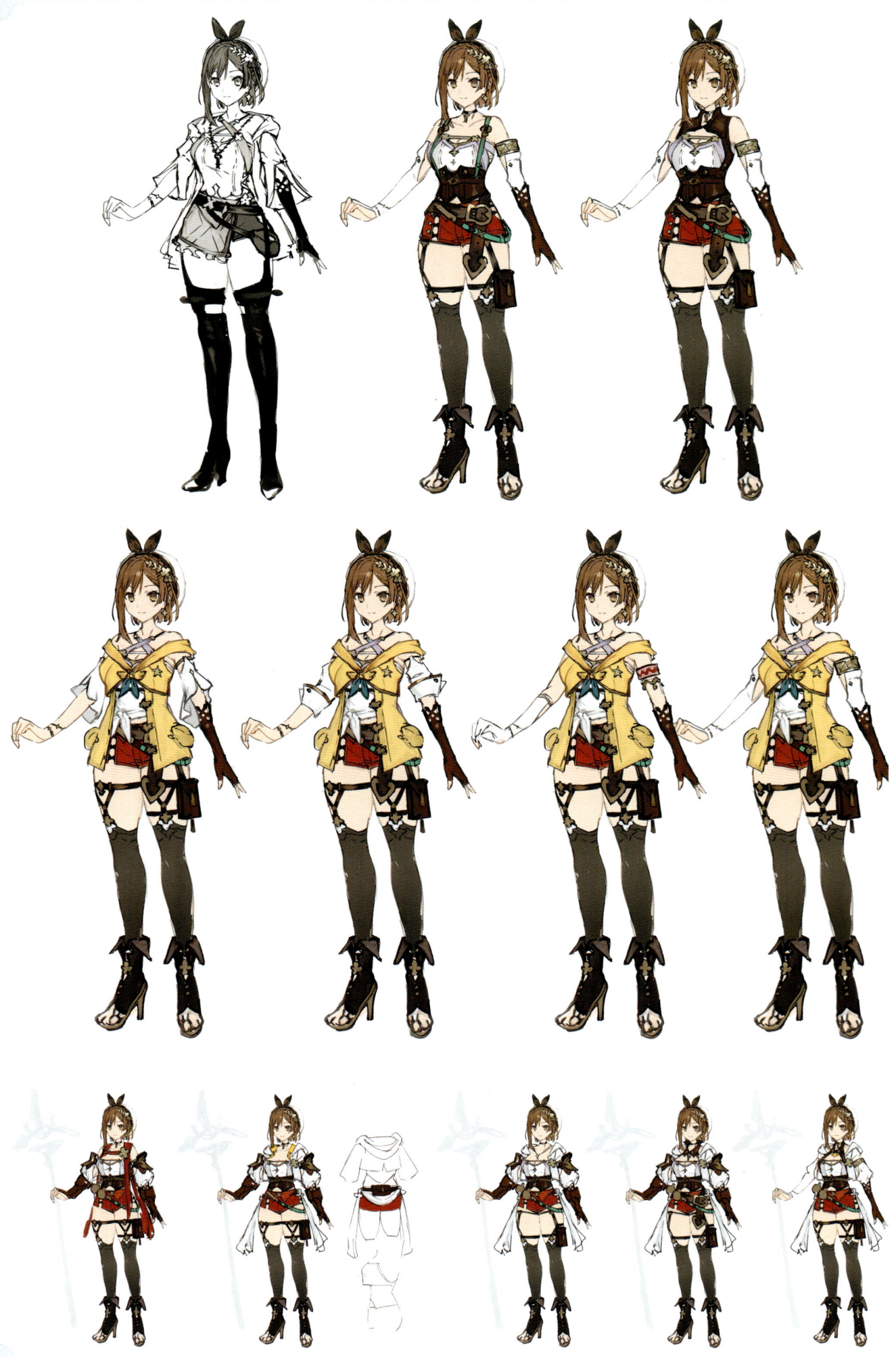

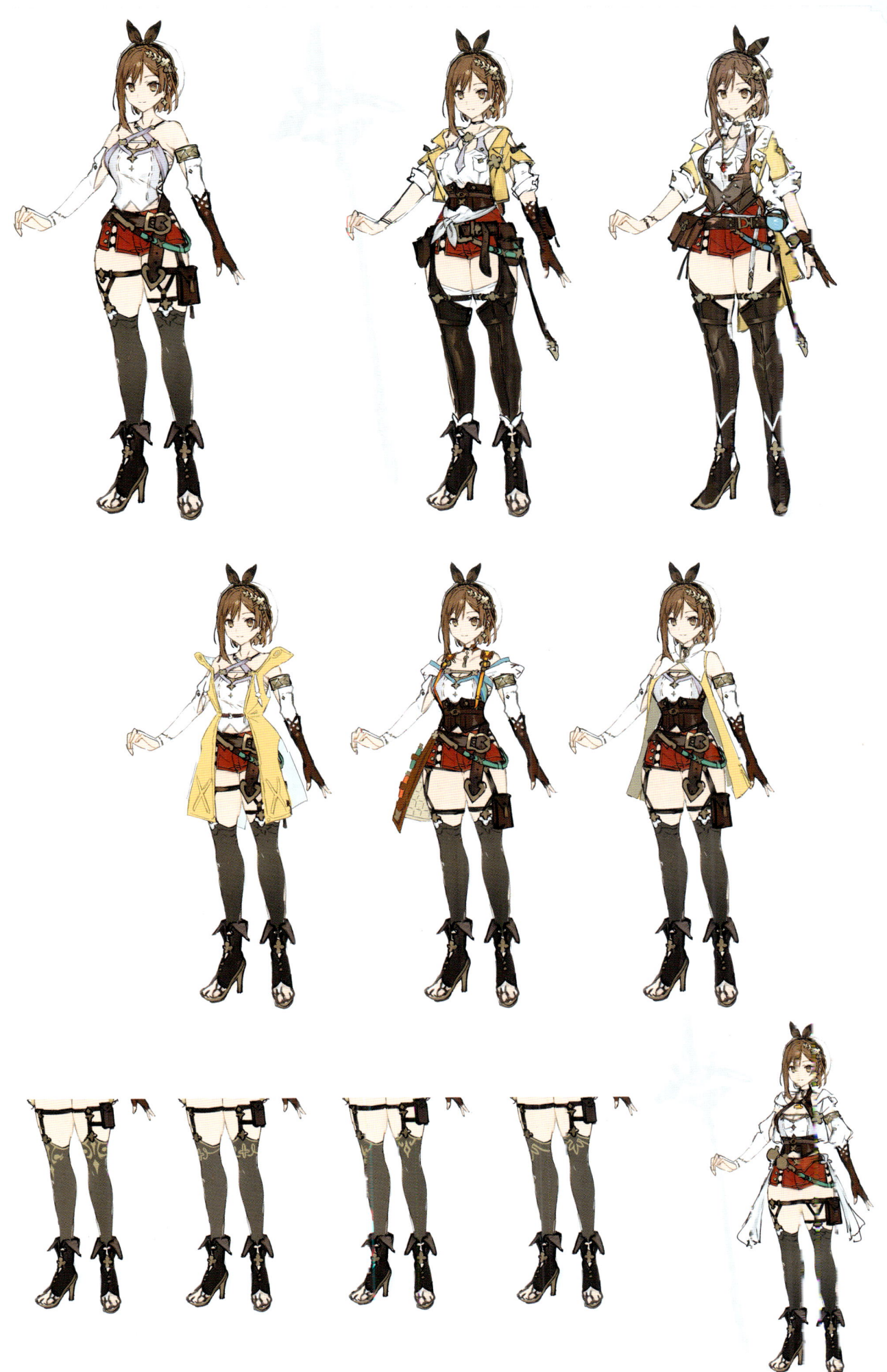

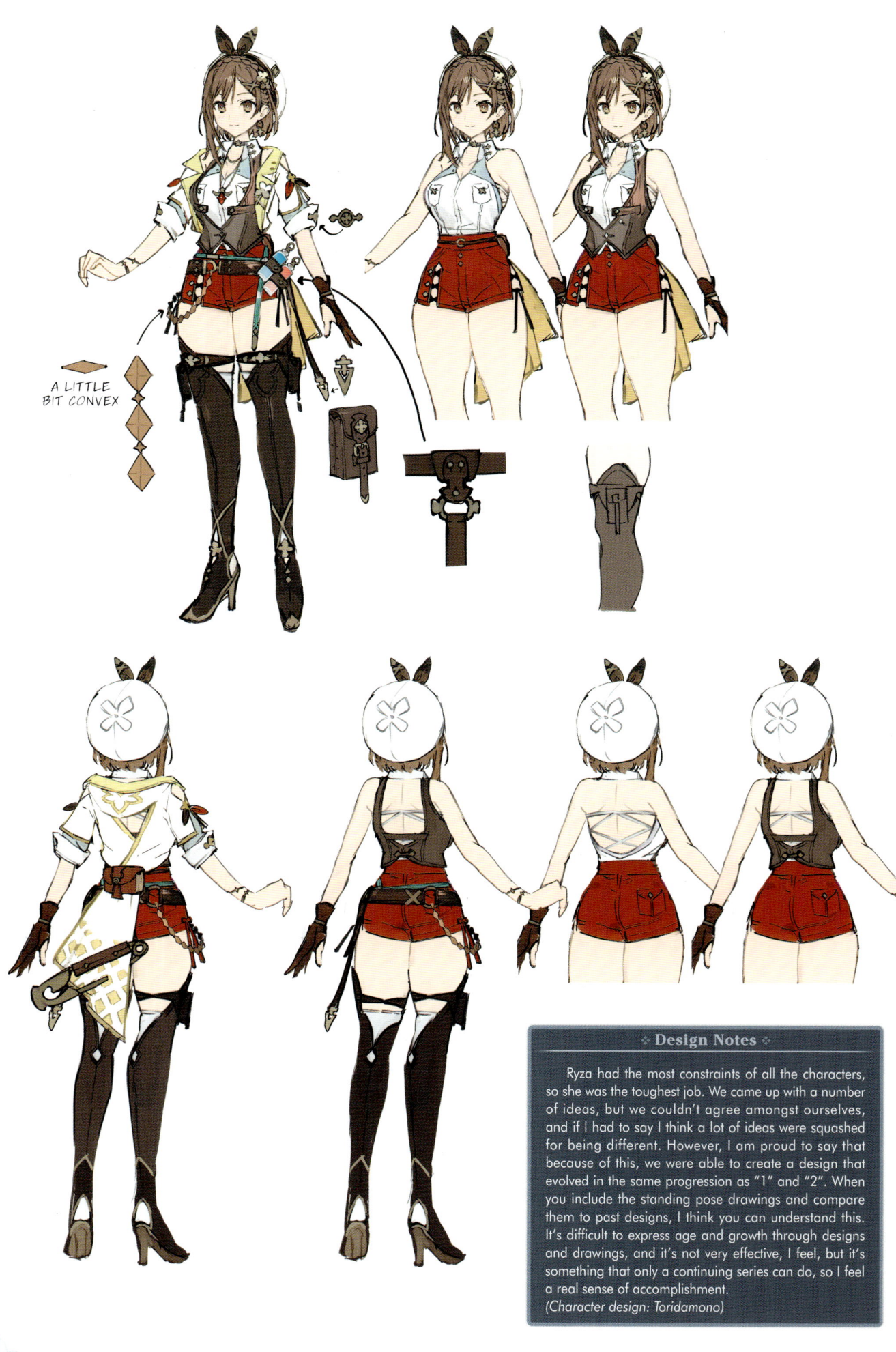

✦ Design Notes ✦

Ryza had the most constraints of all the characters, so she was the toughest job. We came up with a number of ideas, but we couldn't agree amongst ourselves, and if I had to say I think a lot of ideas were squashed for being different. However, I am proud to say that because of this, we were able to create a design that evolved in the same progression as "1" and "2". When you include the standing pose drawings and compare them to past designs, I think you can understand this. It's difficult to express age and growth through designs and drawings, and it's not very effective, I feel, but it's something that only a continuing series can do, so I feel a real sense of accomplishment.
(Character design: Toridamono)

* REGARDING HAIR COLOR
IN 2, THE HAIR WAS CONSCIOUSLY A LITTLE BROWNER, BUT IN 3, IT'S BACK TO WHAT IT WAS LIKE IN 1, WITH A MORE SUBDUED, CHESTNUT-TONED FEEL.

* REGARDING HAIRSTYLE
THE OVERALL FEEL IS MATURE, GLOSSY, AND DELICATE. THE HAIR IS THINNED OUT AND THE VOLUME IS REDUCED A LITTLE. KIND OF A CROSS BETWEEN 1 AND 2.

SHOULD FEEL LIKE THERE'S ALMOST NO KINKY HAIR, AND IT FALLS STRAIGHT DOWN. MORE OF A MATURE WOMAN THAN A TOMBOY FEEL.

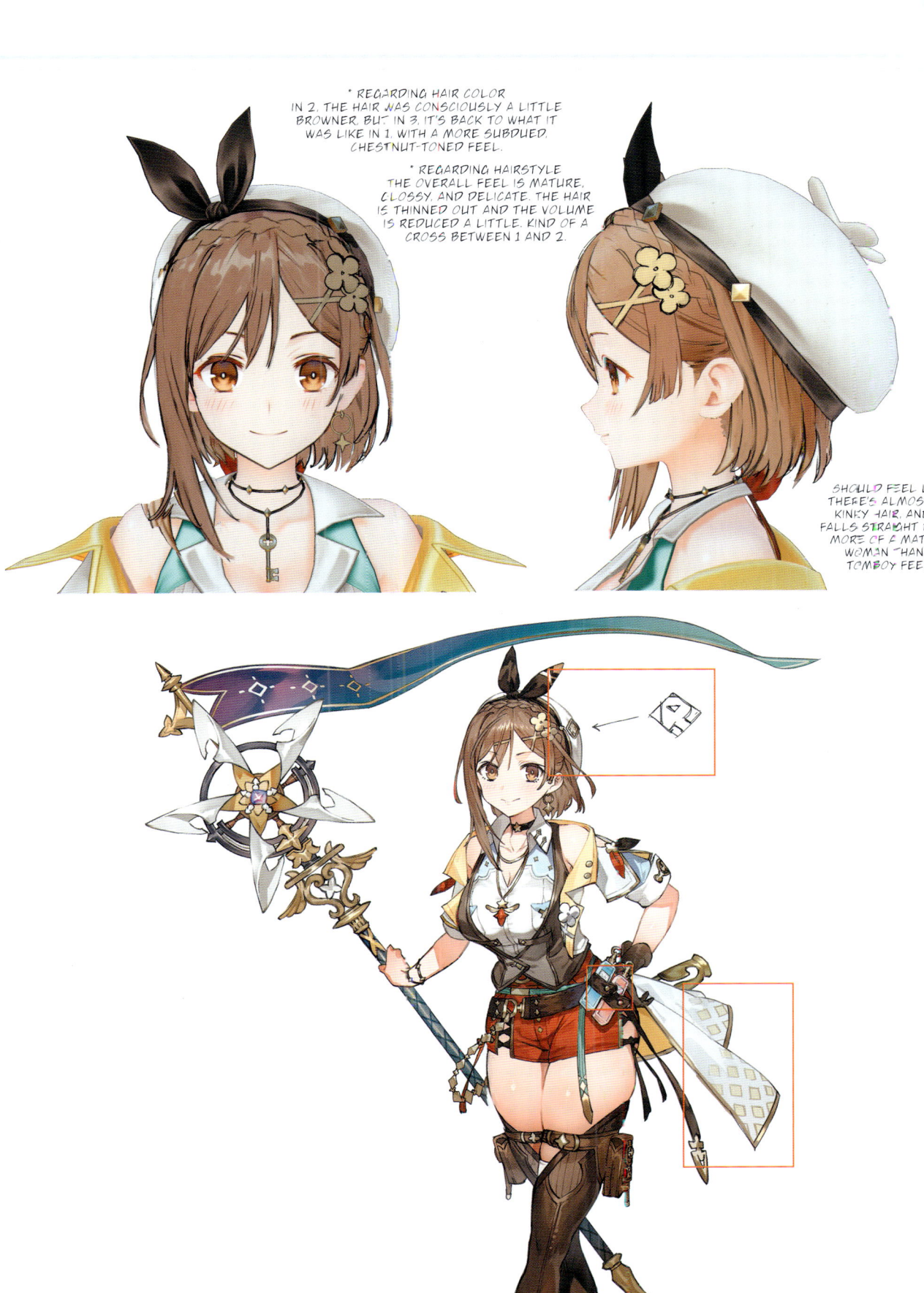

Klaudia Design Sketches

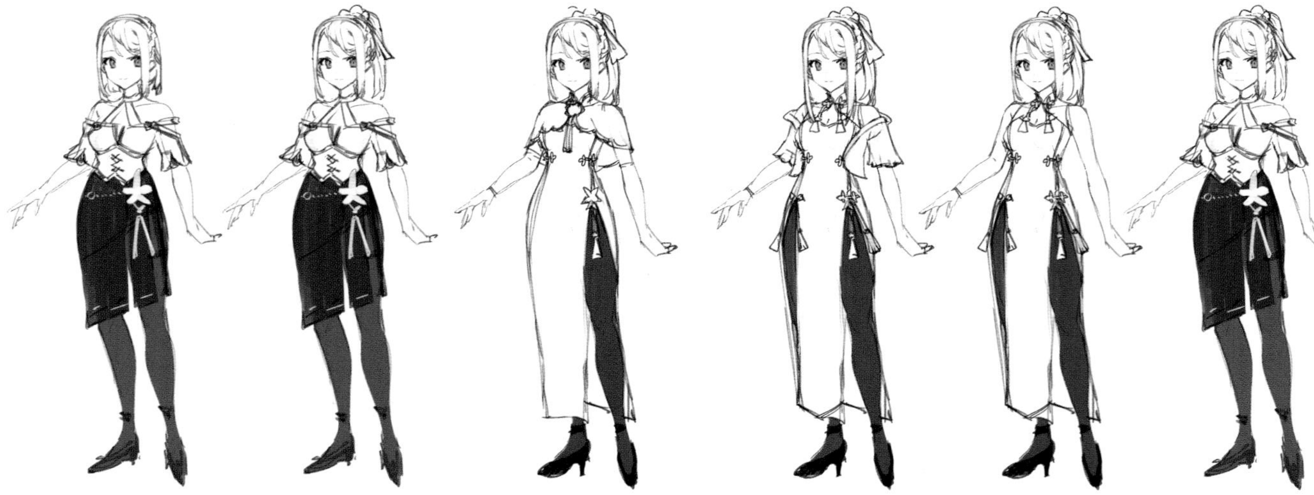

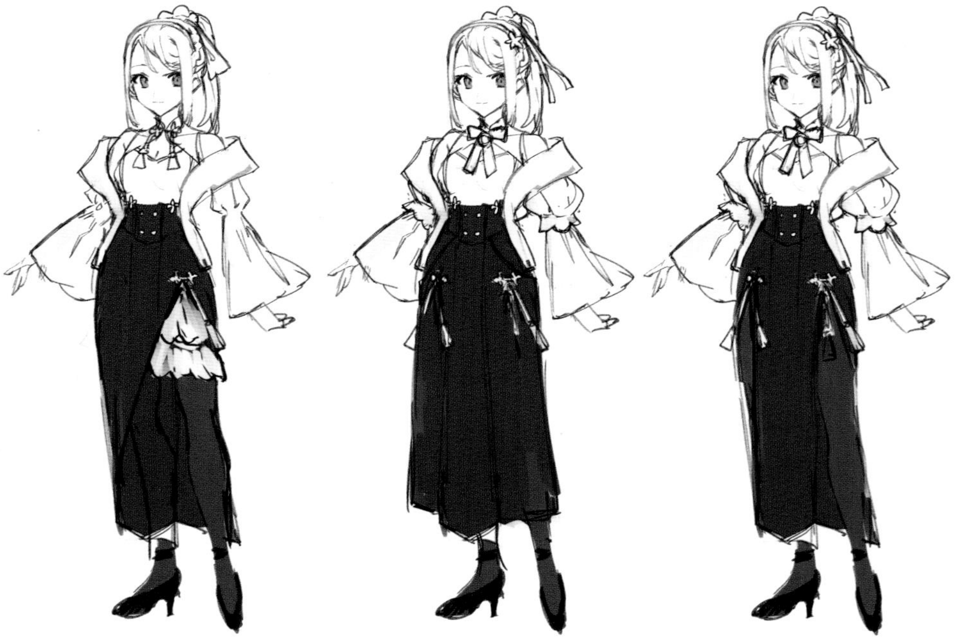

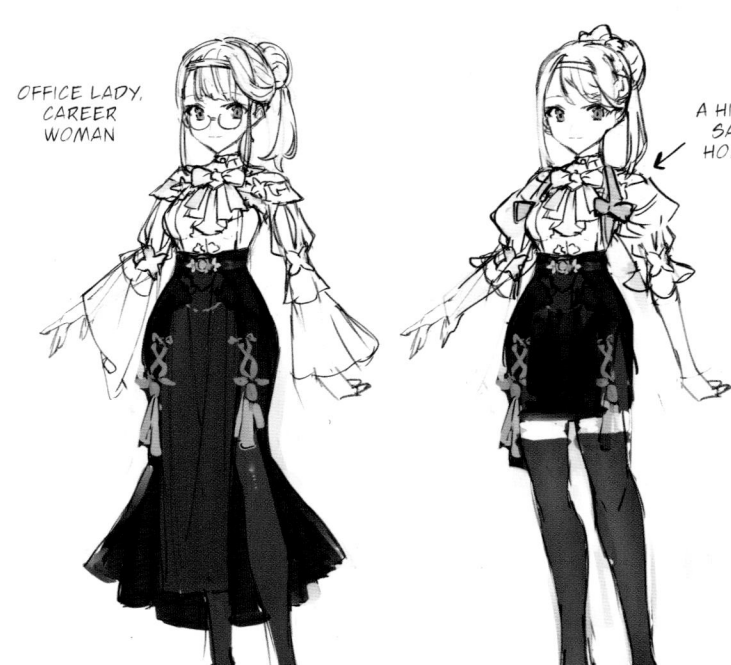

OFFICE LADY, CAREER WOMAN

A HINT OF THE TASUKI SASHES USED FOR HOLDING UP KIMONO SLEEVES

❖ Design Notes ❖

The point I fixated on most is the accessory on her left wrist. Anyone who notices this has a wonderful eye for observation. It was actually given to her by Ryza as a gift in a sub-event in "2". The overall design is unchanged from the concept in "2", which is of a Klaudia who has matured into more of an adult woman, but I feel like this point I obsessed about was the only thing I enjoyed telling the development team about.
(Character Design: Toridamono)

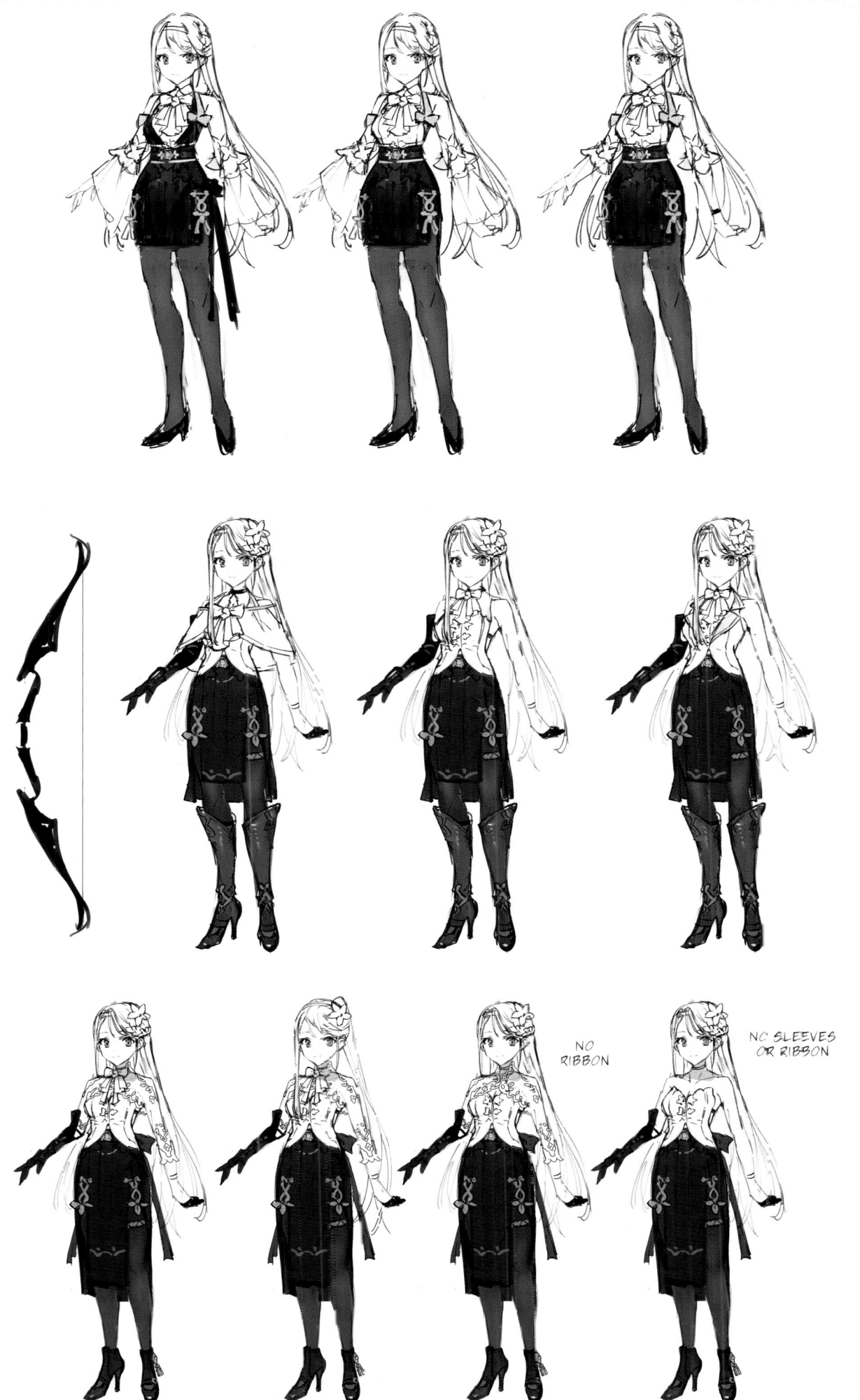

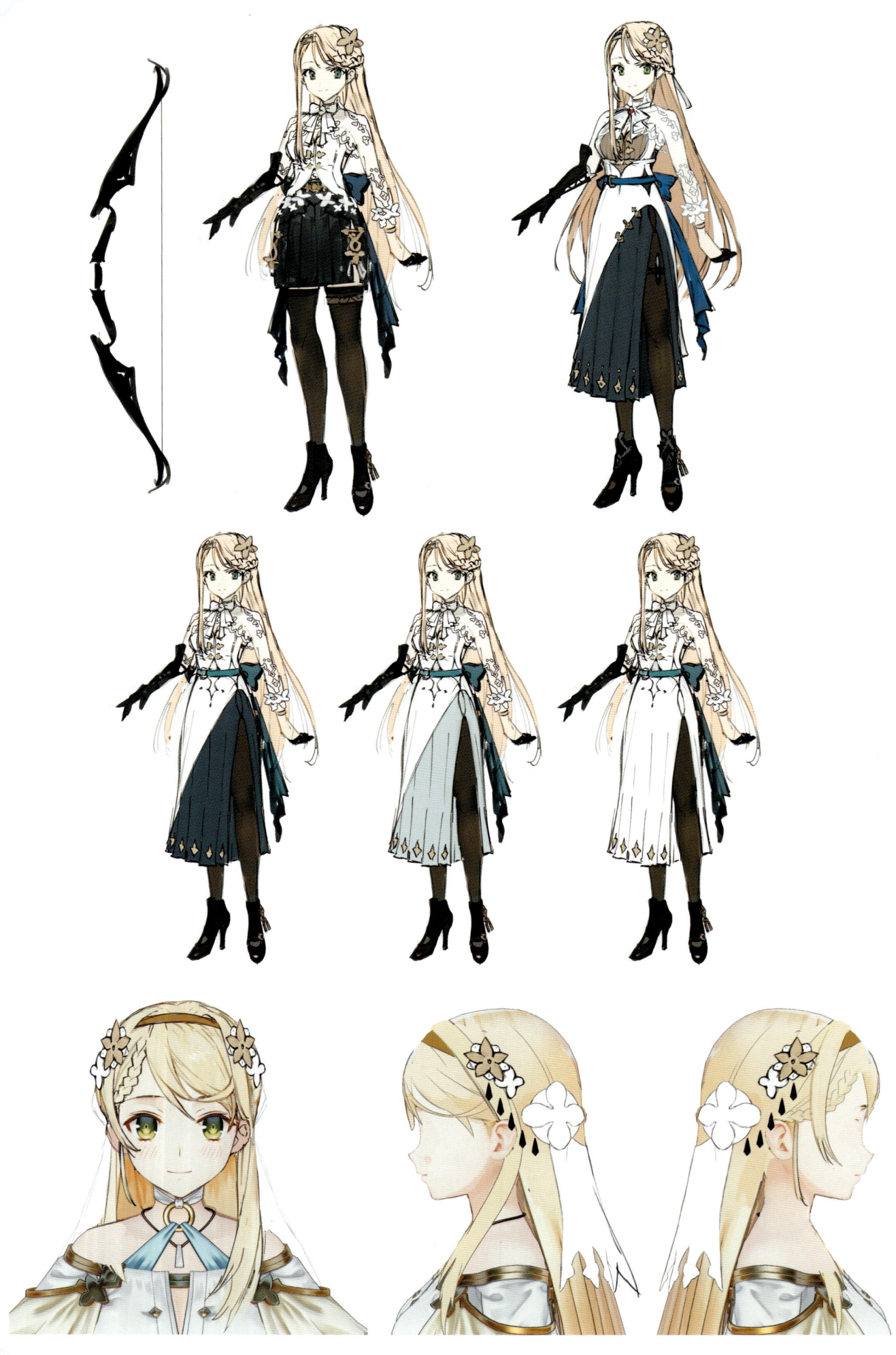

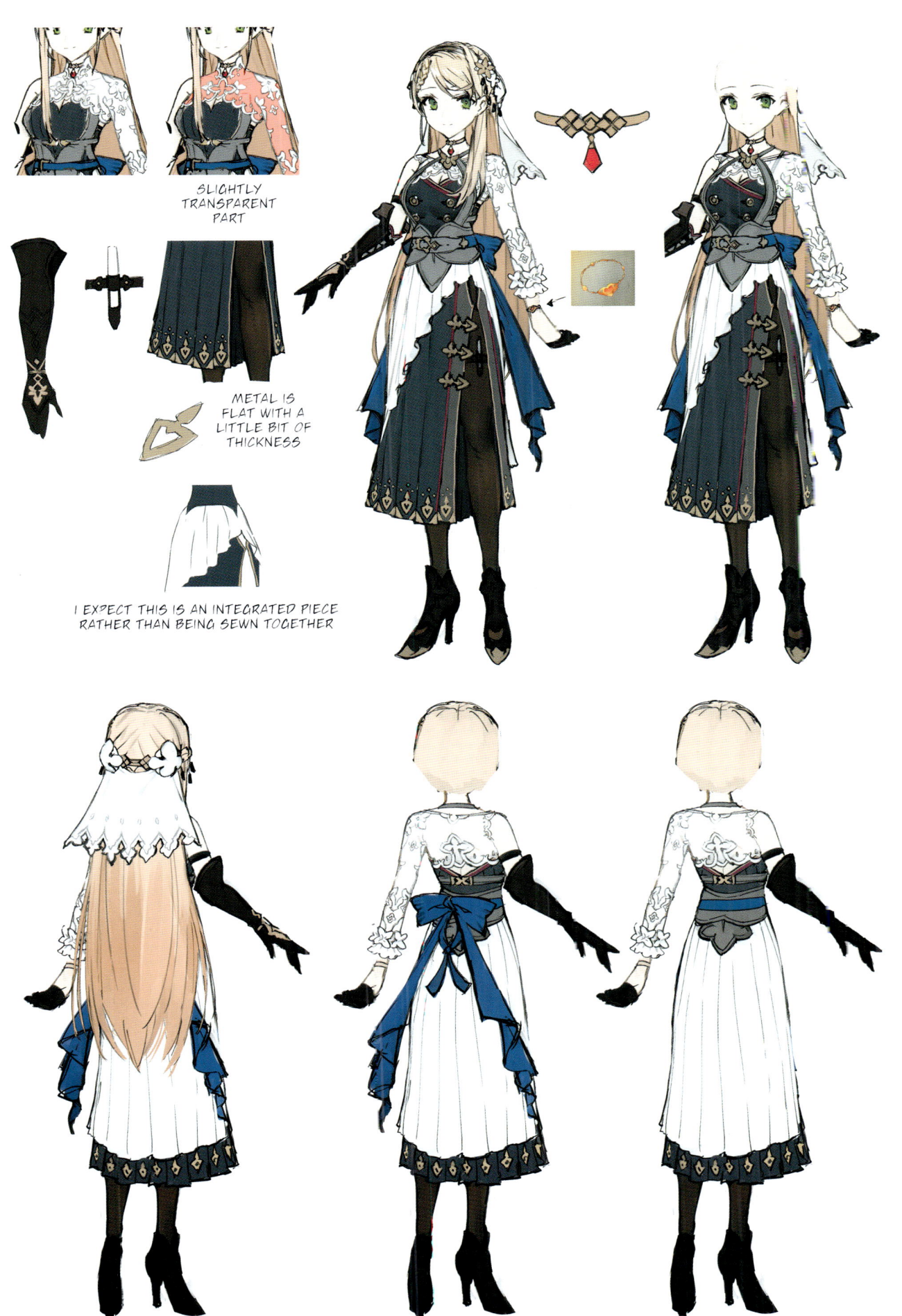

Lent Design Sketches

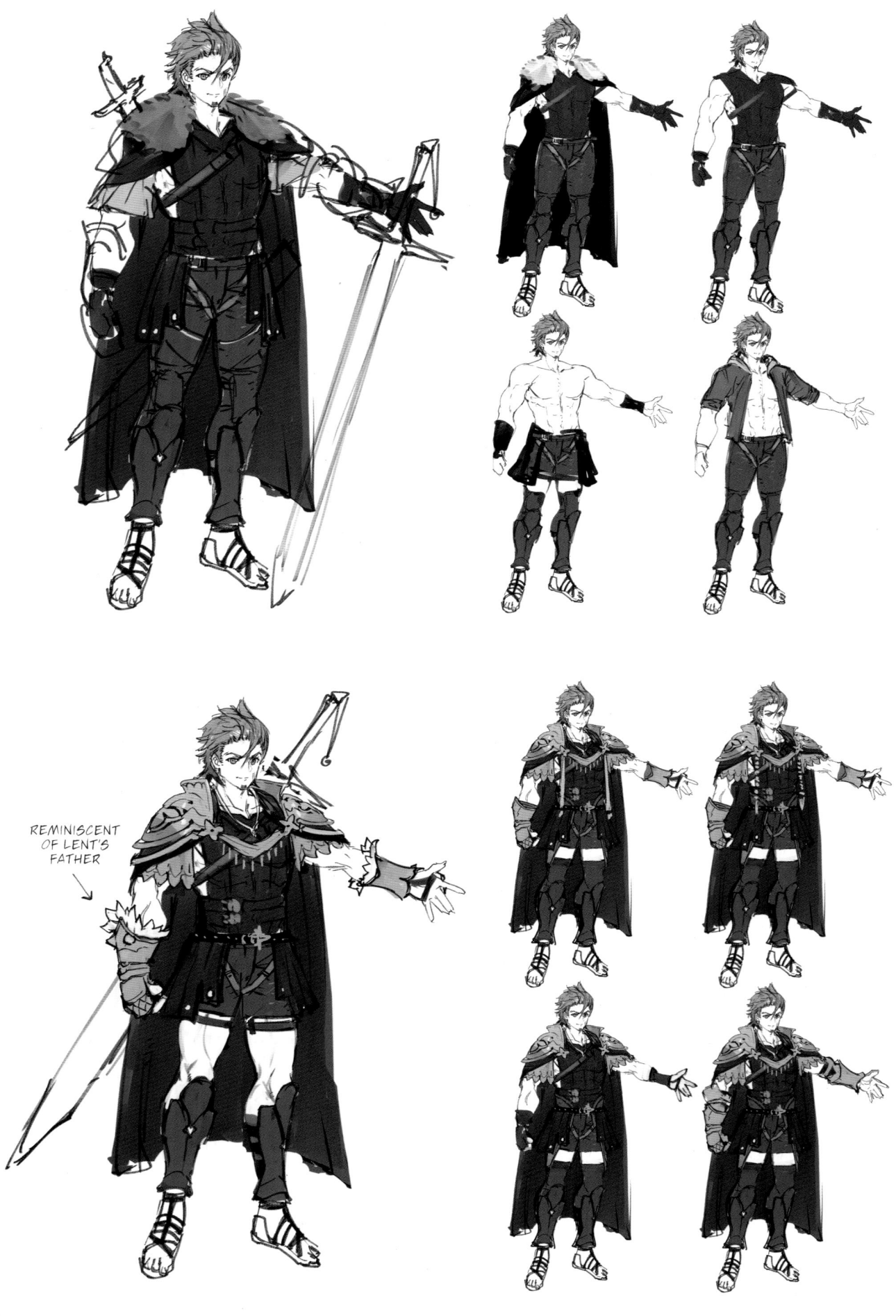

REMINISCENT OF LENT'S FATHER

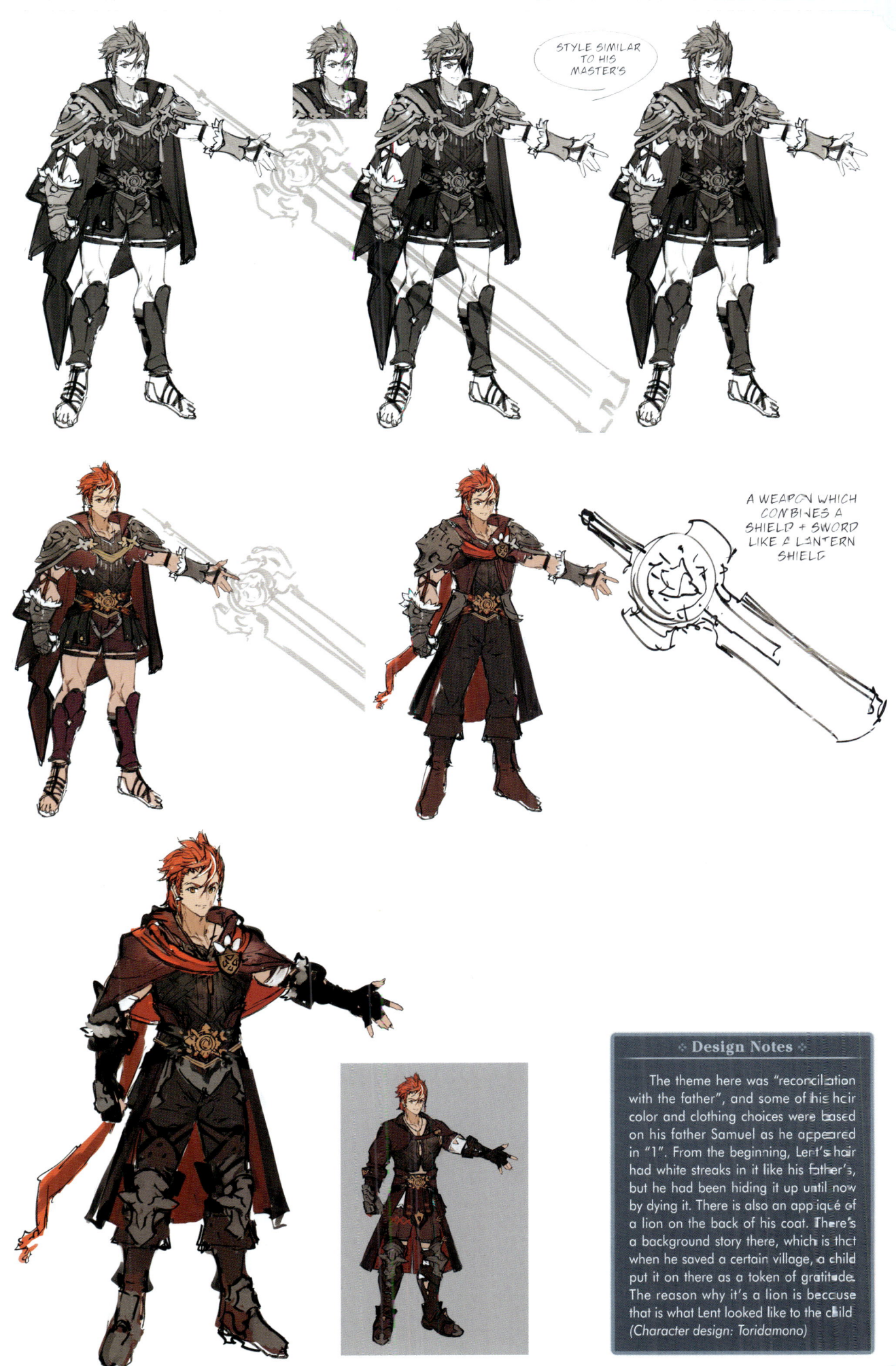

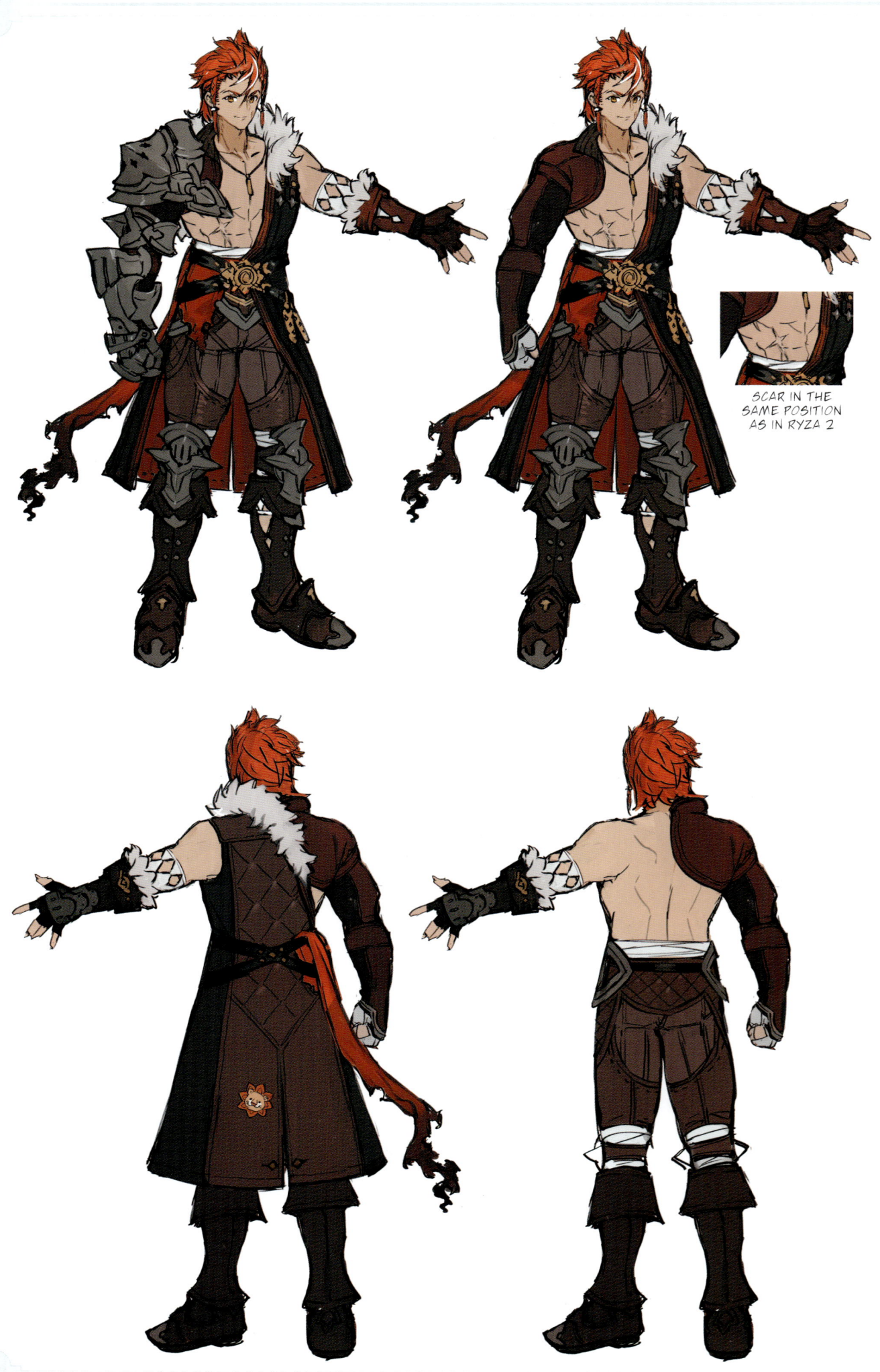

SCAR IN THE SAME POSITION AS IN RYZA 2

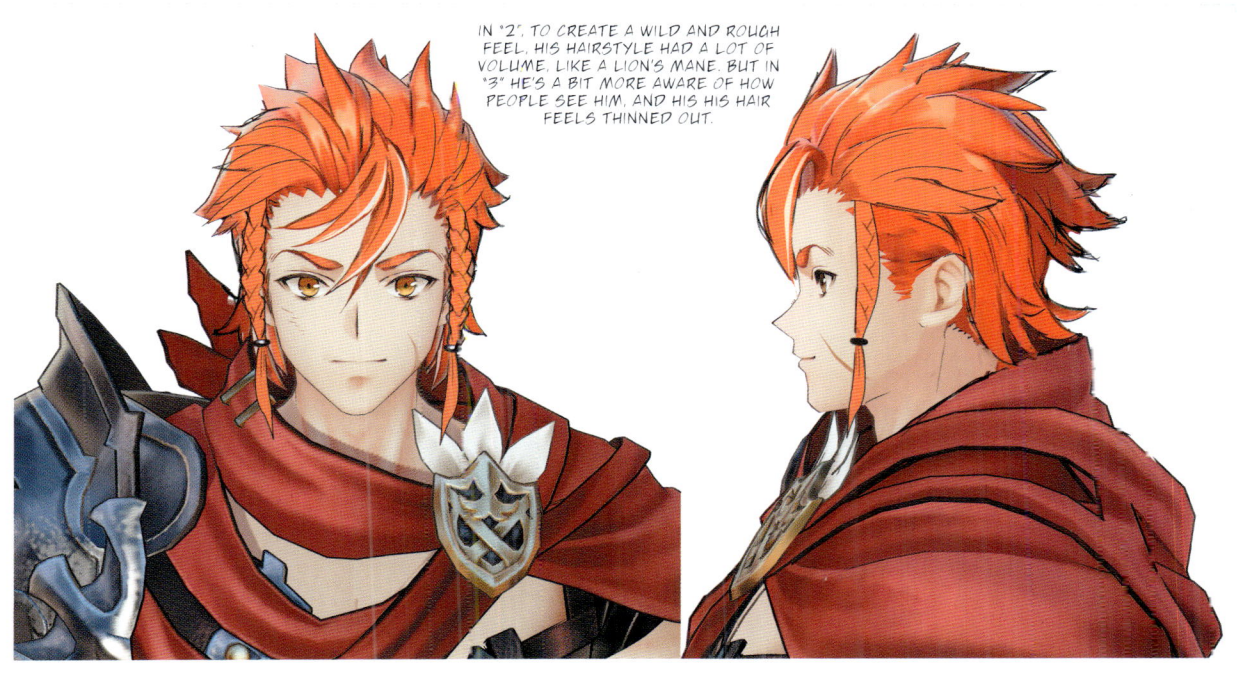

IN "2", TO CREATE A WILD AND ROUGH FEEL, HIS HAIRSTYLE HAD A LOT OF VOLUME, LIKE A LION'S MANE. BUT IN "3" HE'S A BIT MORE AWARE OF HOW PEOPLE SEE HIM, AND HIS HAIR FEELS THINNED OUT.

《 Tao Design Sketches 》

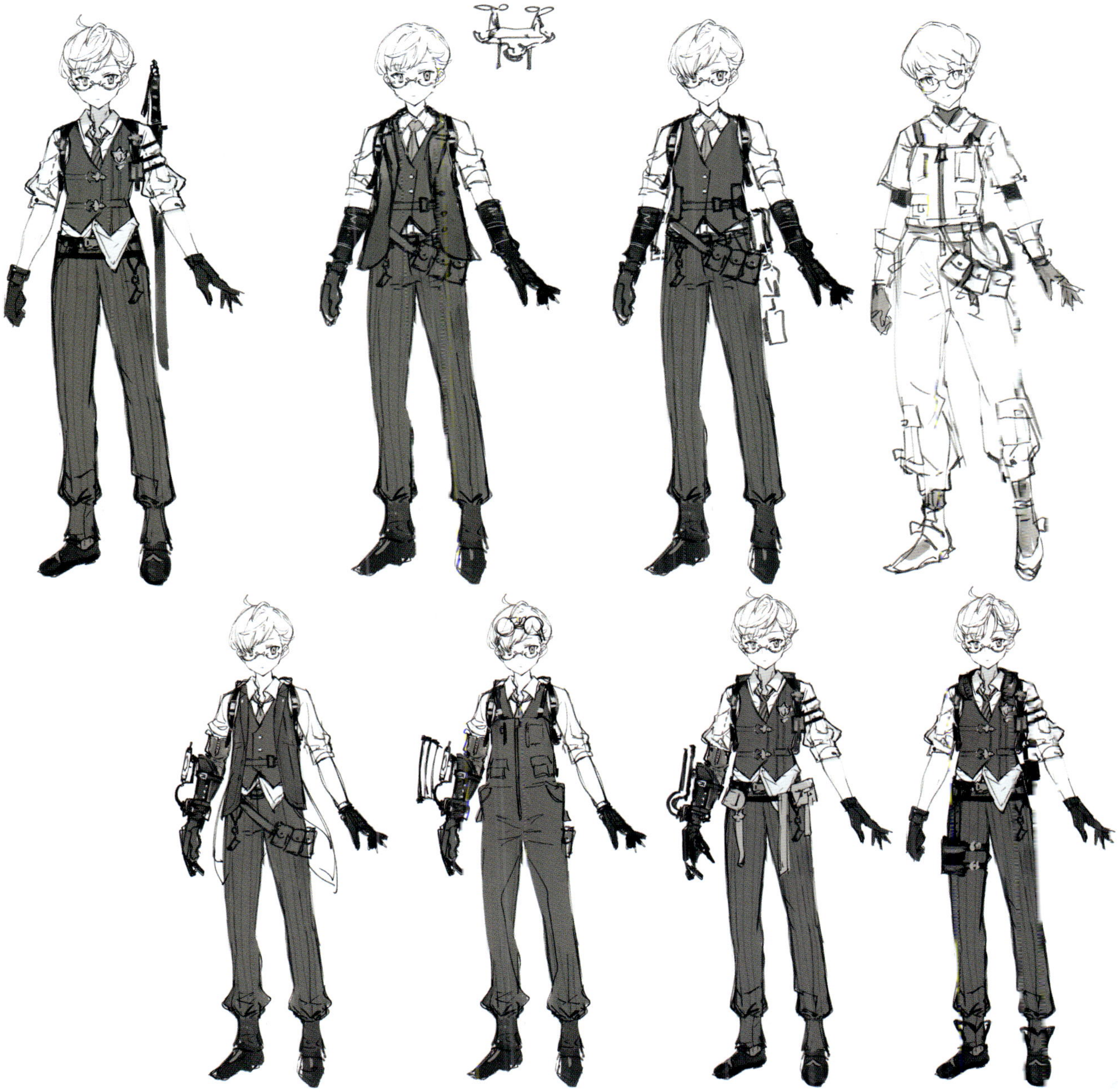

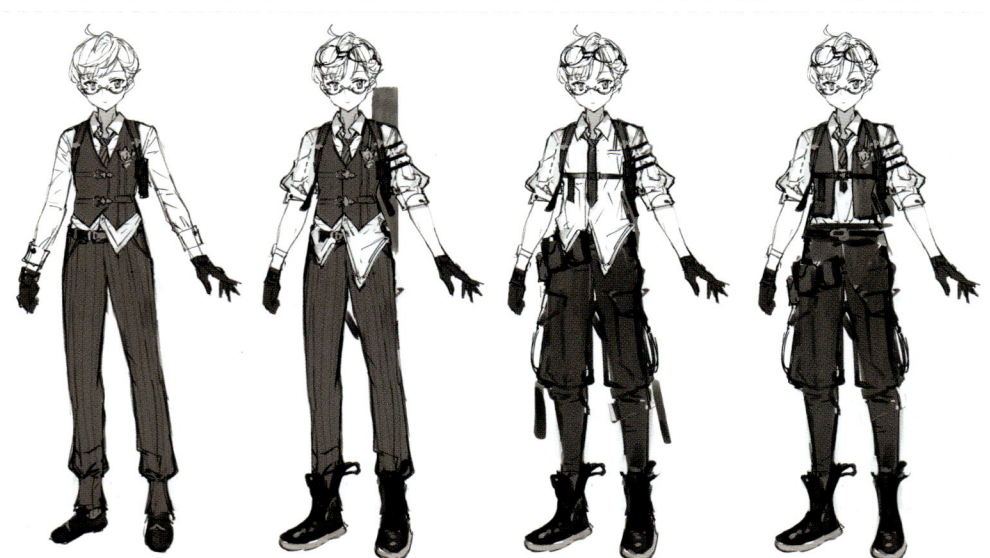

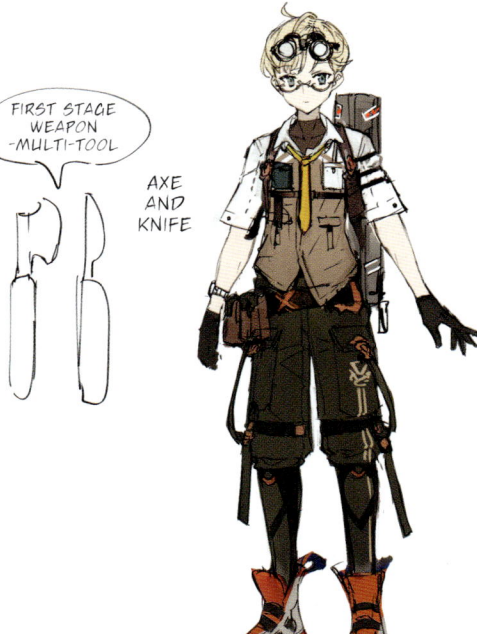

FIRST STAGE WEAPON -MULTI-TOOL

AXE AND KNIFE

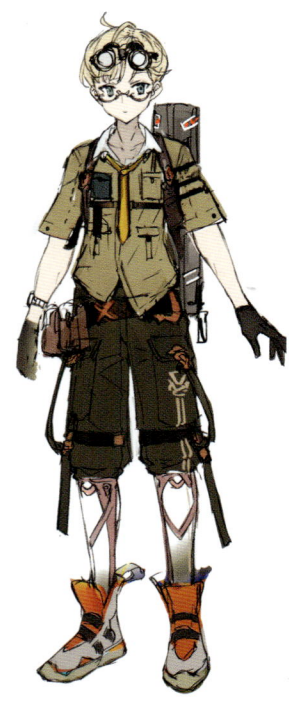

> ### ◆ Design Notes ◆
>
> This was actually in my Top 3 most difficult struggles with characters in this game. At first, I was going with a formal design like in "2", but in order to further develop the character's personality, I tried steering towards a scientist with messy hair and sloppy clothes, but the impression that he was unkempt became too strong, so I gave up on the idea. In the end, I changed direction to a more fieldwork-oriented style.
> *(Character design: Toridamono)*

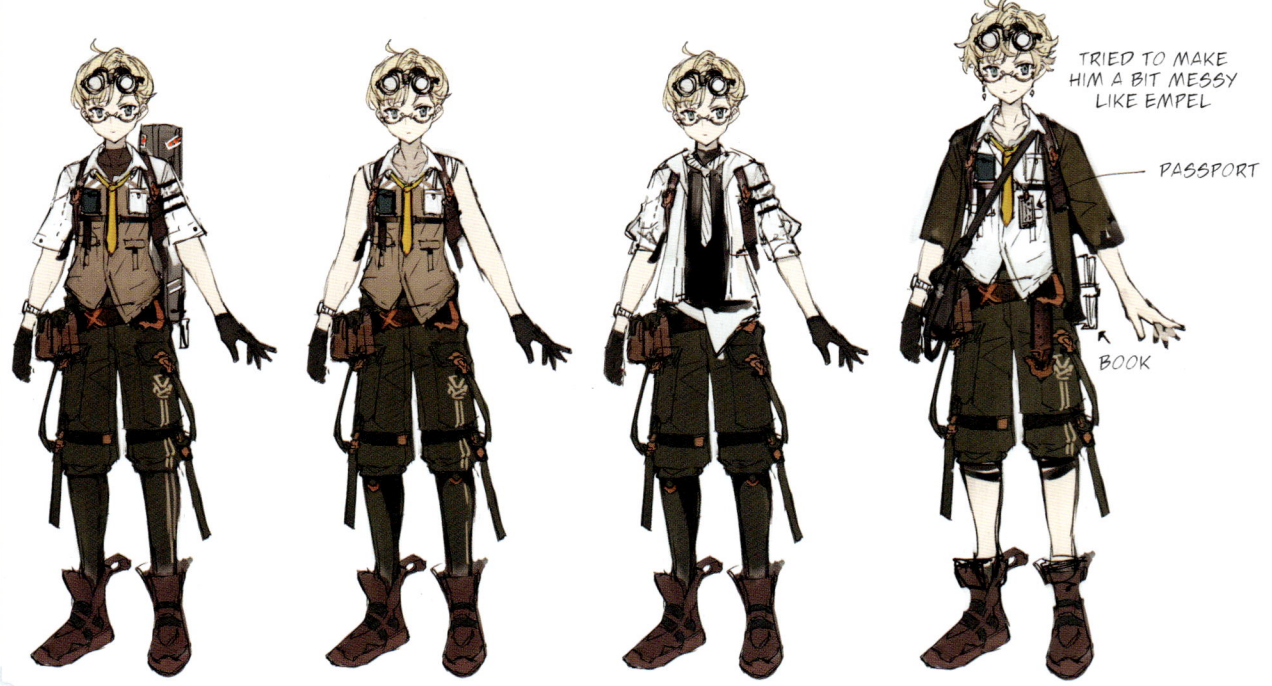

TRIED TO MAKE HIM A BIT MESSY LIKE EMPEL

PASSPORT

BOOK

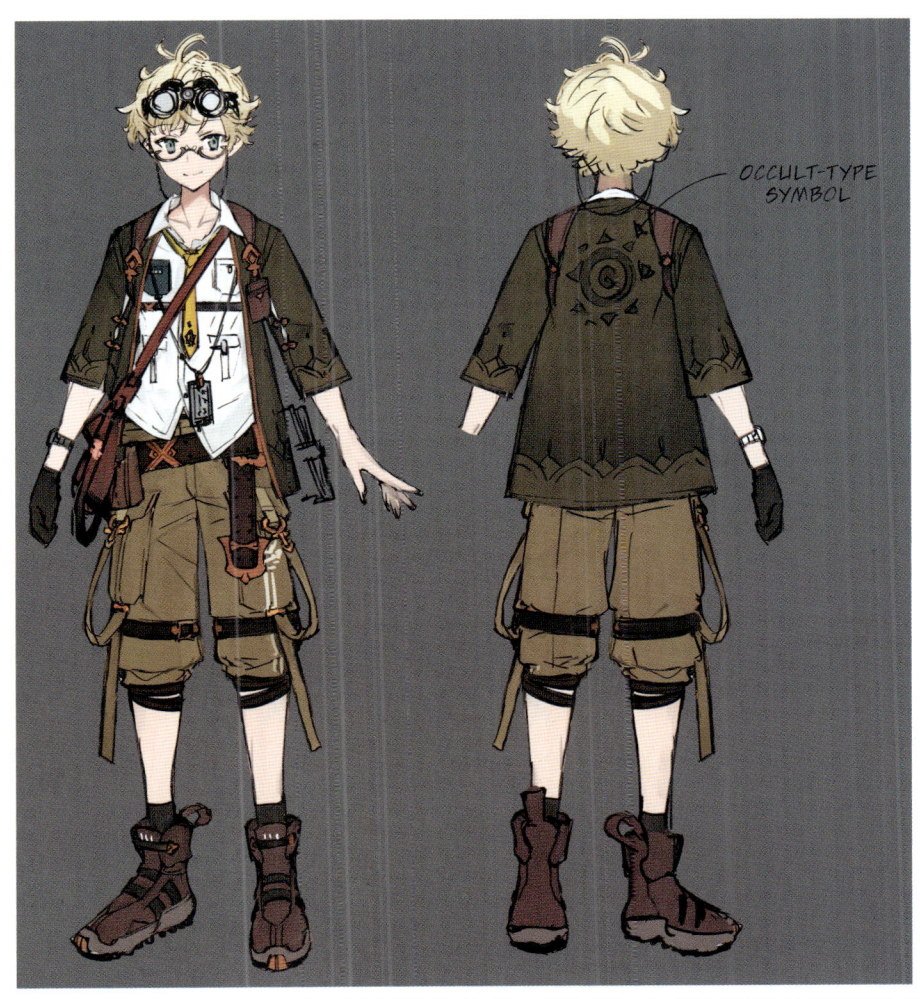

OCCULT-TYPE SYMBOL

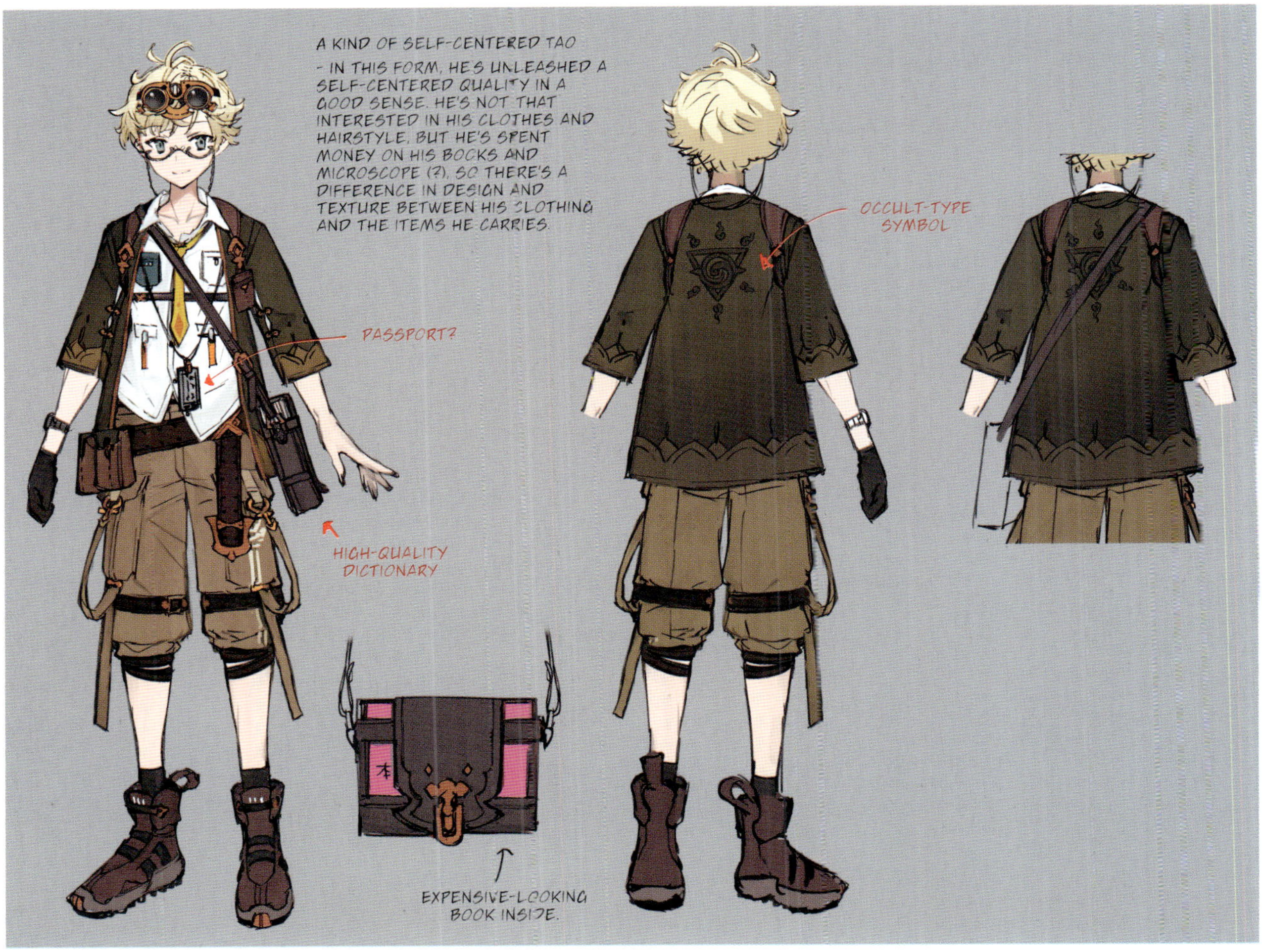

A KIND OF SELF-CENTERED TAO
- IN THIS FORM, HE'S UNLEASHED A SELF-CENTERED QUALITY IN A GOOD SENSE. HE'S NOT THAT INTERESTED IN HIS CLOTHES AND HAIRSTYLE, BUT HE'S SPENT MONEY ON HIS BOOKS AND MICROSCOPE (?), SO THERE'S A DIFFERENCE IN DESIGN AND TEXTURE BETWEEN HIS CLOTHING AND THE ITEMS HE CARRIES.

PASSPORT?

HIGH-QUALITY DICTIONARY.

OCCULT-TYPE SYMBOL

EXPENSIVE-LOOKING BOOK INSIDE.

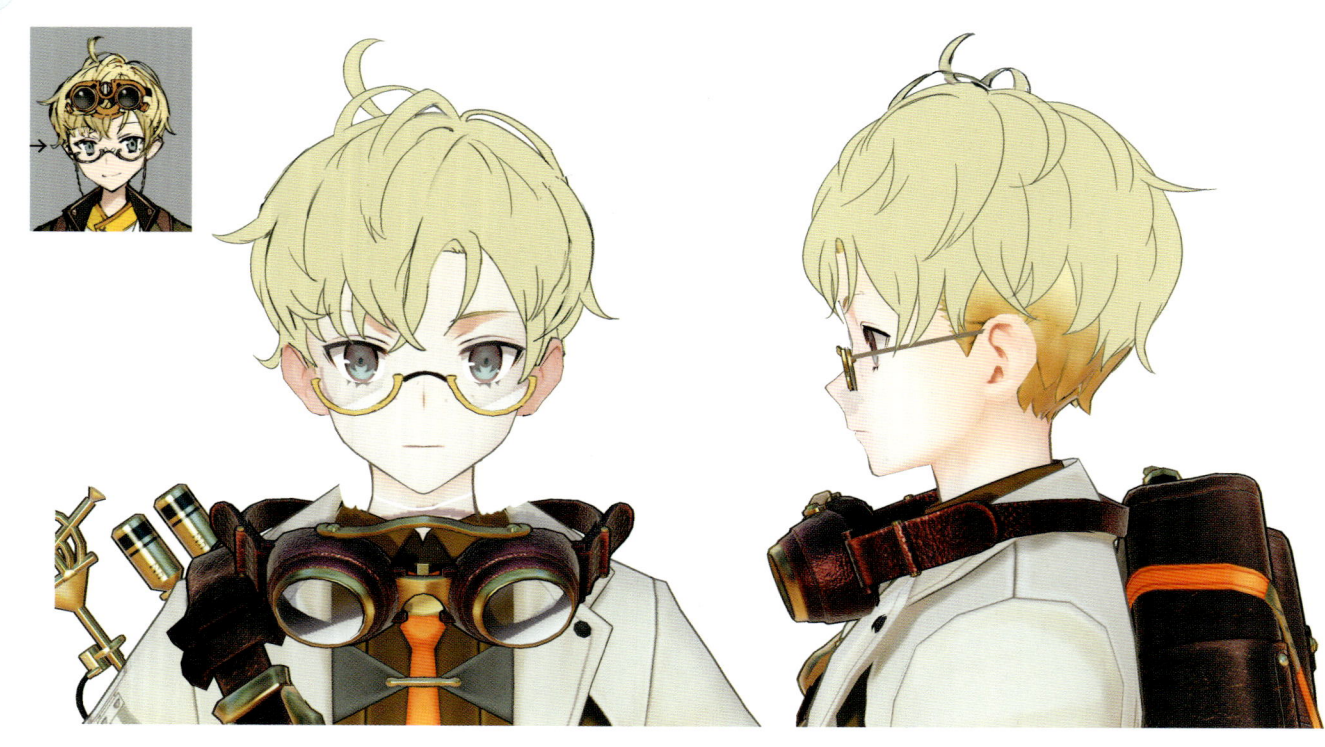

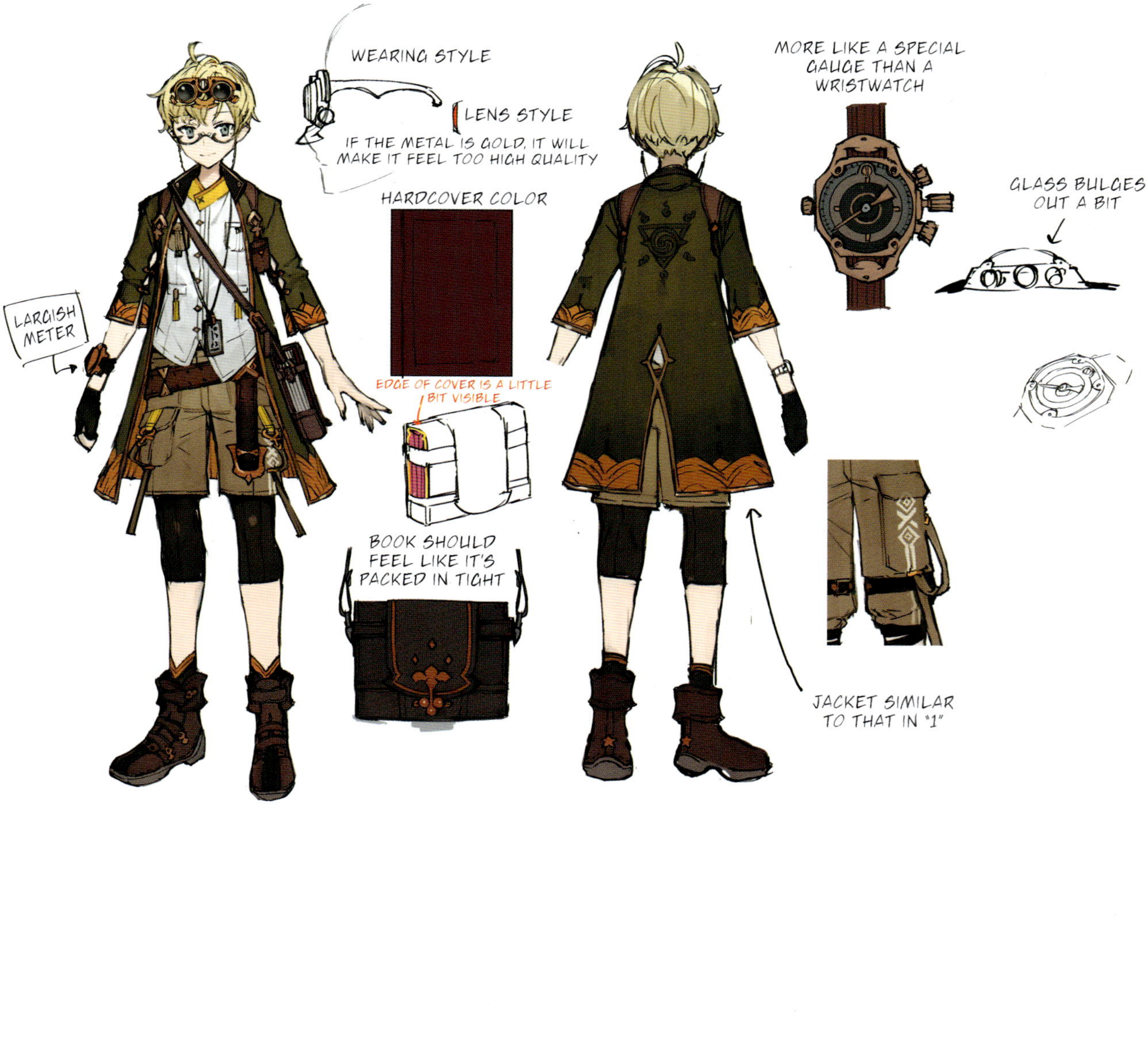

WEARING STYLE

LENS STYLE

IF THE METAL IS GOLD, IT WILL MAKE IT FEEL TOO HIGH QUALITY

MORE LIKE A SPECIAL GAUGE THAN A WRISTWATCH

GLASS BULGES OUT A BIT

HARDCOVER COLOR

LARGISH METER

EDGE OF COVER IS A LITTLE BIT VISIBLE

BOOK SHOULD FEEL LIKE IT'S PACKED IN TIGHT

JACKET SIMILAR TO THAT IN "1"

Patricia Design Sketches

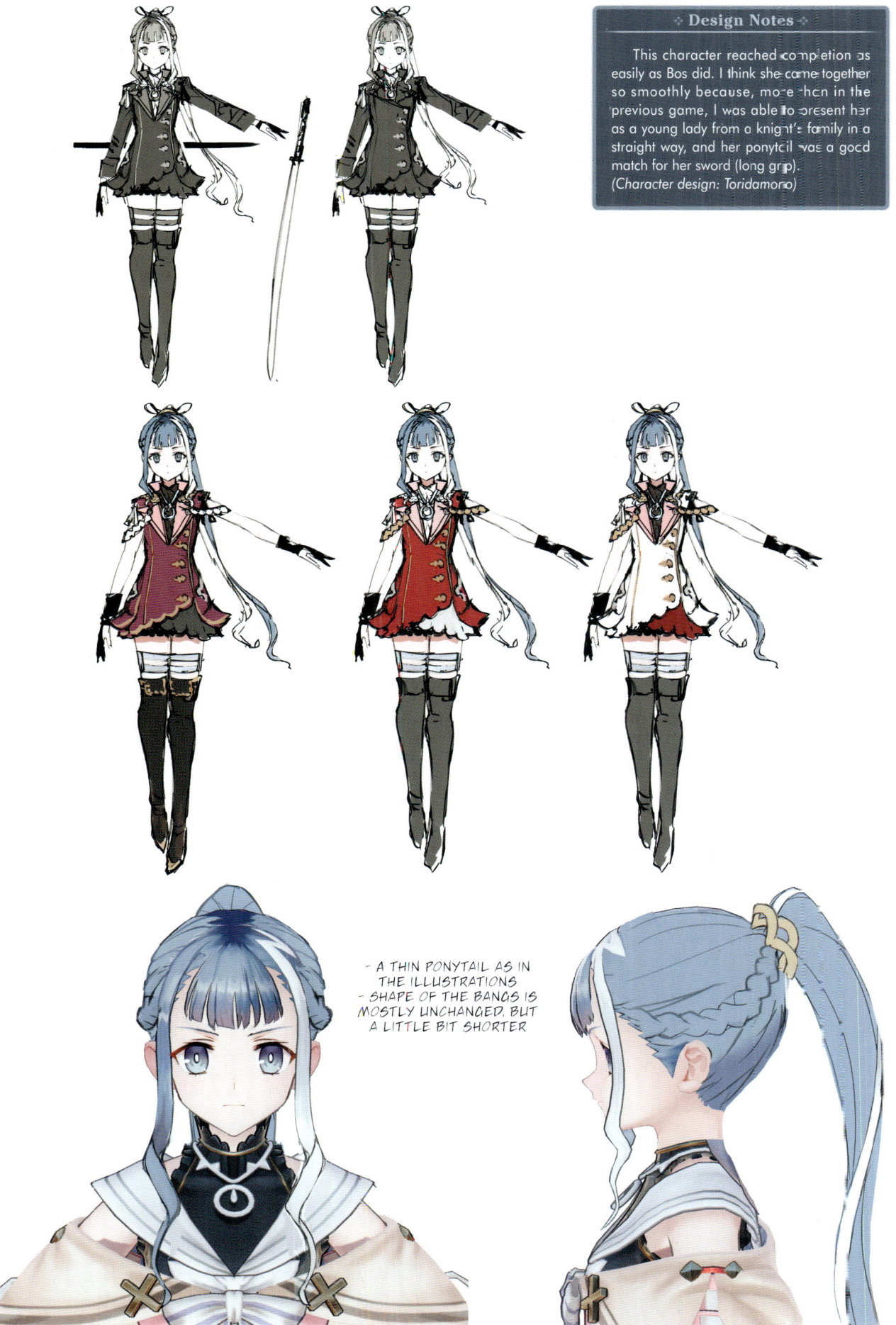

Design Notes

This character reached completion as easily as Bos did. I think she came together so smoothly because, more than in the previous game, I was able to present her as a young lady from a knight's family in a straight way, and her ponytail was a good match for her sword (long grip).
(Character design: Toridamono)

- A THIN PONYTAIL AS IN THE ILLUSTRATIONS
- SHAPE OF THE BANGS IS MOSTLY UNCHANGED, BUT A LITTLE BIT SHORTER

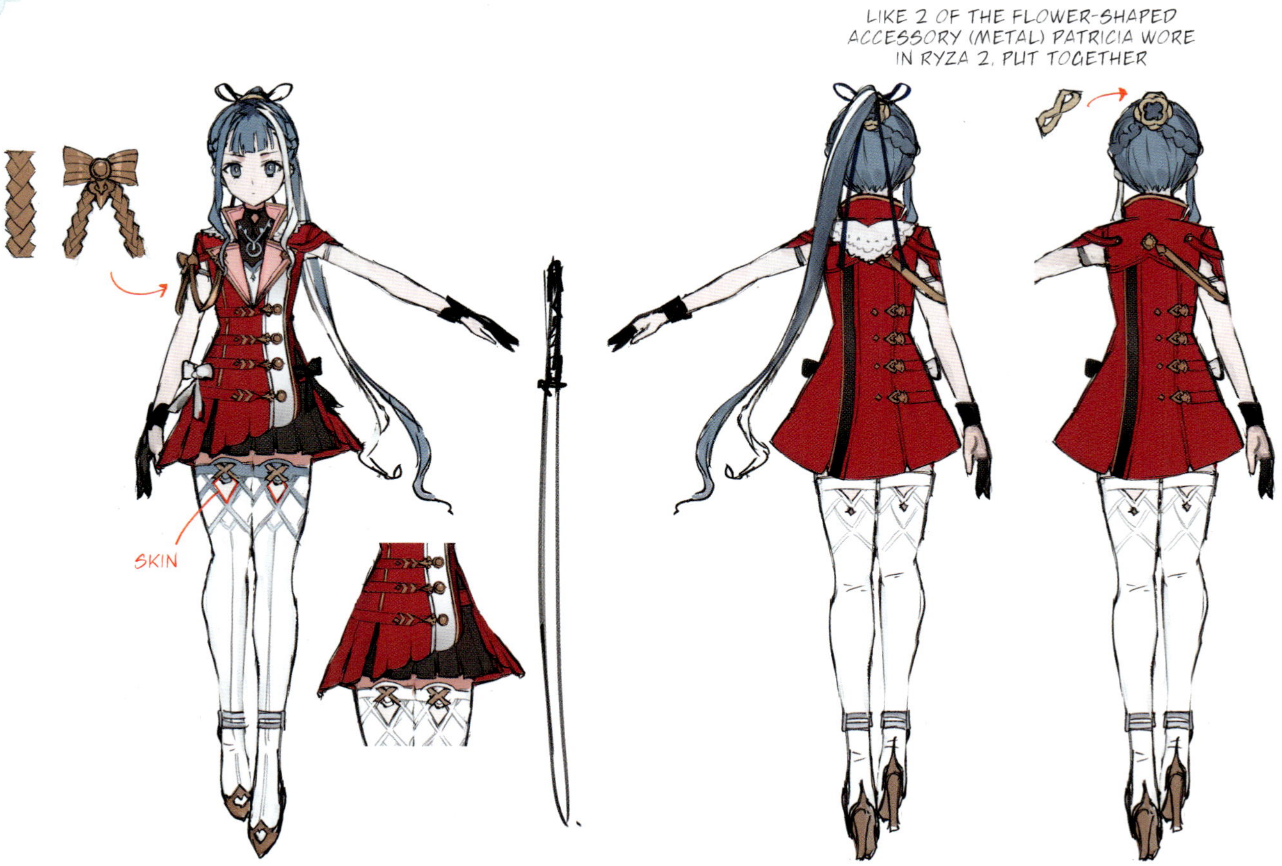

LIKE 2 OF THE FLOWER-SHAPED ACCESSORY (METAL) PATRICIA WORE IN RYZA 2, PUT TOGETHER

SKIN

Bos Design Sketches

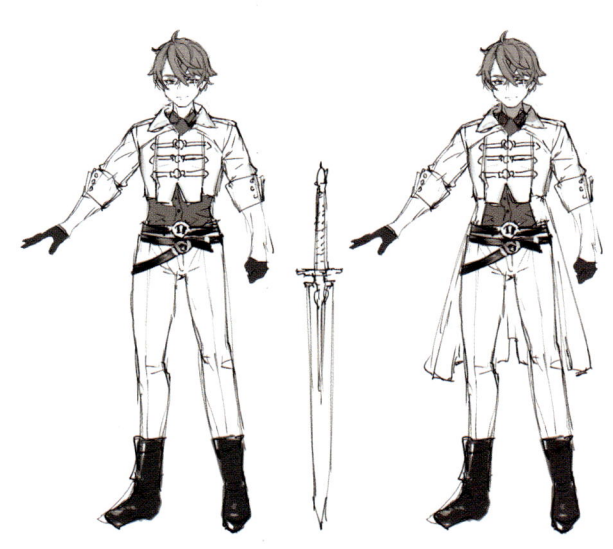
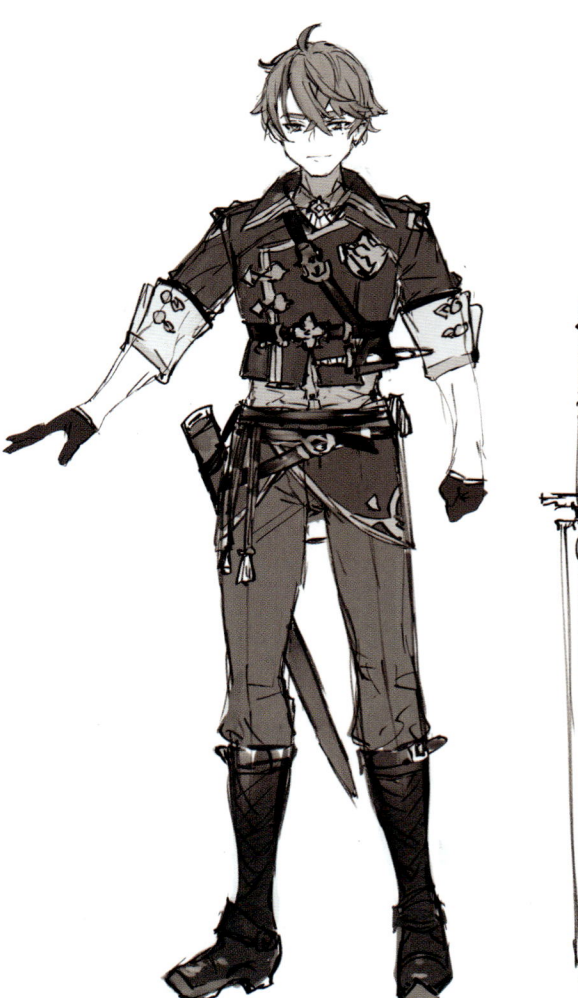

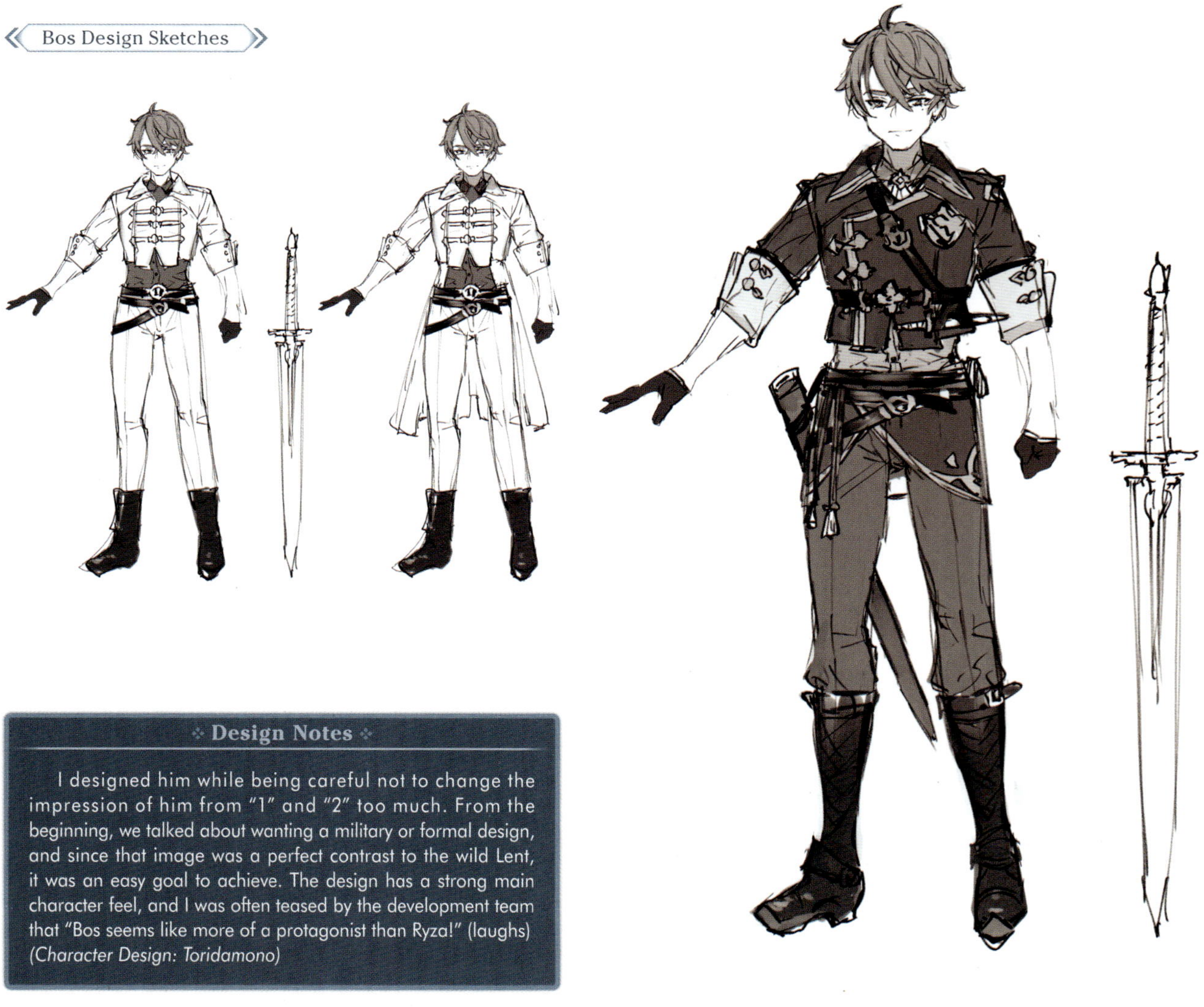

❖ Design Notes ❖

I designed him while being careful not to change the impression of him from "1" and "2" too much. From the beginning, we talked about wanting a military or formal design, and since that image was a perfect contrast to the wild Lent, it was an easy goal to achieve. The design has a strong main character feel, and I was often teased by the development team that "Bos seems like more of a protagonist than Ryza!" (laughs) (Character Design: Toridamono)

THE METAL PARTS ARE NEUTRAL COLORS LIKE SILVER OR PLATINUM

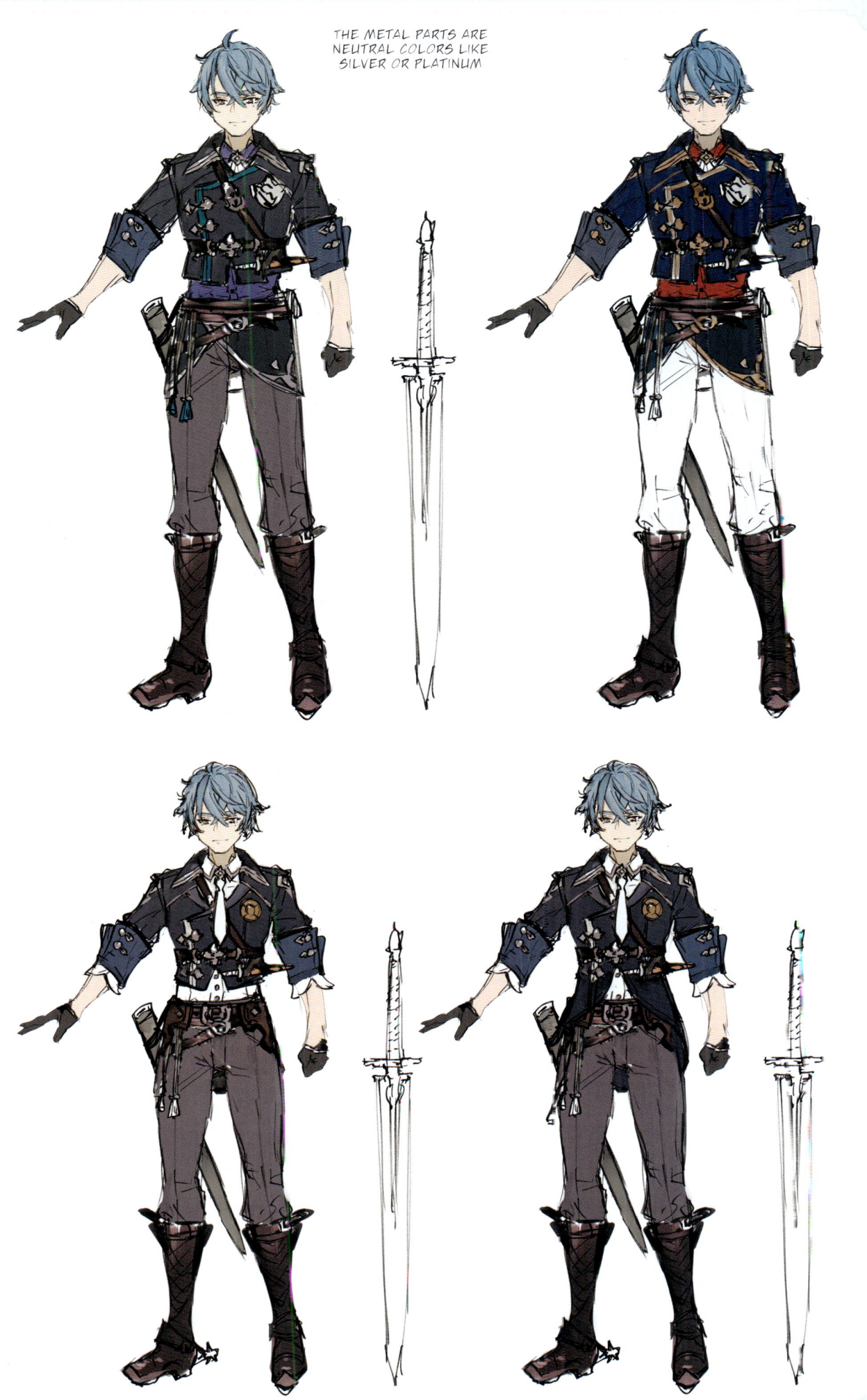

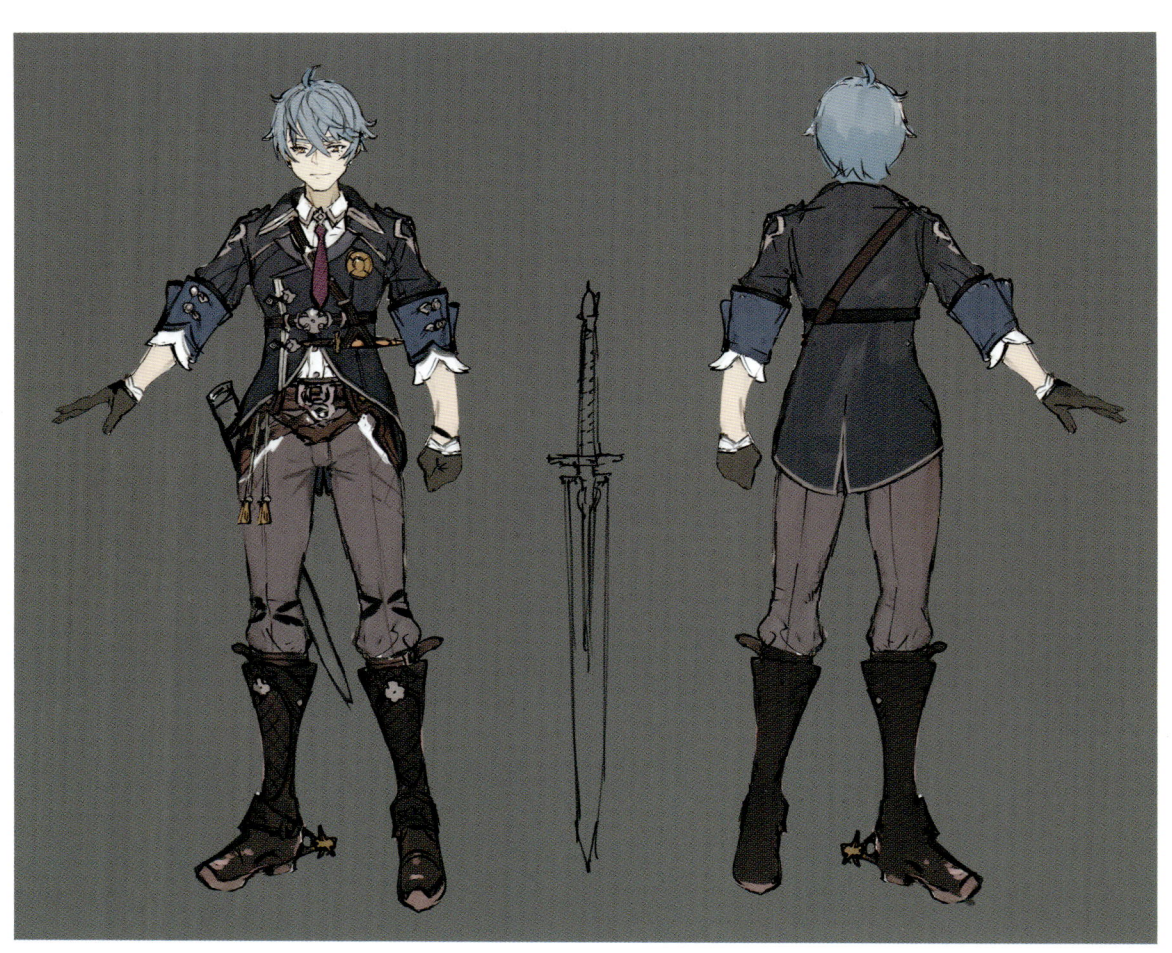

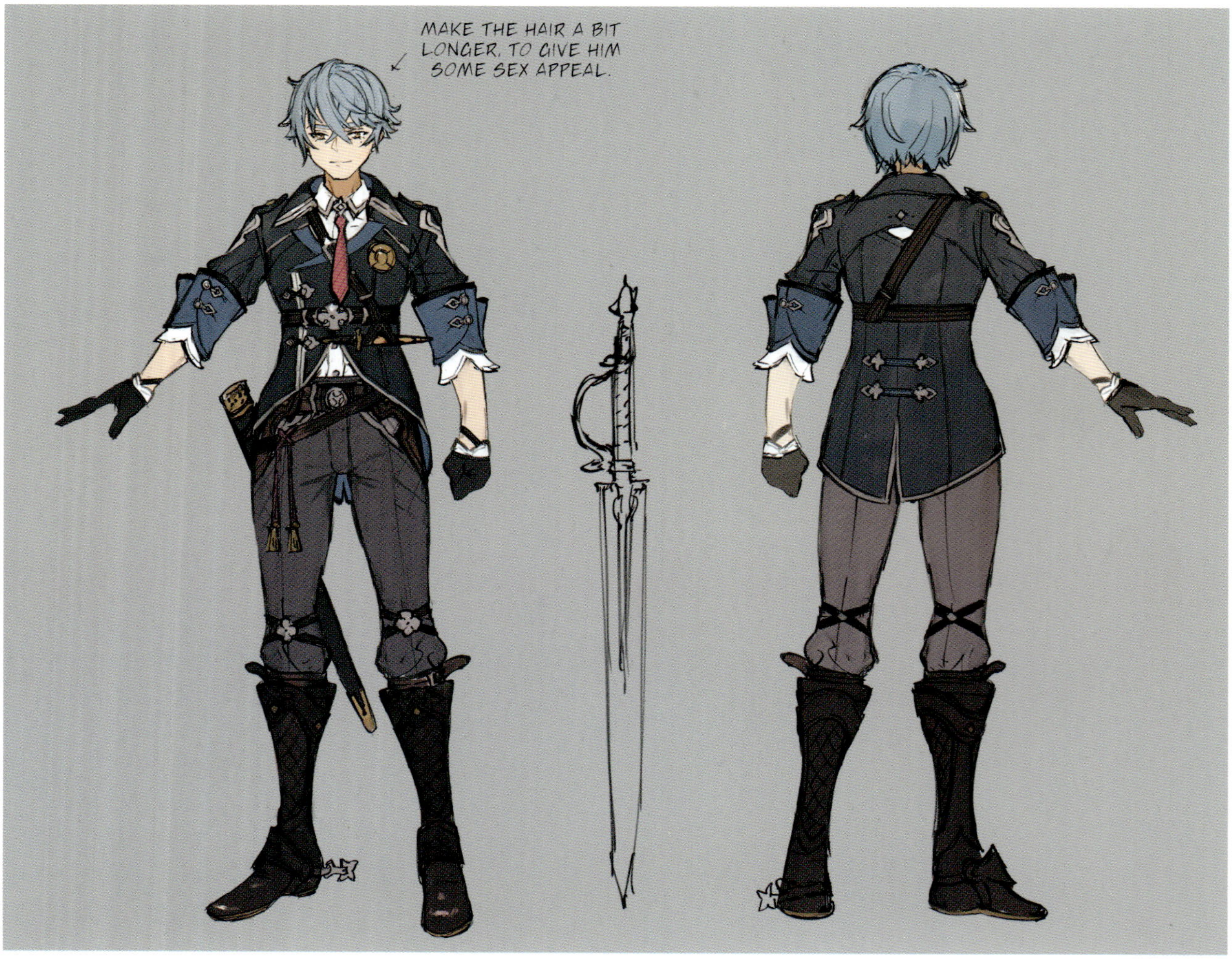

MAKE THE HAIR A BIT LONGER, TO GIVE HIM SOME SEX APPEAL.

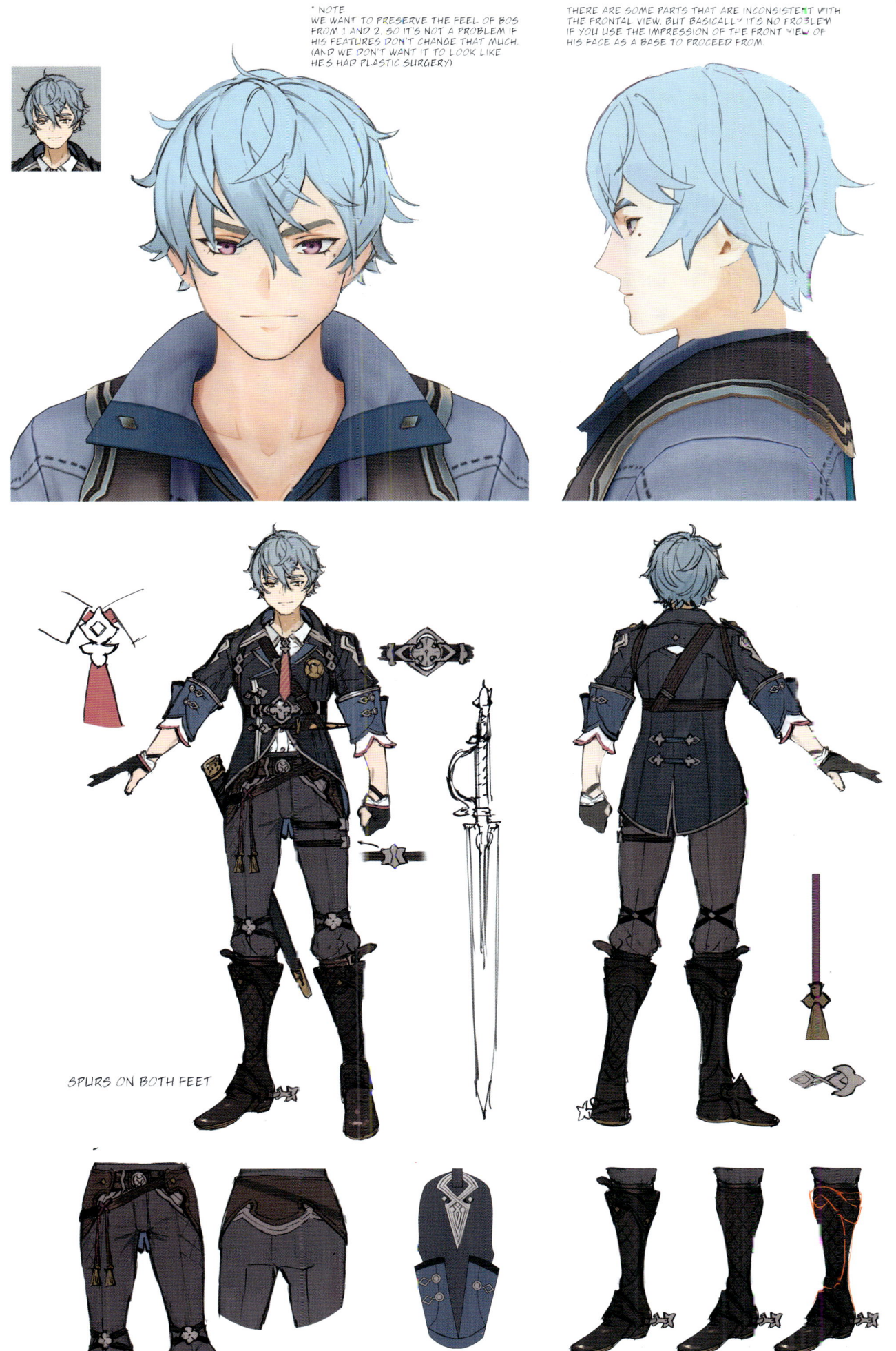

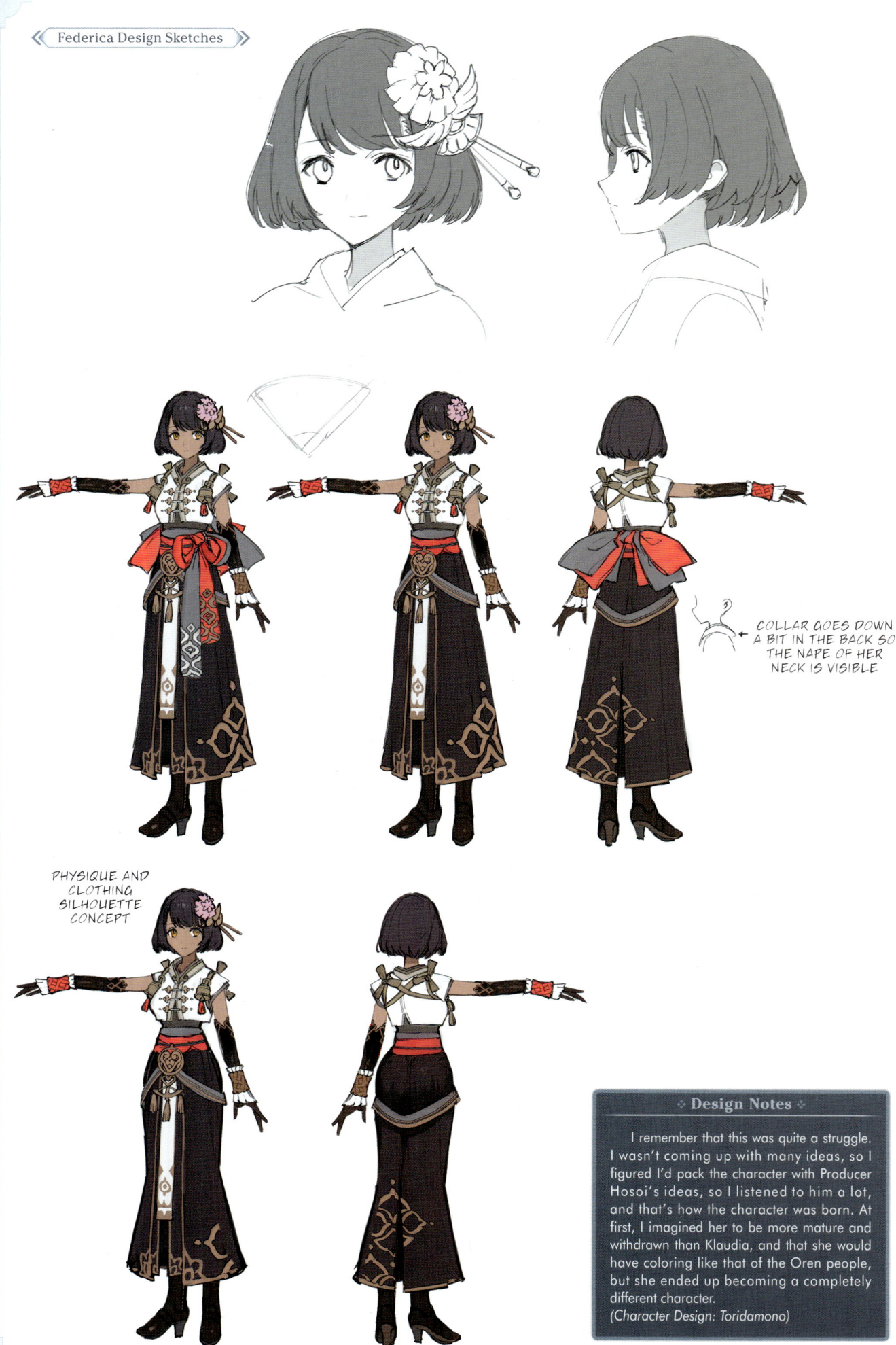

Federica Design Sketches

COLLAR GOES DOWN A BIT IN THE BACK SO THE NAPE OF HER NECK IS VISIBLE

PHYSIQUE AND CLOTHING SILHOUETTE CONCEPT

❖ Design Notes ❖

I remember that this was quite a struggle. I wasn't coming up with many ideas, so I figured I'd pack the character with Producer Hosoi's ideas, so I listened to him a lot, and that's how the character was born. At first, I imagined her to be more mature and withdrawn than Klaudia, and that she would have coloring like that of the Oren people, but she ended up becoming a completely different character.
(Character Design: Toridamono)

« Dian Design Sketches »

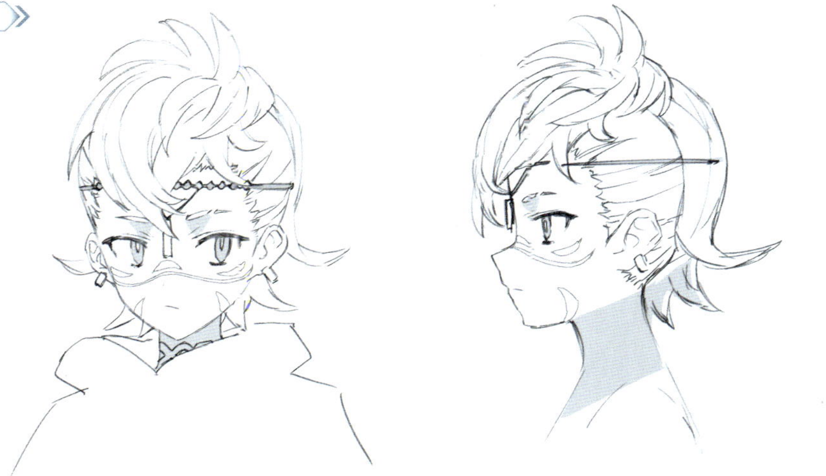

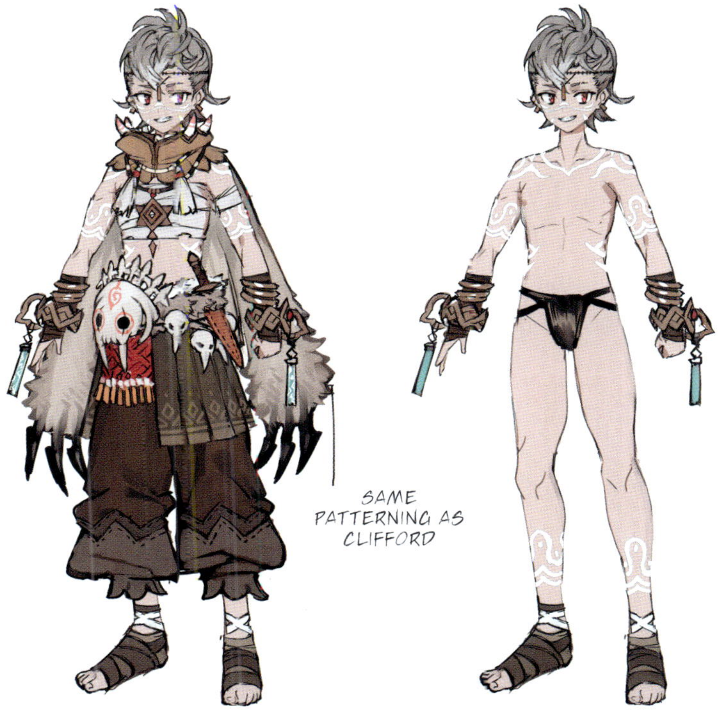

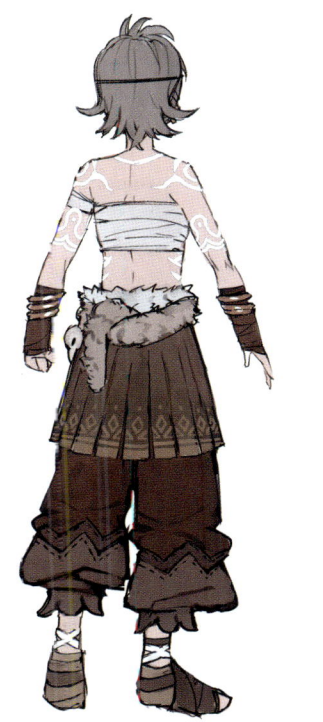

SAME PATTERNING AS CLIFFORD

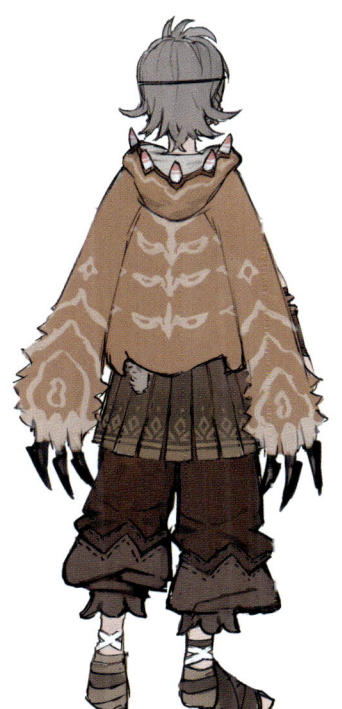

✧ Design Notes ✧

In terms of his specs, he was easy to understand, but he didn't jump out at you as an individual. His personality was a bit thin. We were concerned about that, and we talked it over, and we said, "What if we added some delinquent kind of elements?". So we came up with a pompadour-style haircut and loose pants, and it we were able to finalize him easily after that. As part of his backstory, he's from the same hometown as Clifford when he appeared in "2".
(Character design: Toridamono)

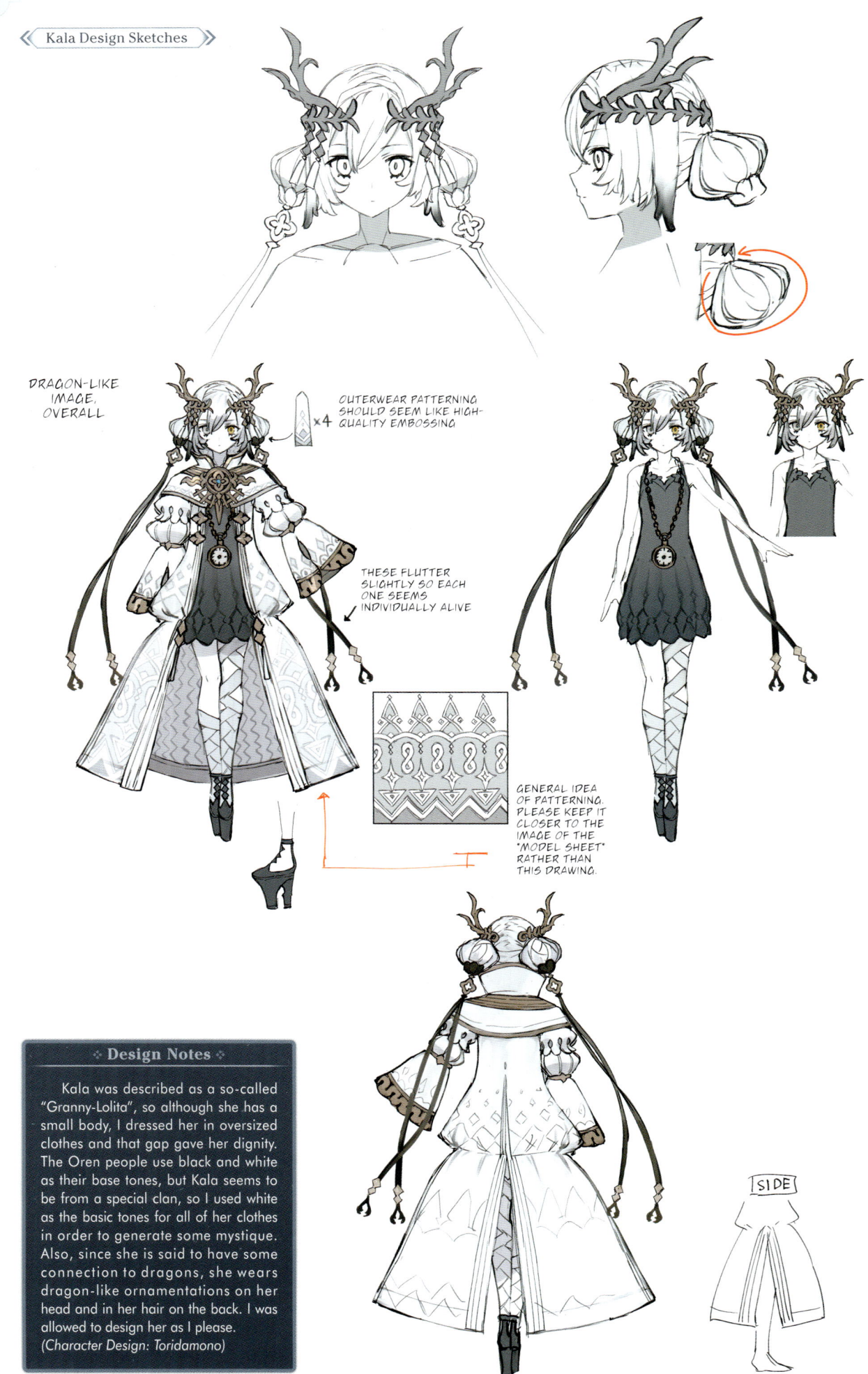

Alberta Design Sketches

FABRIC ON THE INSIDE ON THE LEFT SIDE OF THE KIMONO ONLY

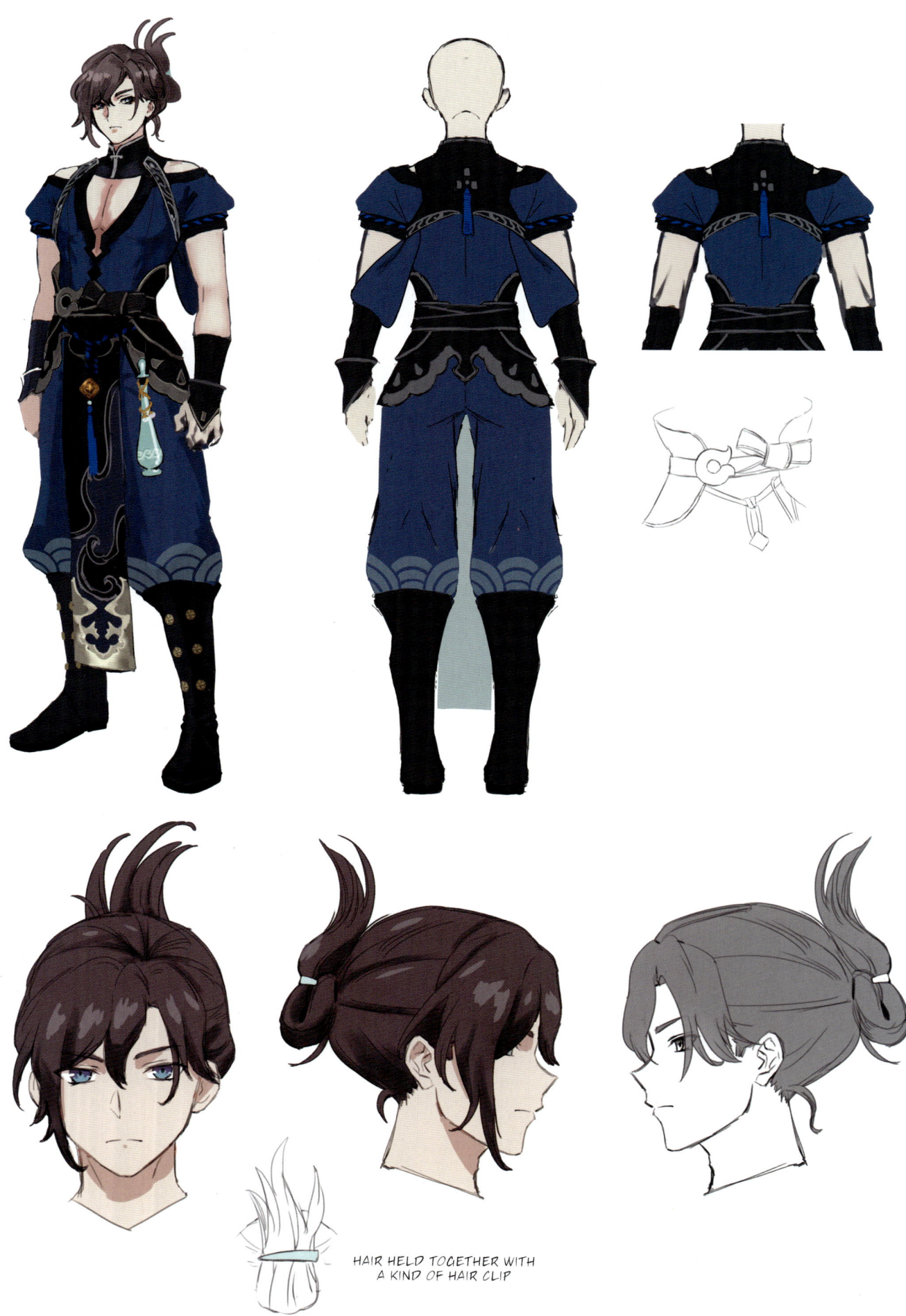

Saverio Design Sketches

HAIR HELD TOGETHER WITH A KIND OF HAIR CLIP

Anna Design Sketches

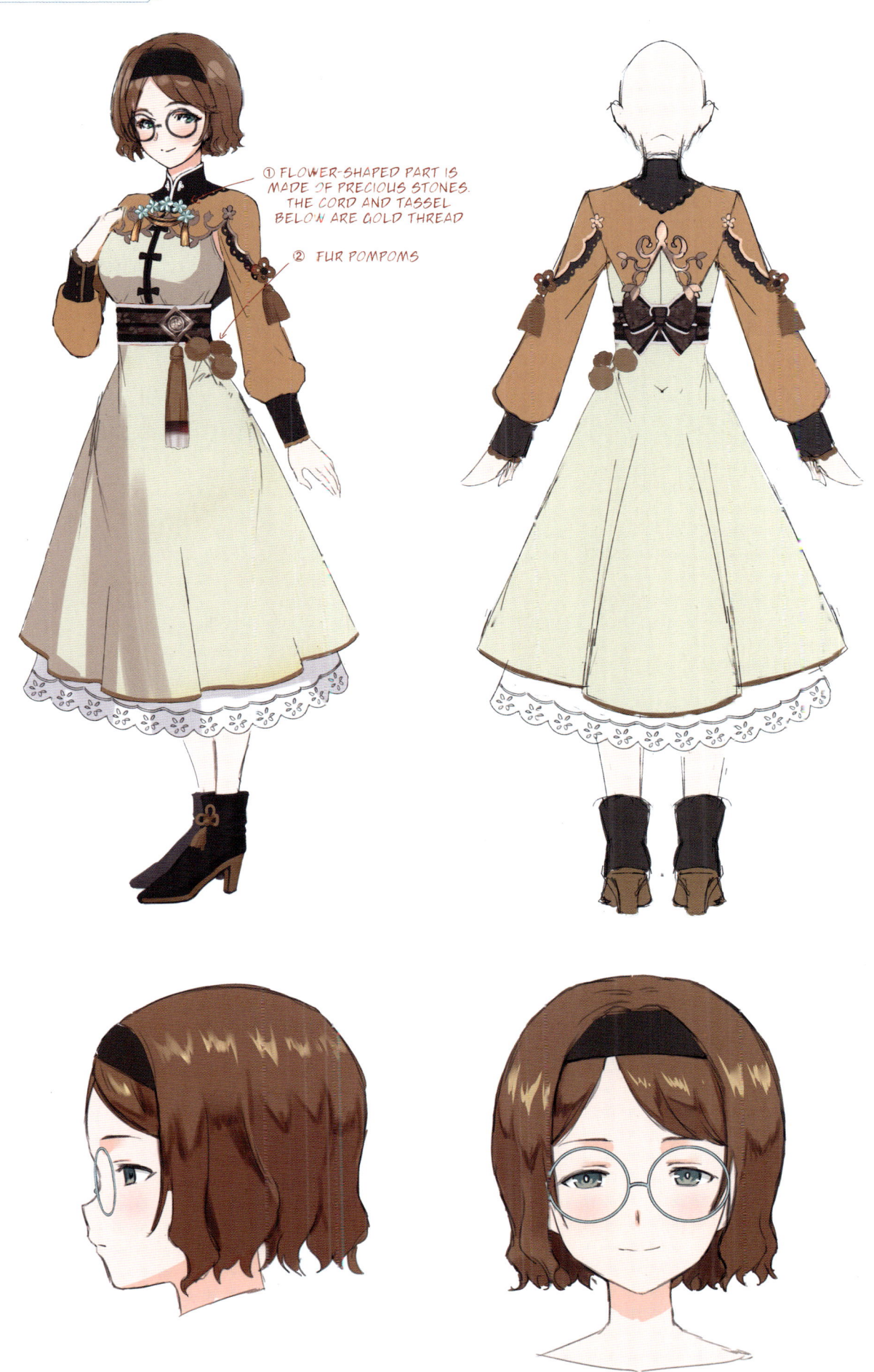

① FLOWER-SHAPED PART IS MADE OF PRECIOUS STONES. THE CORD AND TASSEL BELOW ARE GOLD THREAD

② FUR POMPOMS

Dolto Design Sketches

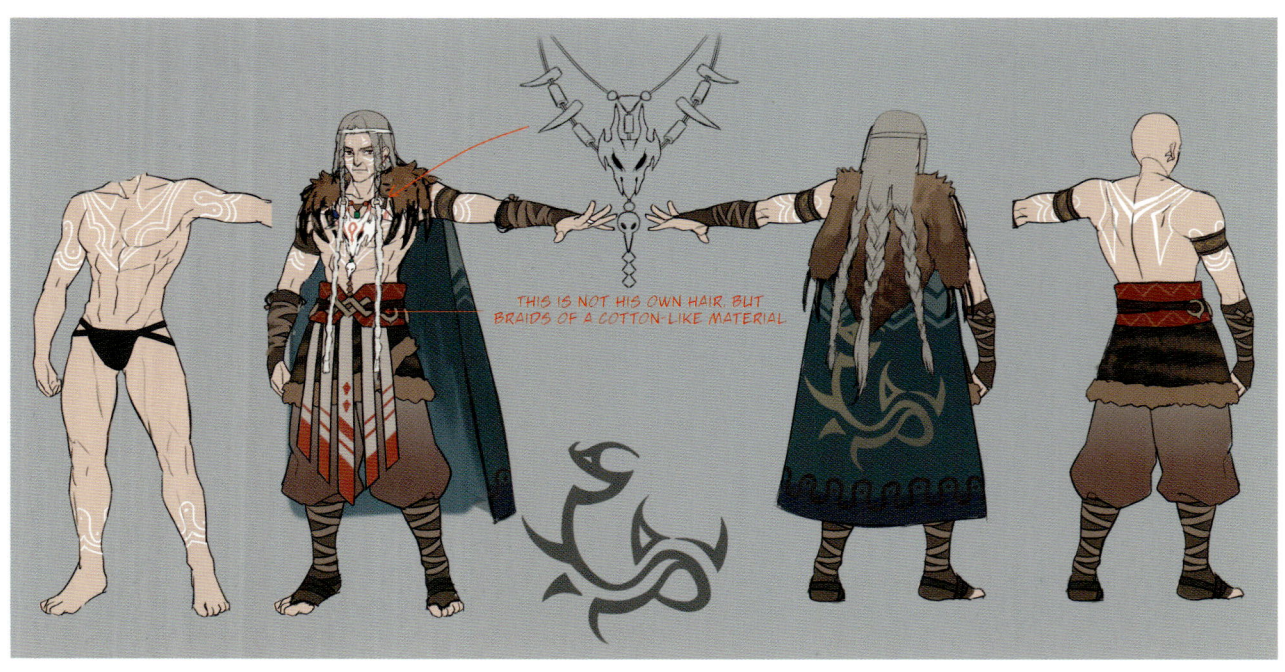

THIS IS NOT HIS OWN HAIR, BUT BRAIDS OF A COTTON-LIKE MATERIAL

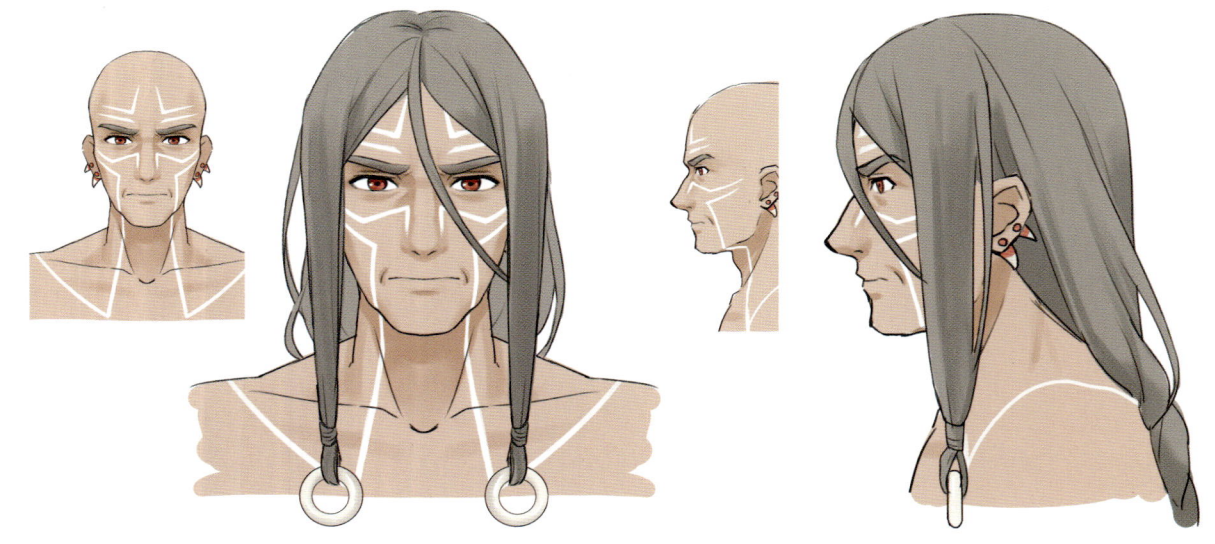

Deirdre Design Sketches

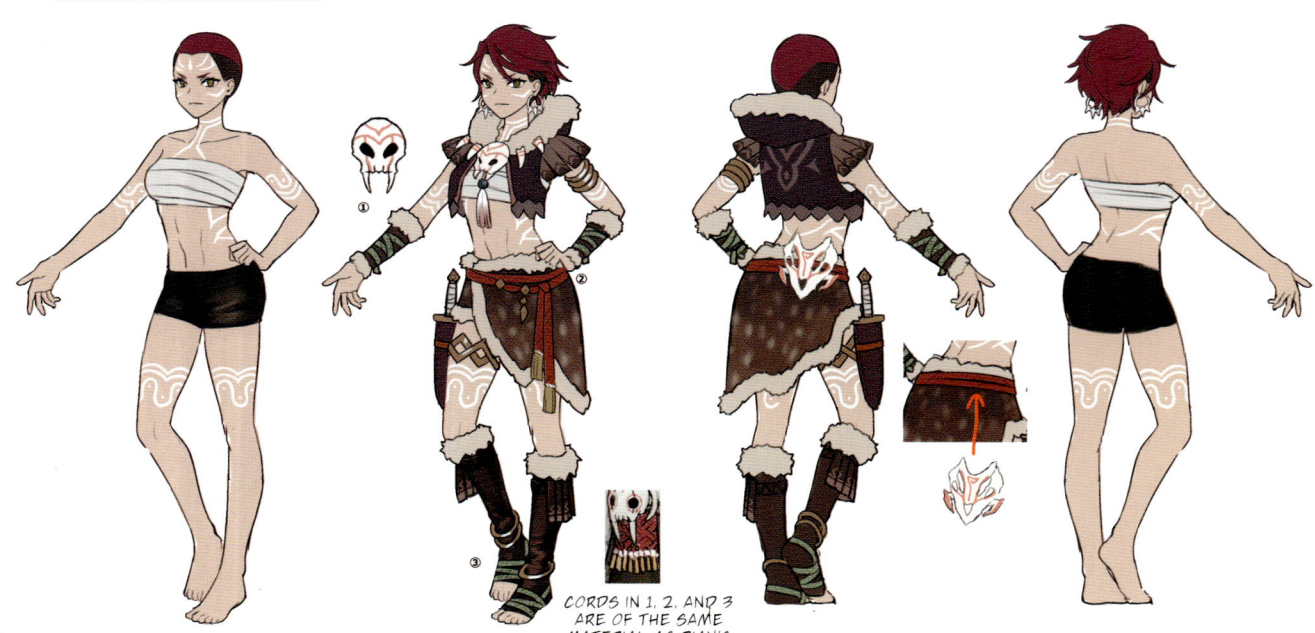

CORDS IN 1, 2, AND 3 ARE OF THE SAME MATERIAL AS DIAN'S

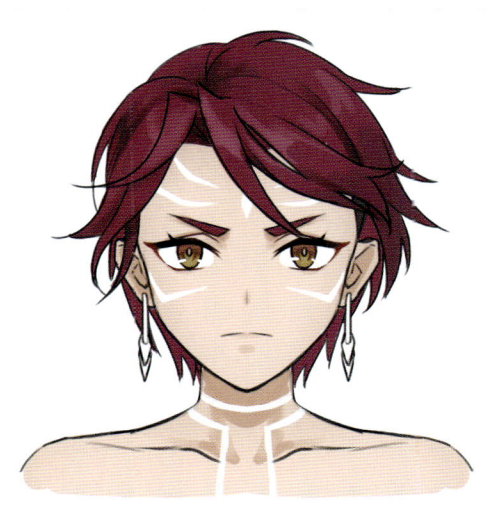
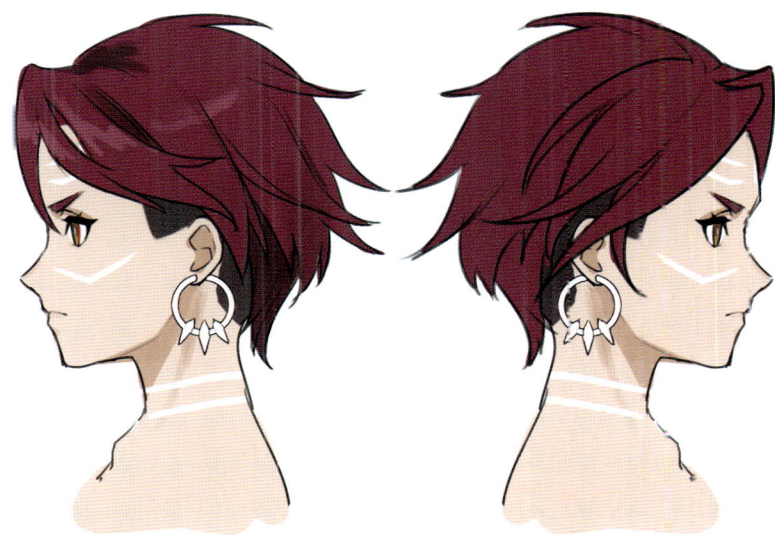
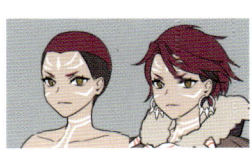
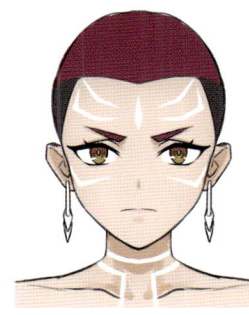
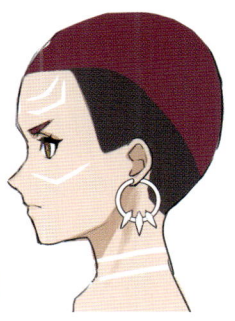

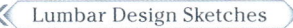

《 Lumbar Design Sketches 》

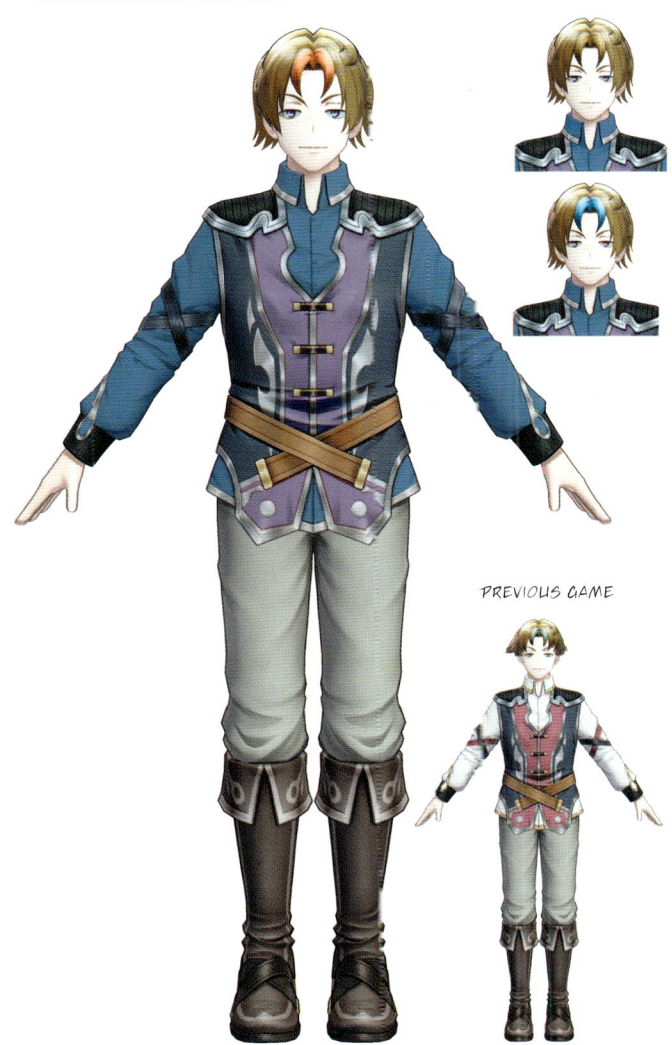
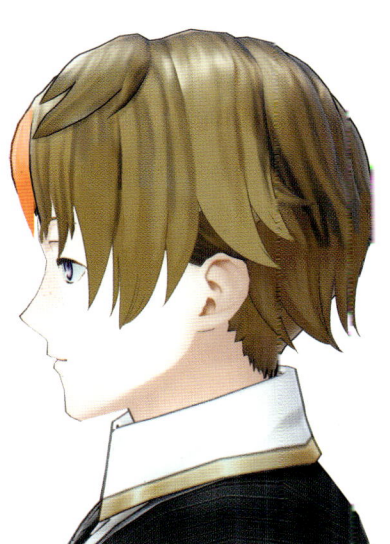

PREVIOUS GAME

Oren Warrior Design Sketches

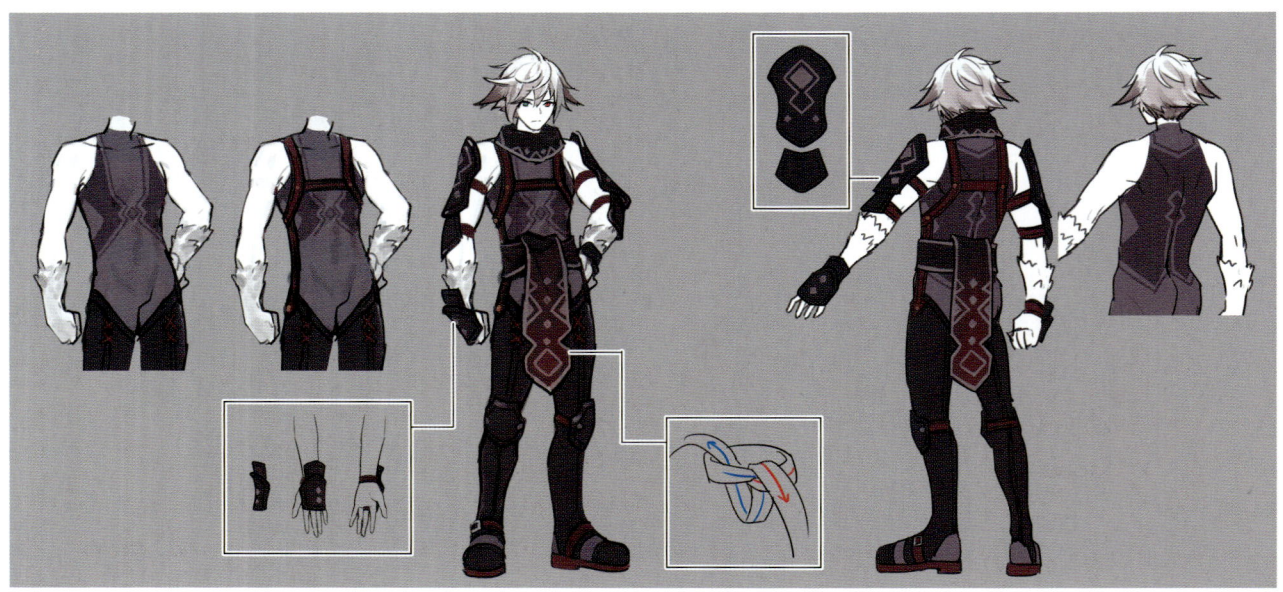
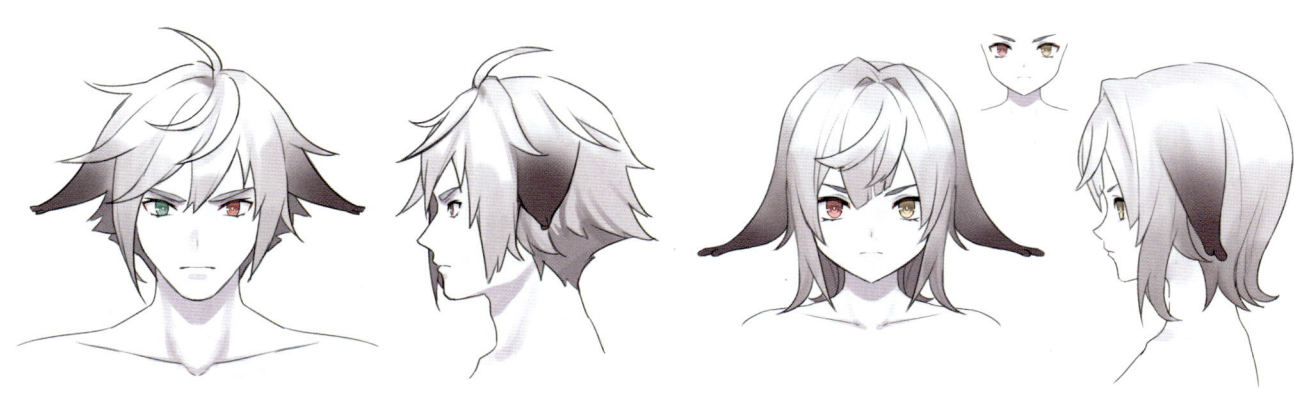
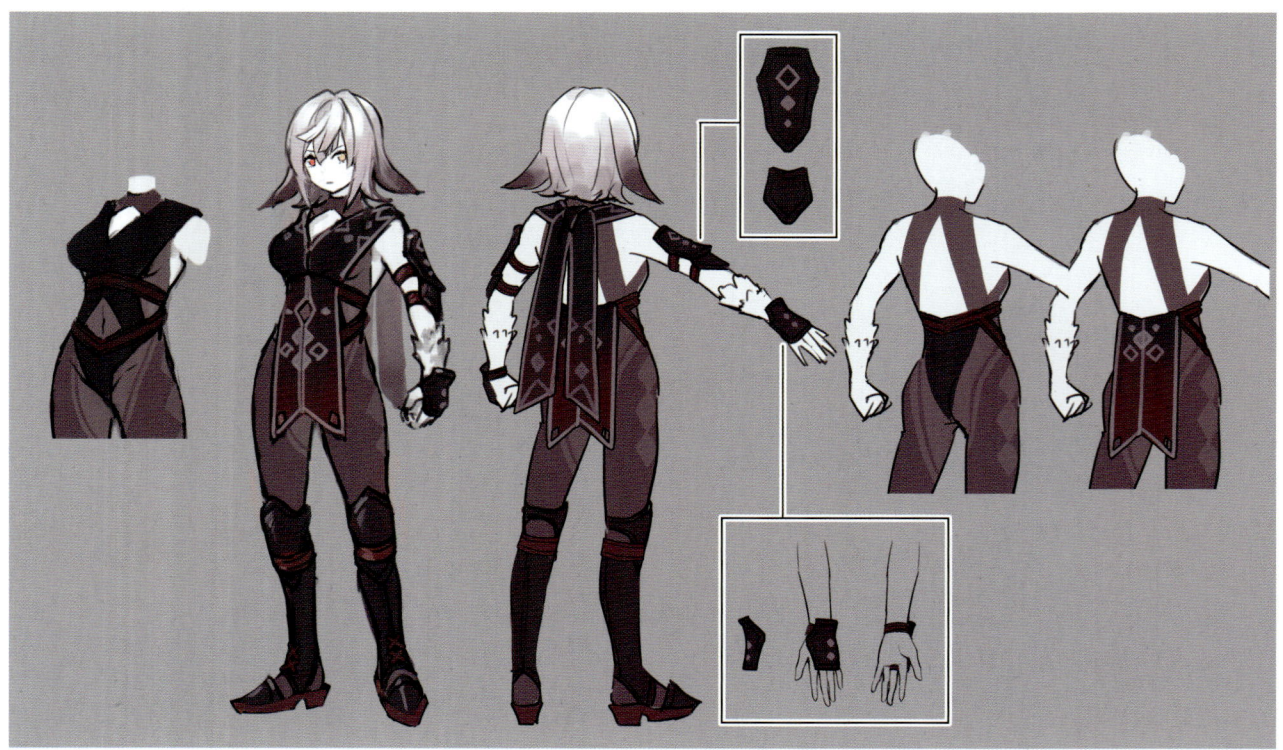

Oren Mage Design Sketches

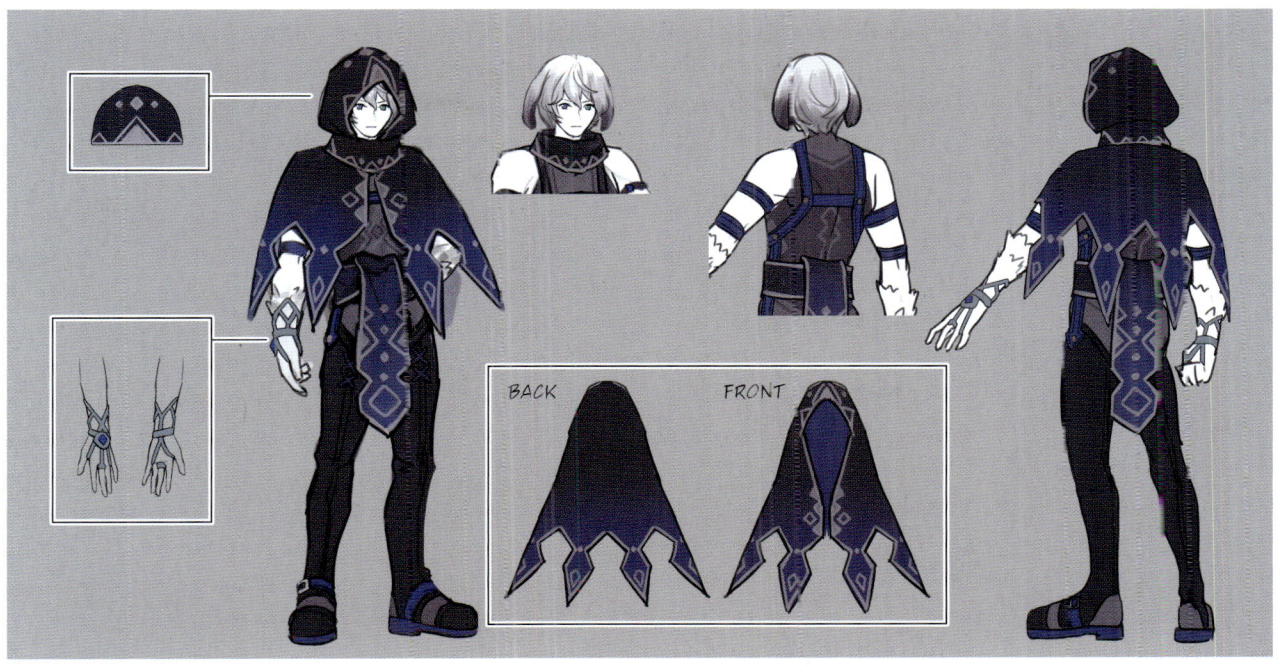
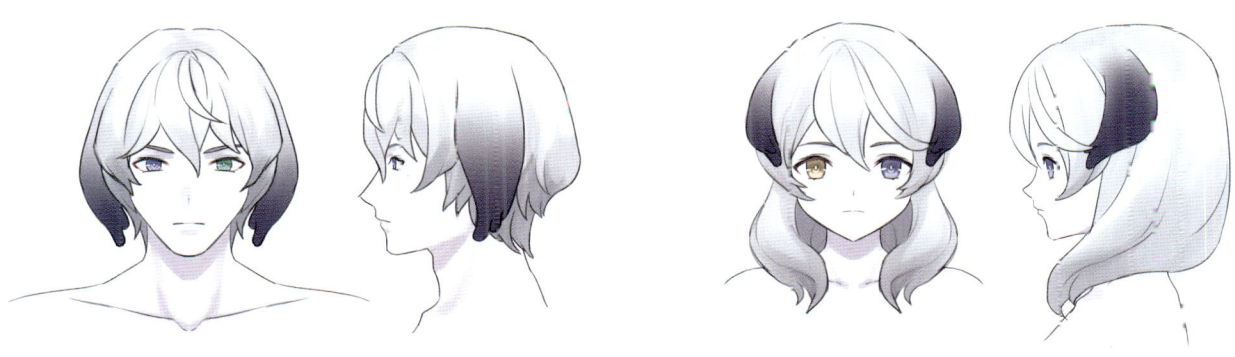
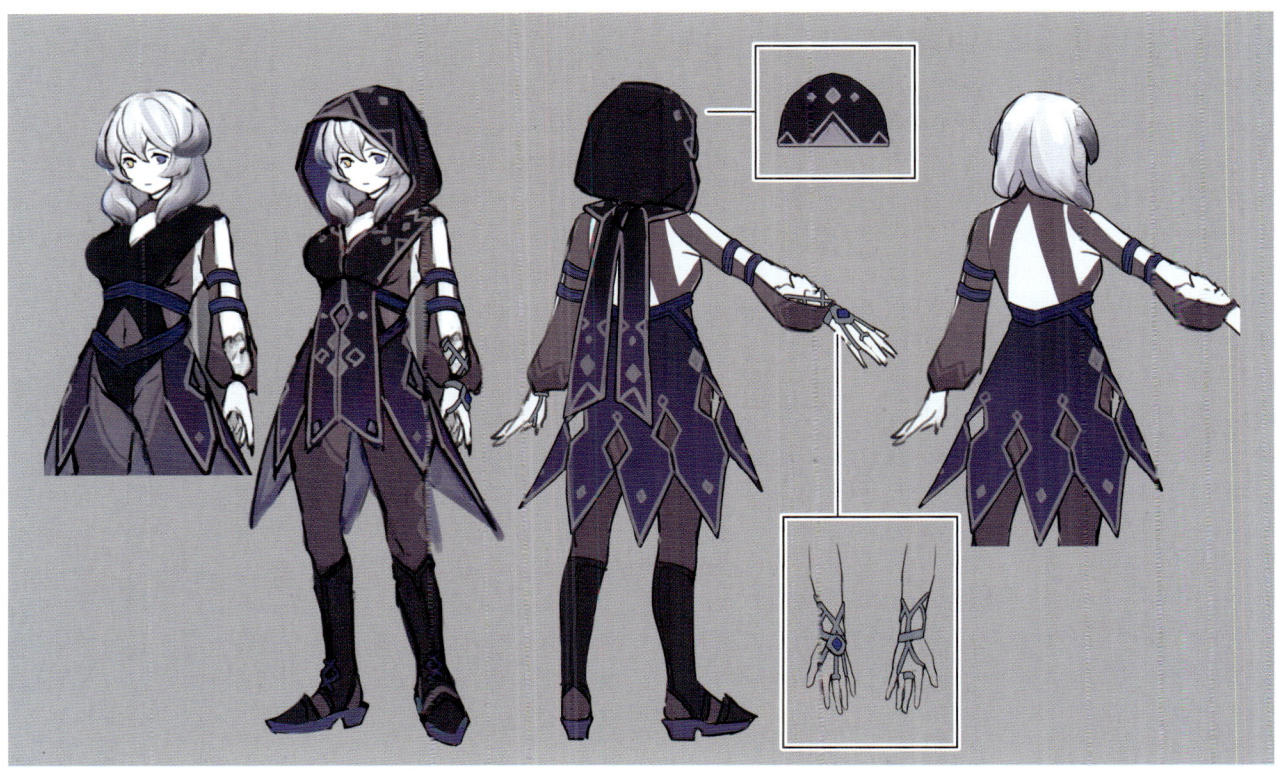

《 Unused Character Design Sketches 》

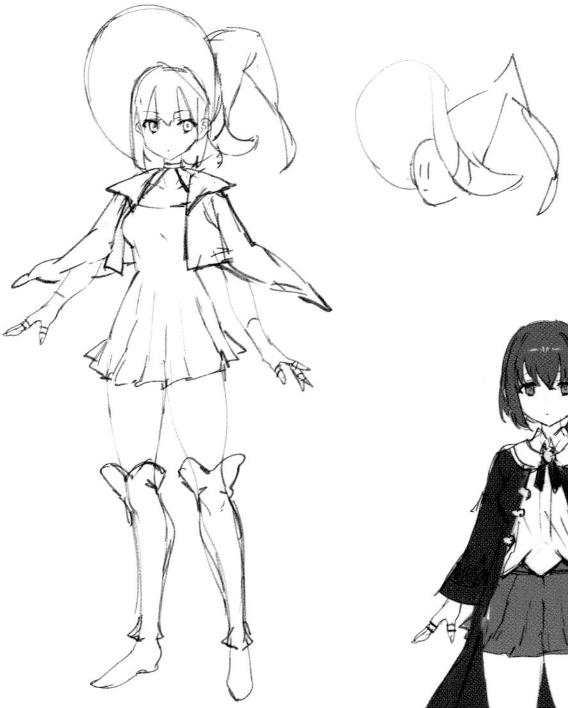

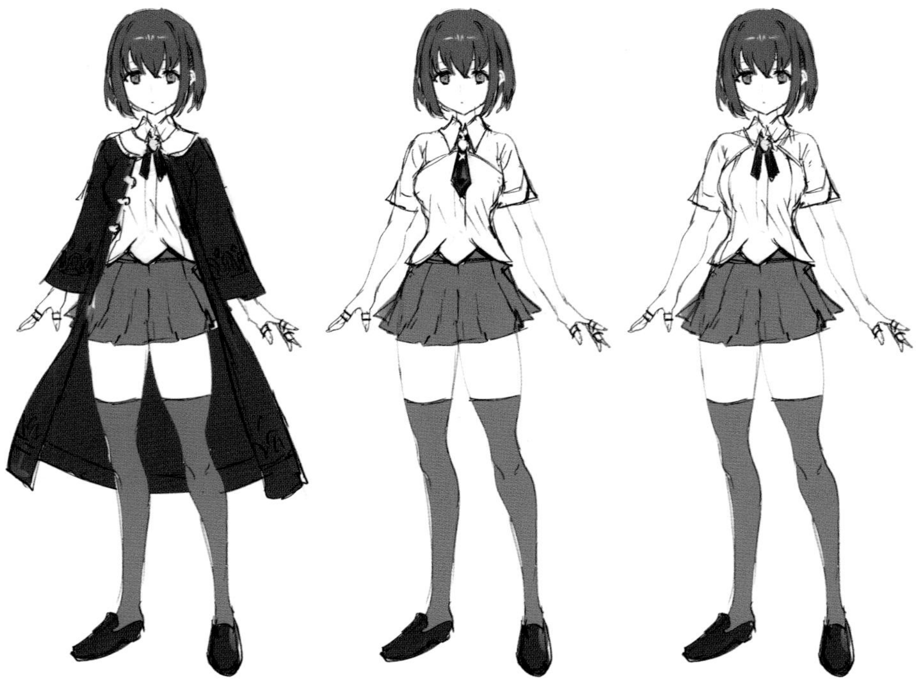

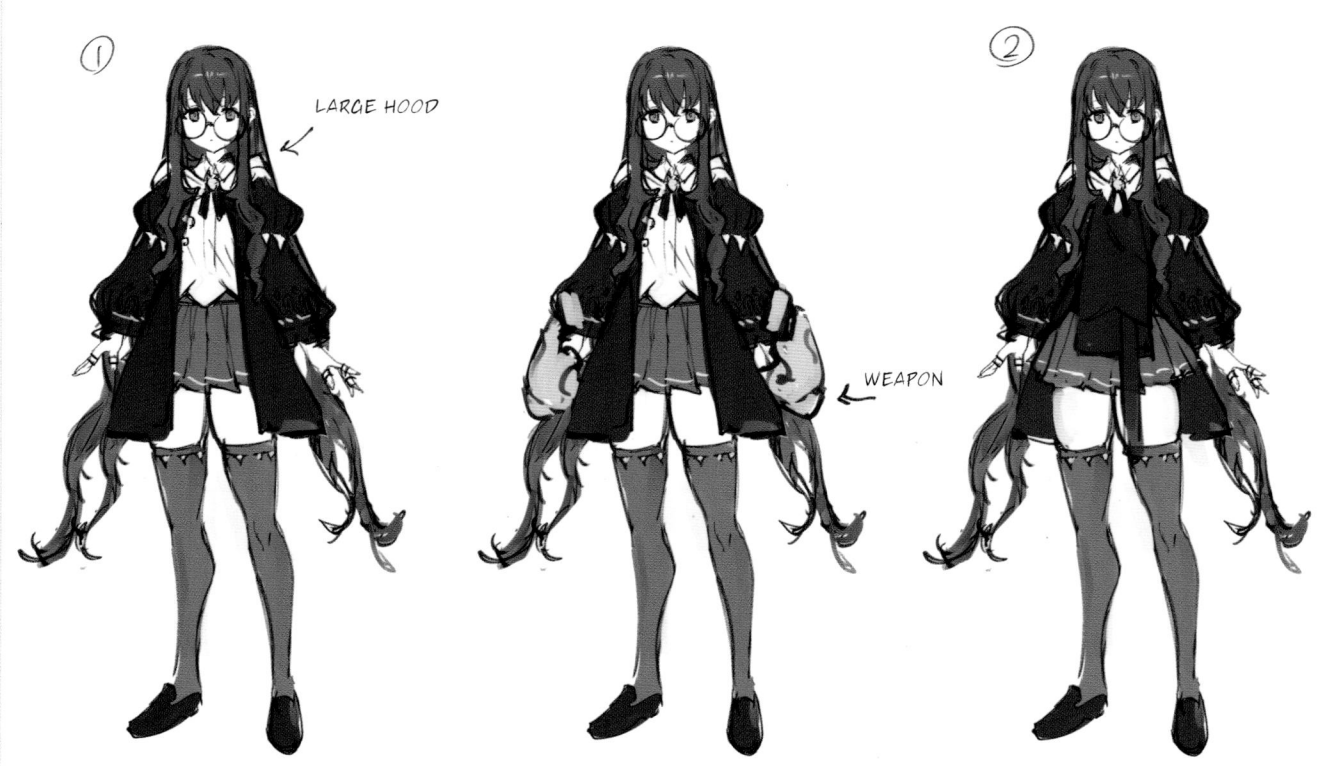

Costume Designs

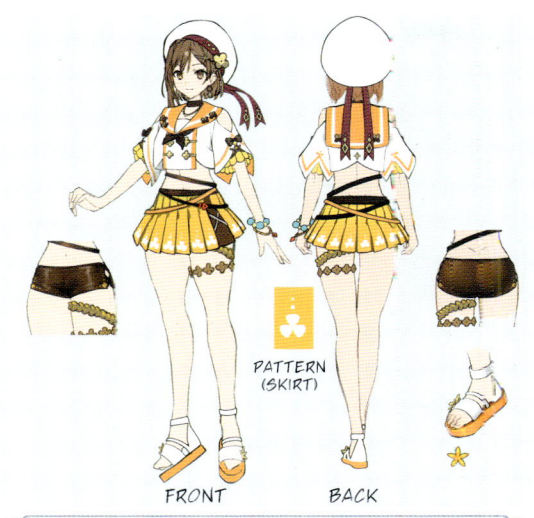

Ryza "Marine Look of Kurken Shore" Design Sketches

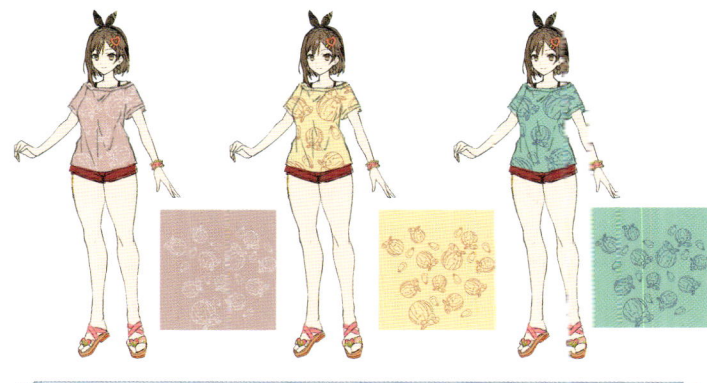

Ryza Exclusive T-Shirts "Freshly Picked! Kurken Fruits" Design Sketches

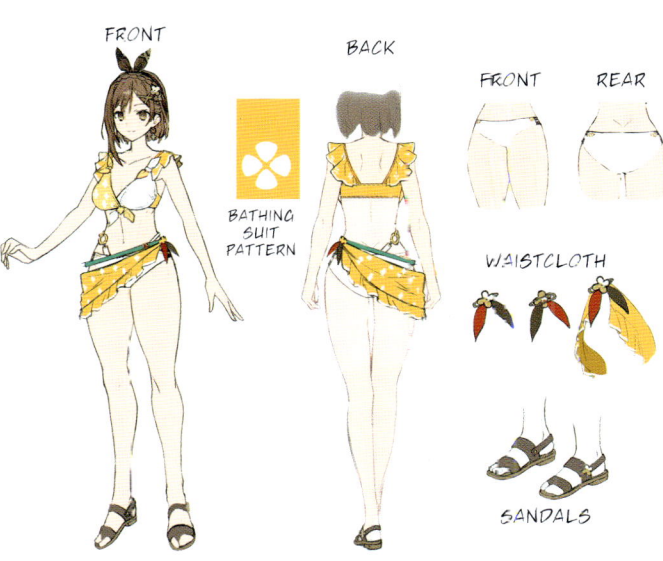

Ryza "Happy Sunshine" Design Sketches

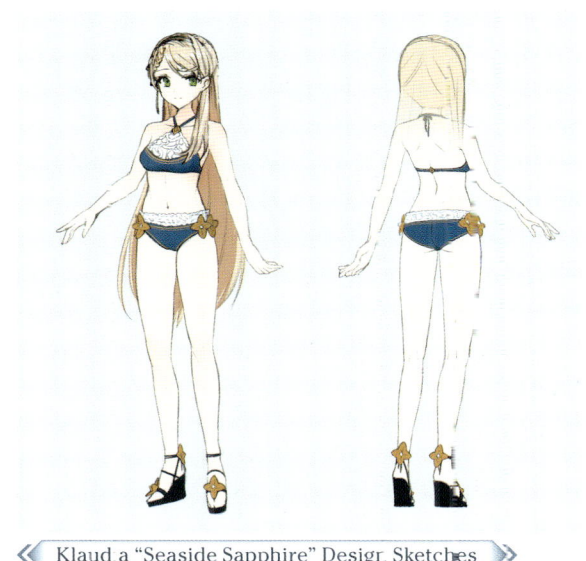

Klaudia "Seaside Sapphire" Design Sketches

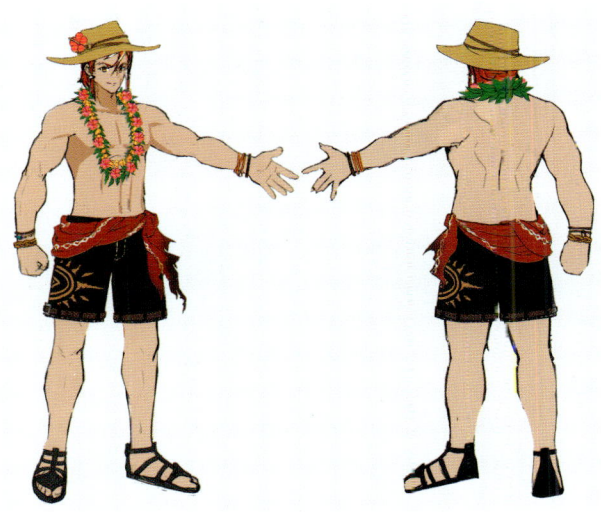

Lent "King of Summer" Design Sketches

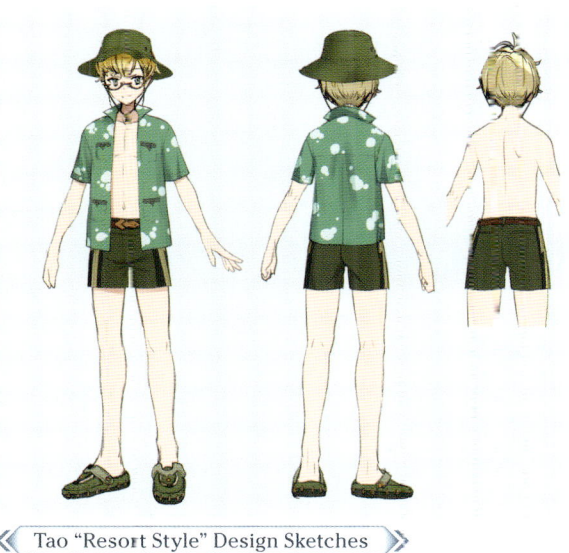

Tao "Resort Style" Design Sketches

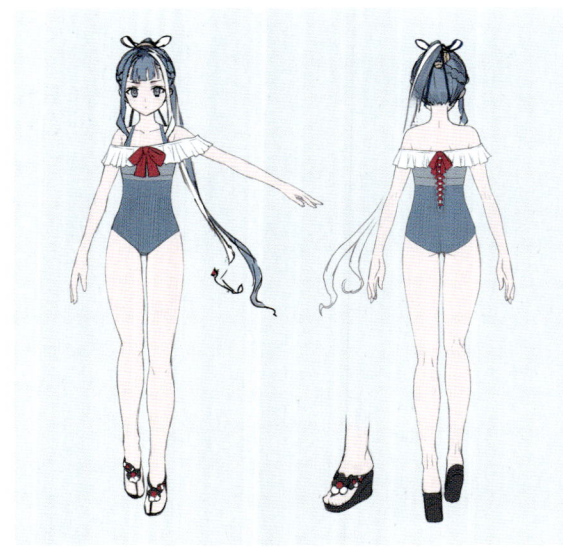

《 Patricia "Fresh Fairy" Design Sketches 》

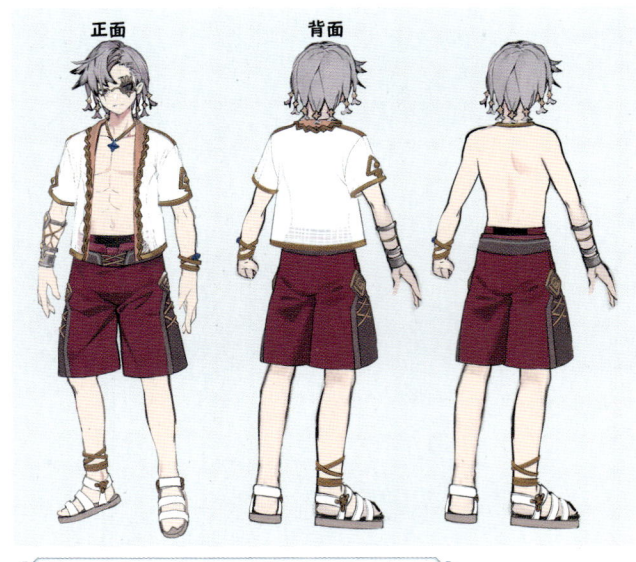

《 Empel "Long Holiday" Design Sketches 》

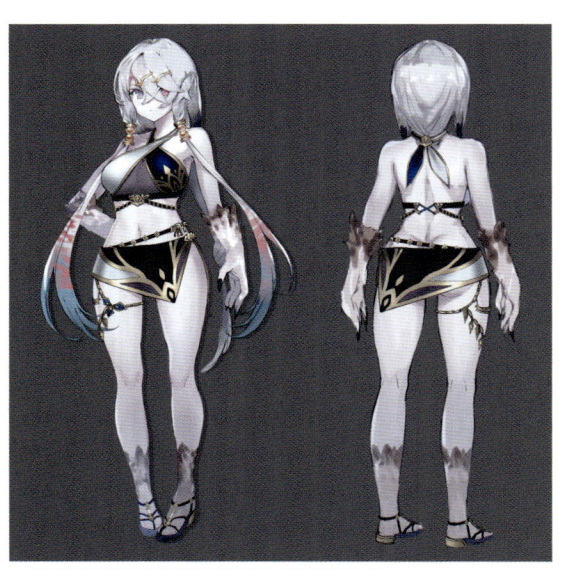

《 Lila "Lady Pirate" Design Sketches 》

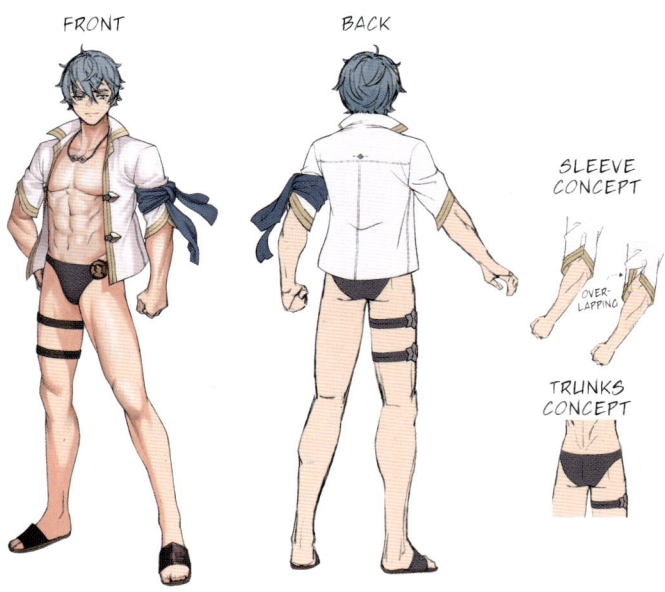

《 Bos "Hot Hurricane" Design Sketches 》

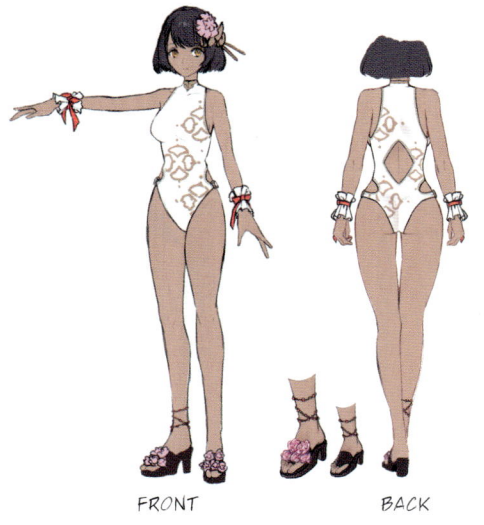

《 Federica "Coral Lagoon" Design Sketches 》

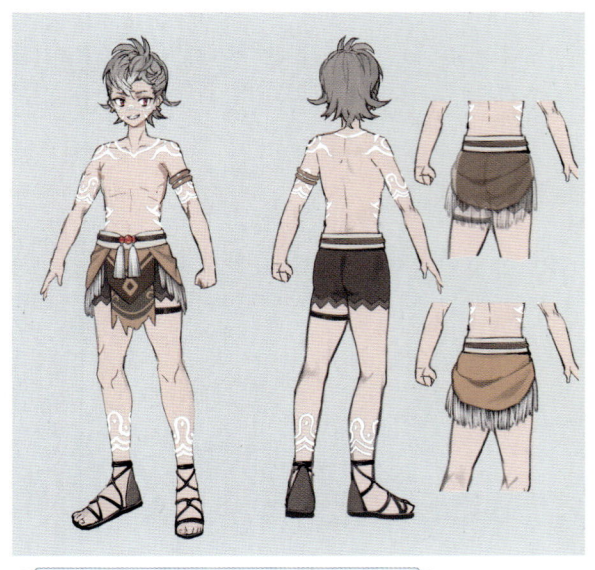

《 Dian "Splash Beast" Design Sketches 》

Kala "Beach Wind Chime" Design Sketches

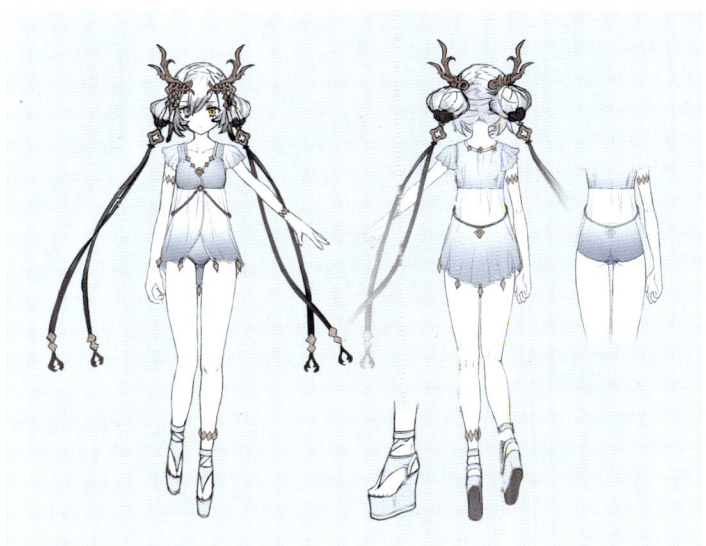

Costume Set "Far East Travelers" / Ryza "Summer Festival Star" Design Sketches

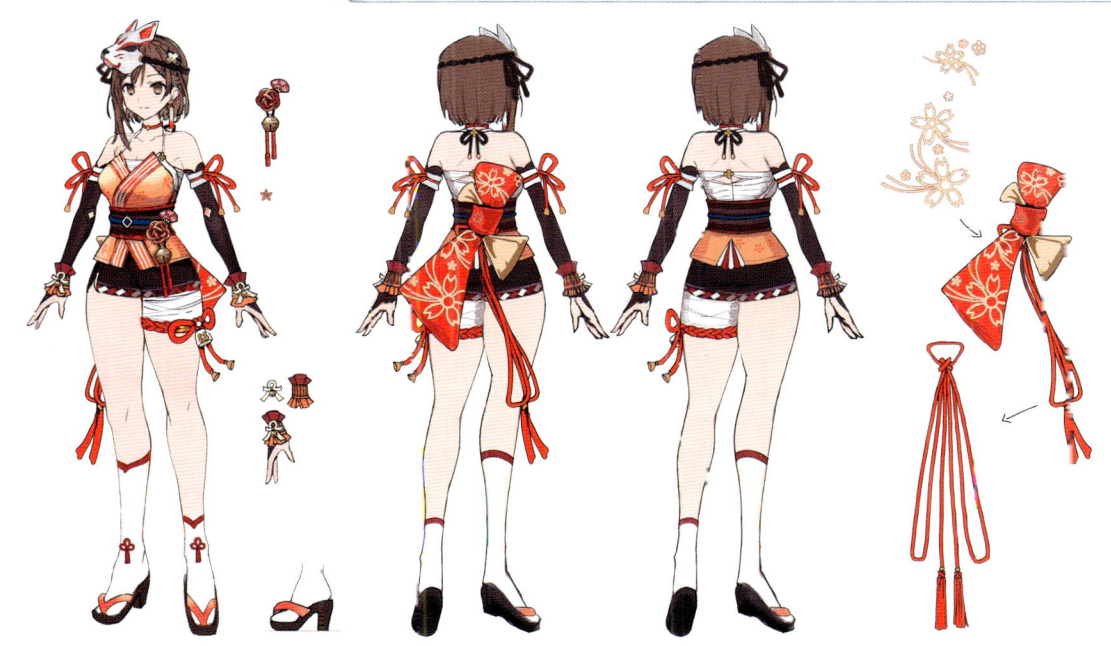

Costume Set "Far East Travelers" / Klaudia "Master Samurai" Design Sketches

CHERRY BLOSSOM COLOR + UPPER BODY WHITE VERSION

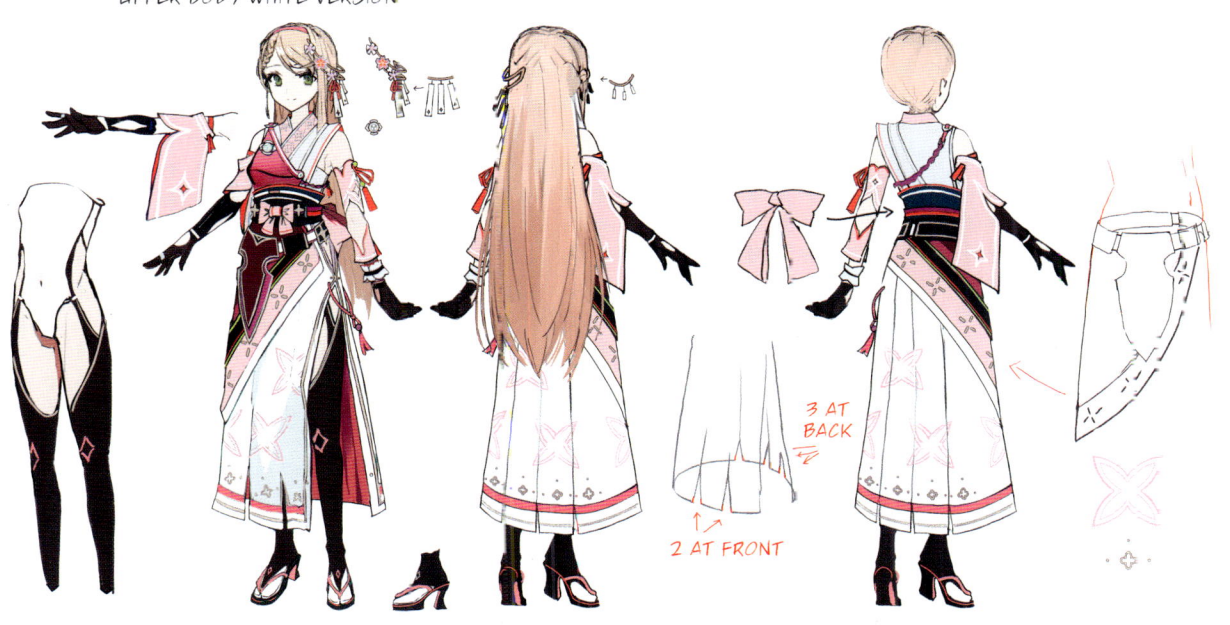

3 AT BACK

2 AT FRONT

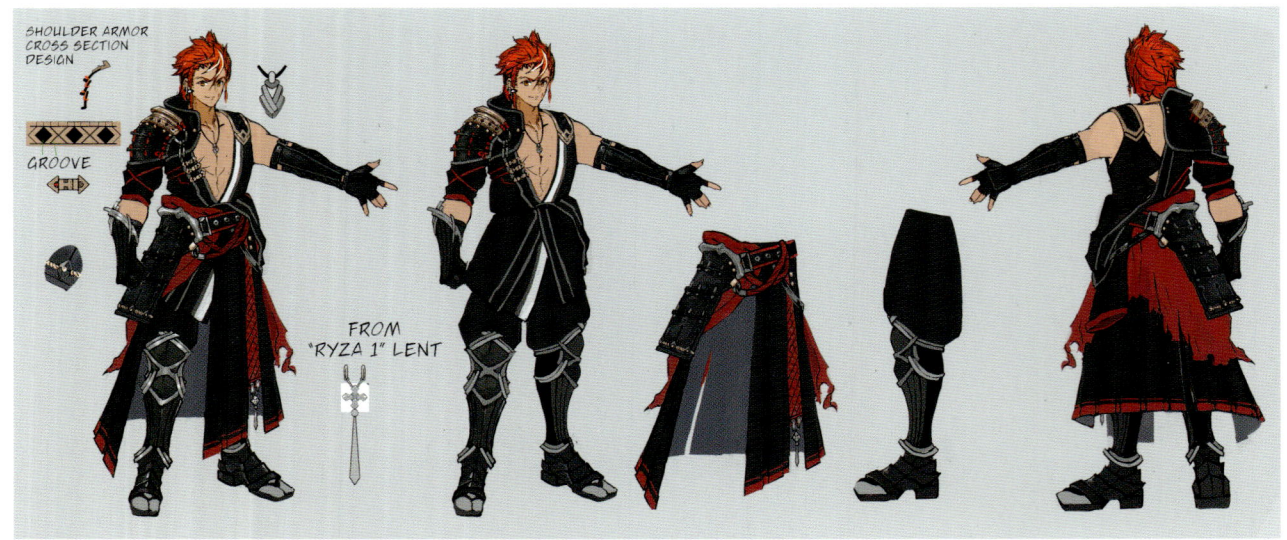

《 Costume Set "Far East Travelers" / Lent "THE SAMURAI" Design Sketches 》

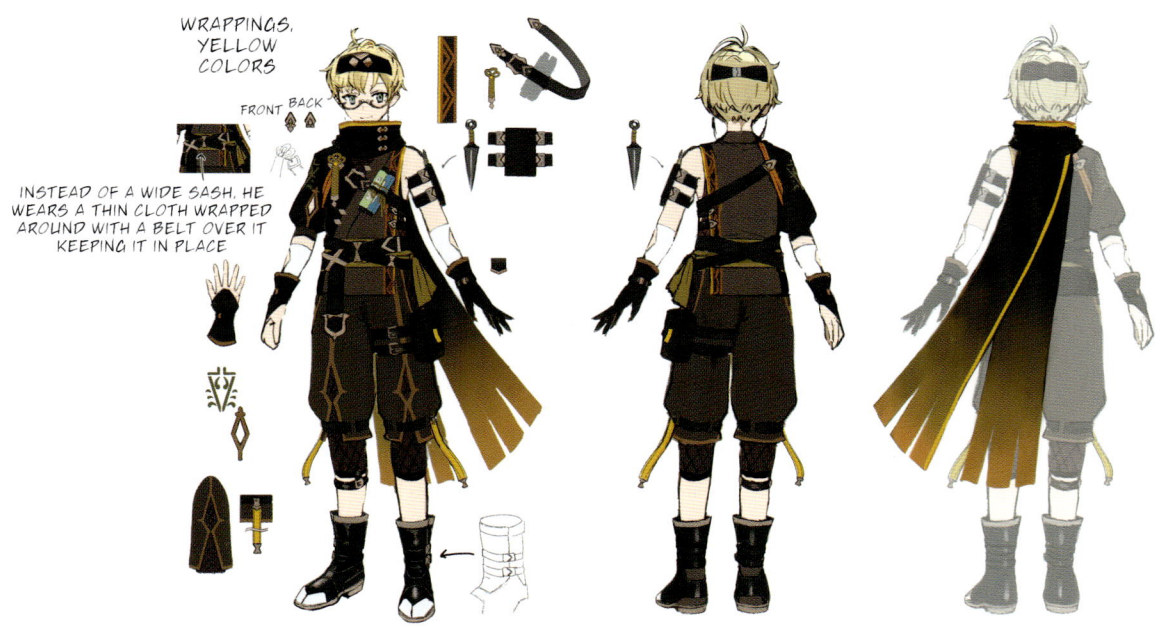

《 Costume Set "Far East Travelers" / Tao "Master of Jet Black" Design Sketches 》

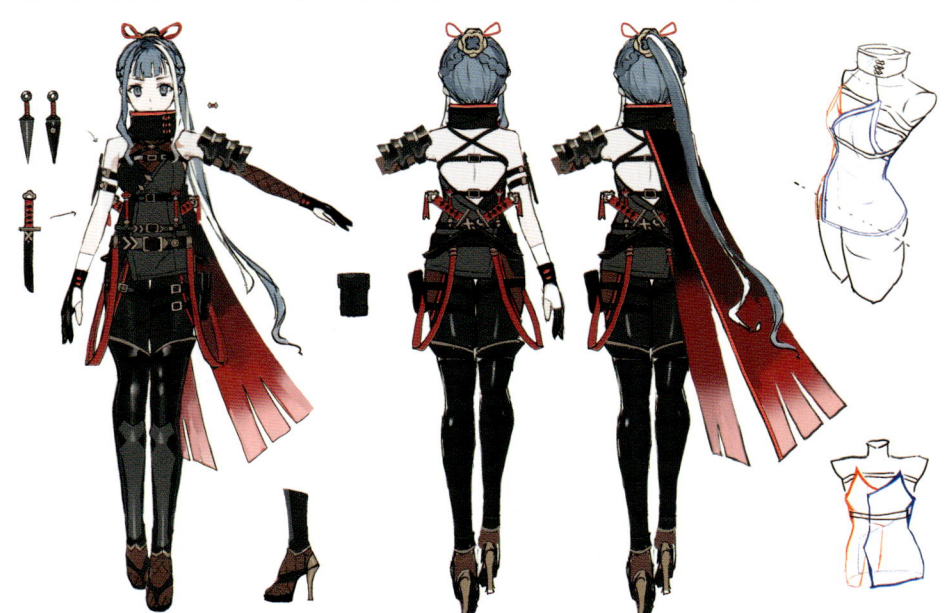

《 Costume Set "Far East Travelers" / Patricia "Master of Silence" Design Sketches 》

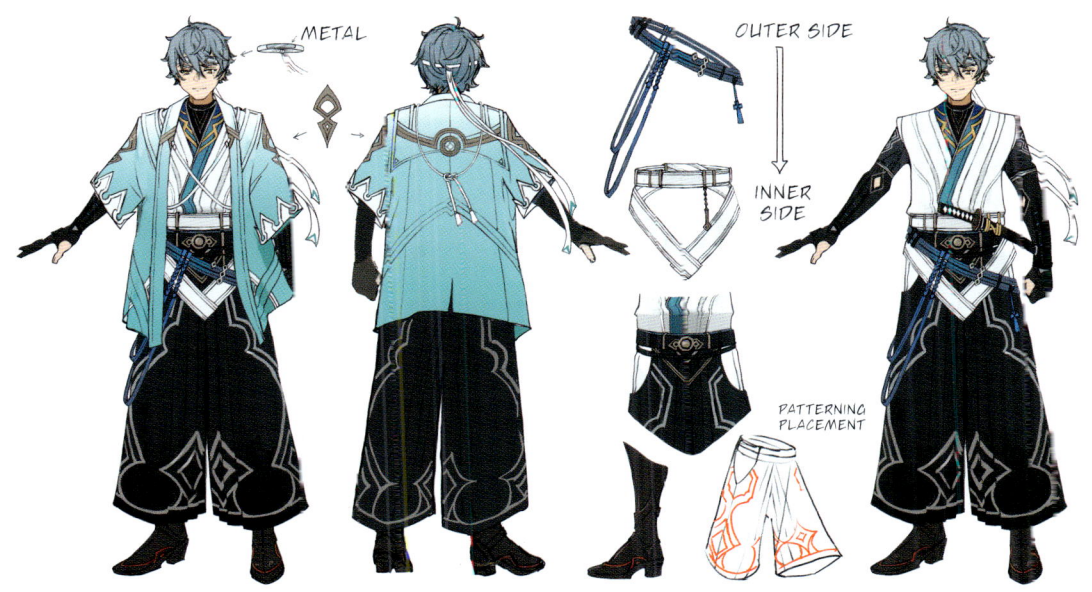

《 Costume Set "Far East Travelers" / Bos "Bakumatsu Sword Master" Design Sketches 》

《 Costume Set "Far East Travelers" / Federica "Princess of the Keep" Design Sketches 》

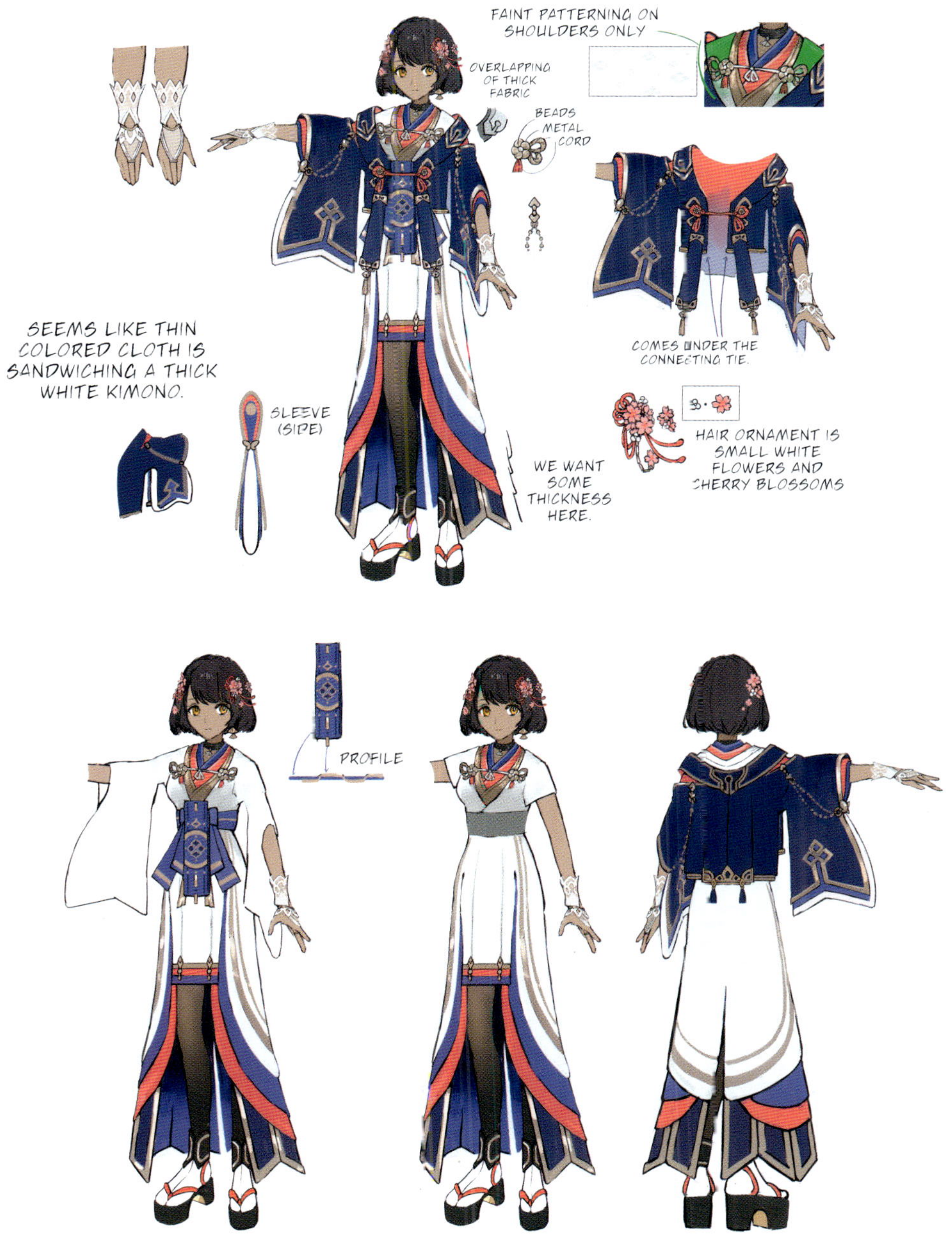

《 Costume Set "Far East Travelers" / Dian "Warrior in the Arena" Design Sketches 》

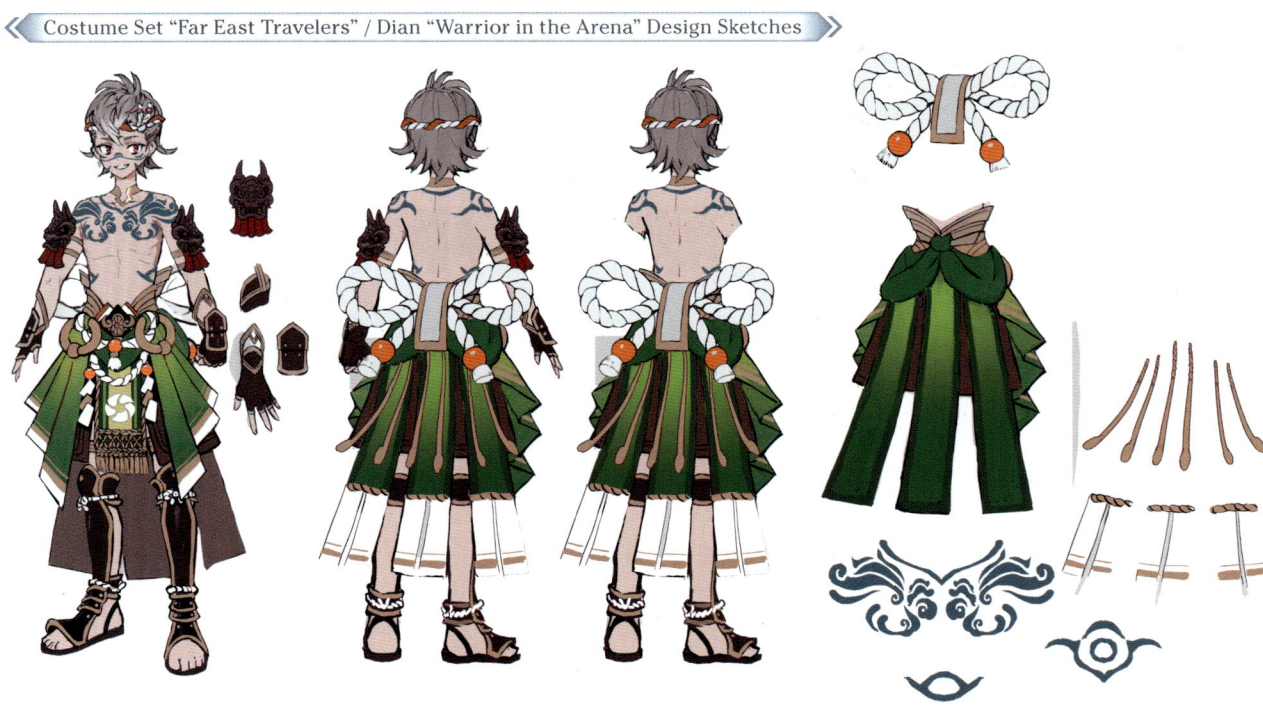

《 Costume Set "Far East Travelers" / Kala "Specter of Joy" Design Sketches 》

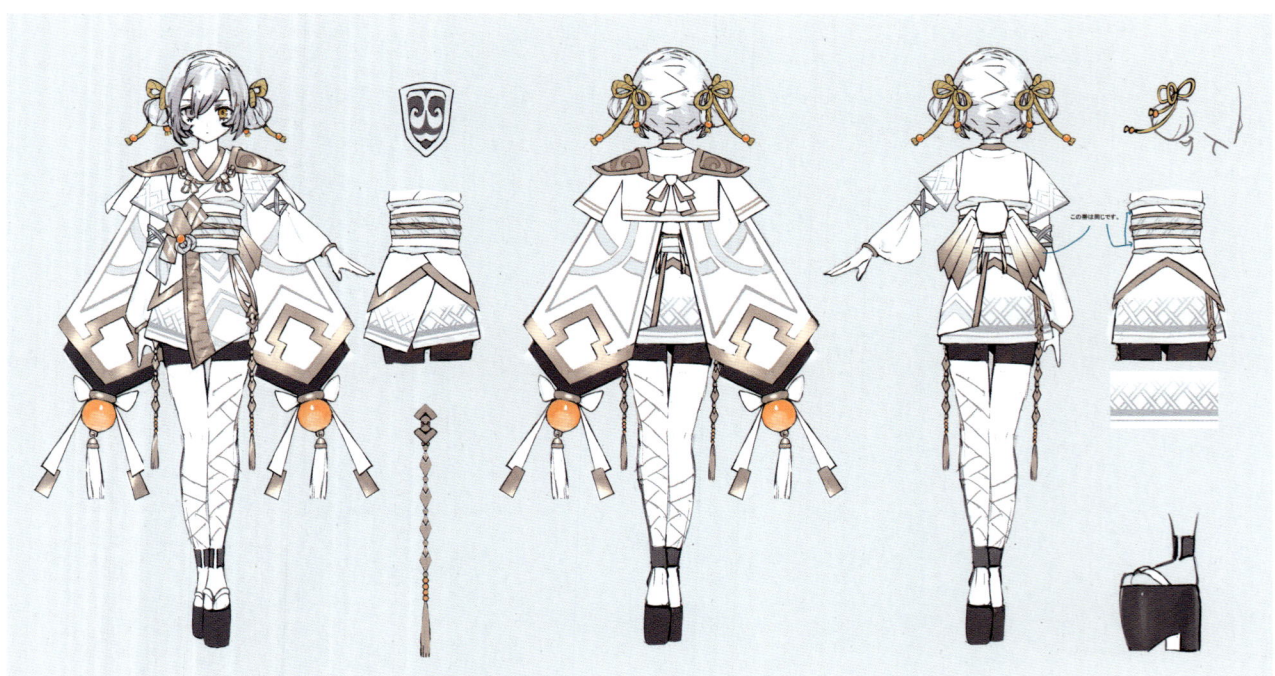

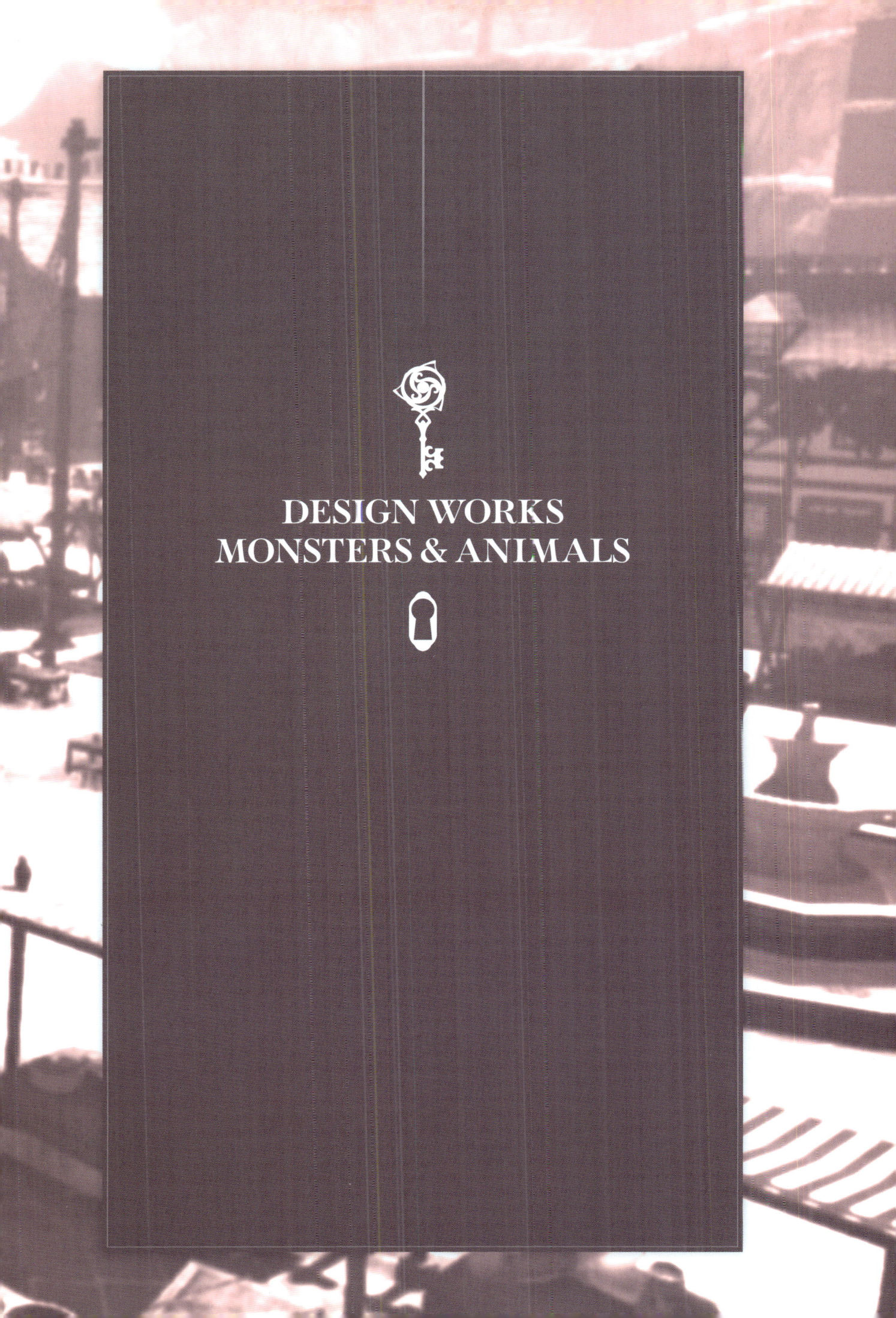

DESIGN WORKS
MONSTERS & ANIMALS

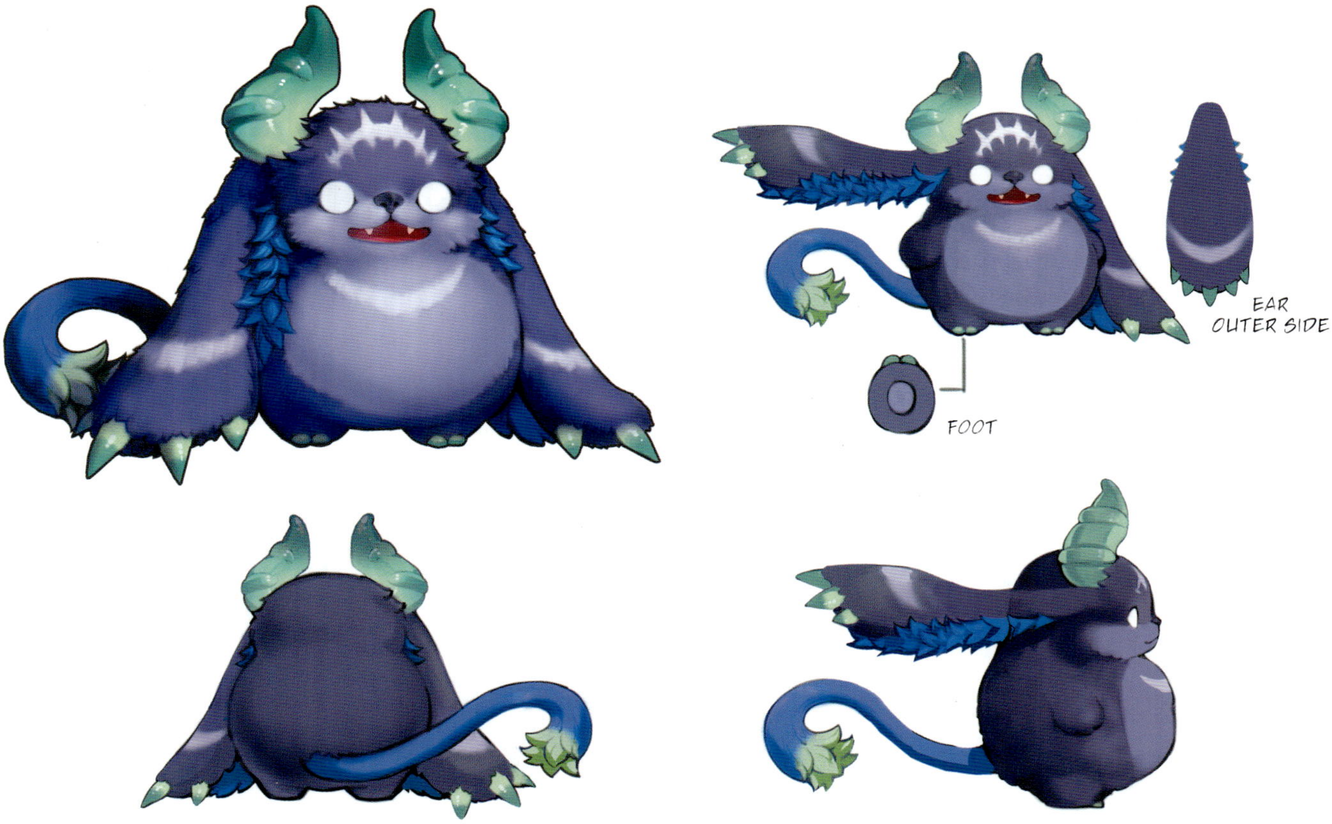

Small Devil type Design Sketches

EAR OUTER SIDE

FOOT

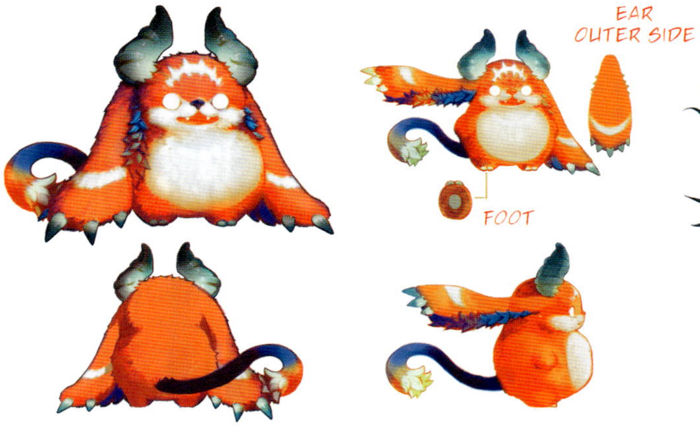

EAR OUTER SIDE

FOOT

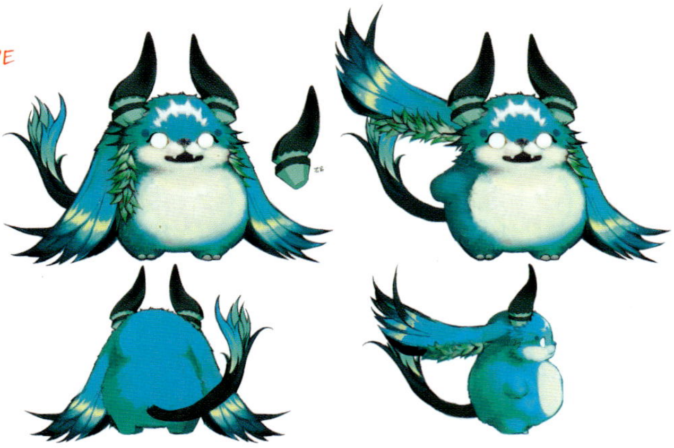

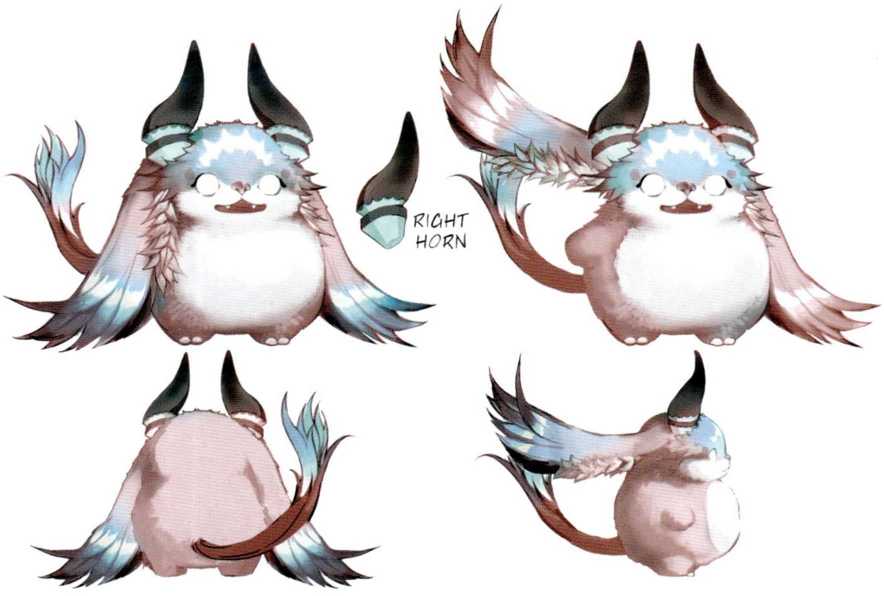

RIGHT HORN

Elemental type Design Sketches

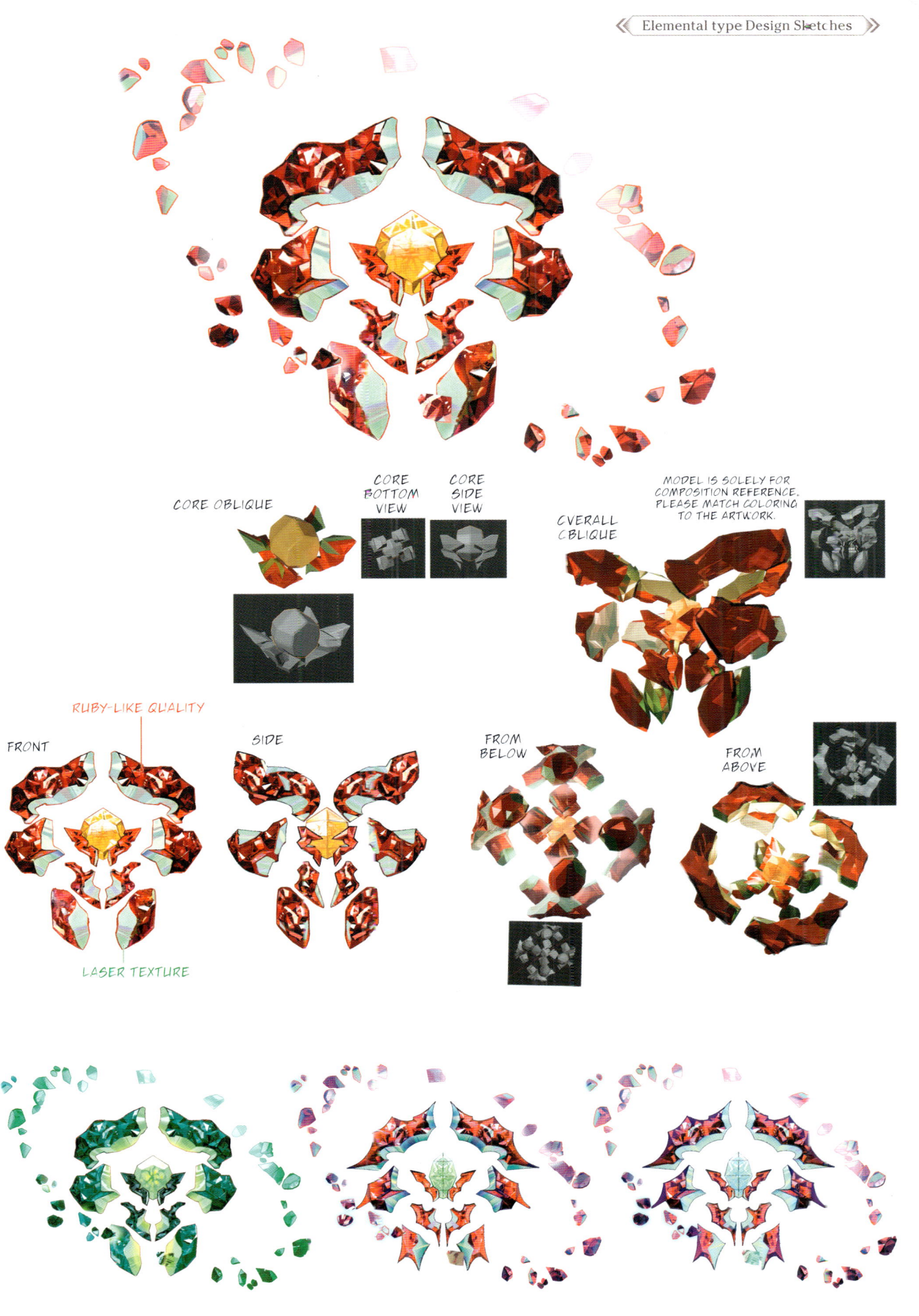

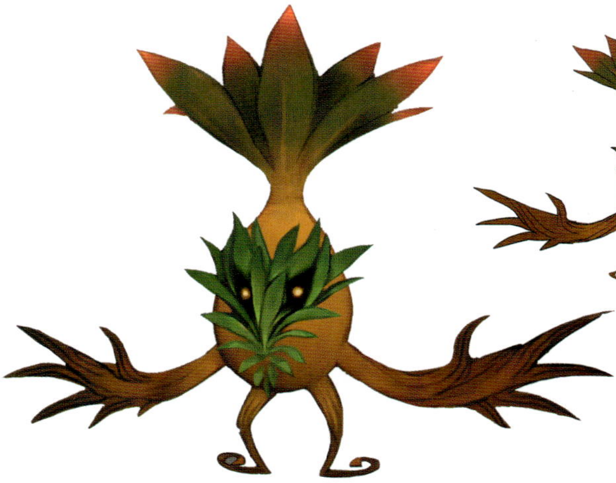

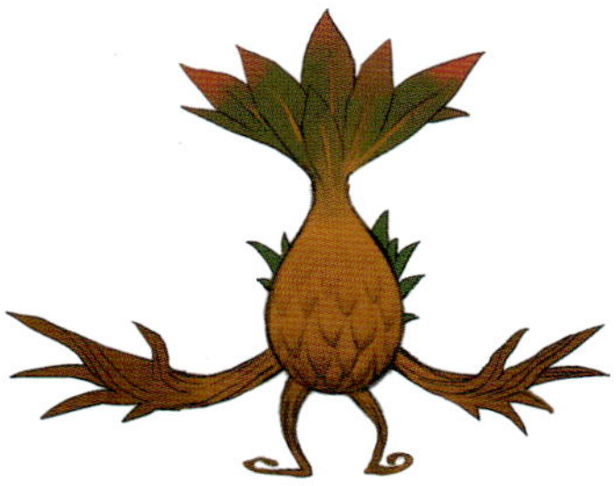

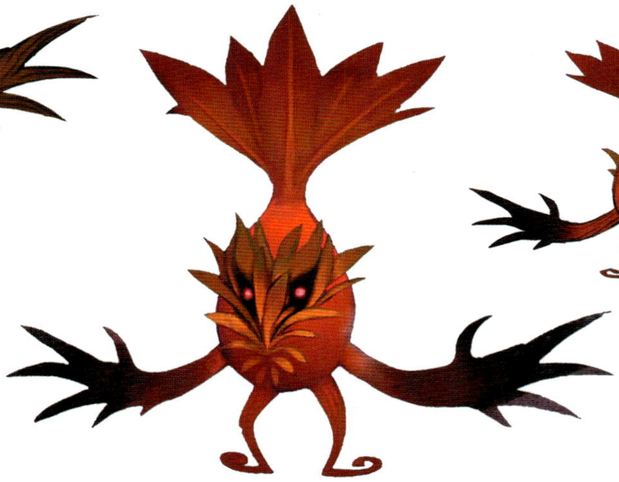

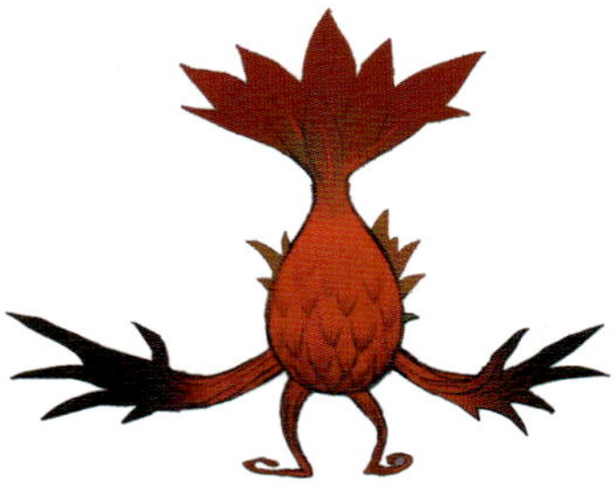

《 Dryad type Design Sketches 》

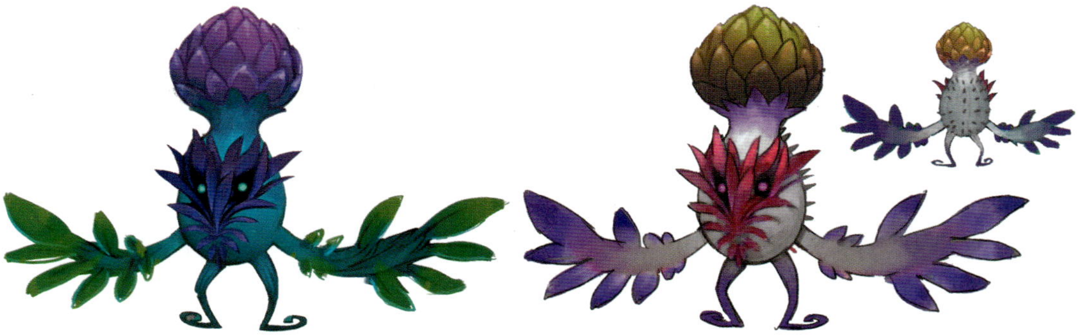

《 Lazybones type Design Sketches 》

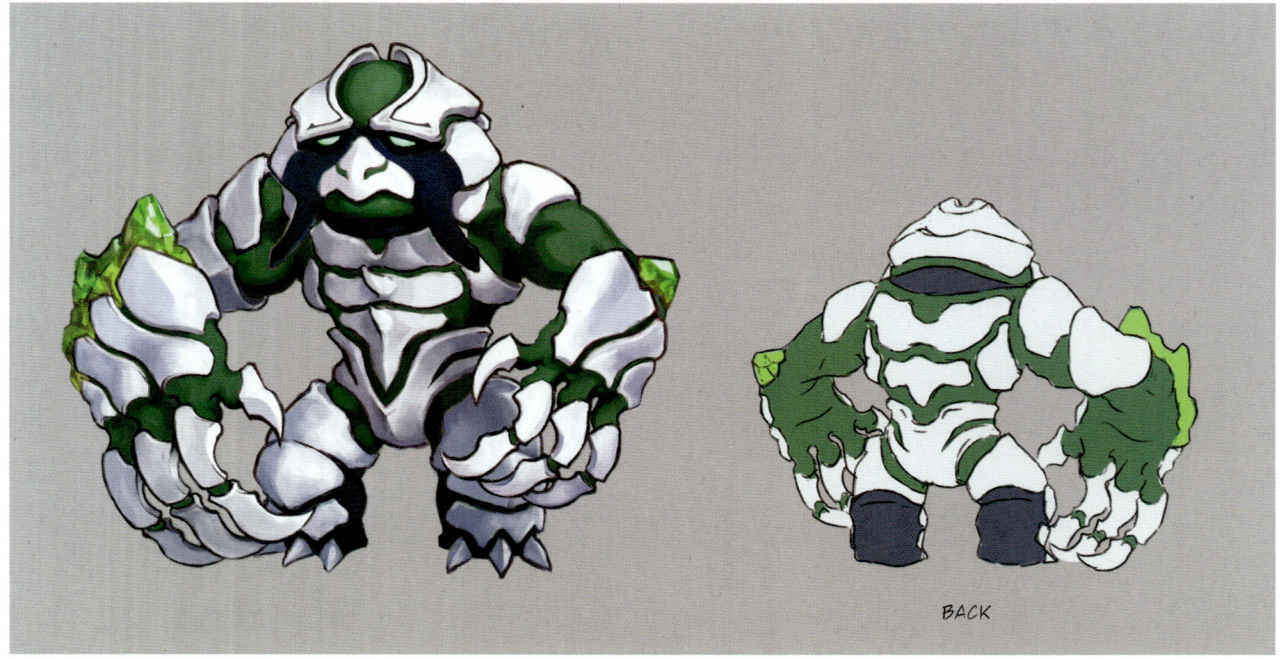

BACK

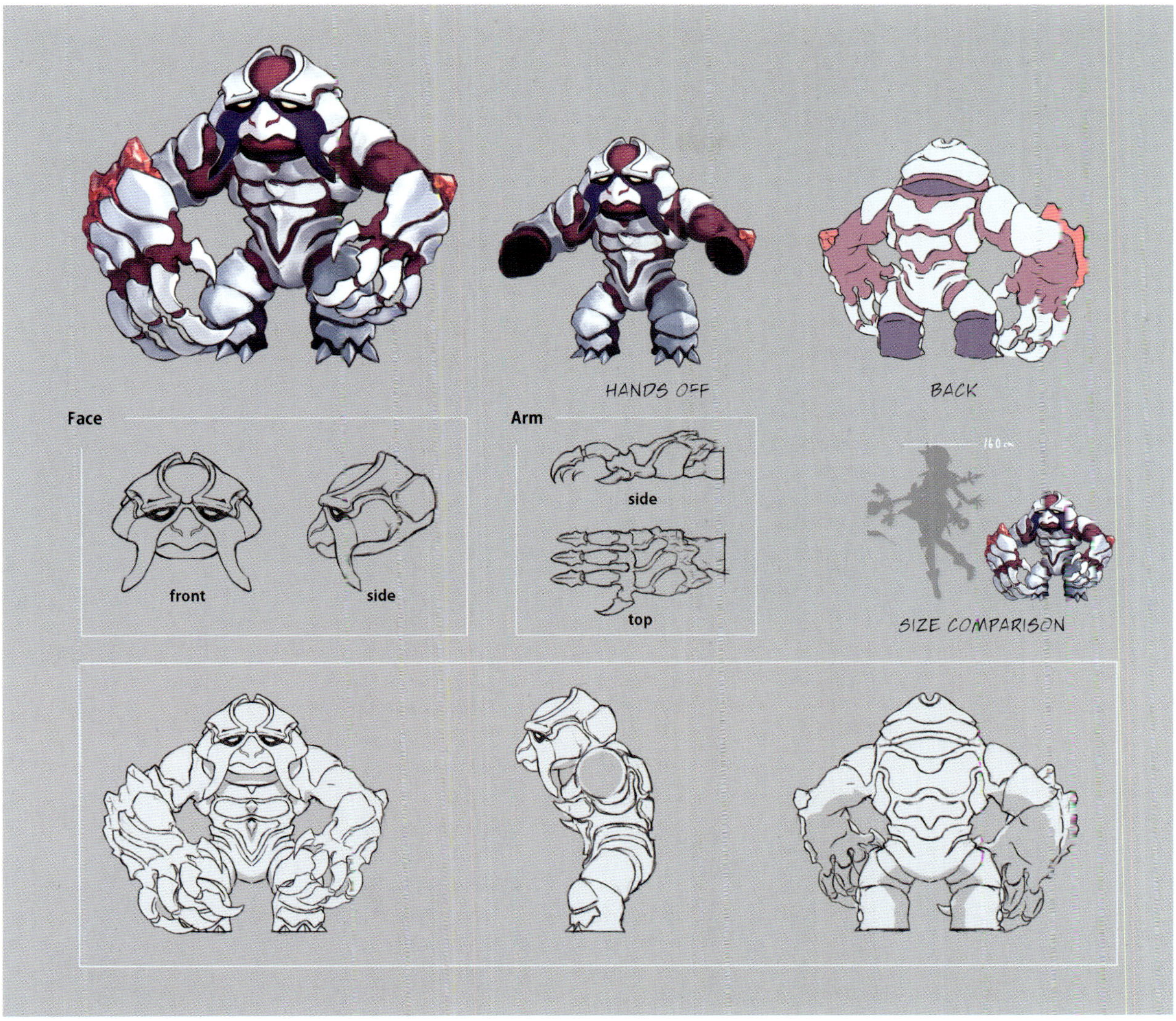

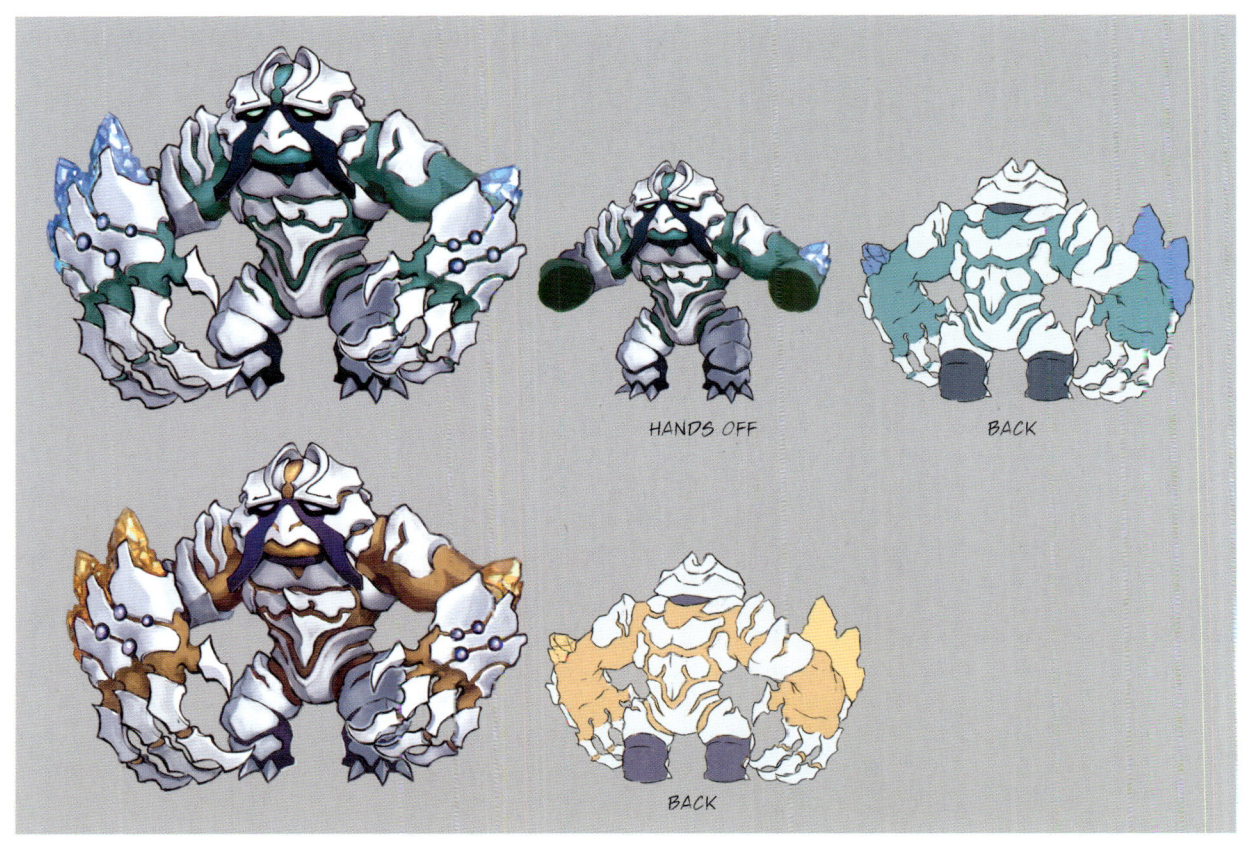

Raptor type Design Sketches

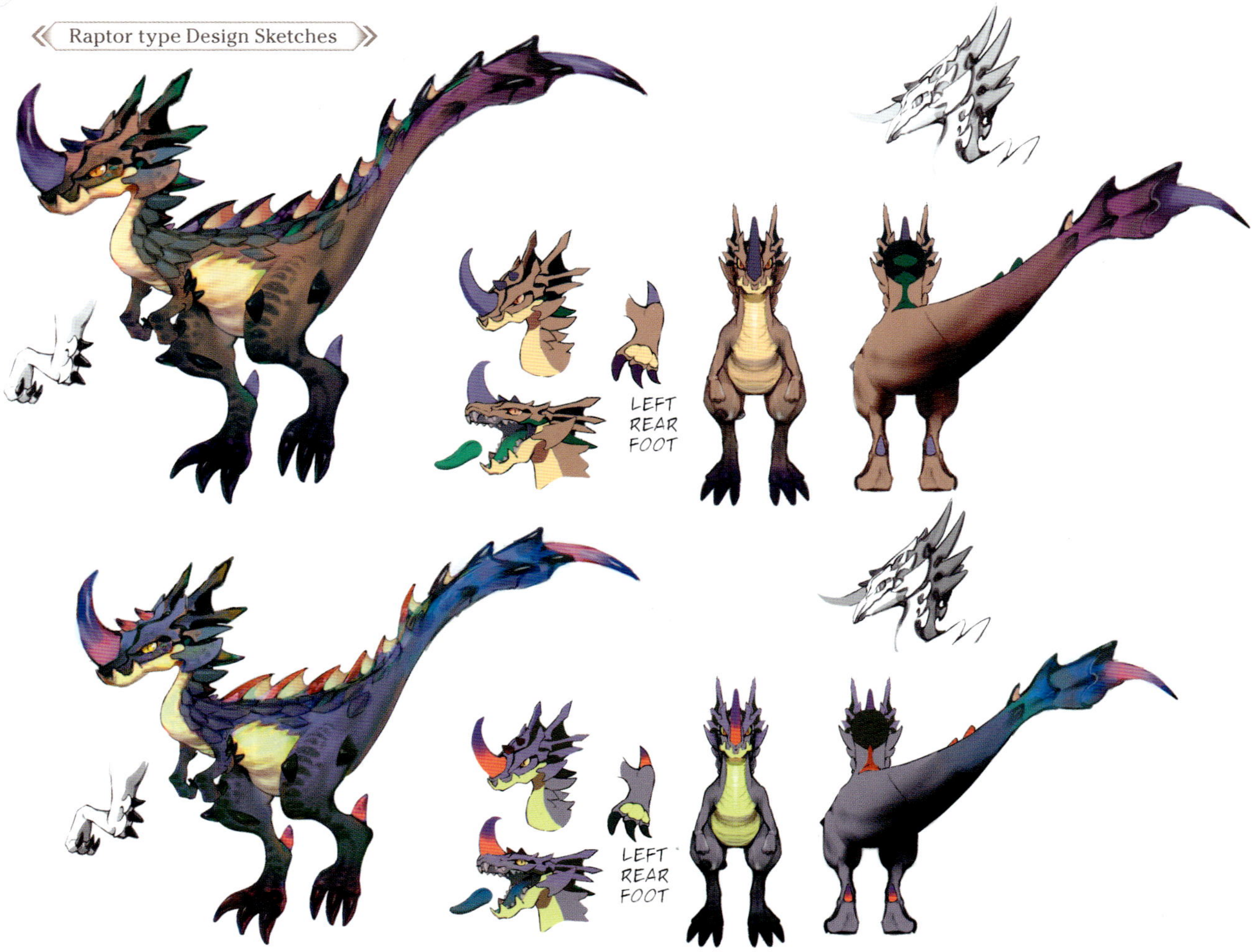

LEFT REAR FOOT

LEFT REAR FOOT

Chameleon type Design Sketches

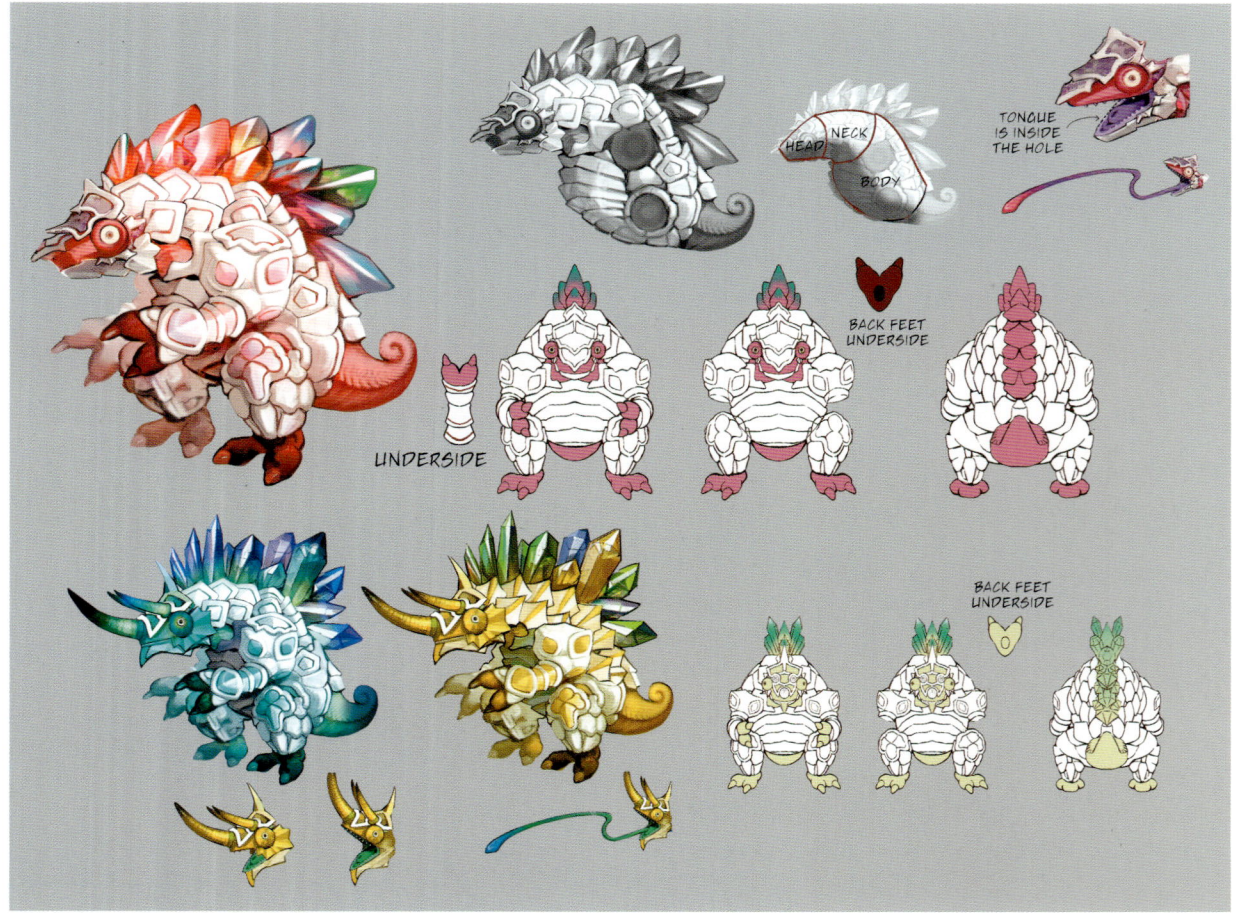

HEAD / NECK / BODY

TONGUE IS INSIDE THE HOLE

UNDERSIDE

BACK FEET UNDERSIDE

BACK FEET UNDERSIDE

Fenrir type Design Sketches

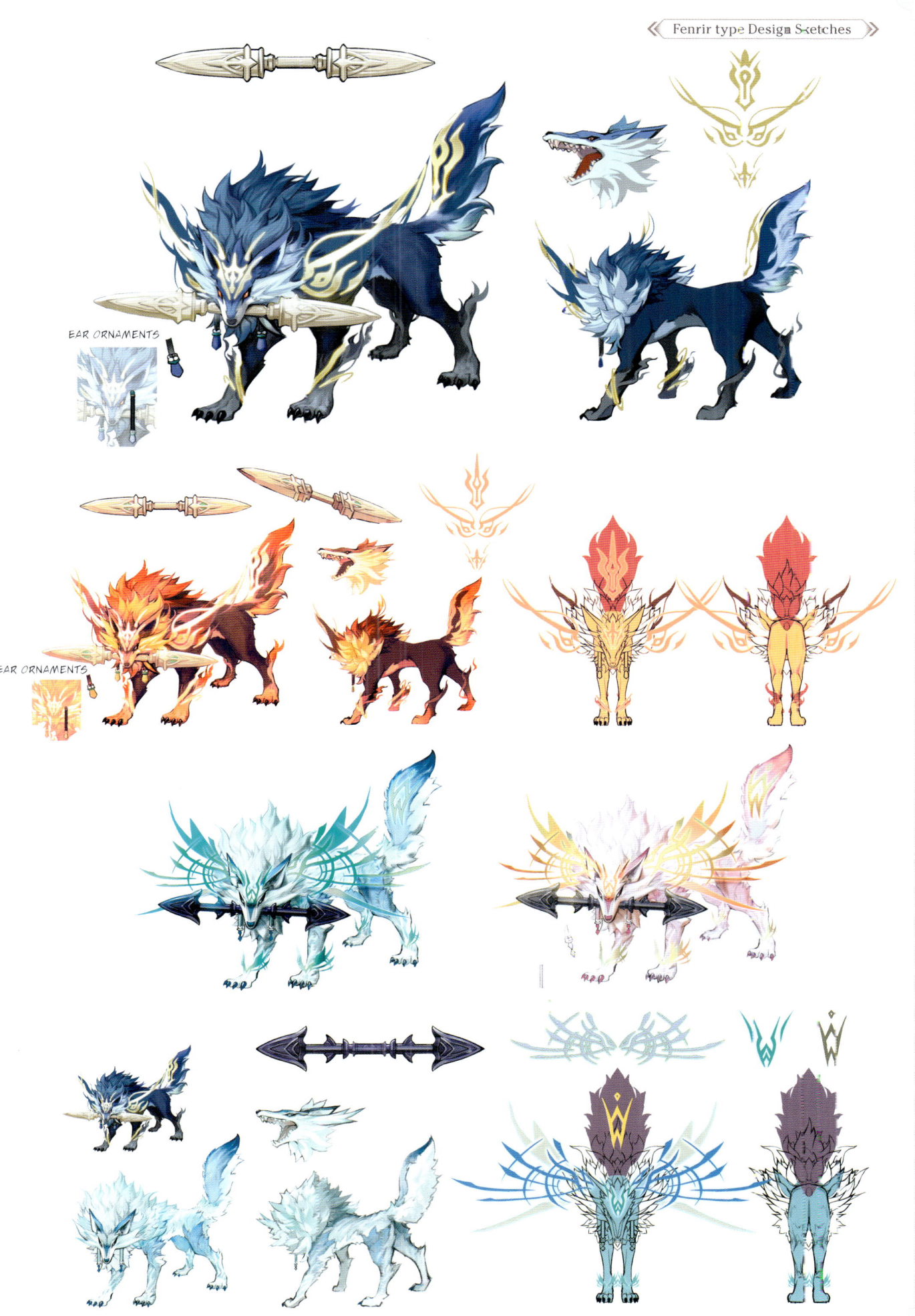

EAR ORNAMENTS

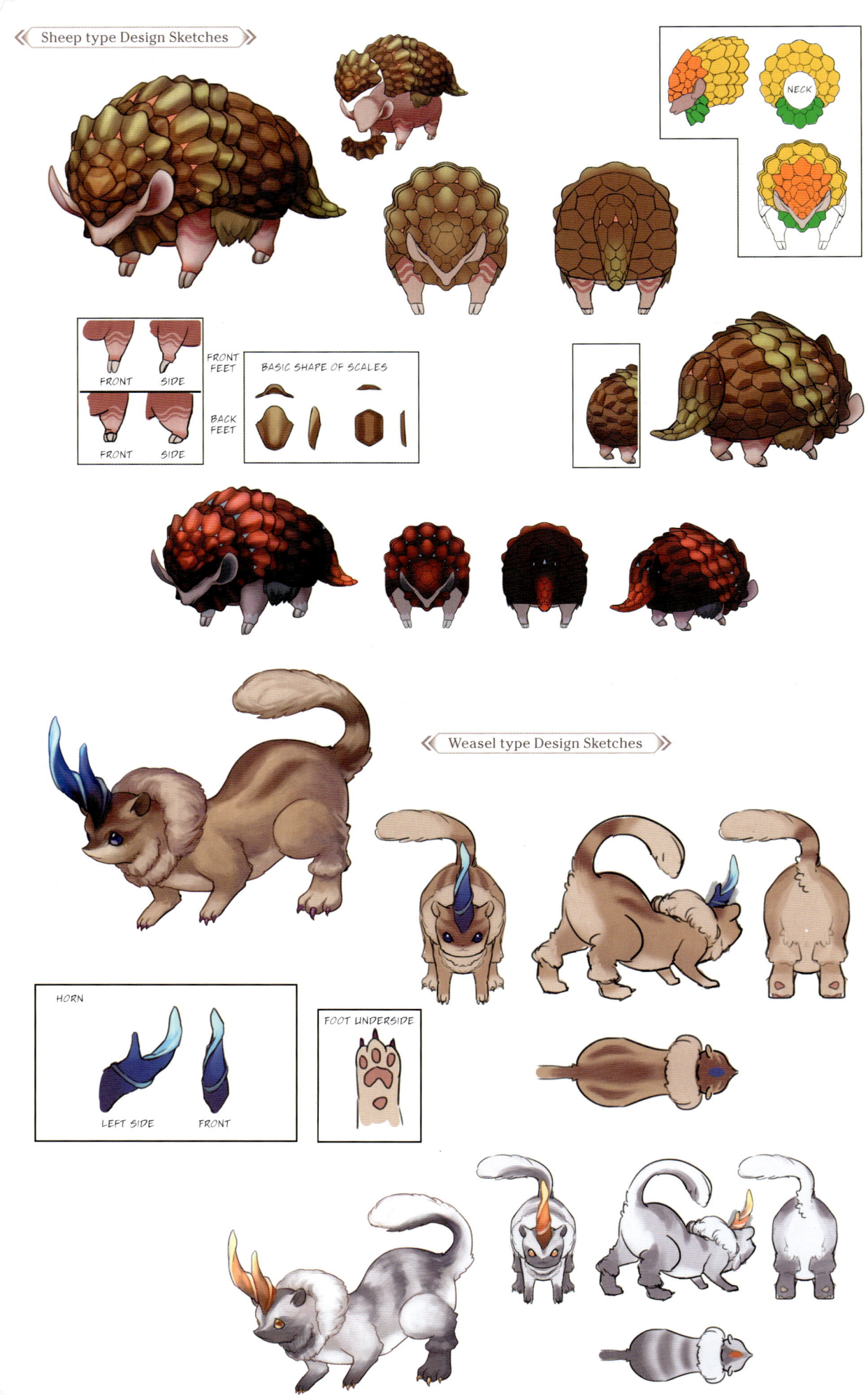

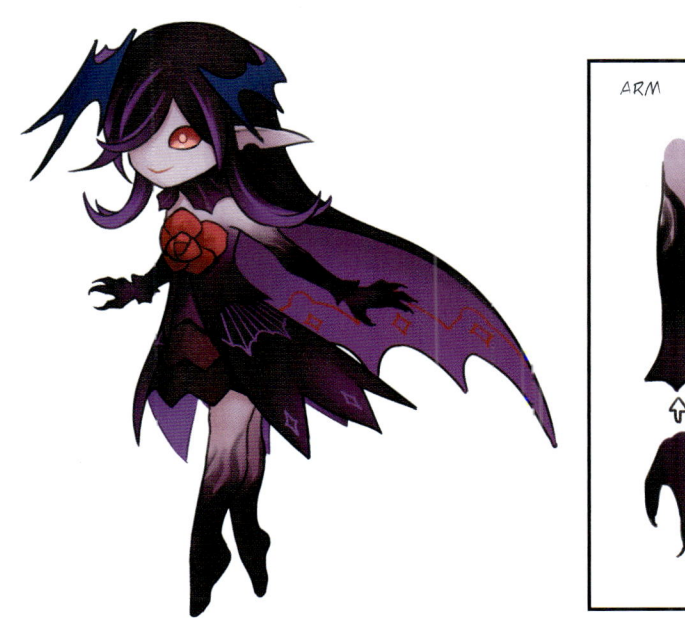
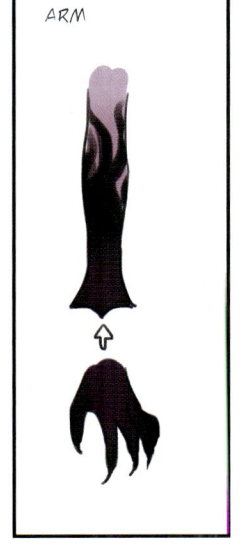

ARM

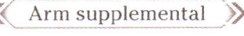

《 Arm supplemental 》

SIDE

BACK OF HAIR   FRONT

《 Knight type Design Sketches 》

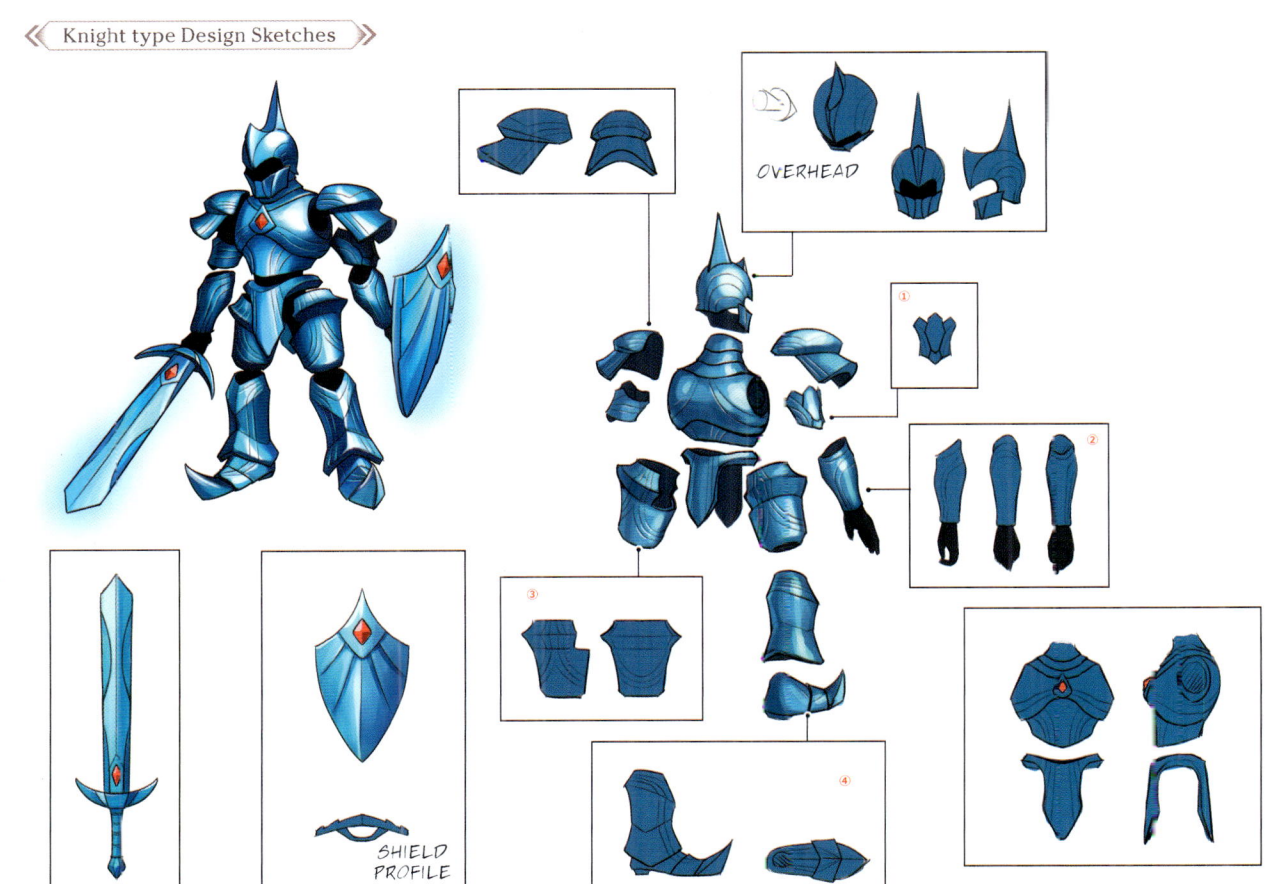

OVERHEAD

SHIELD PROFILE

Ratite type Design Sketches

Shark type Design Sketches

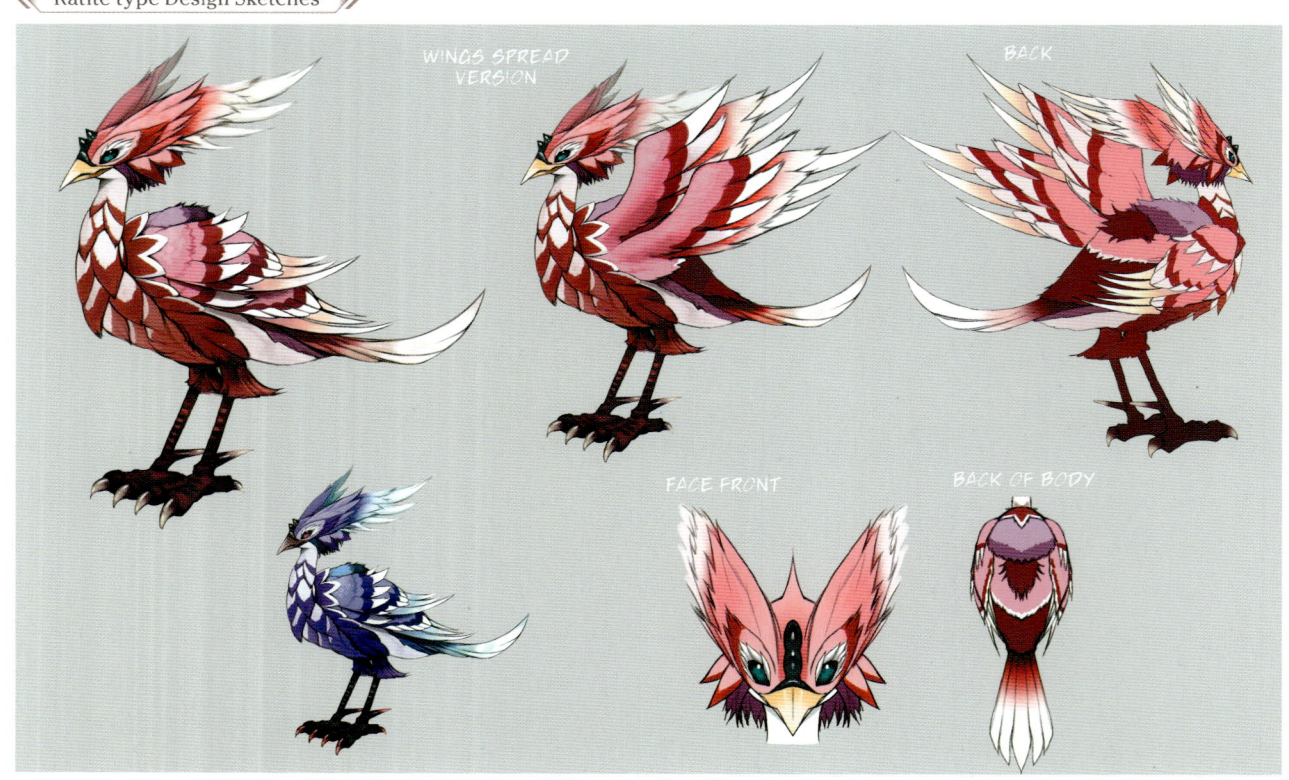

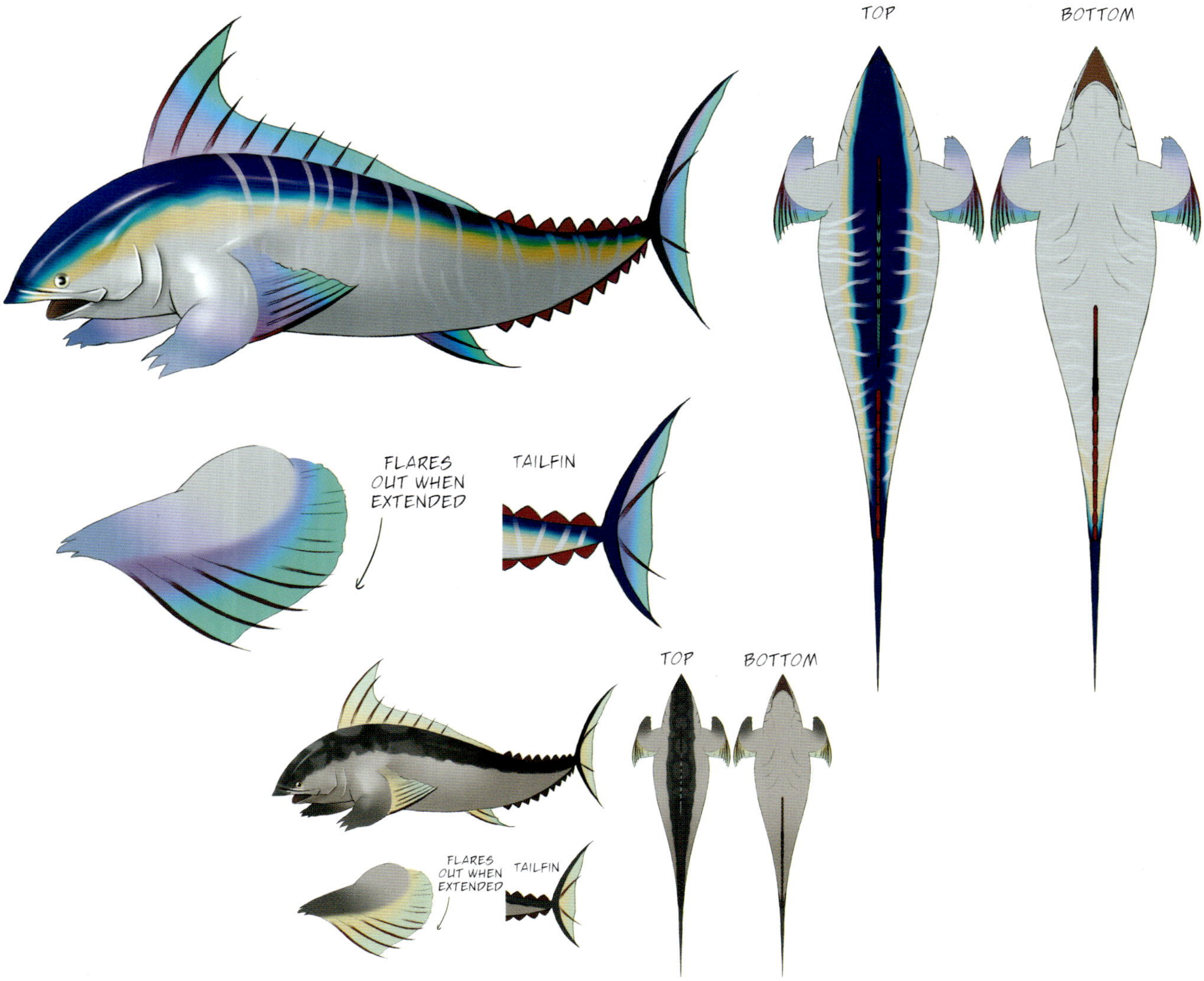

« Mini Golem type Design Sketches »

« Pterosaur type Design Sketches »

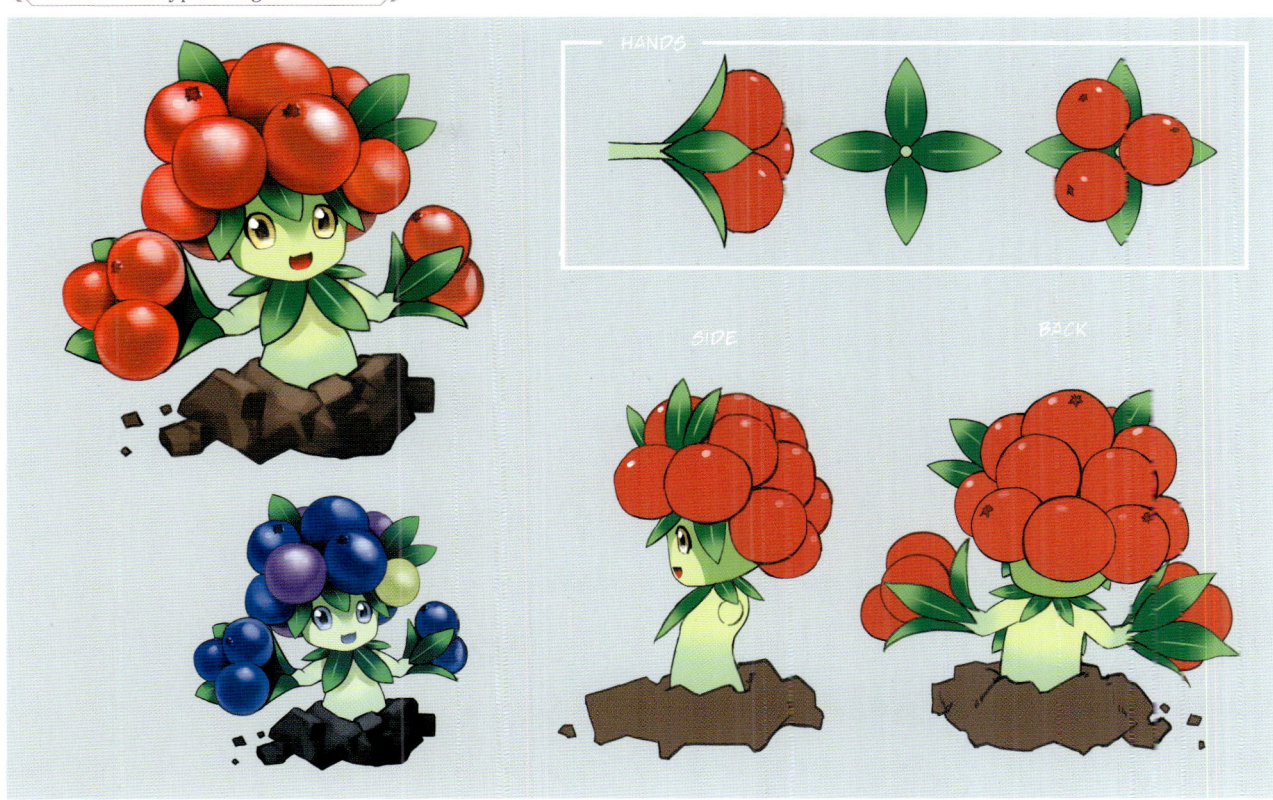

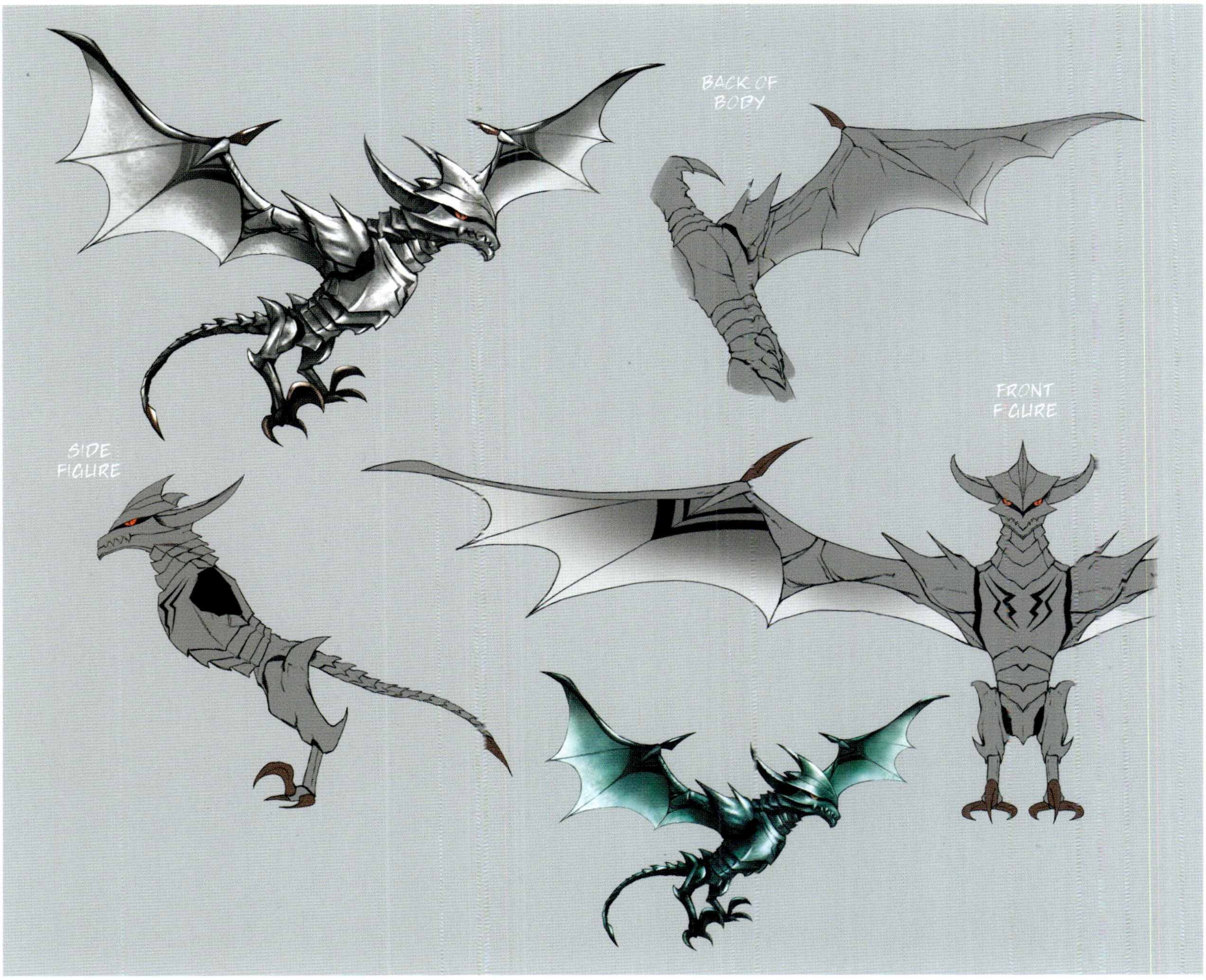

Skeleton type Design Sketches

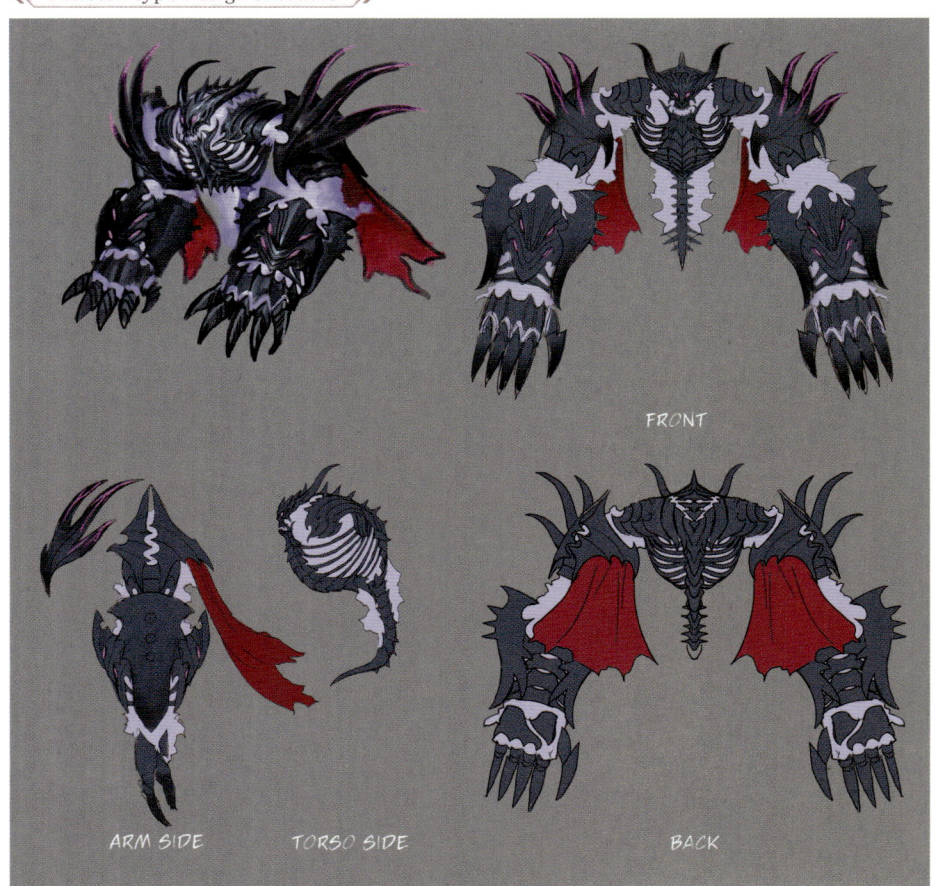

FRONT

ARM SIDE TORSO SIDE BACK

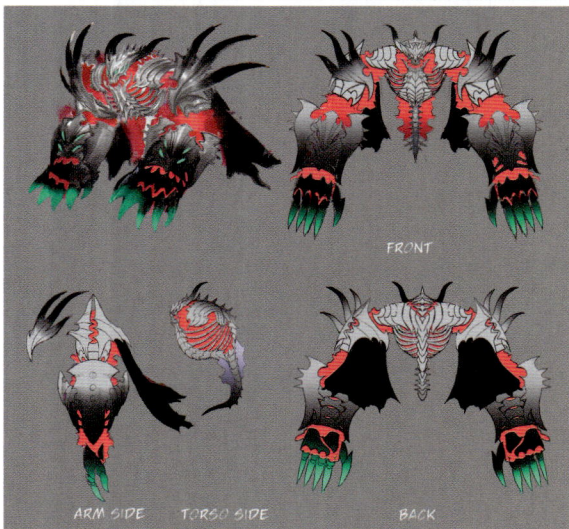

FRONT

ARM SIDE TORSO SIDE BACK

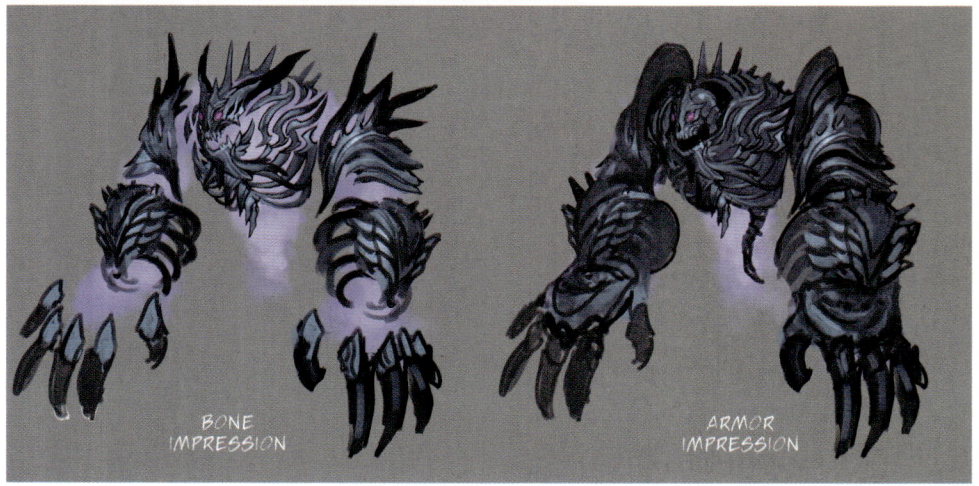

BONE IMPRESSION ARMOR IMPRESSION

Golem type Design Sketches

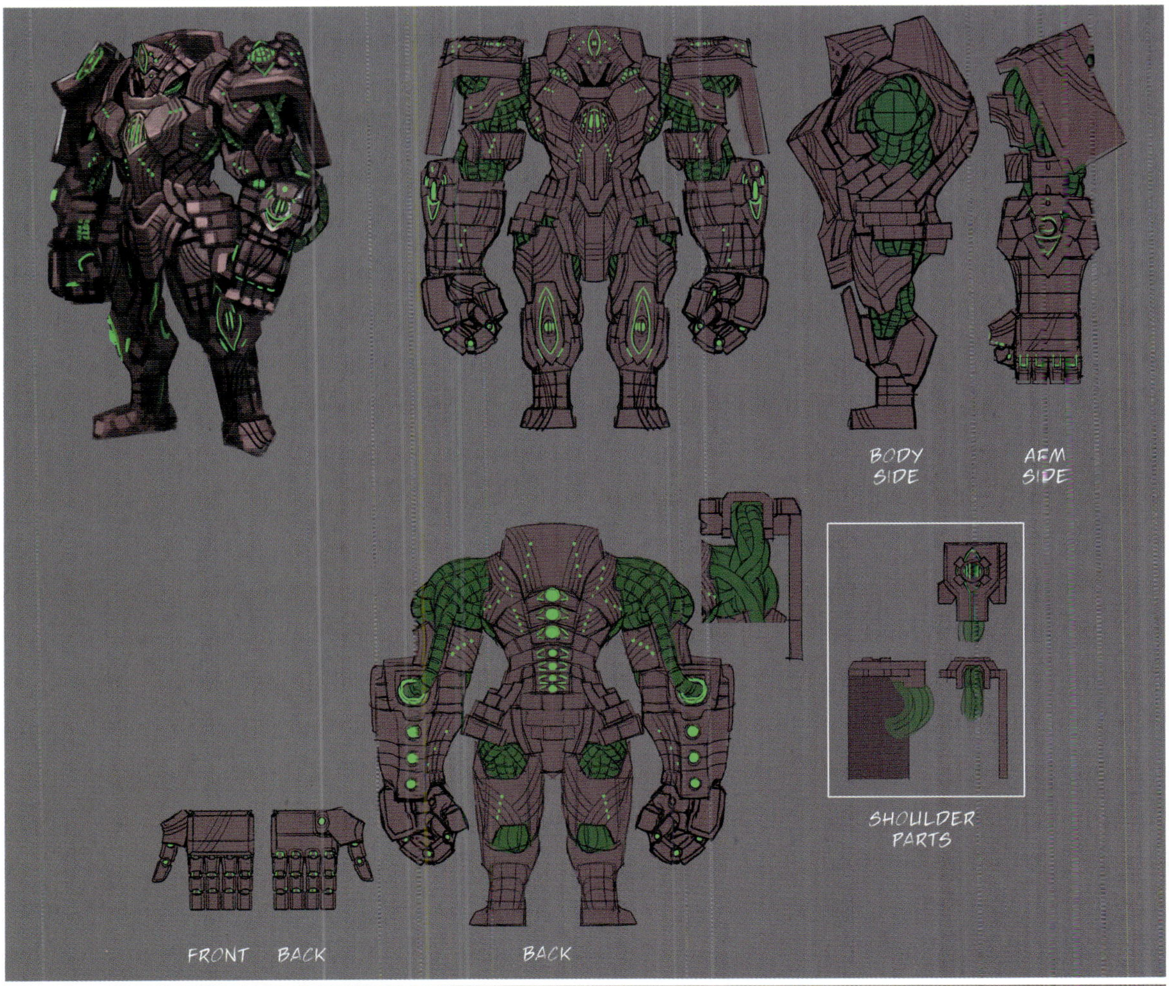

BODY SIDE ARM SIDE

FRONT BACK BACK SHOULDER PARTS

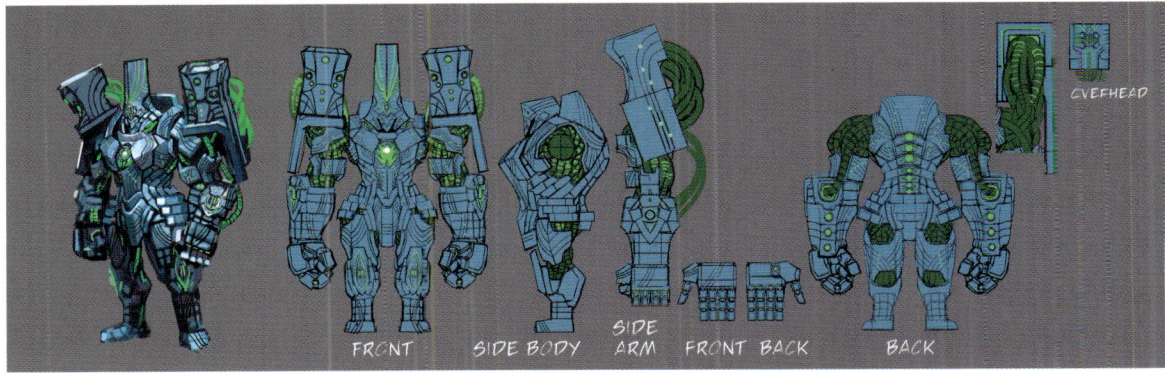

FRONT SIDE BODY SIDE ARM FRONT BACK BACK OVERHEAD

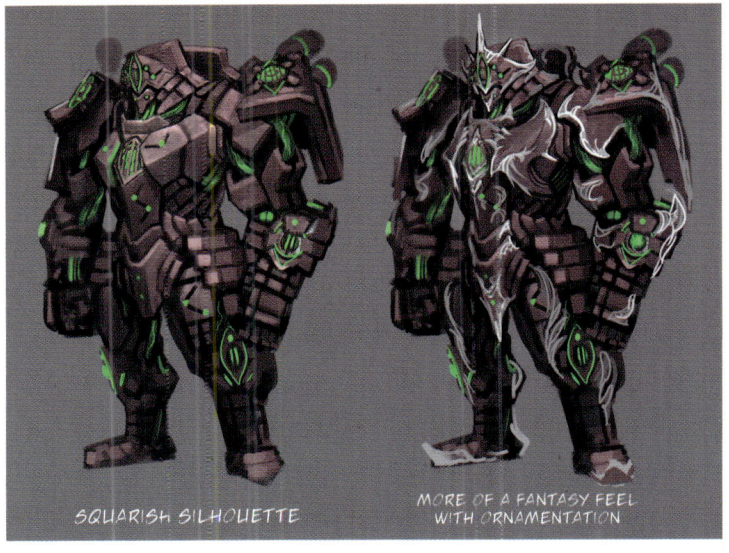

SQUARISH SILHOUETTE MORE OF A FANTASY FEEL WITH ORNAMENTATION

Elder Treant type Design Sketches

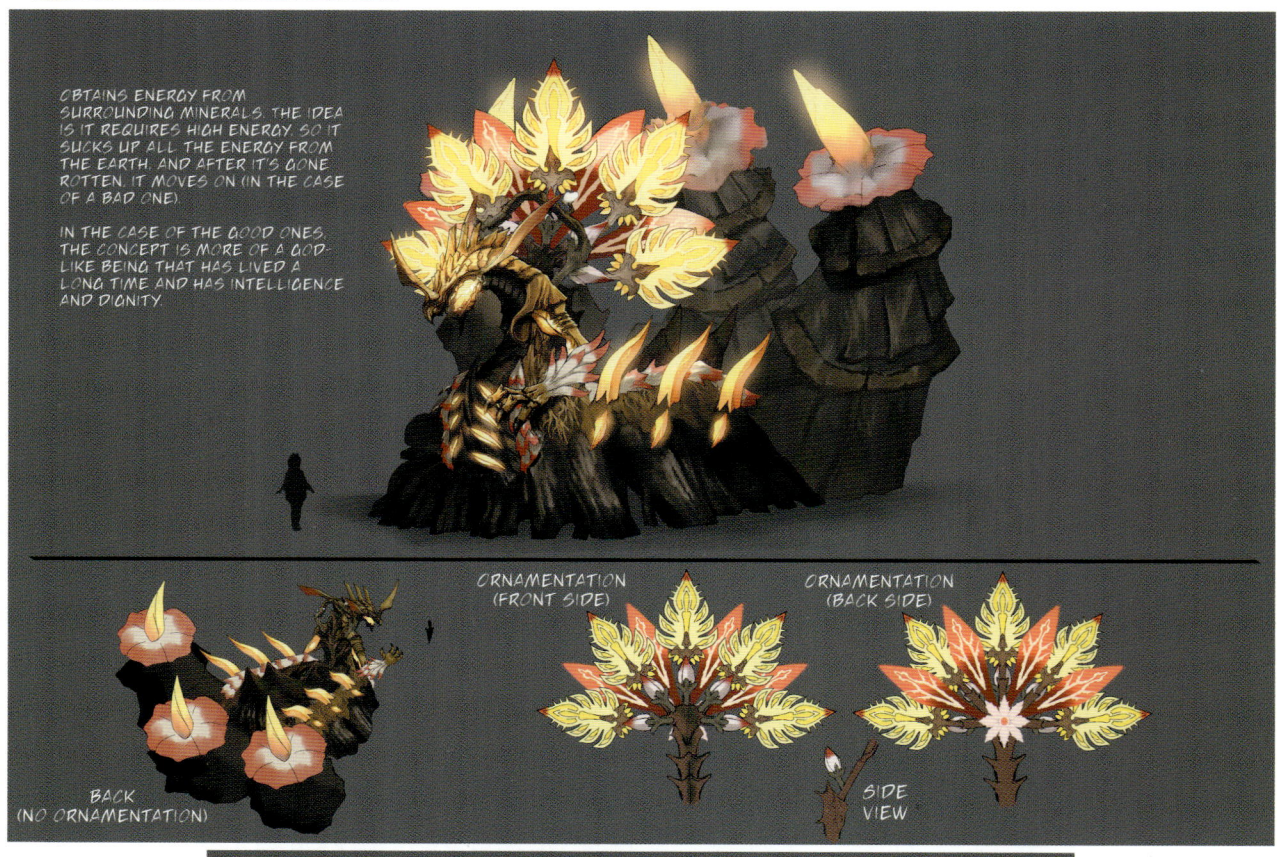

OBTAINS ENERGY FROM SURROUNDING MINERALS. THE IDEA IS IT REQUIRES HIGH ENERGY, SO IT SUCKS UP ALL THE ENERGY FROM THE EARTH, AND AFTER IT'S GONE ROTTEN, IT MOVES ON (IN THE CASE OF A BAD ONE).

IN THE CASE OF THE GOOD ONES, THE CONCEPT IS MORE OF A GOD-LIKE BEING THAT HAS LIVED A LONG TIME AND HAS INTELLIGENCE AND DIGNITY.

BACK (NO ORNAMENTATION)

ORNAMENTATION (FRONT SIDE)

ORNAMENTATION (BACK SIDE)

SIDE VIEW

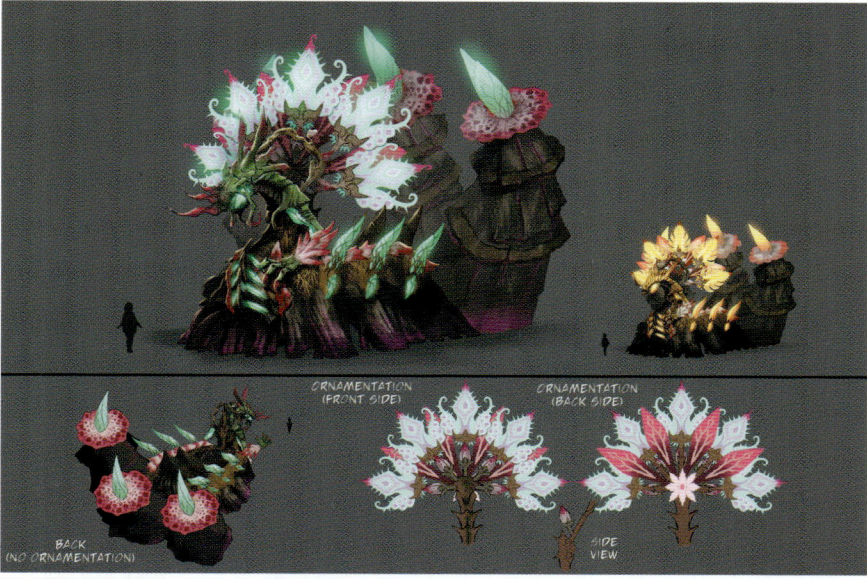

BACK (NO ORNAMENTATION)

ORNAMENTATION (FRONT SIDE)

ORNAMENTATION (BACK SIDE)

SIDE VIEW

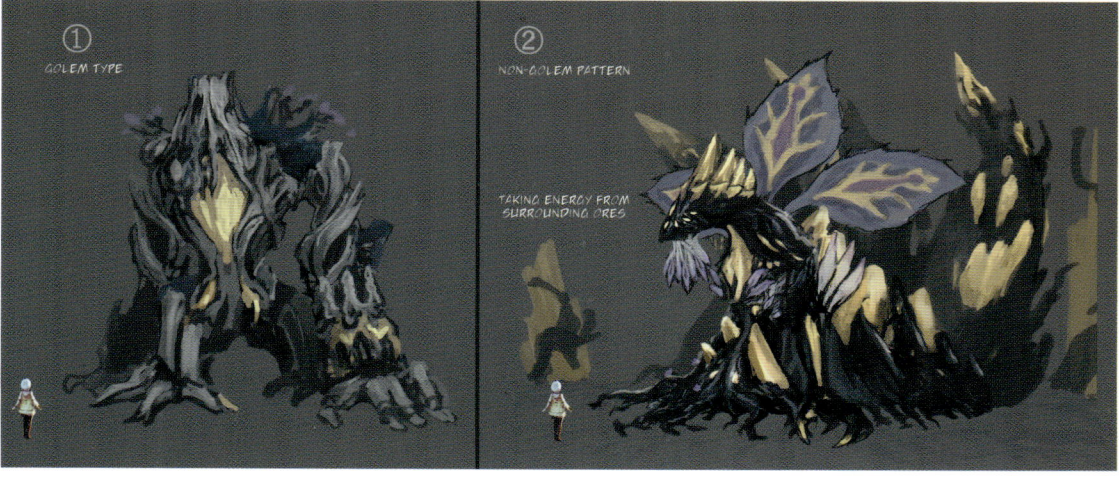

① GOLEM TYPE

② NON-GOLEM PATTERN

TAKING ENERGY FROM SURROUNDING ORES

King Philuscha type Design Sketches

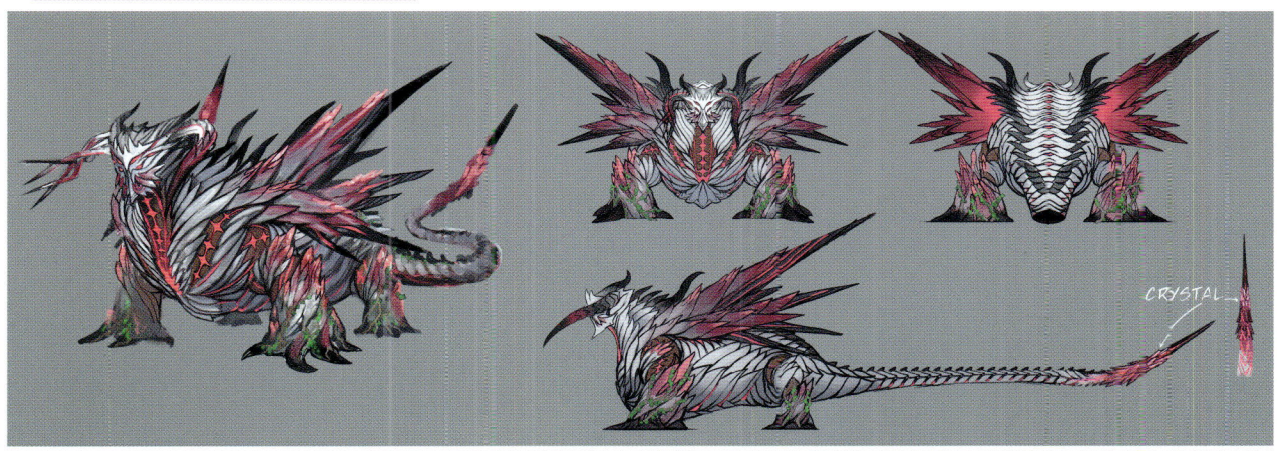

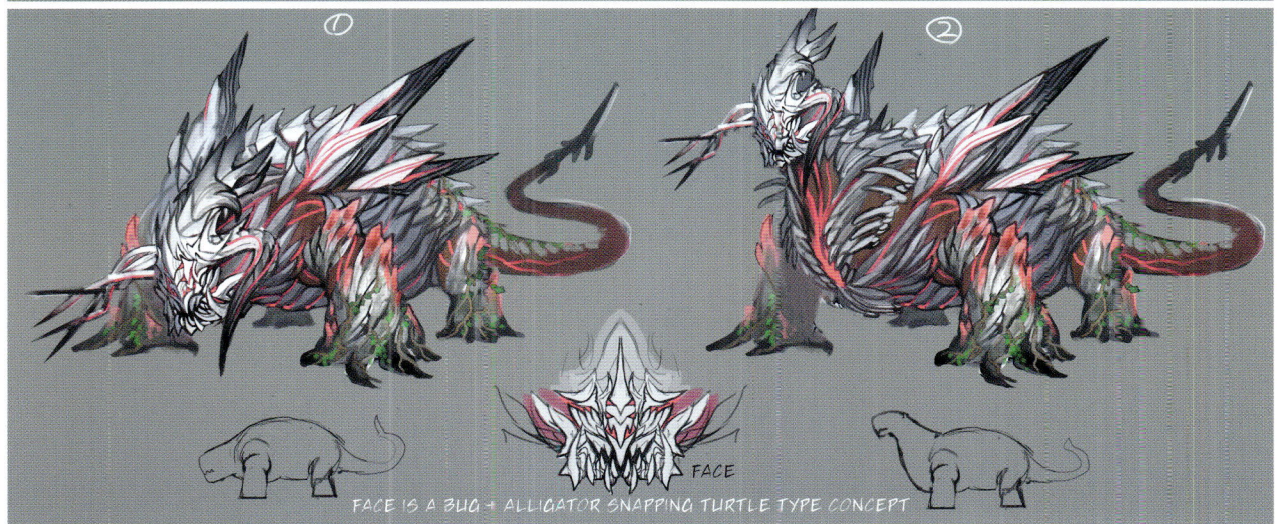

FACE IS A BUG + ALLIGATOR SNAPPING TURTLE TYPE CONCEPT

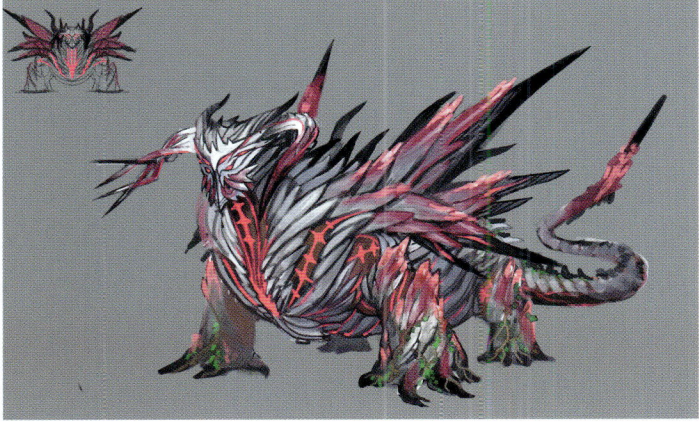

Machine Soldier type Design Sketches

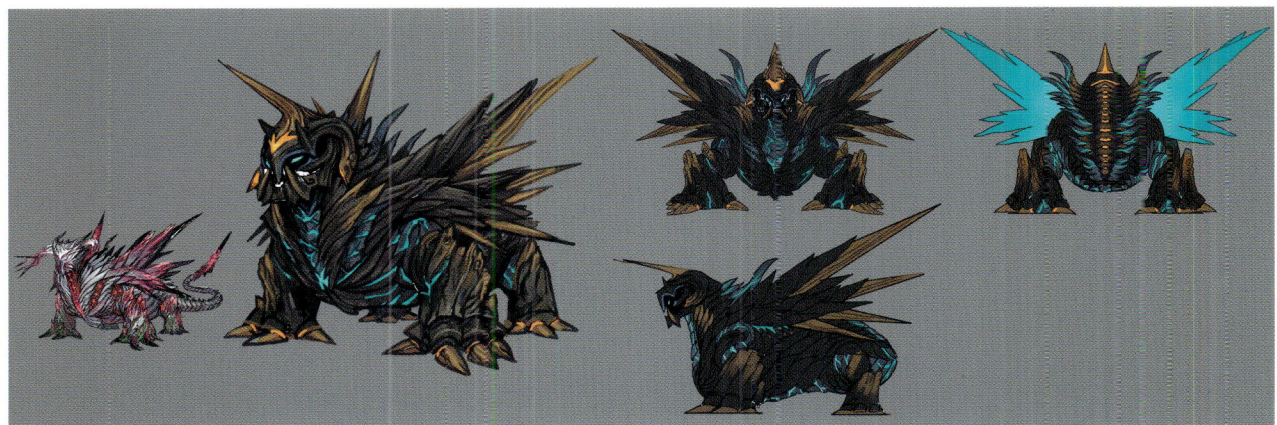

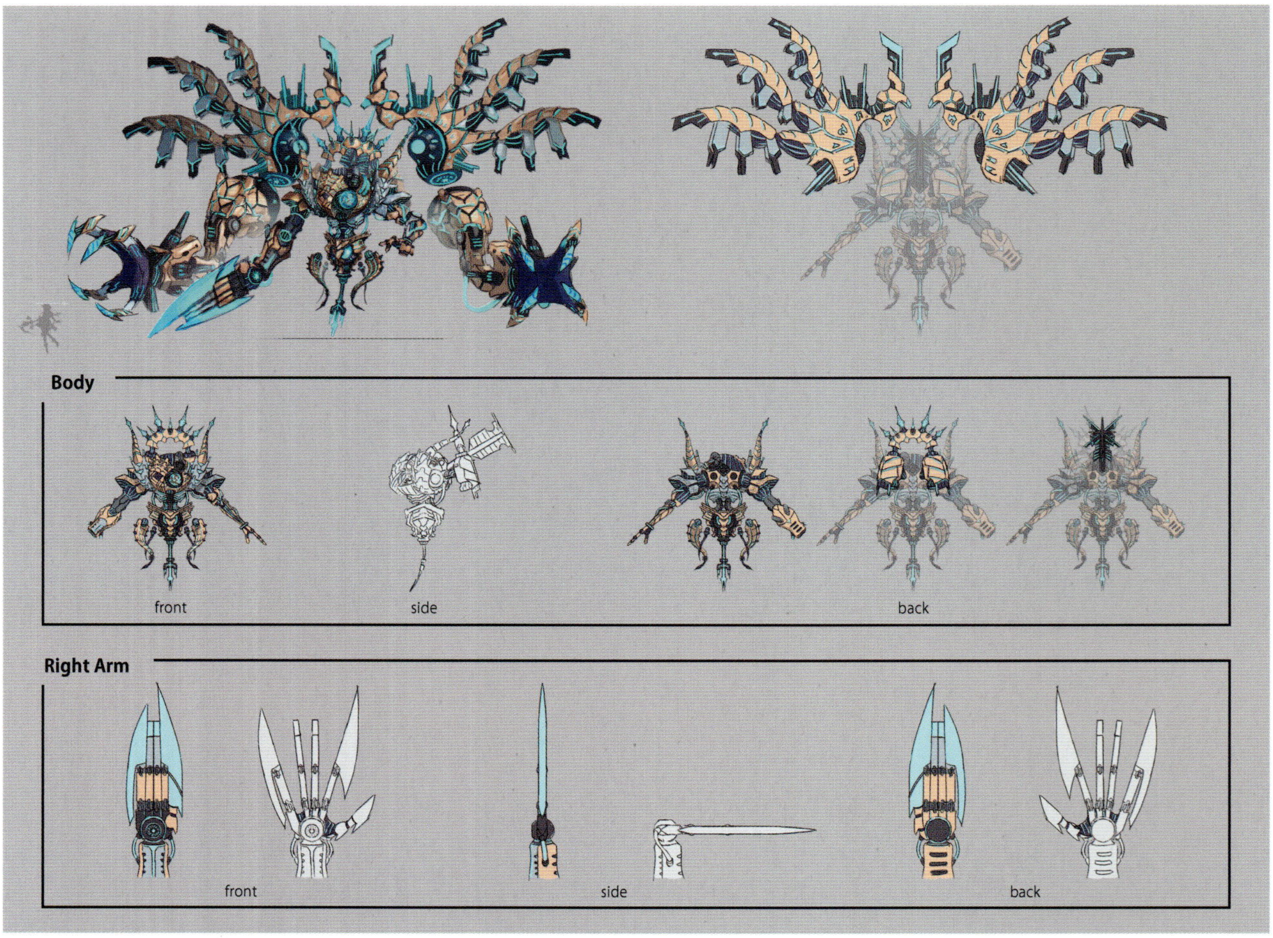

Code of the Universe type Design Sketches

Body

front | side | back

Right Arm

front | side | back

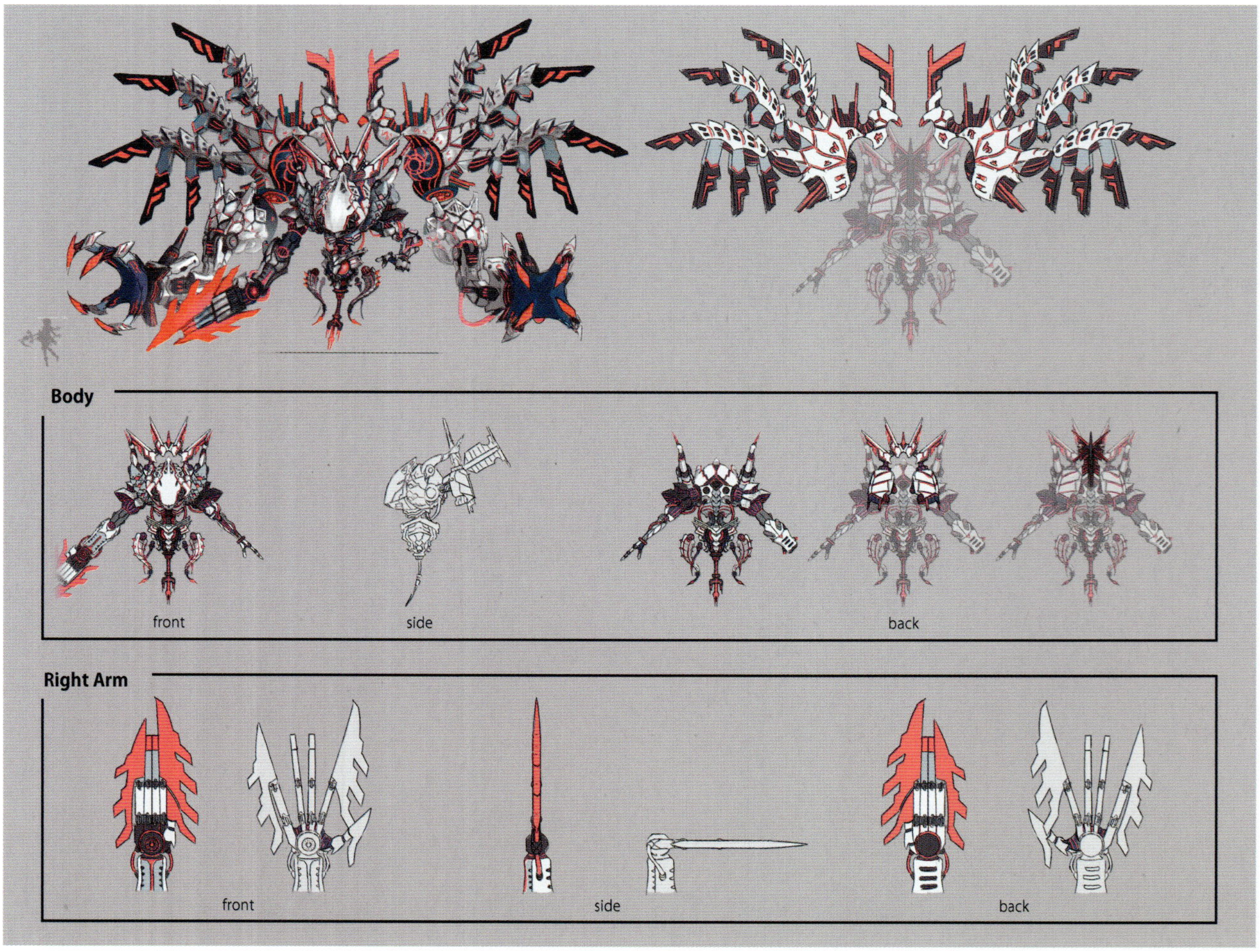

Body

front | side | back

Right Arm

front | side | back

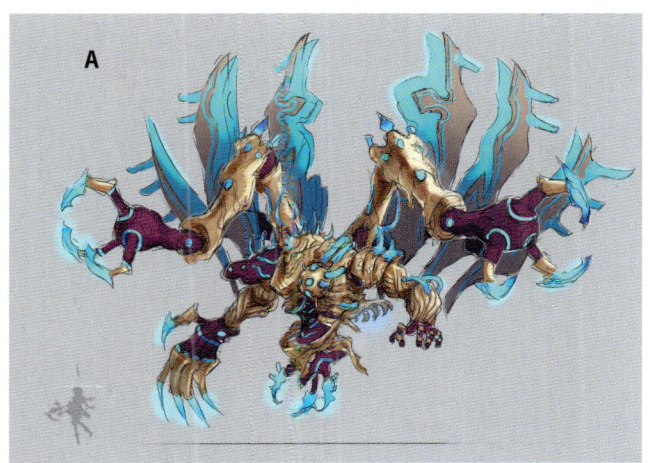

A

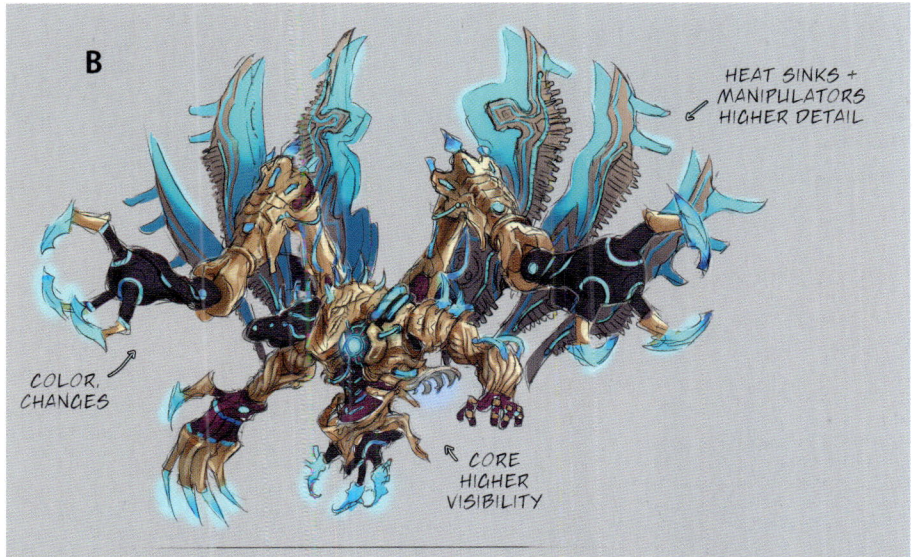

B

HEAT SINKS + MANIPULATORS HIGHER DETAIL

COLOR CHANGES

CORE HIGHER VISIBILITY

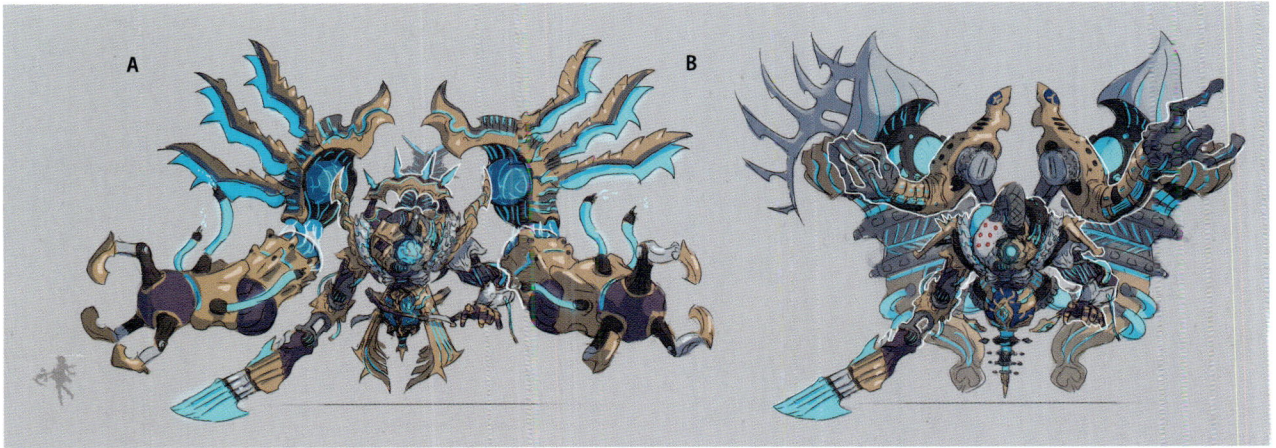

A B

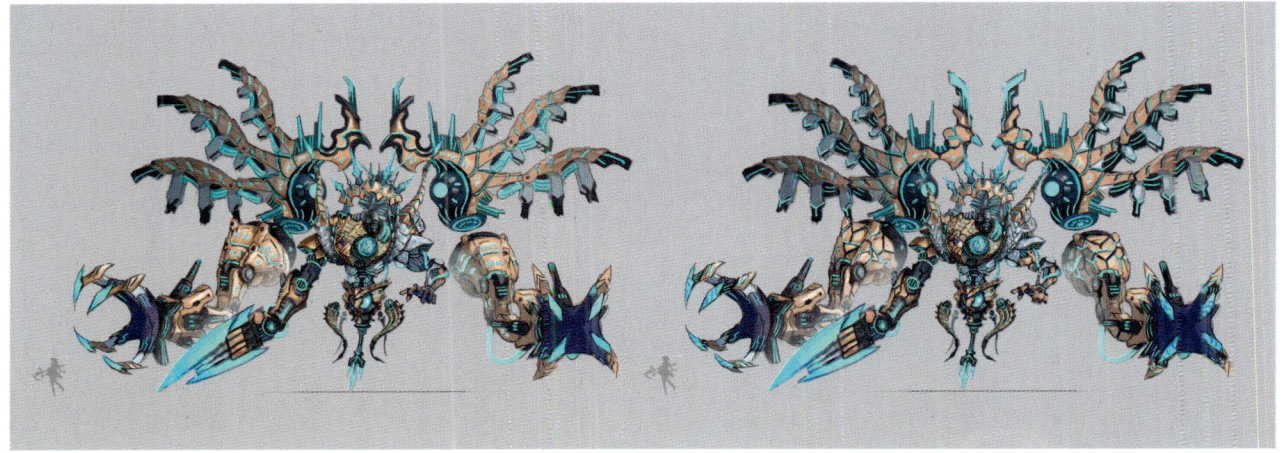

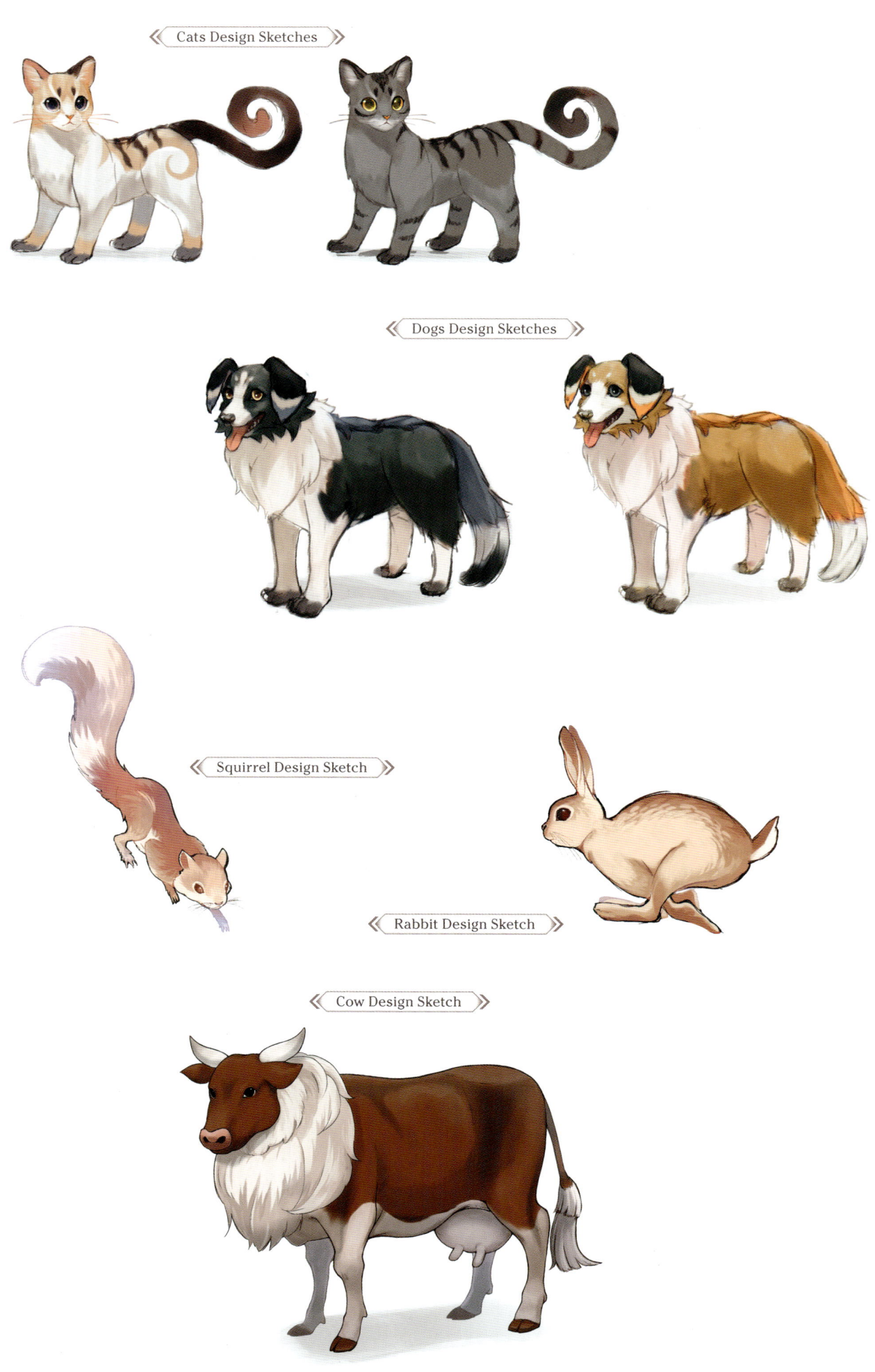

BACK PATTERNING

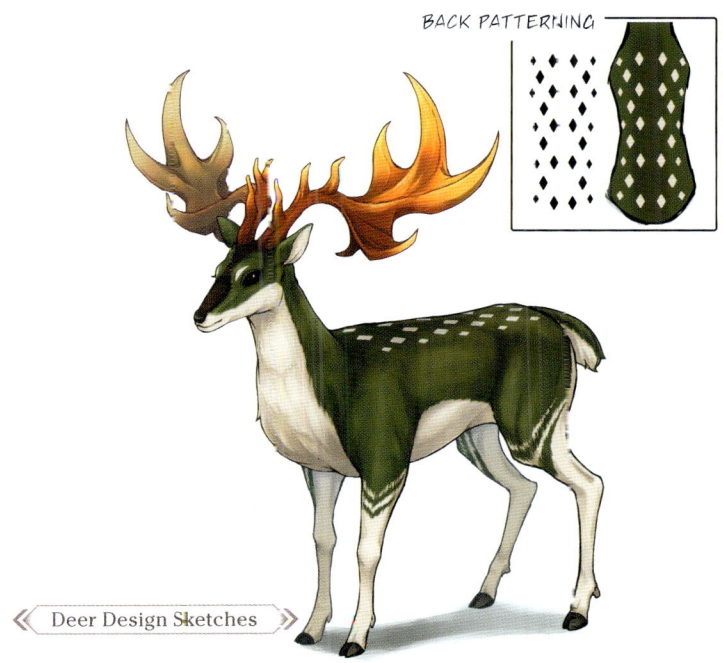

《 Deer Design Sketches 》

《 Fish Design Sketches 》

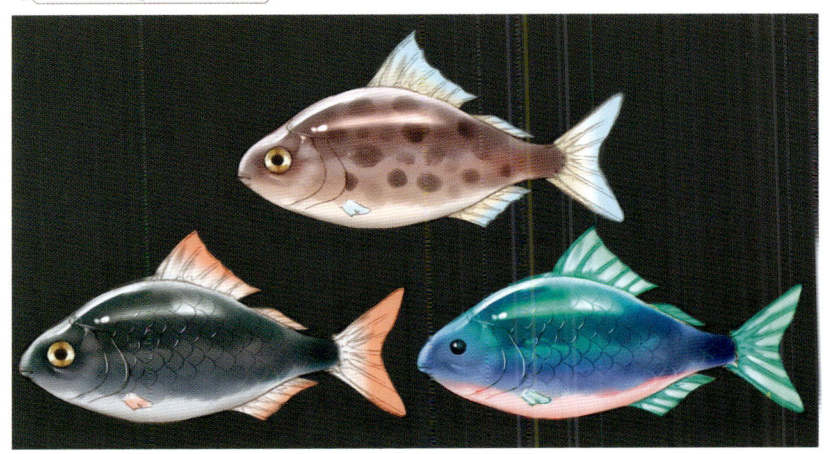

《 Butterfly Design Sketch 》

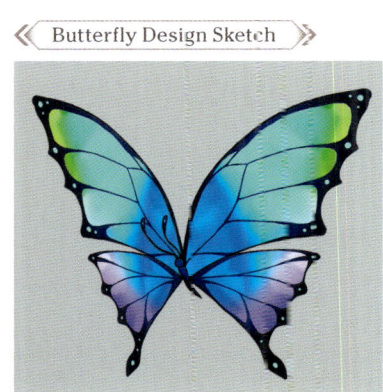

SHELL PATTERNING

UNDERSIDE REFERENCE

《 Dolphin Design Sketch 》

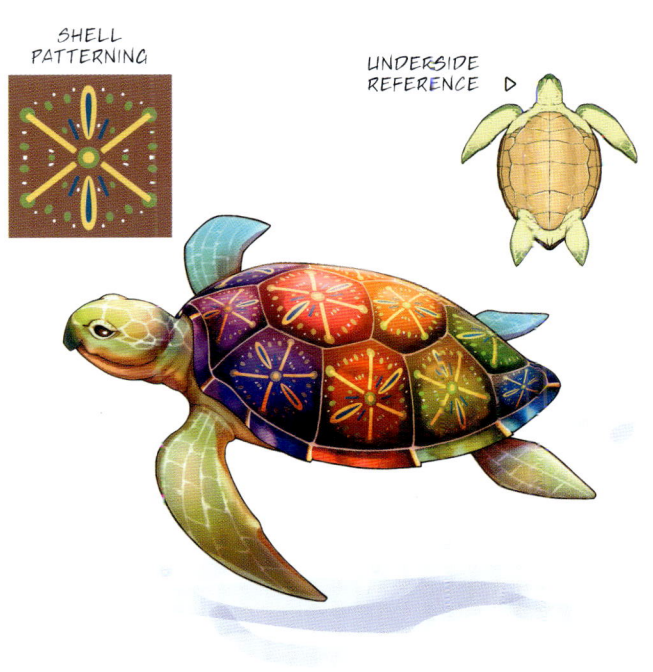

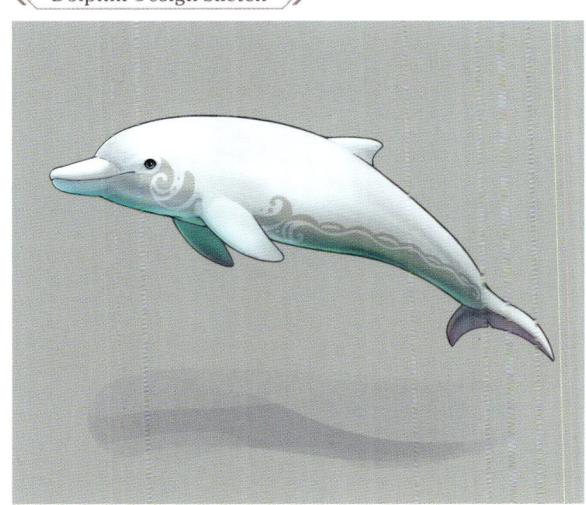

《 Turtle Design Sketches 》

145

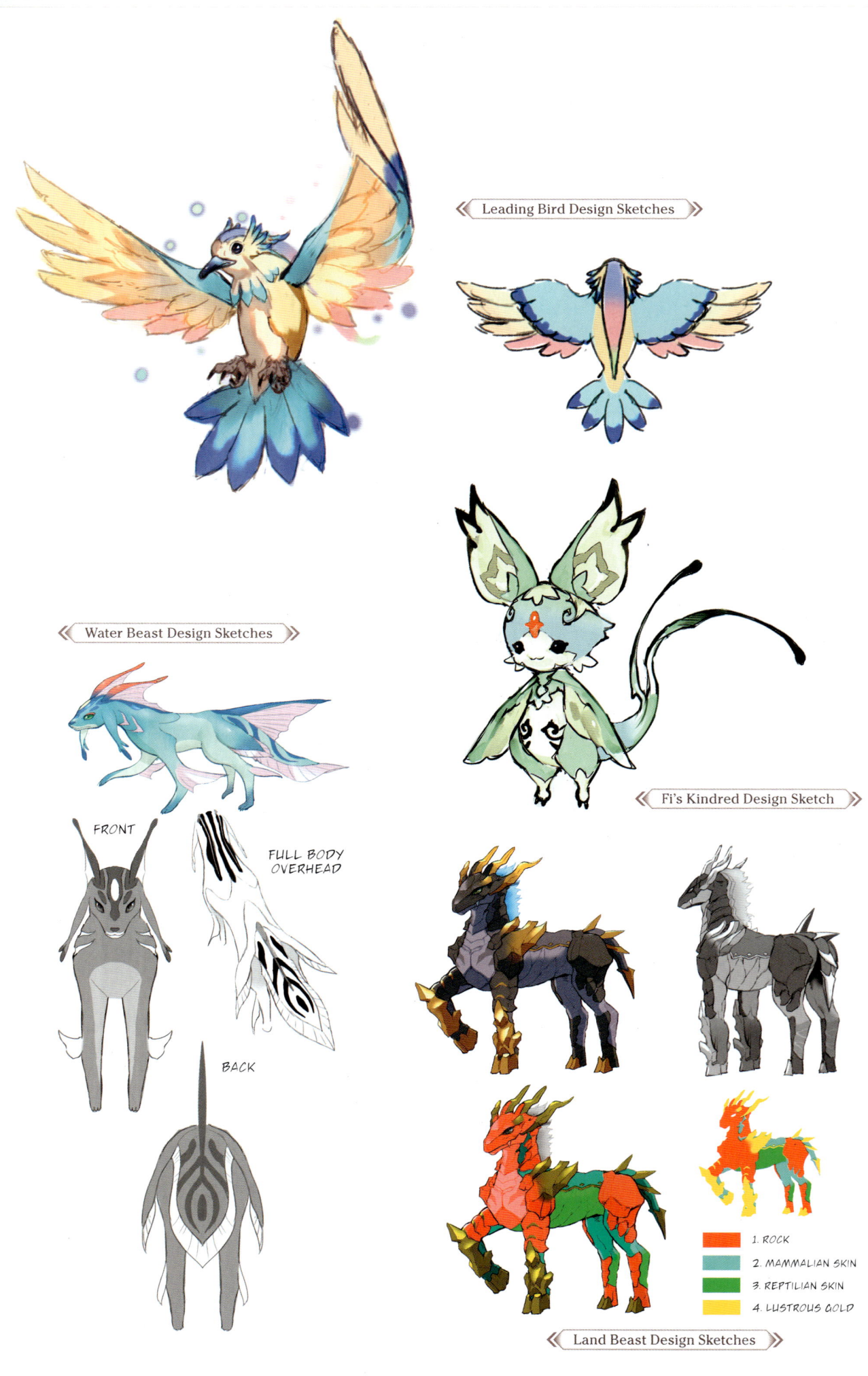

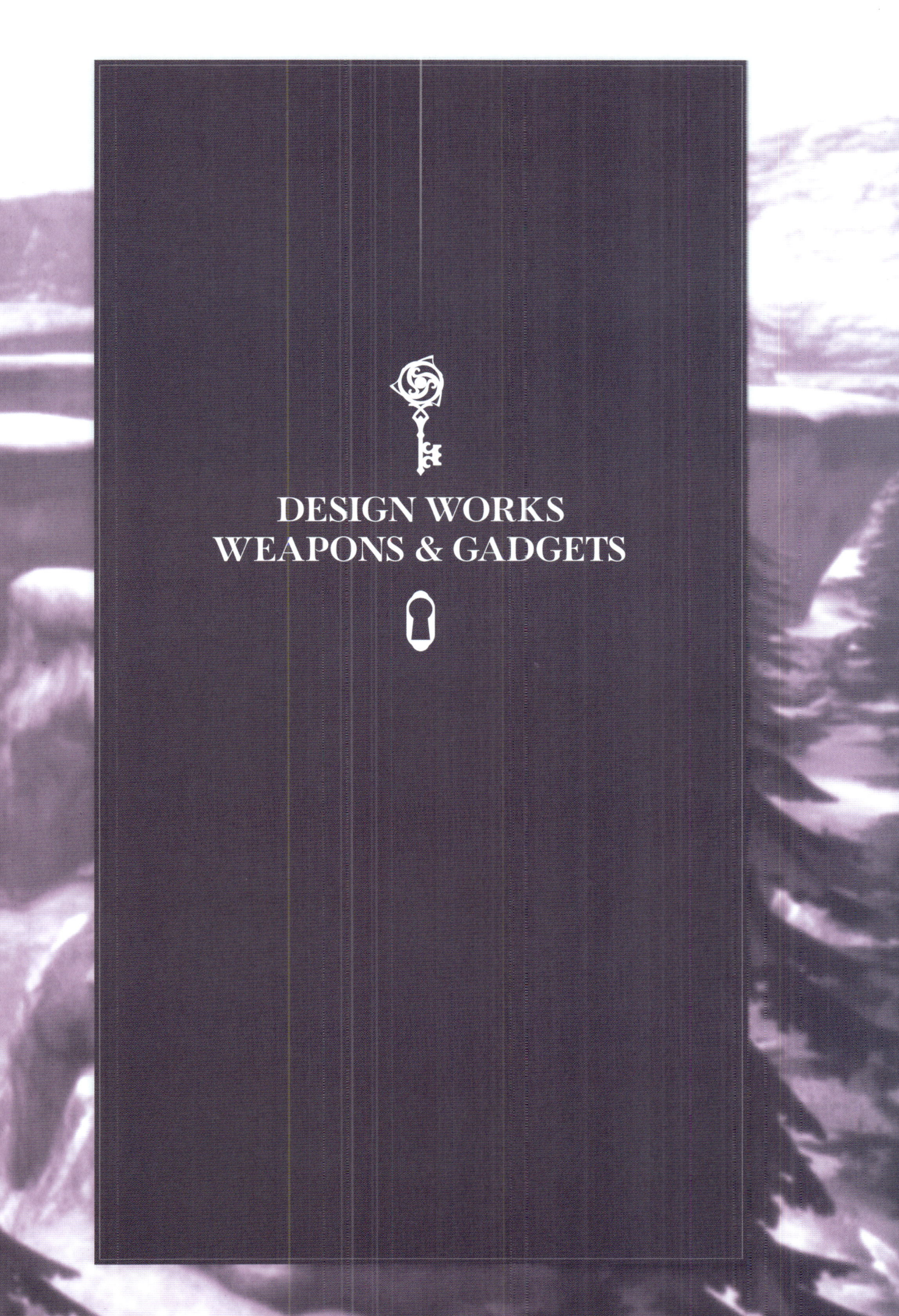

DESIGN WORKS
WEAPONS & GADGETS

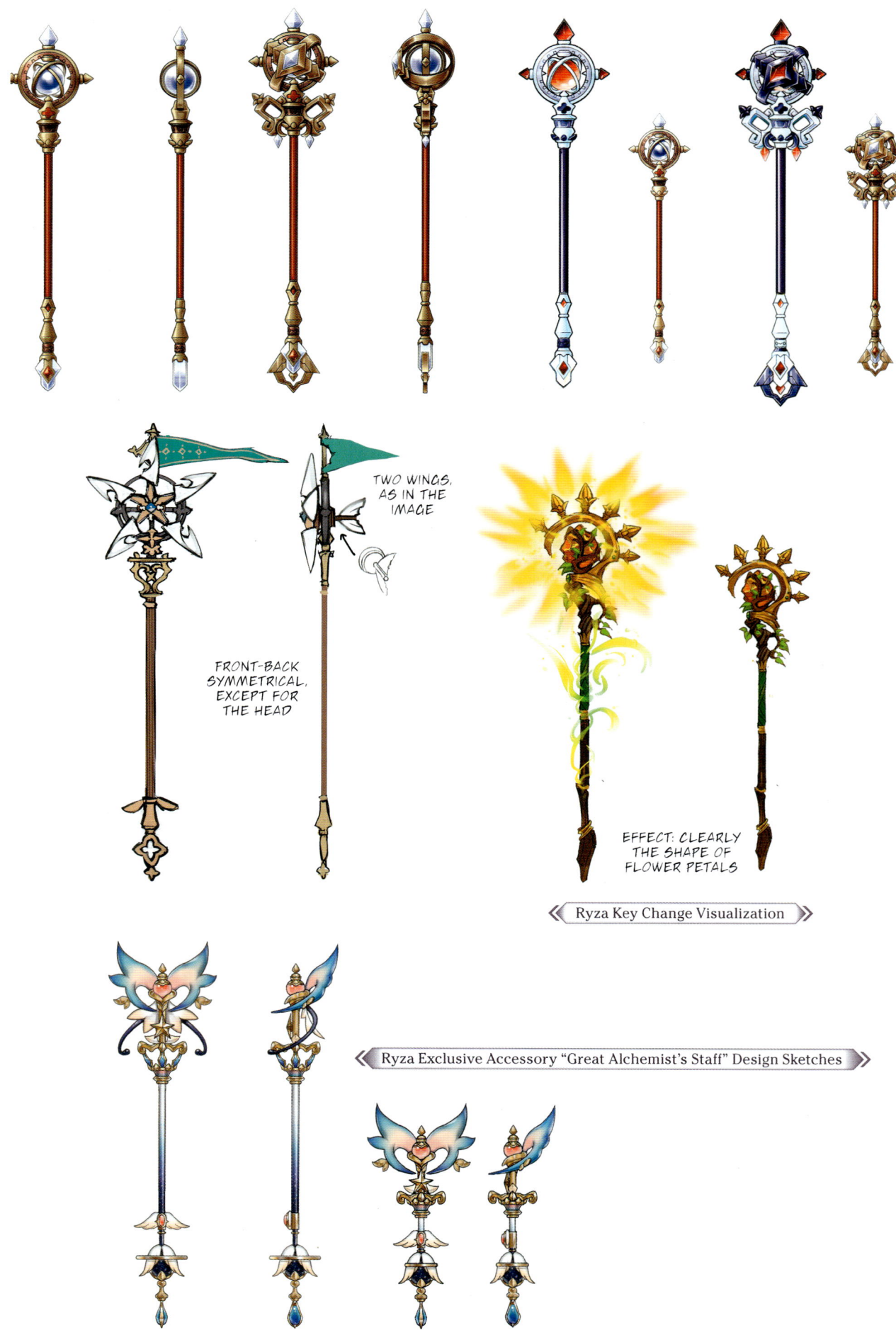といった

Klaudia's Bow Design Sketches

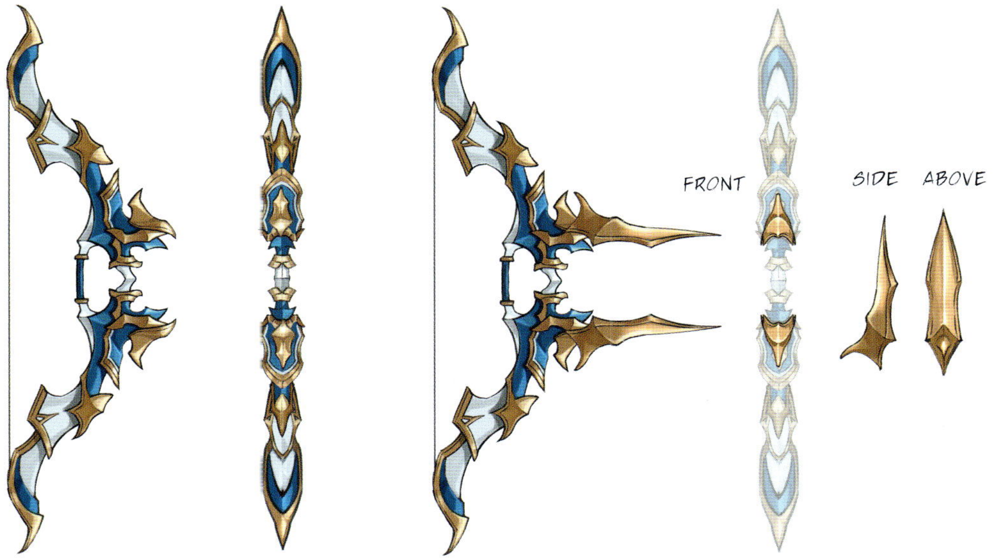

FRONT SIDE ABOVE

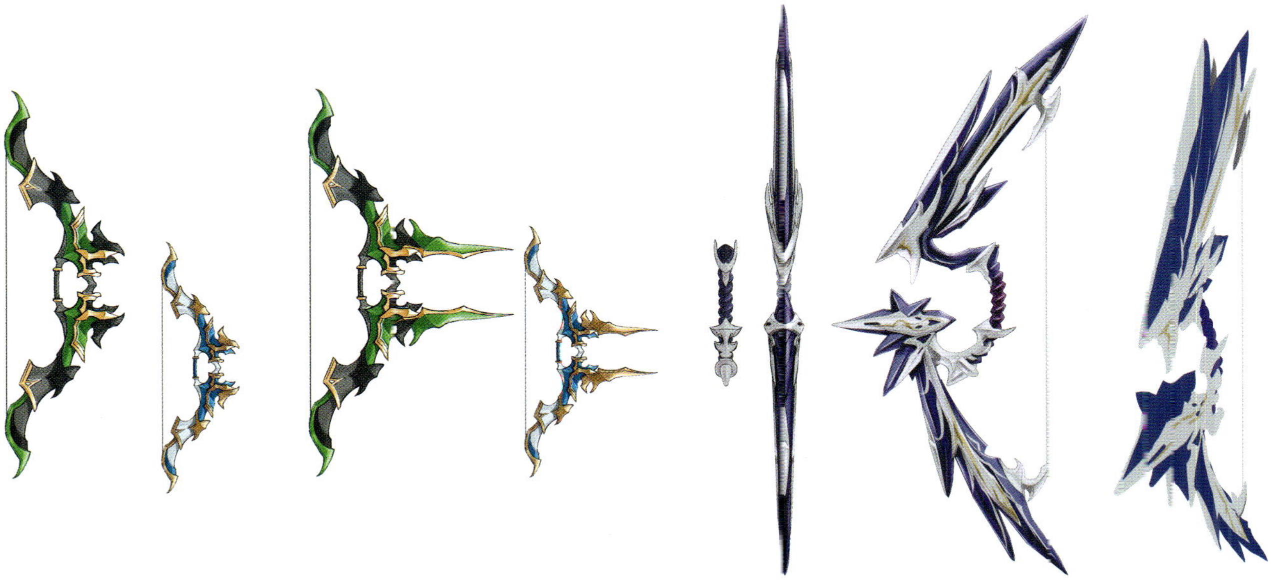

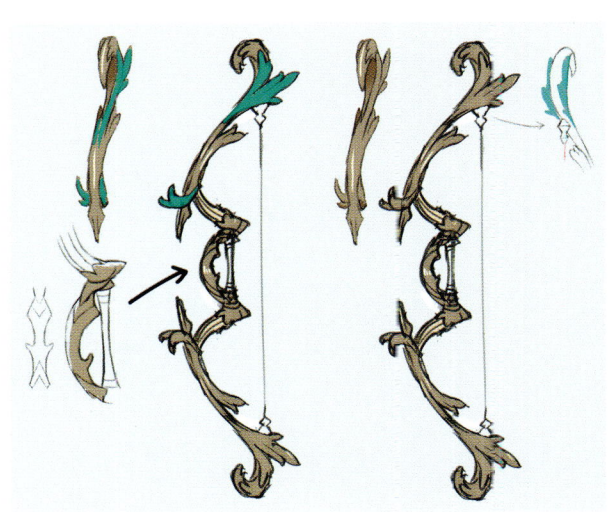

Klaudia Key Change Visualization

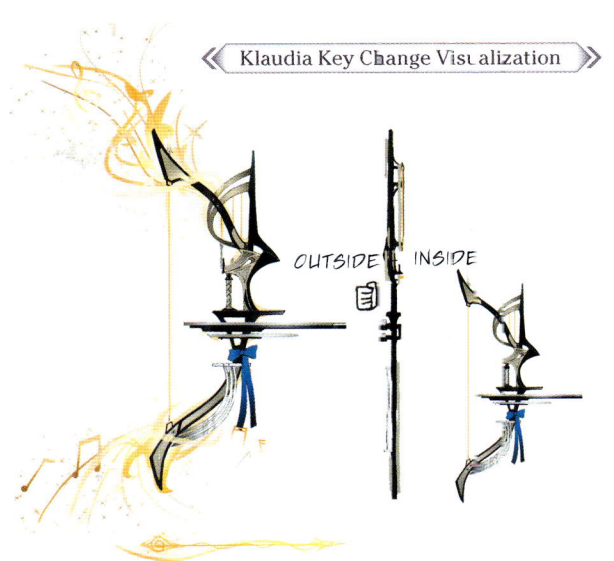

OUTSIDE INSIDE

Lent's Great Sword Design Sketches

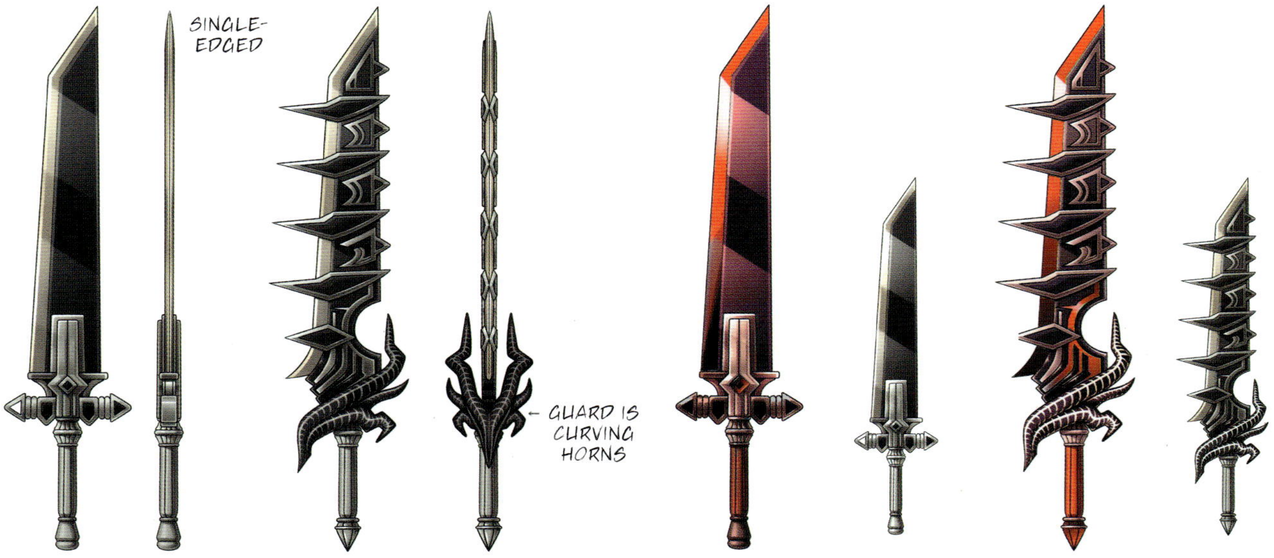

SINGLE-EDGED

GUARD IS CURVING HORNS

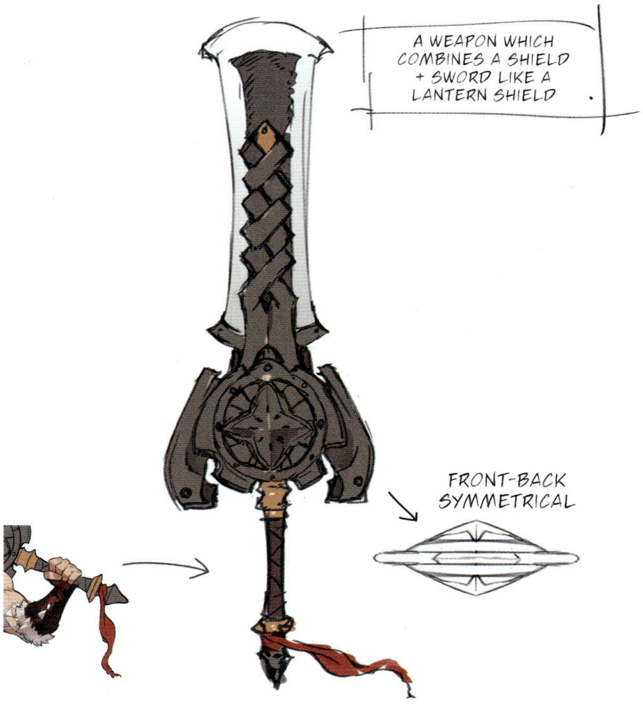

A WEAPON WHICH COMBINES A SHIELD + SWORD LIKE A LANTERN SHIELD

FRONT-BACK SYMMETRICAL

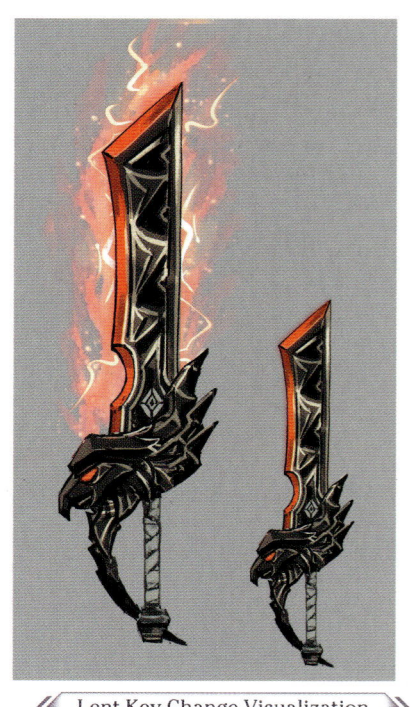

Lent Key Change Visualization

Tao's Dual Daggers Design Sketches

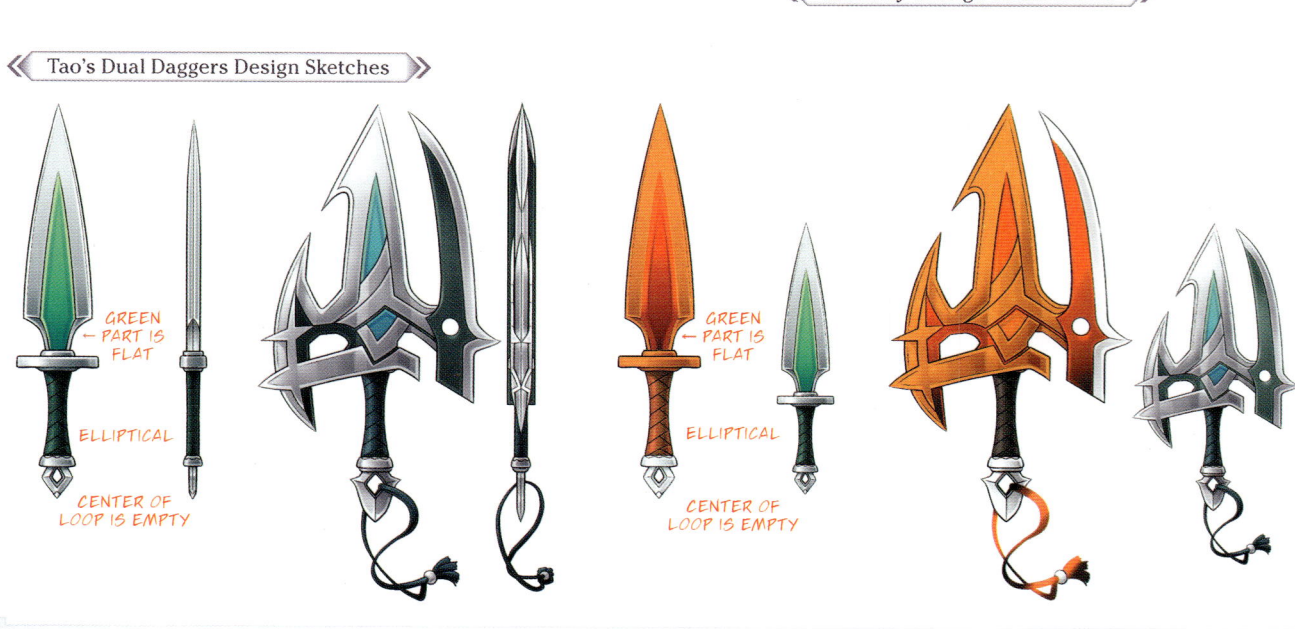

GREEN PART IS FLAT

ELLIPTICAL

CENTER OF LOOP IS EMPTY

GREEN PART IS FLAT

ELLIPTICAL

CENTER OF LOOP IS EMPTY

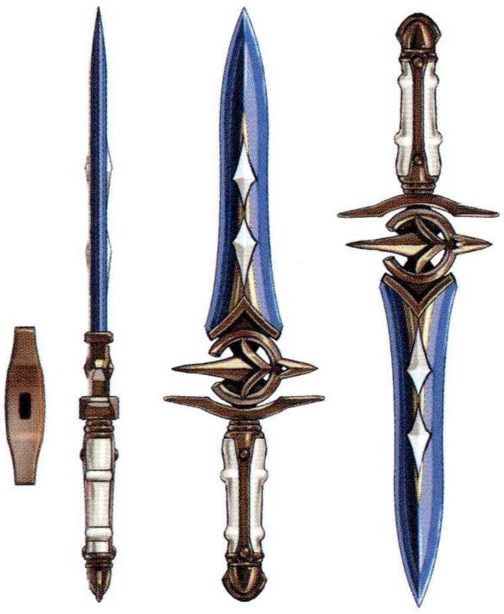

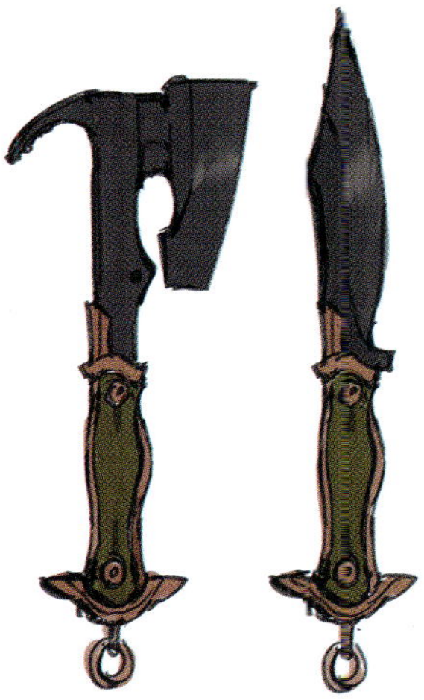

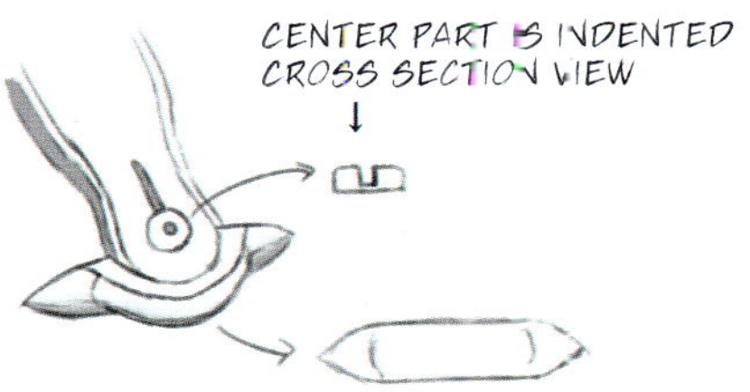

CENTER PART IS INDENTED
CROSS SECTION VIEW

《 Tao Key Change Visualization 》

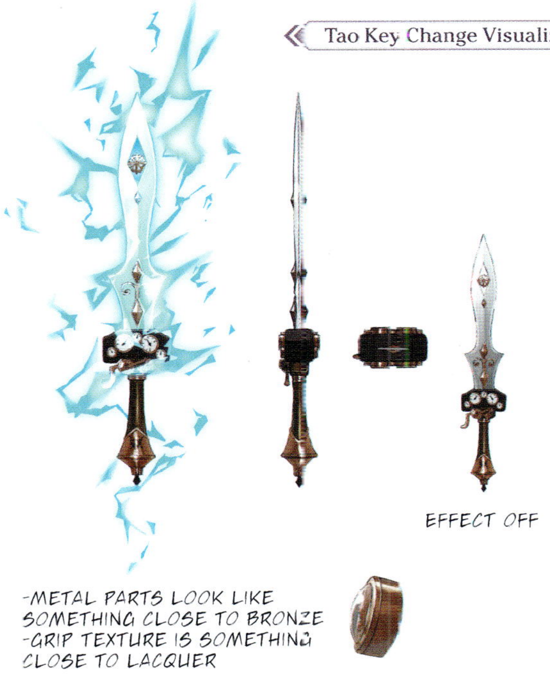

EFFECT OFF

- METAL PARTS LOOK LIKE SOMETHING CLOSE TO BRONZE
- GRIP TEXTURE IS SOMETHING CLOSE TO LACQUER

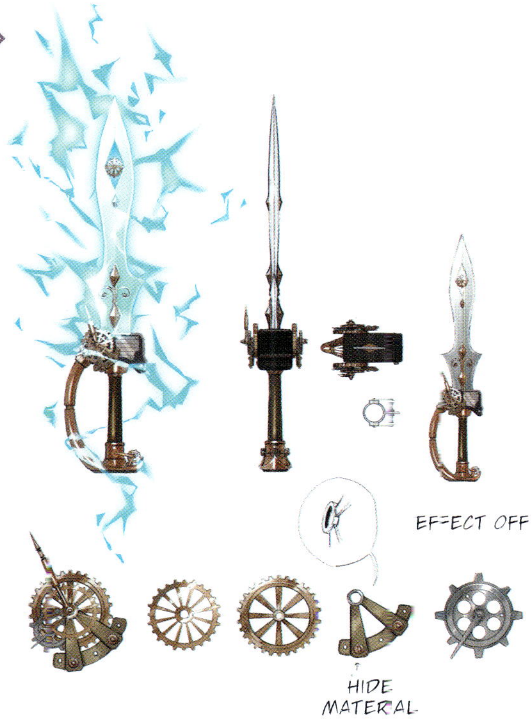

EFFECT OFF

HIDE MATERIAL

《 Patricia's Nagamaki (swords with long grip) Design Sketches 》

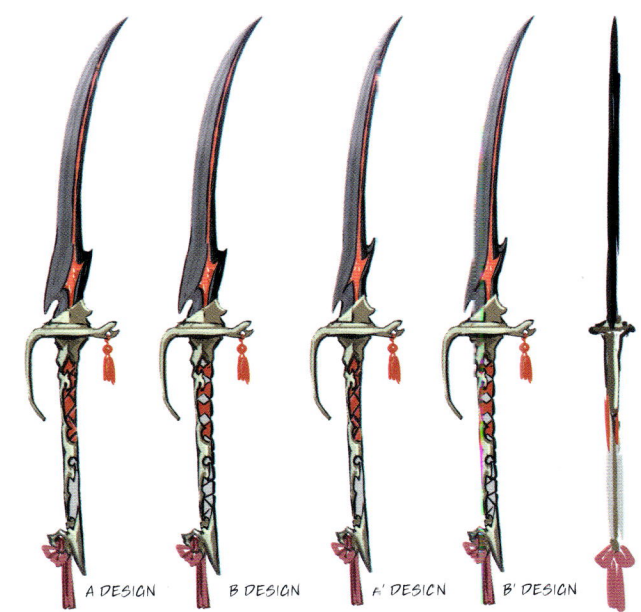

A DESIGN   B DESIGN   A' DESIGN   B' DESIGN

DESIGNS WITH AND WITHOUT CLOTH-WRAPPED HANDLE.

DESIGNS WITH THE BLADE ADJUSTED TO BE A LITTLE NARROWER.

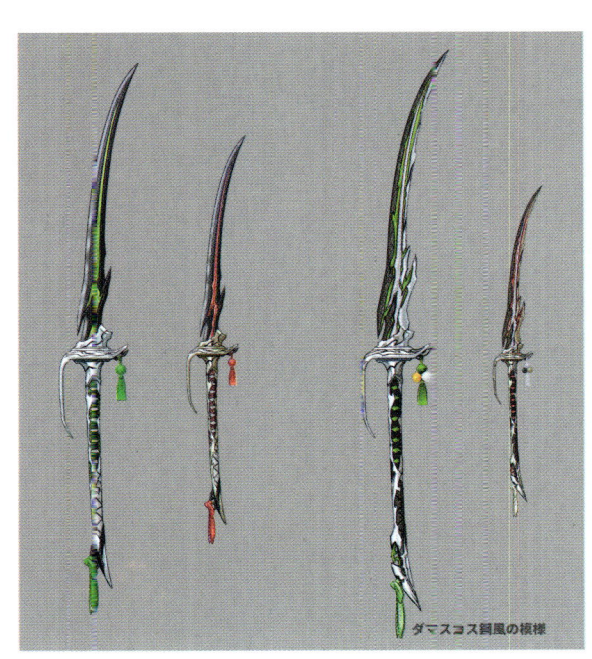

ダマスコス鋼風の模様

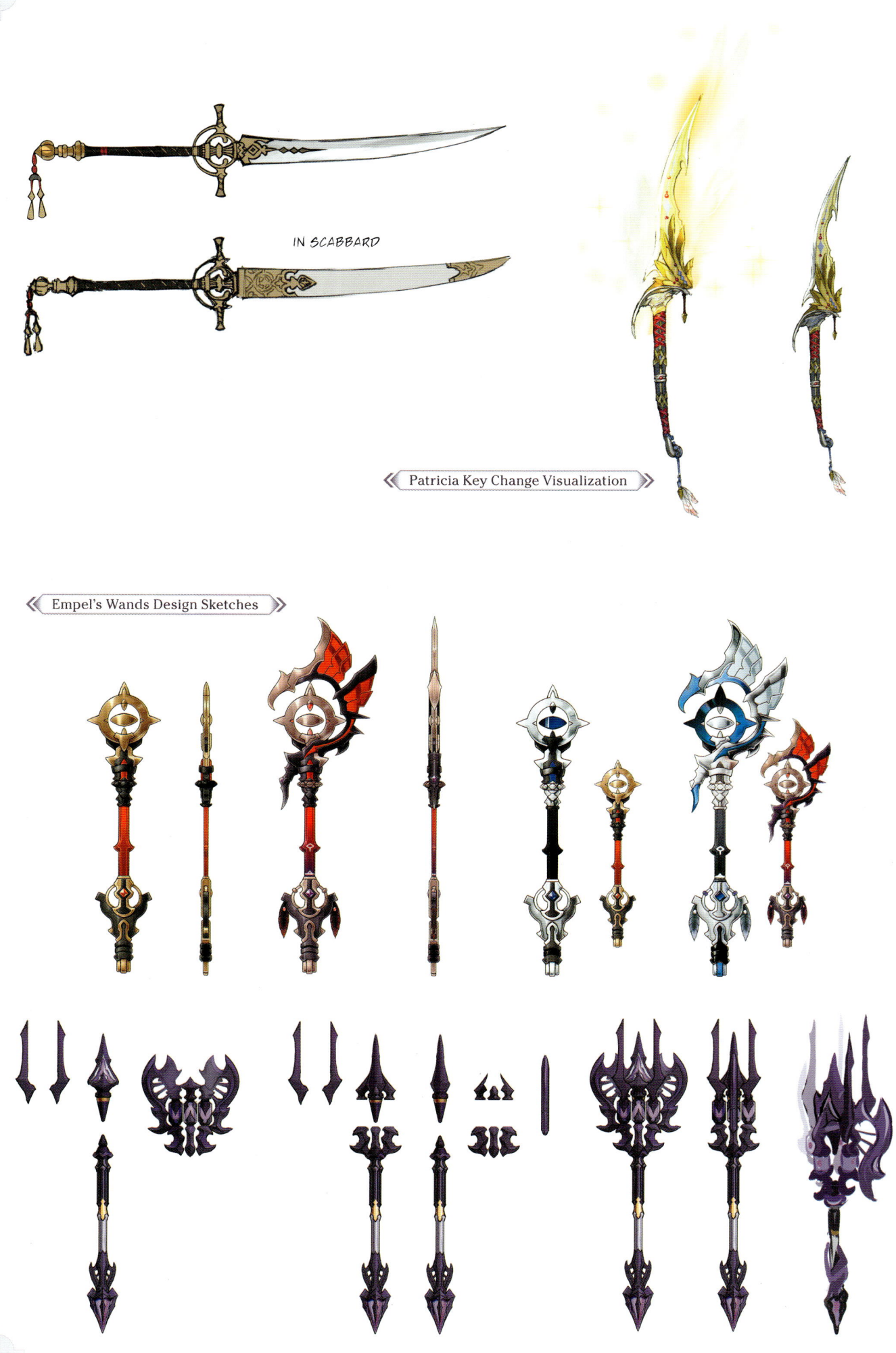

IN SCABBARD

Patricia Key Change Visualization

Empel's Wands Design Sketches

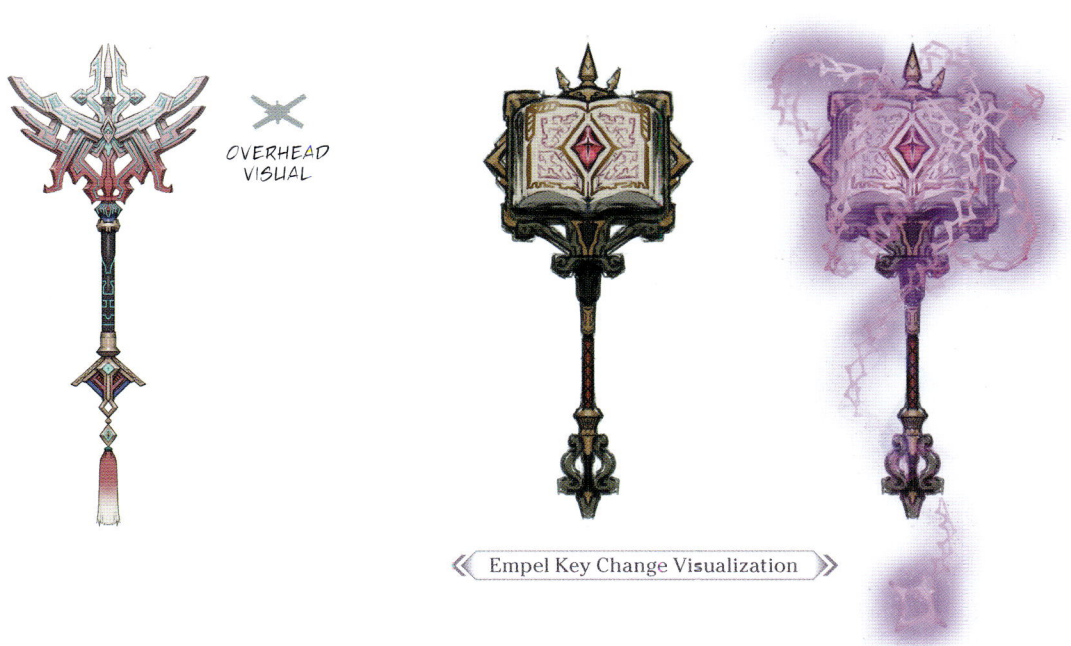

OVERHEAD VISUAL

《 Empel Key Change Visualization 》

《 Lila's Claws Design Sketches 》

《 Lila Key Change Visualization 》

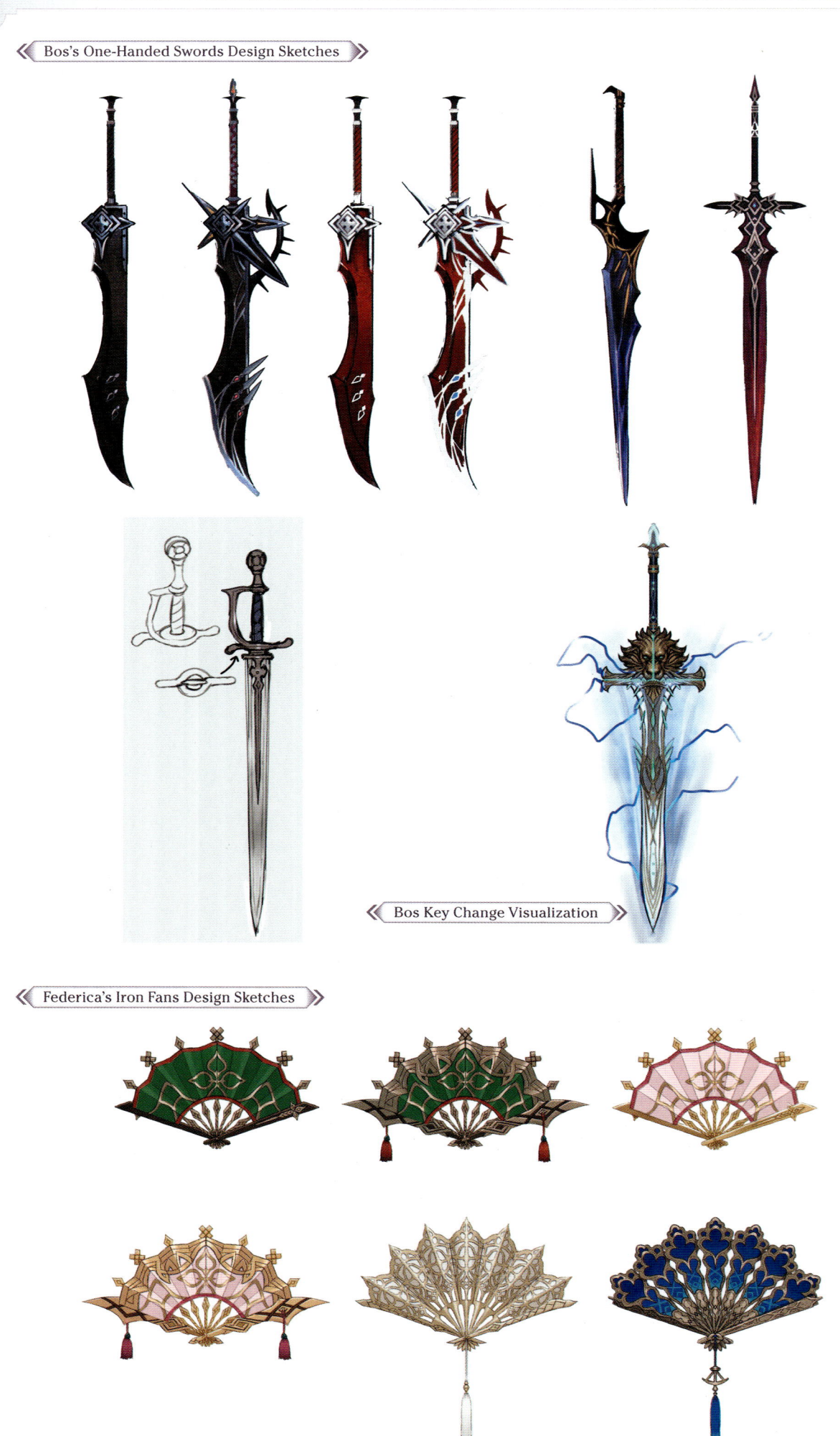

Bos's One-Handed Swords Design Sketches

Bos Key Change Visualization

Federica's Iron Fans Design Sketches

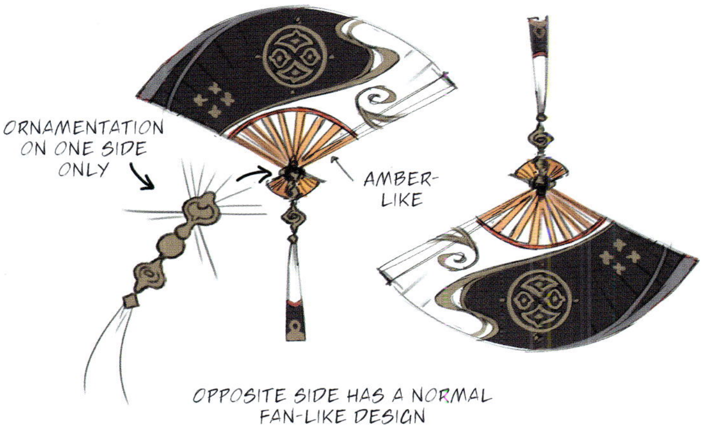

ORNAMENTATION ON ONE SIDE ONLY

AMBER-LIKE

OPPOSITE SIDE HAS A NORMAL FAN-LIKE DESIGN

《 Federica Key Change Visualization 》

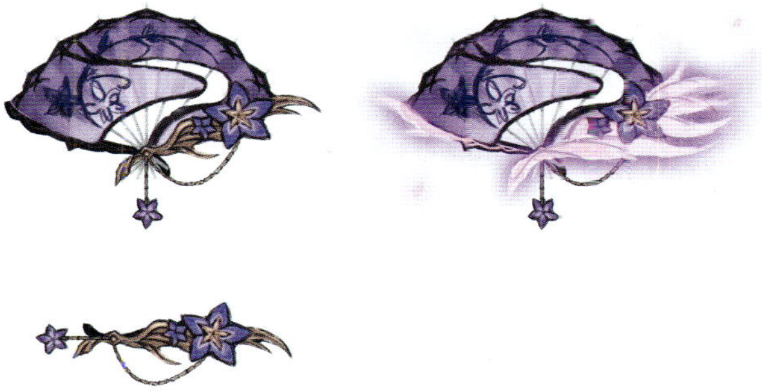

《 Dian's Battleaxes Design Sketches 》

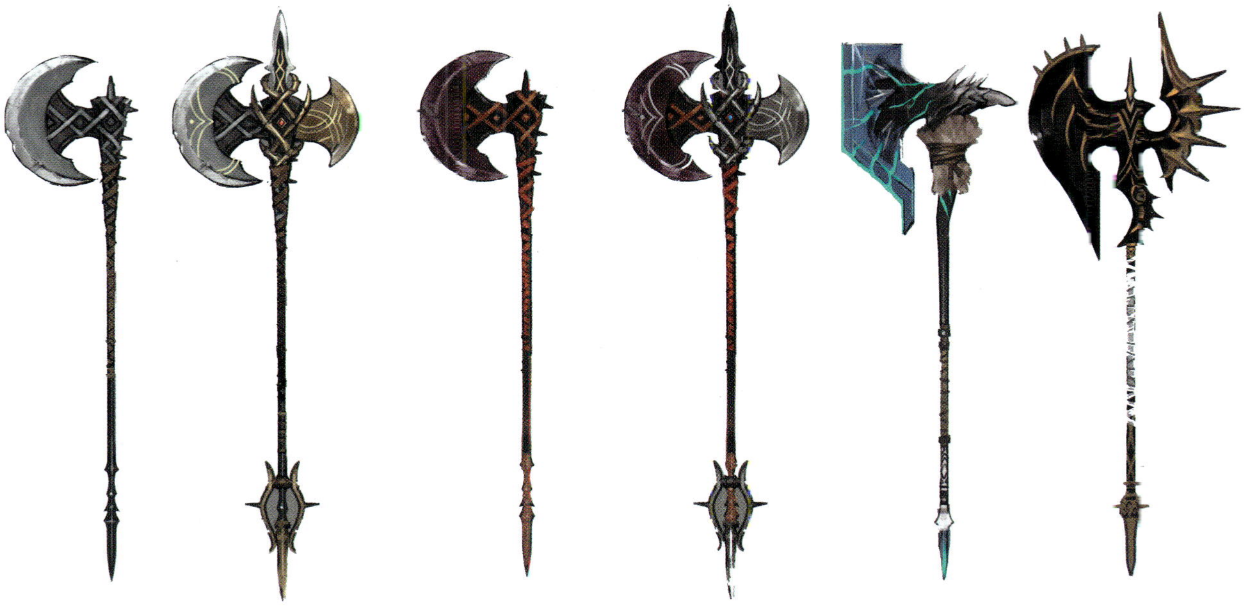

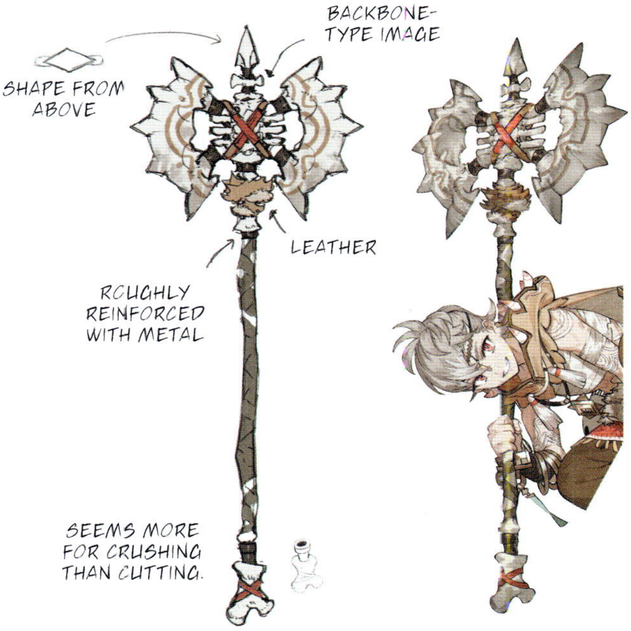

SHAPE FROM ABOVE

BACKBONE-TYPE IMAGE

LEATHER

ROUGHLY REINFORCED WITH METAL

SEEMS MORE FOR CRUSHING THAN CUTTING.

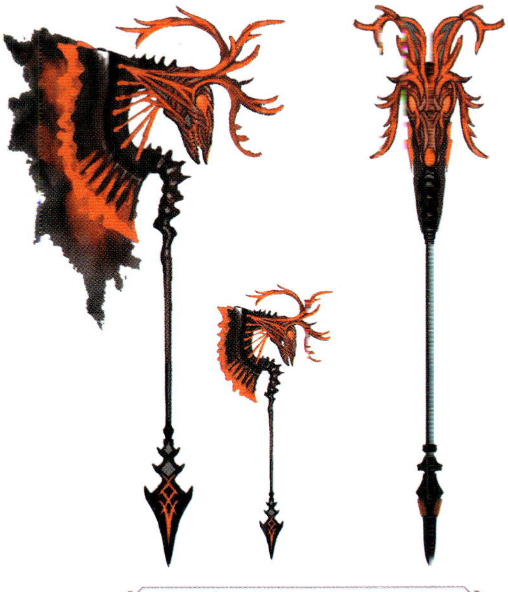

《 Dian Key Change Visualization 》

《 Kala's Warhammers Design Sketches 》

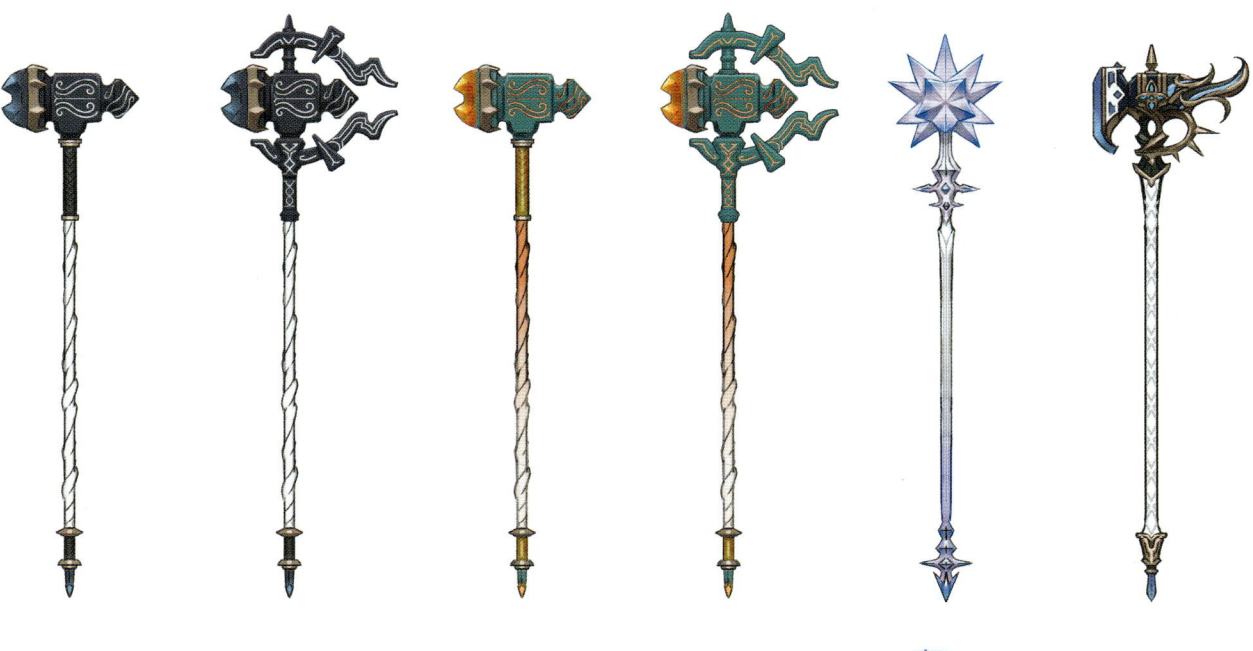

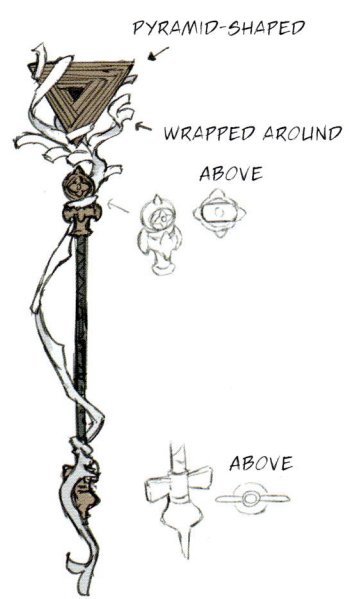

PYRAMID-SHAPED
WRAPPED AROUND
ABOVE
ABOVE

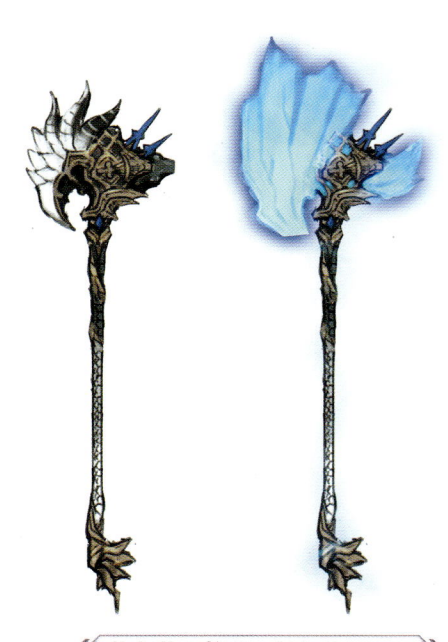

《 Kala Key Change Visualization 》

《 Federica's Pendant Design Sketch 》

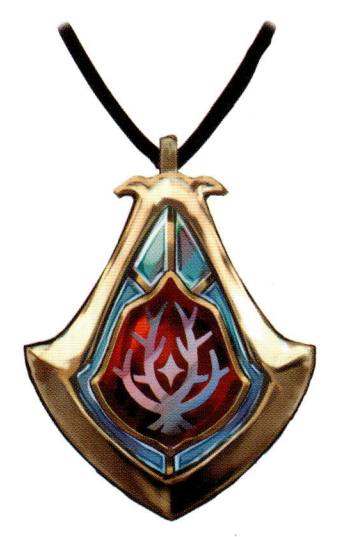

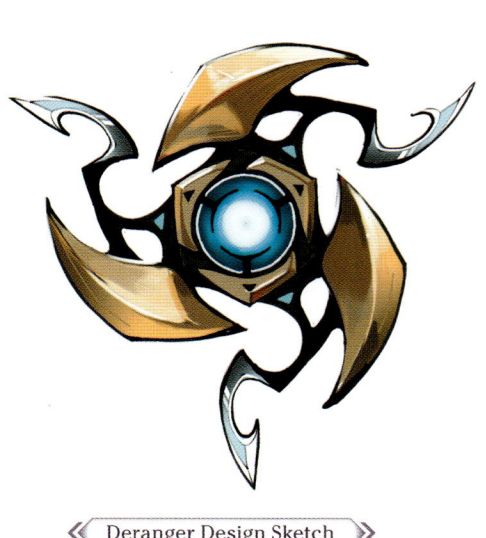

《 Deranger Design Sketch 》

《 Emil's Tablets Design Sketches 》

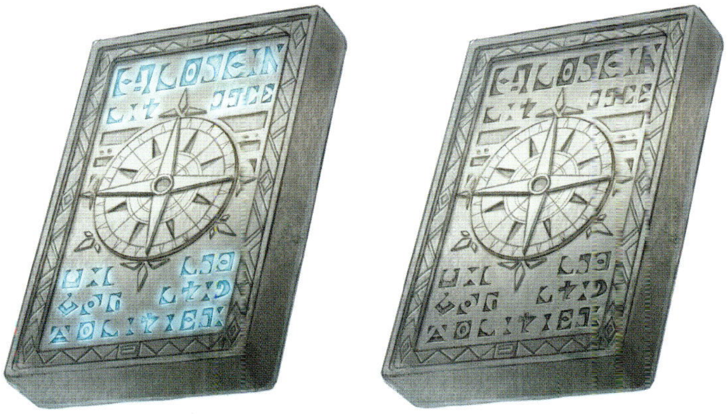

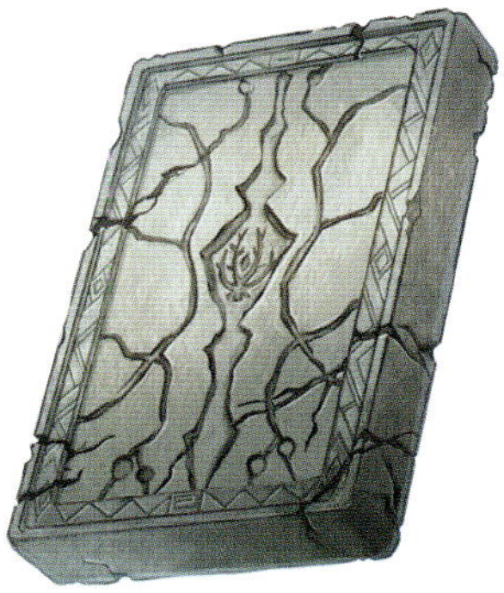

《 Old Tablet Design Sketches 》

《 Fairystone Light - Improved Design Sketches 》

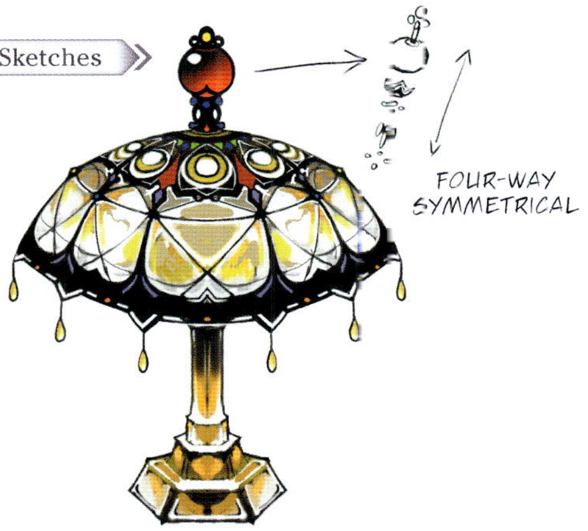

《 Fairystone Light Design Sketches 》

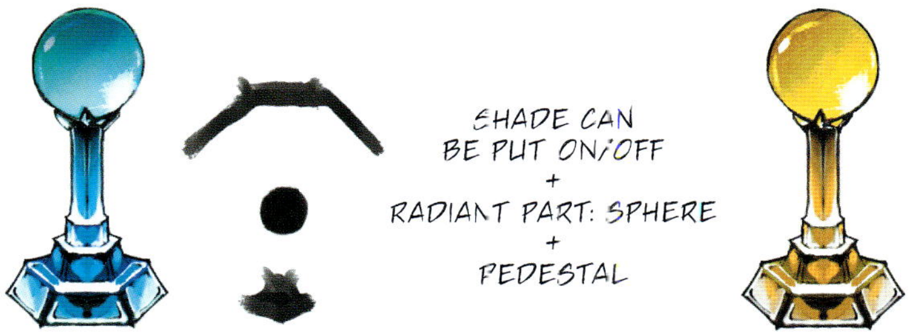

SHADE CAN
BE PUT ON/OFF
+
RADIANT PART: SPHERE
+
PEDESTAL

FOUR-WAY
SYMMETRICAL

《 Seeds of Light Design Sketches 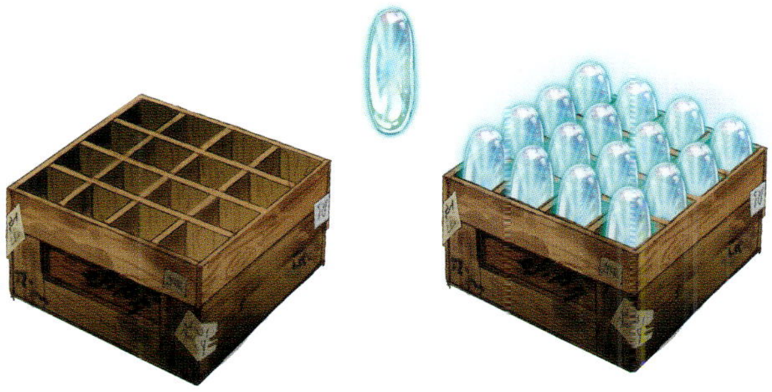 》　　《 Seeds of Light - Improved Design Sketches 》

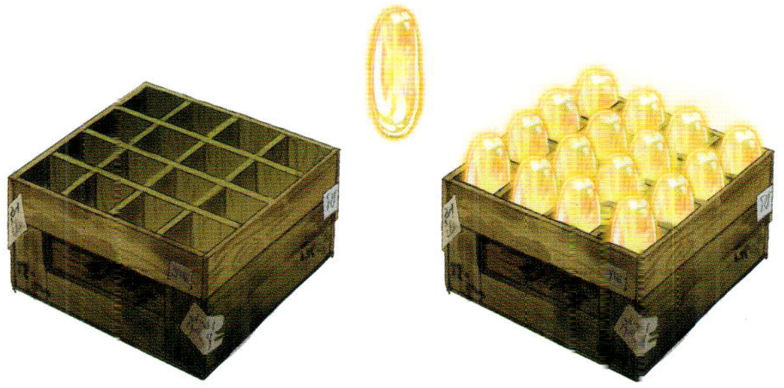

《 Chart of Another Sky Design Sketch 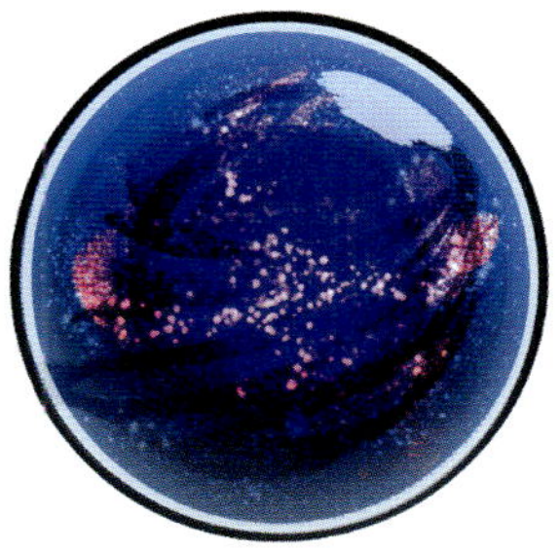 》　　《 Celestial Globe of Another Sky Design Sketch 》

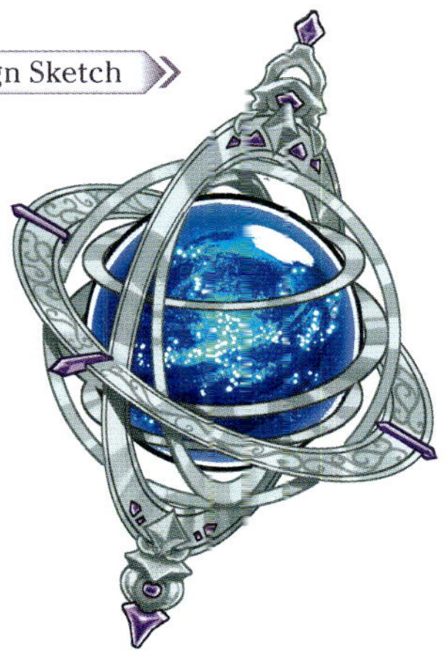

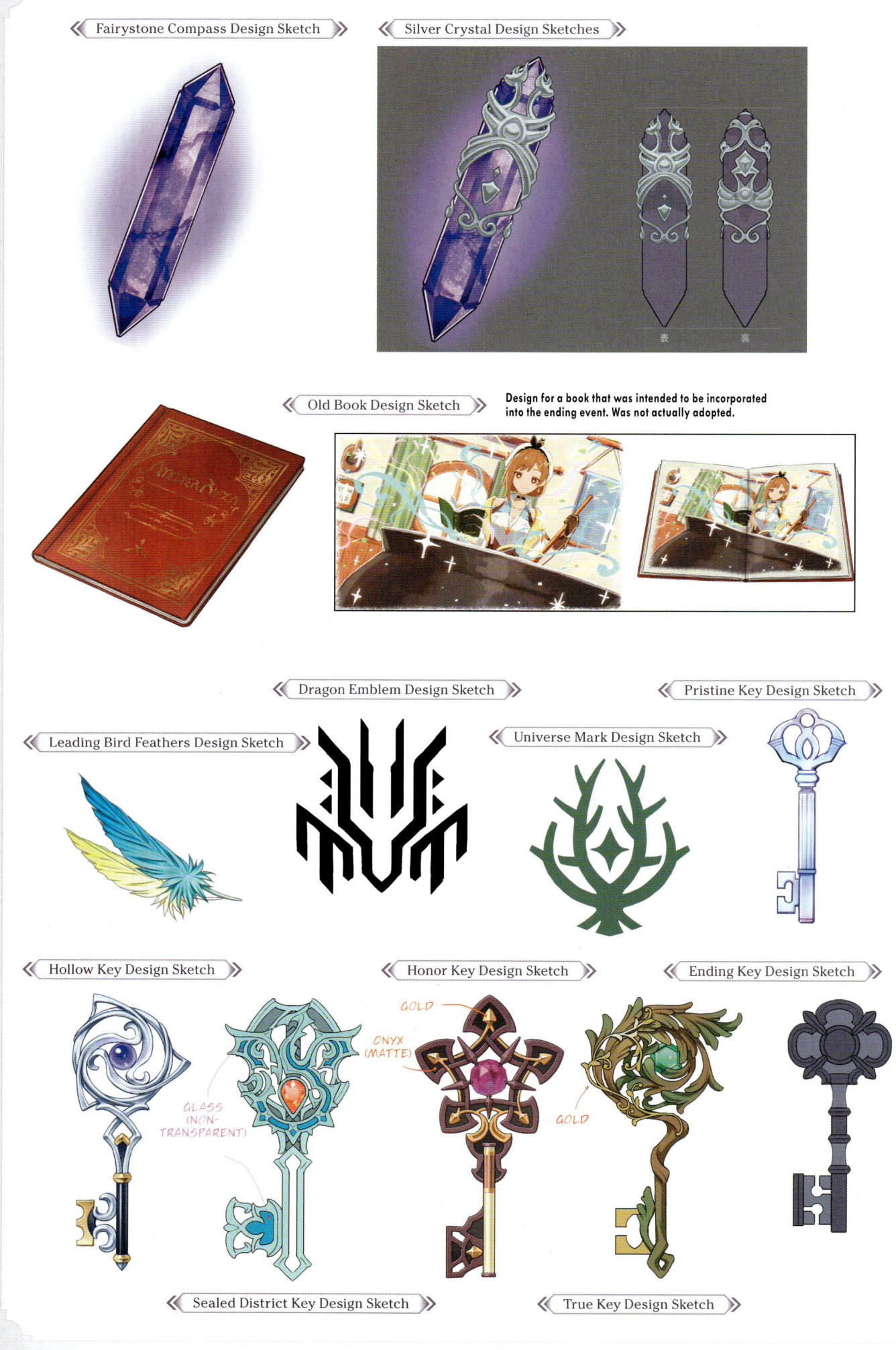

Star-type Keys Design Sketches

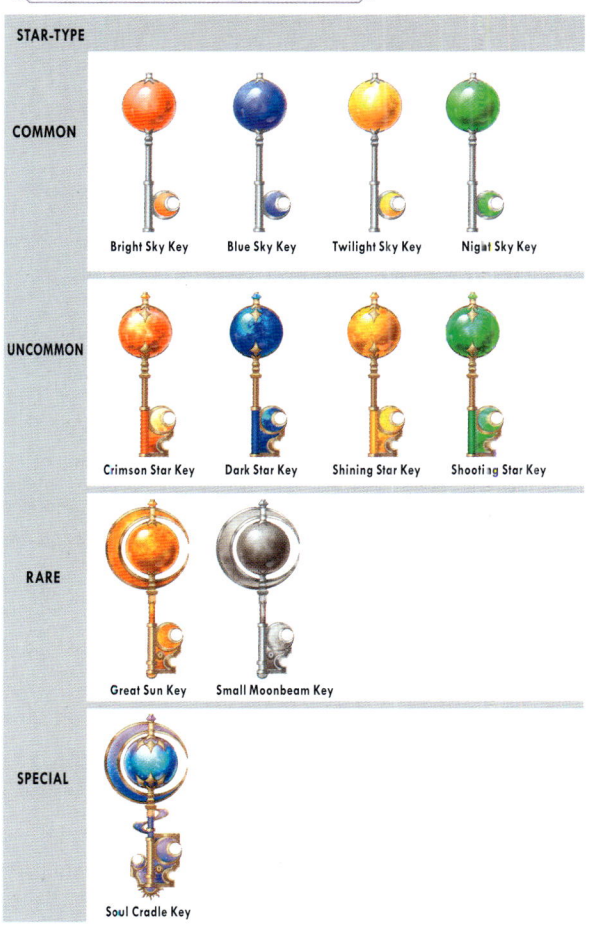

Gear-type Keys Design Sketches

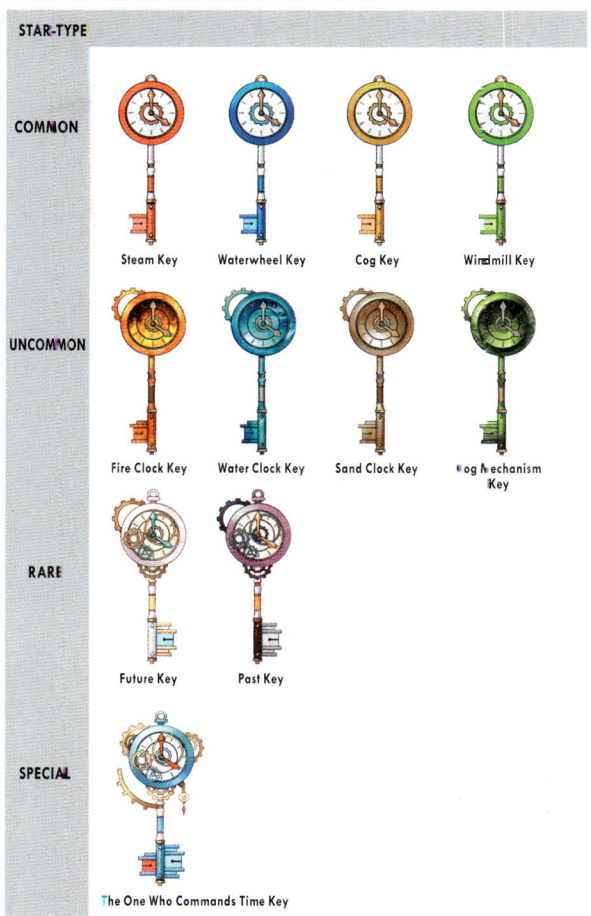

Ore-type Key Design Sketches

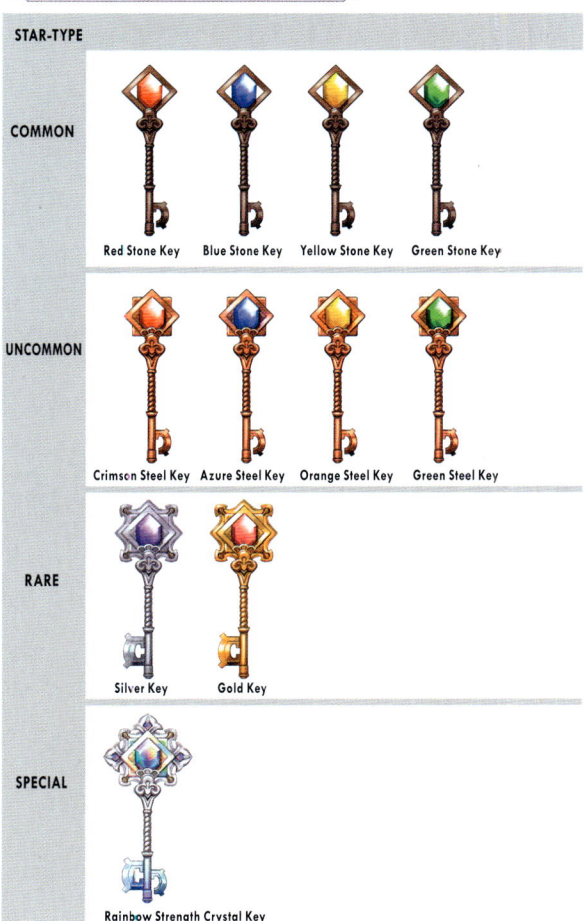

Key Overview Design Sketches

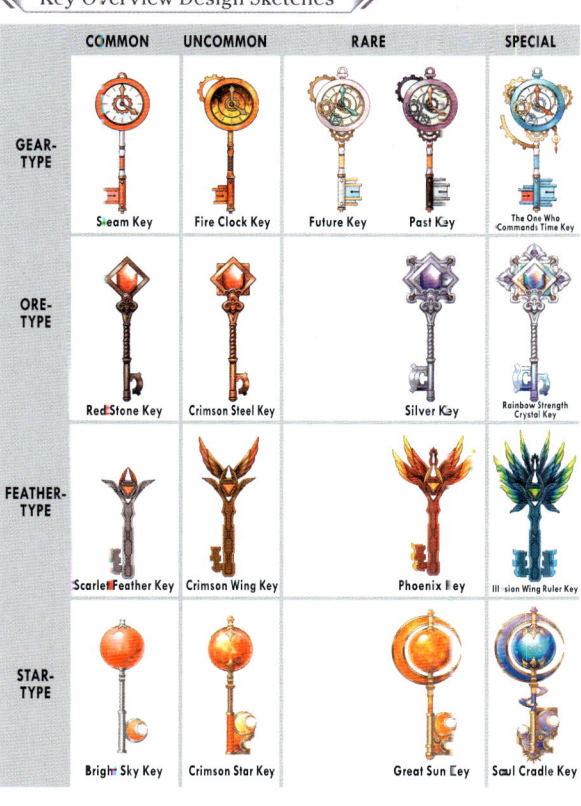

Skill Effect: Ryza Design Sketches

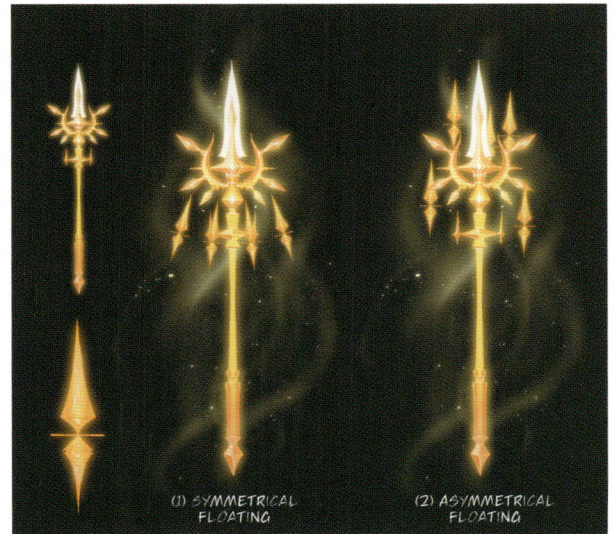

Skill Effect: Klaudia Design Sketches

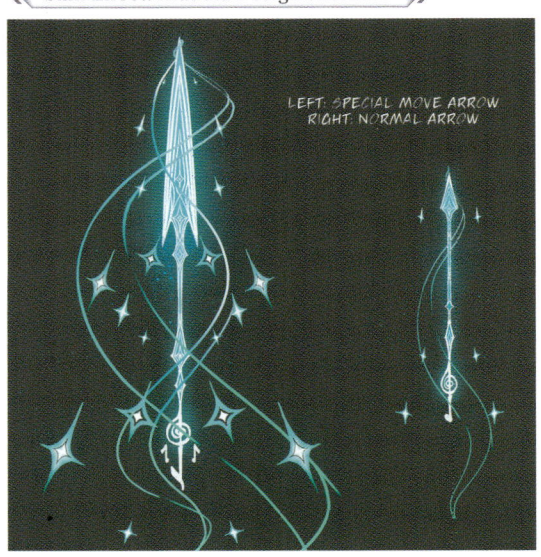

Skill Effect: Empel Design Sketches

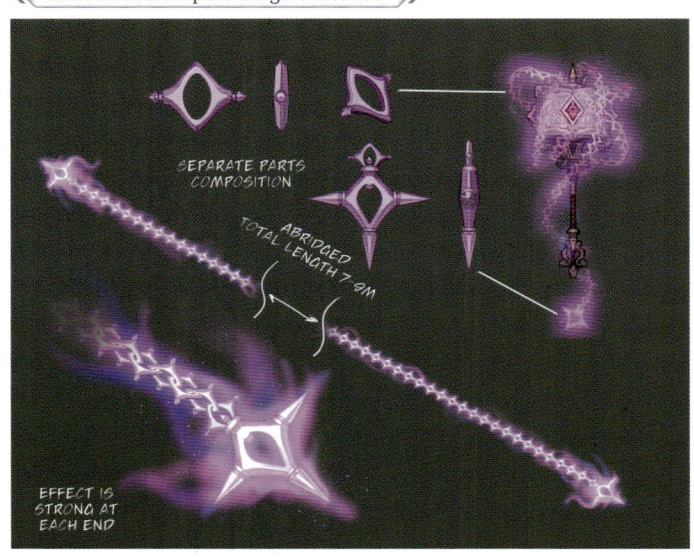

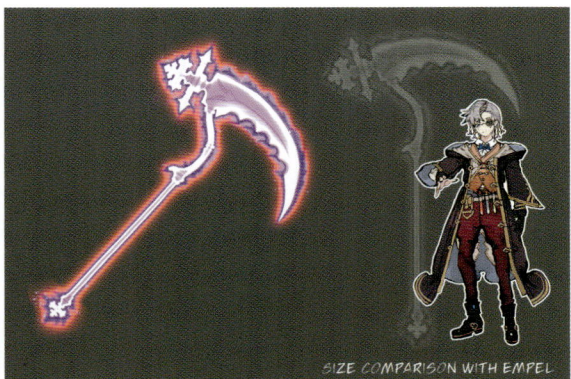

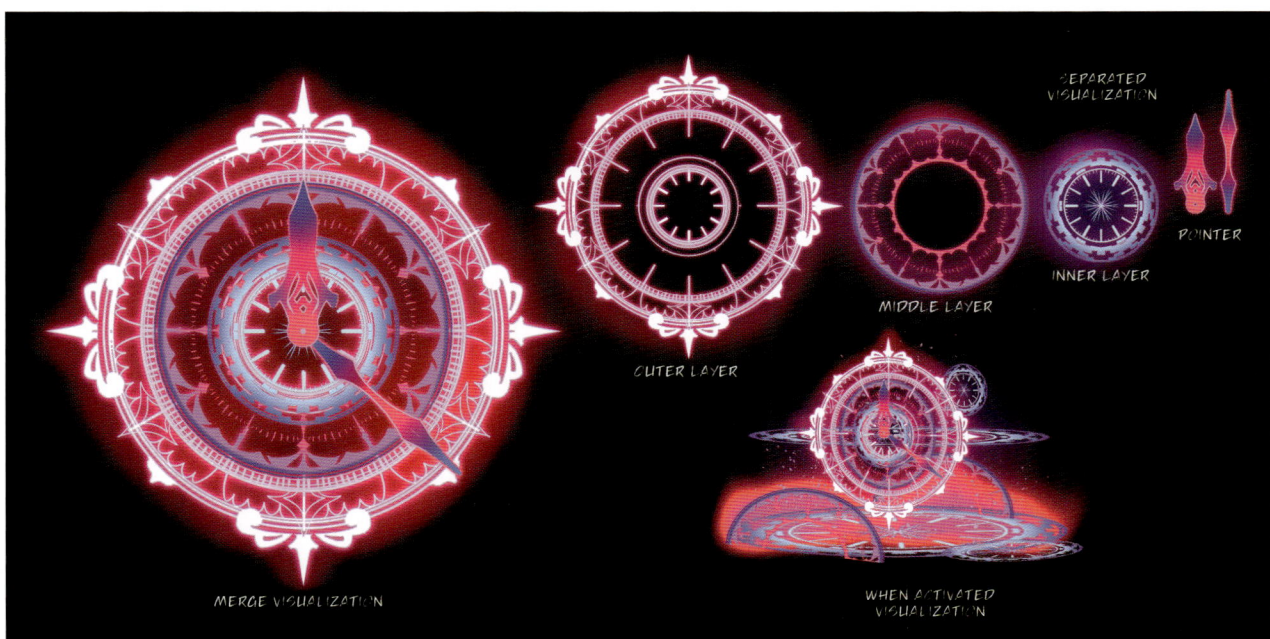

Skill Effect: Federica Design Sketches

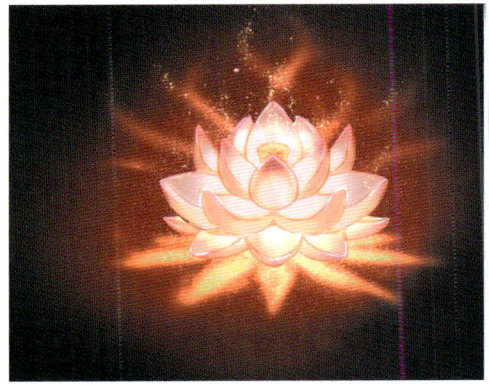
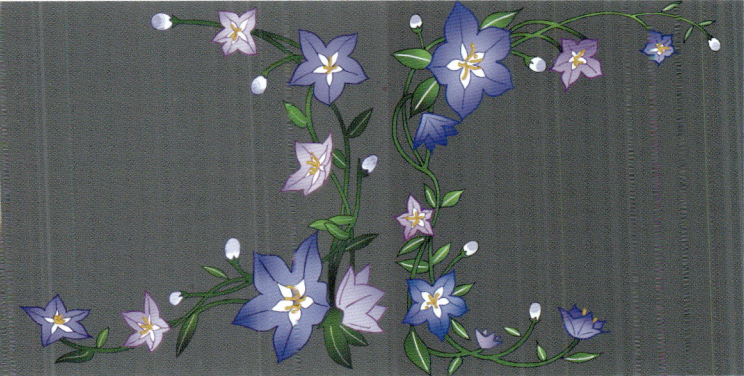

Atelier Exterior Design Sketches

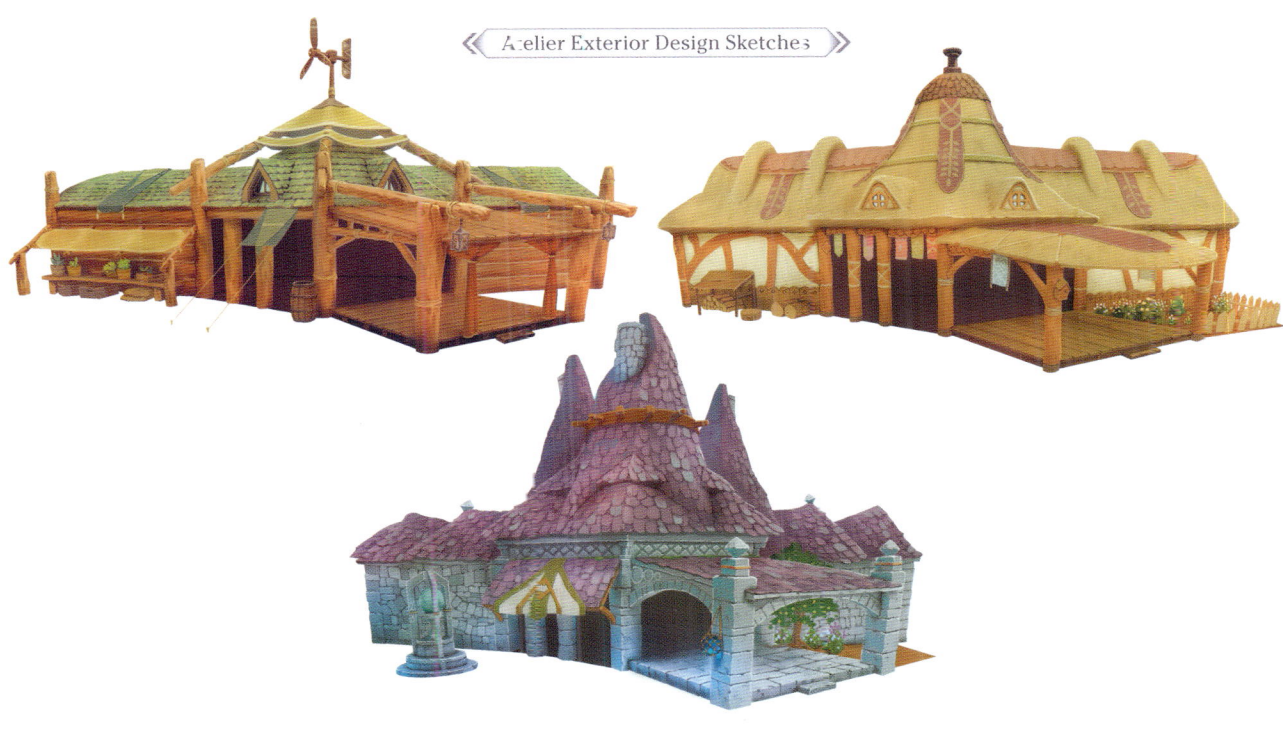

Atelier Exterior Sample Designs

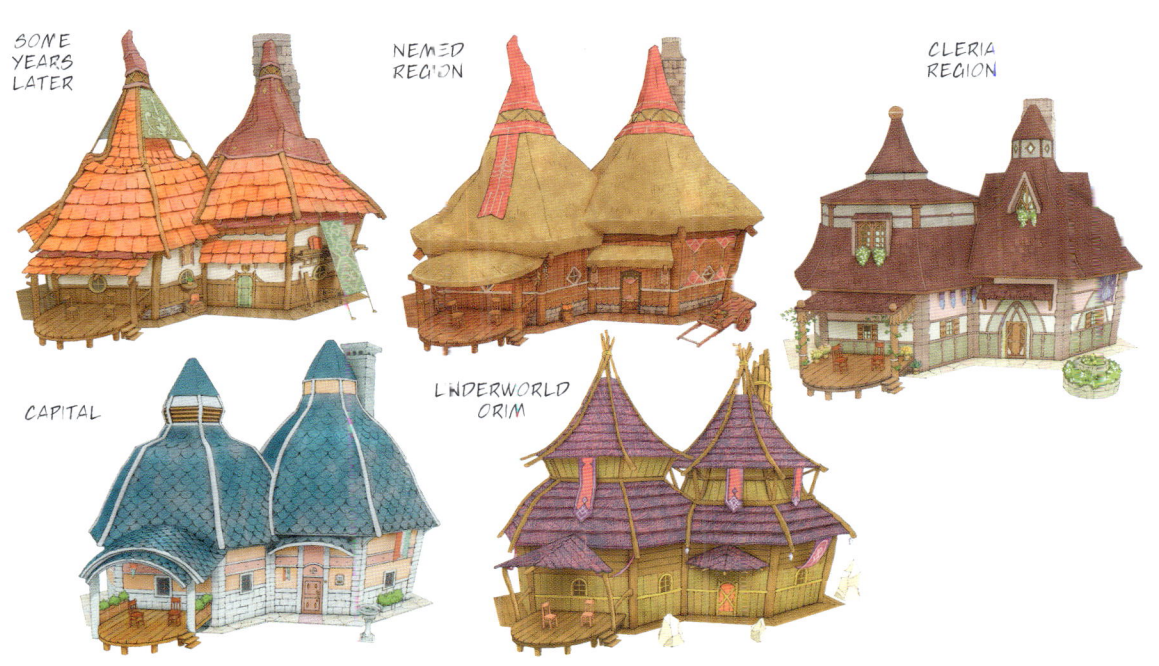

SOME YEARS LATER

NEMED REGION

CLERIA REGION

CAPITAL

UNDERWORLD ORIM

Atelier Interior Sample Designs

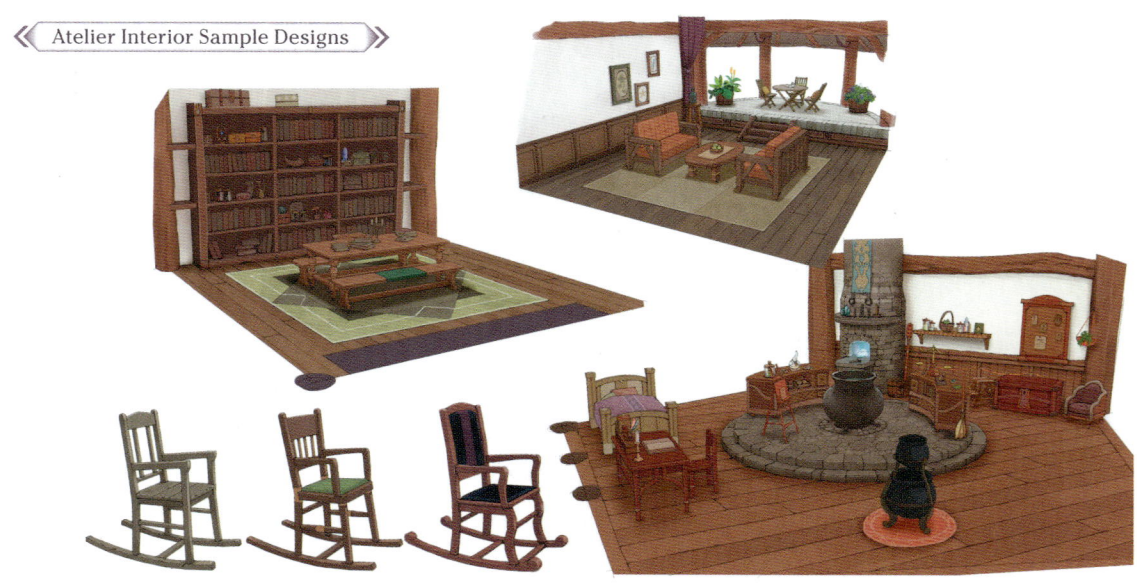

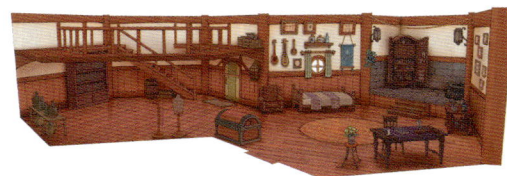
SOME YEARS LATER

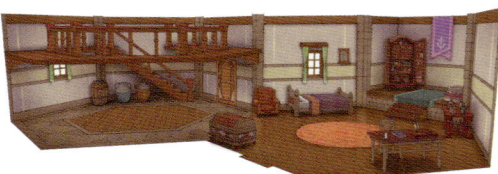
CLERIA REGION

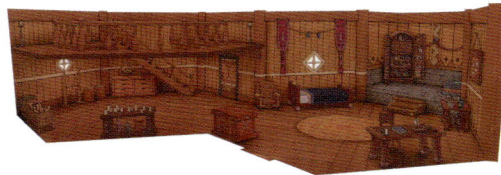
NEMED REGION

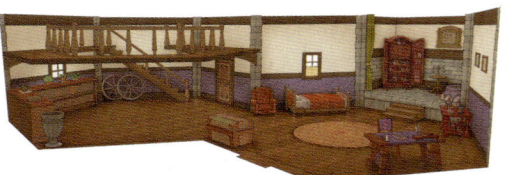
CAPITAL

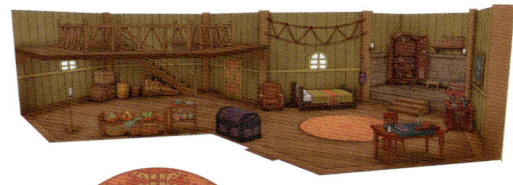
UNDERWORLD ORIM

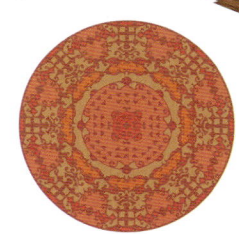

Atelier Additions Design Sketches

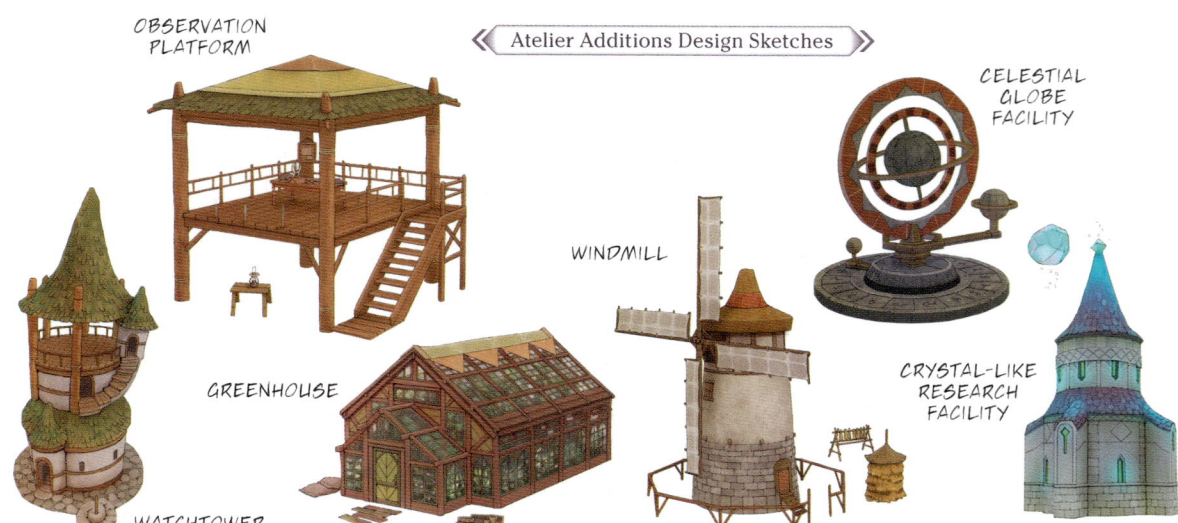

OBSERVATION PLATFORM

CELESTIAL GLOBE FACILITY

WINDMILL

CRYSTAL-LIKE RESEARCH FACILITY

GREENHOUSE

WATCHTOWER

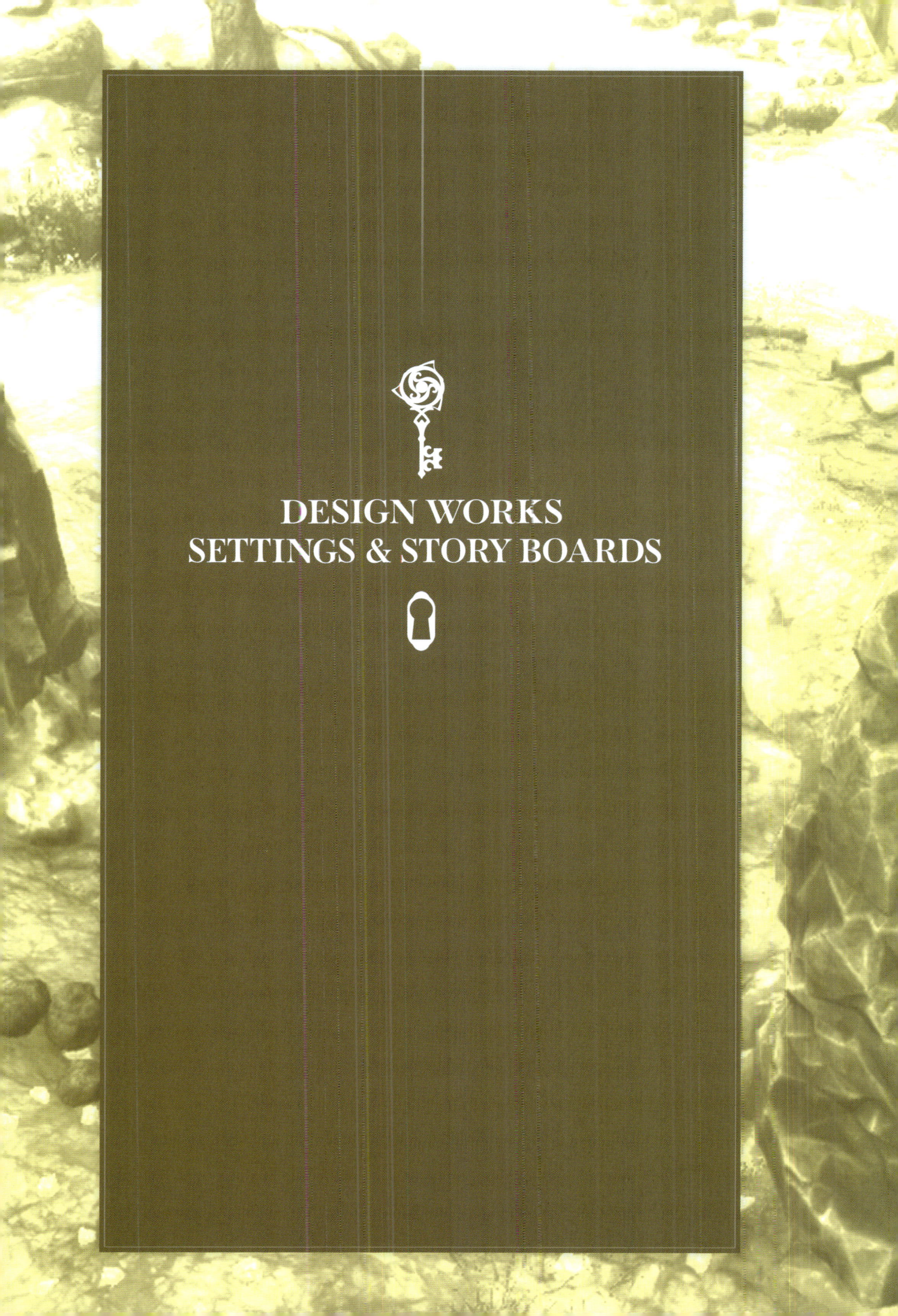

DESIGN WORKS
SETTINGS & STORY BOARDS

Settings

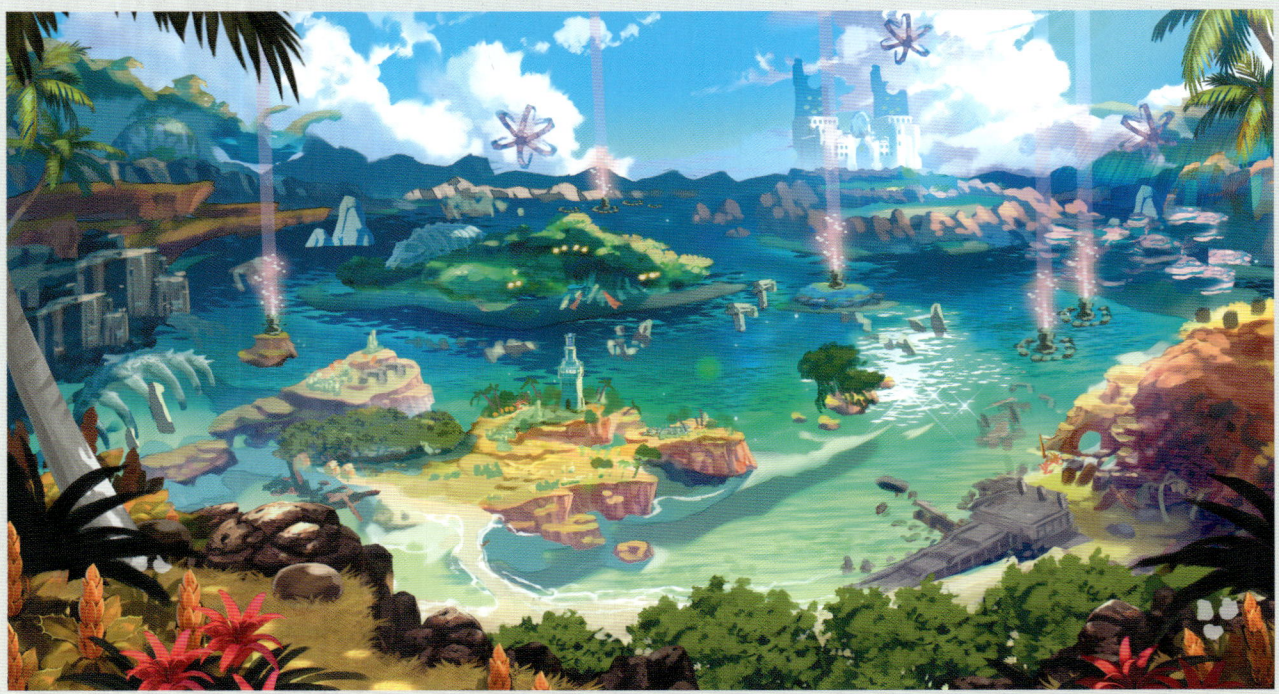

《 Kark Isles bird's eye view 》

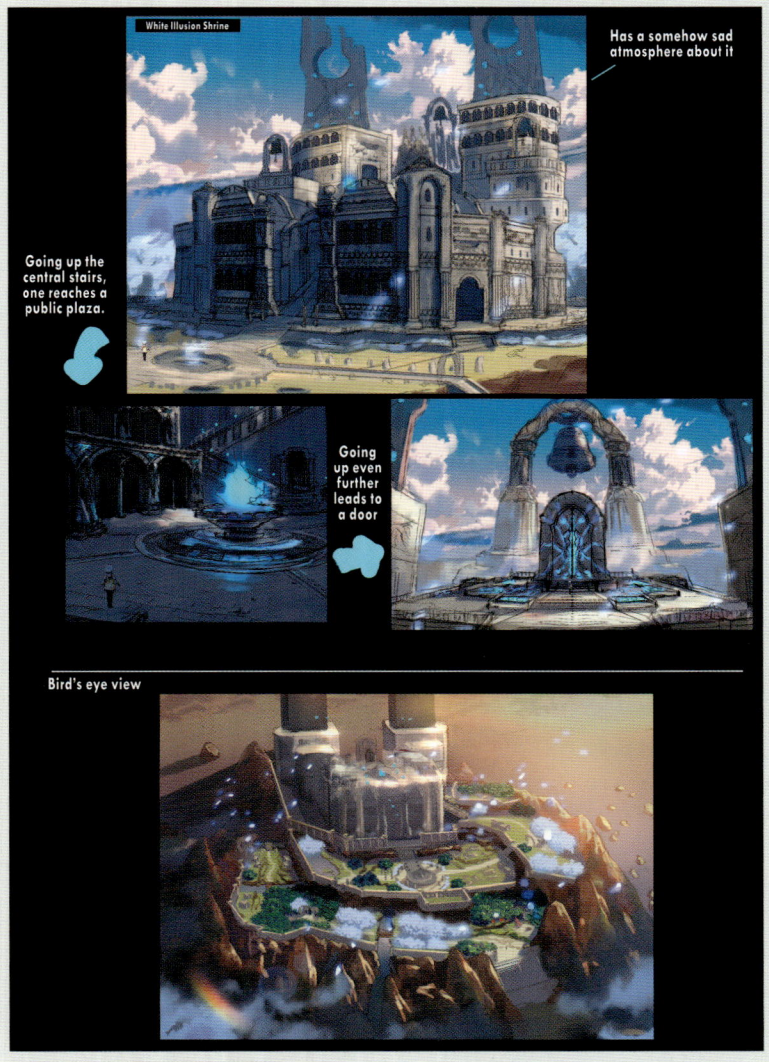

White Illusion Shrine — Has a somehow sad atmosphere about it

Going up the central stairs, one reaches a public plaza.

Going up even further leads to a door

Bird's eye view

《 Kark Isles Ruins Island 》

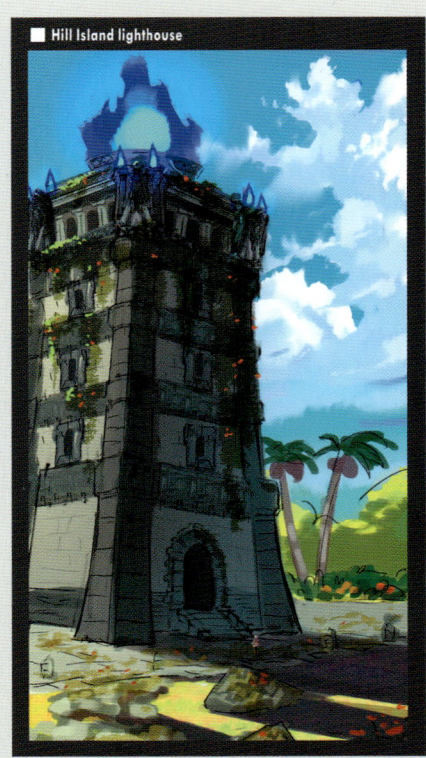

■ Hill Island lighthouse

《 Kark Isles Lighthouse 》

« Kark Isles Rock Island »

■ Rock Island... motifs are roughness and square shapes.

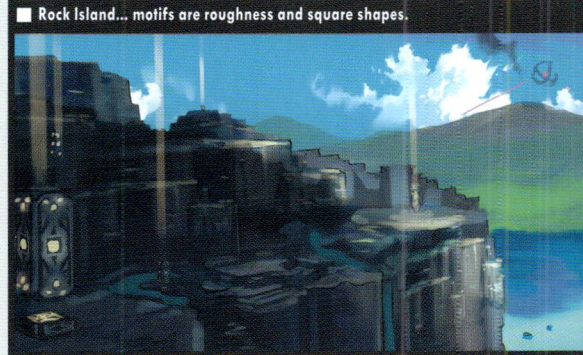

« Kark Isles Reef Island »

■ Reef Island... Feels like a closed off secluded region.
(The following is fantasy) (Delusion) The center of the islands when they were once connected, and older than the civilizations of each island. It was also the center of an energy explosion, and the island was made a forbidden region with a wall of reefs.

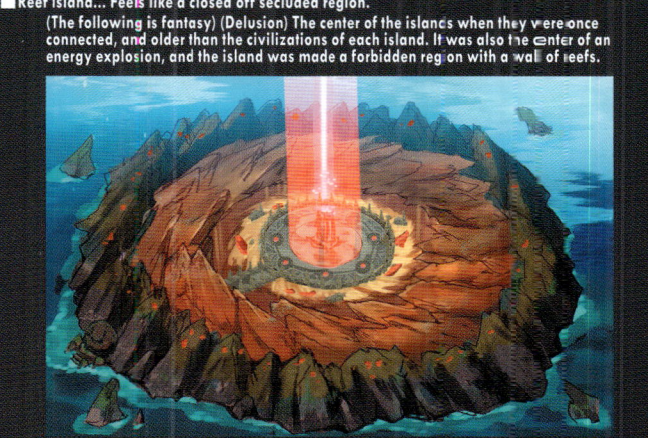

« Kark Isles Coral Island »

■ Coral Island... motif is a beautiful three-dimensional maze.

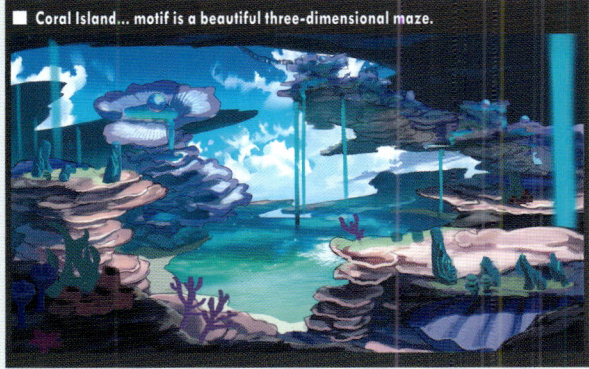

Forest Island... motif is sheltering. Adventures from open spaces to places where visibility is limited.

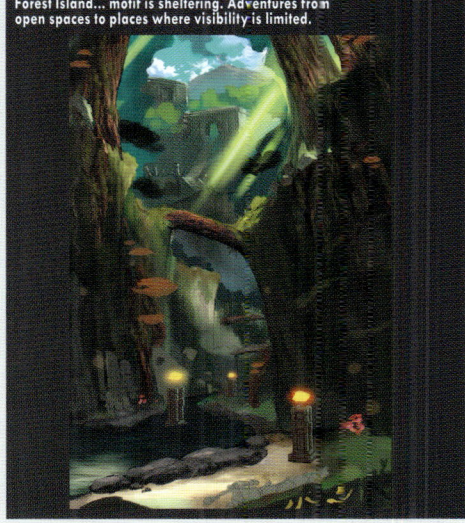

« Kark Isles Island Forest Island »

« Kark Isles Underwater Ruins »

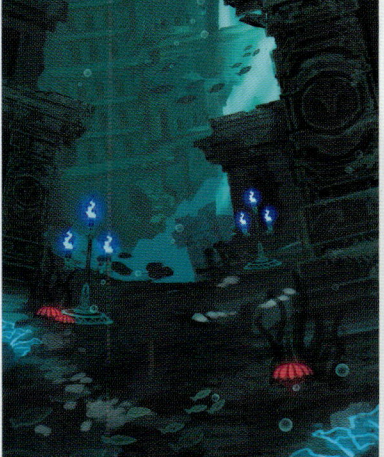

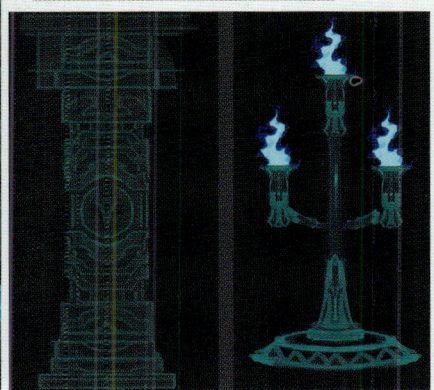

« Zipline Platform »

■ Zipline

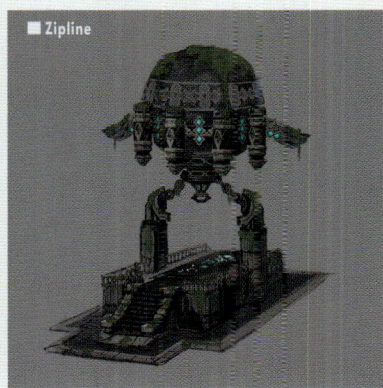

« Control System (not adopted) »

■ Control System

Assuming there will be moss, etc. depending on where it is placed.

When activated

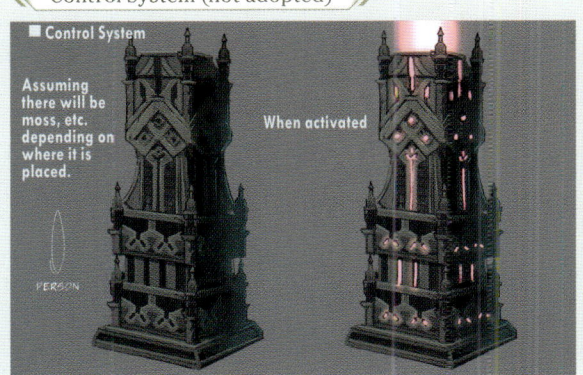

« Floating Object (not adopted) »

■ Floating Object

Assumed to have a stone texture.

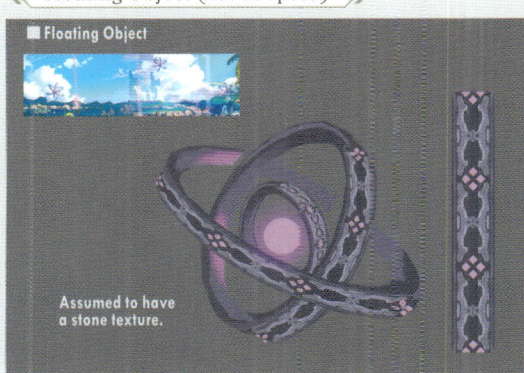

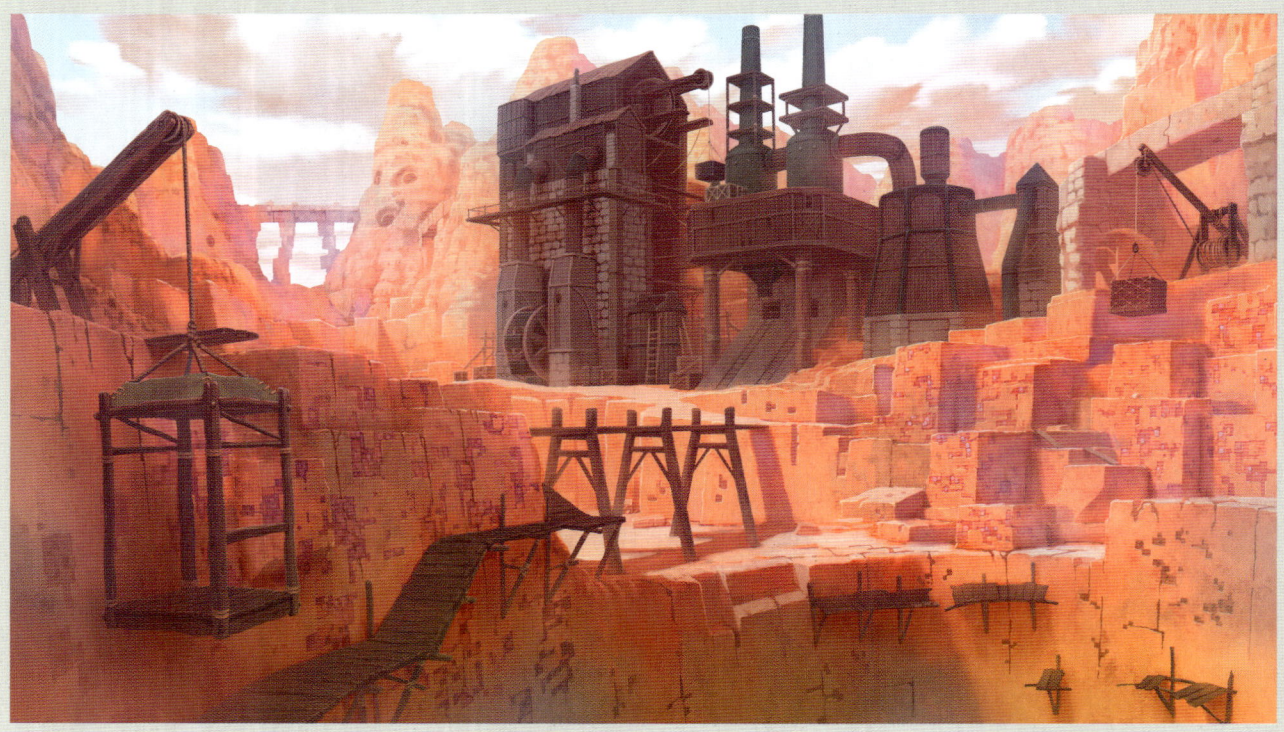

《 Cleria Region mountain district 》

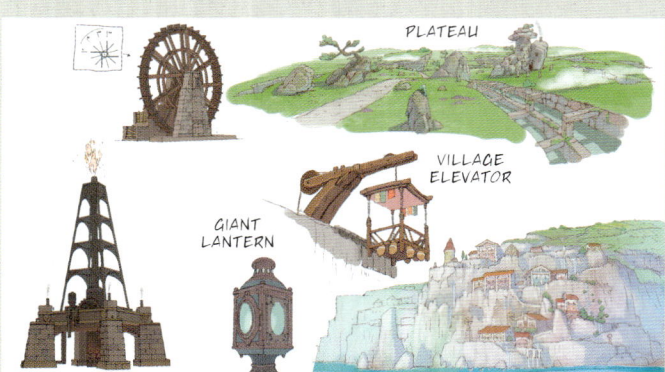

PLATEAU
VILLAGE ELEVATOR
GIANT LANTERN

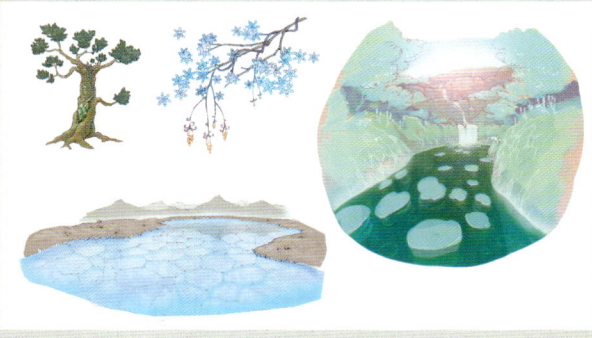

《 Cleria Region model sheets 》

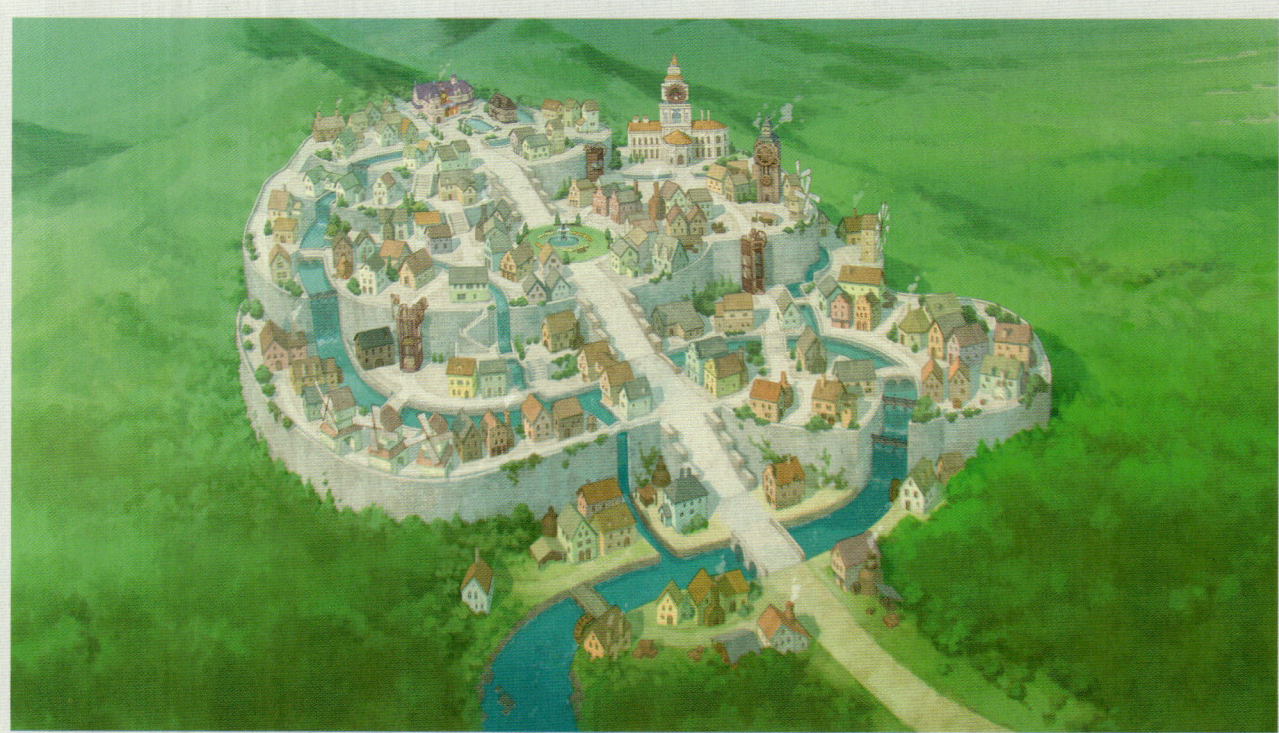

《 Cleria Region bird's eye view 》

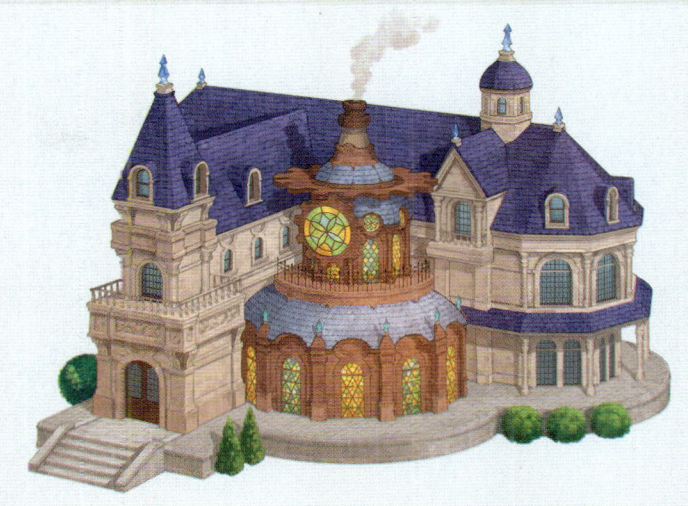
《 Cleria Region Artisan Union Headquarters 》

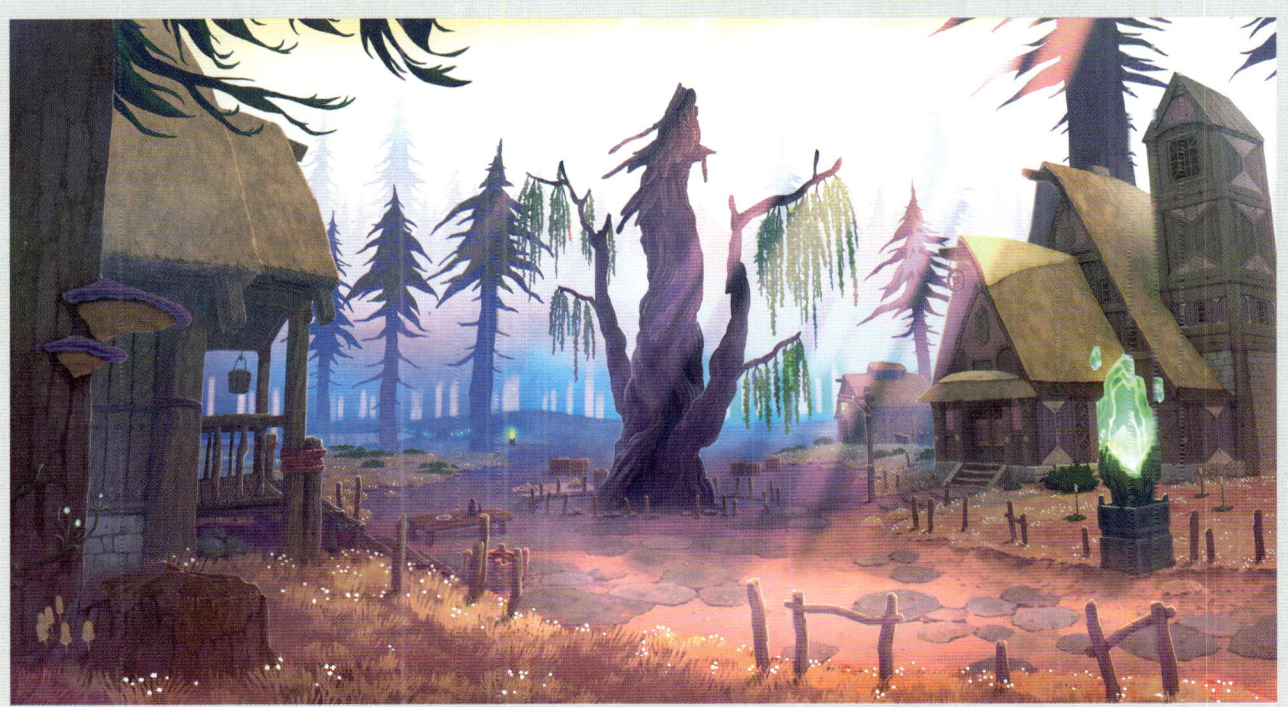
《 Nemed Region Faurre Village 》

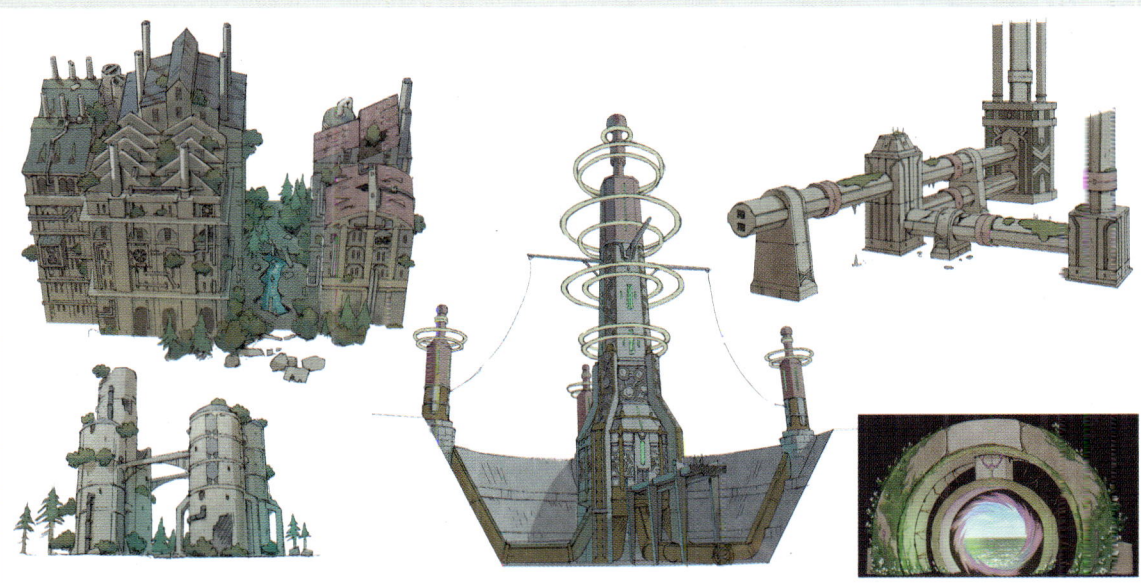
《 Nemed Region model sheets 》

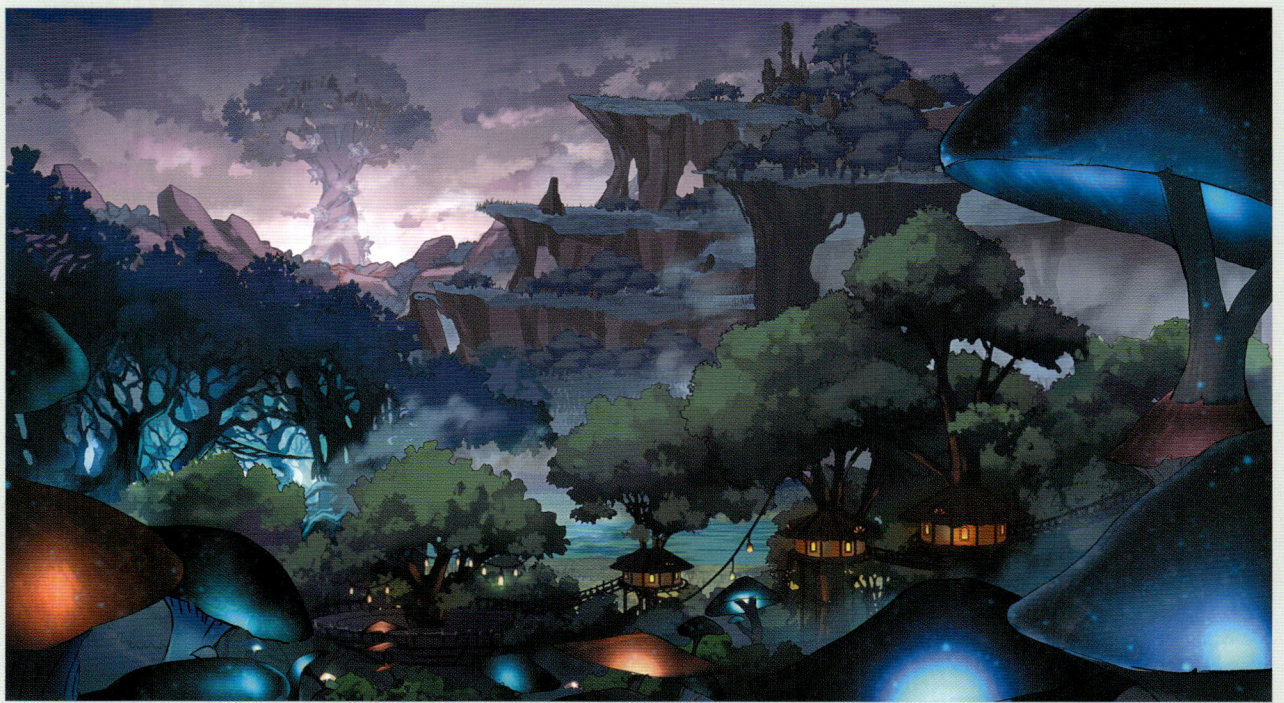
《 Windle panorama 》

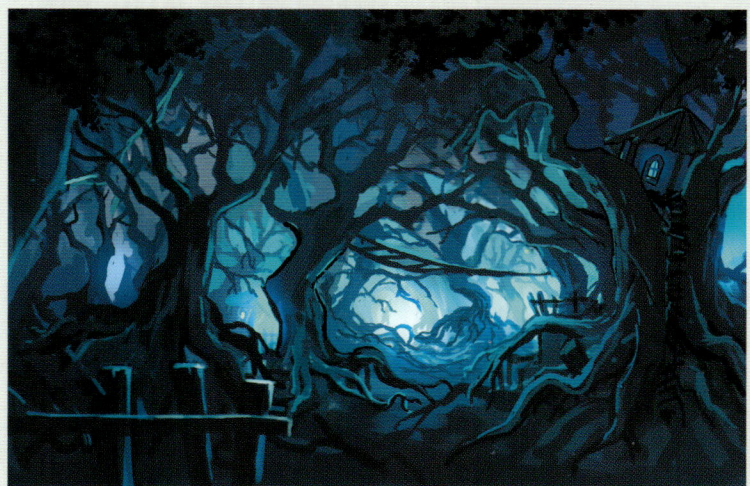
《 Underworld Forest 》

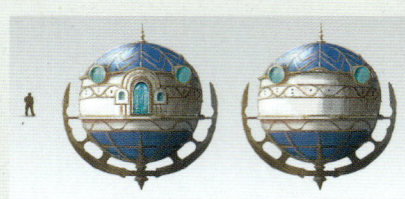
《 Code of the Universe, private home 》

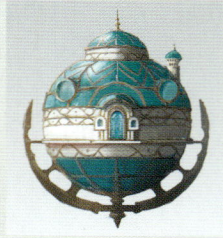
《 Code of the Universe, chief's house 》

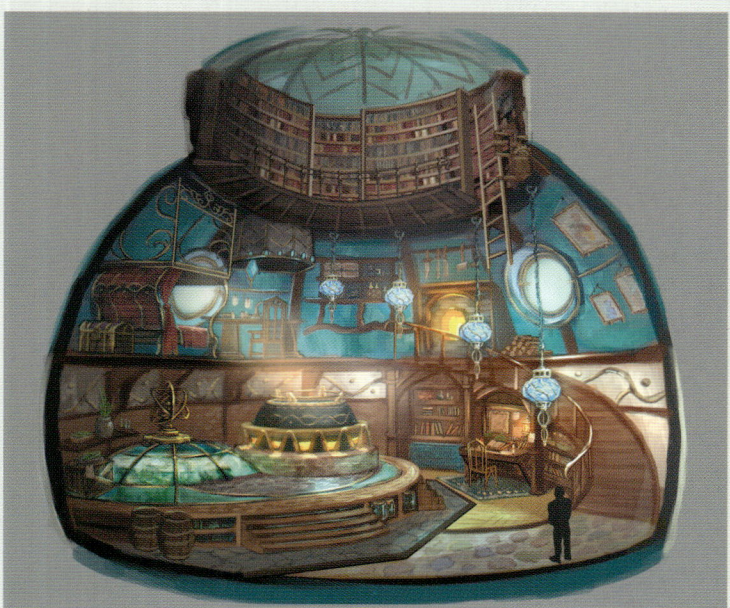
《 Code of the Universe middle level, residential district, chief's house interior 》

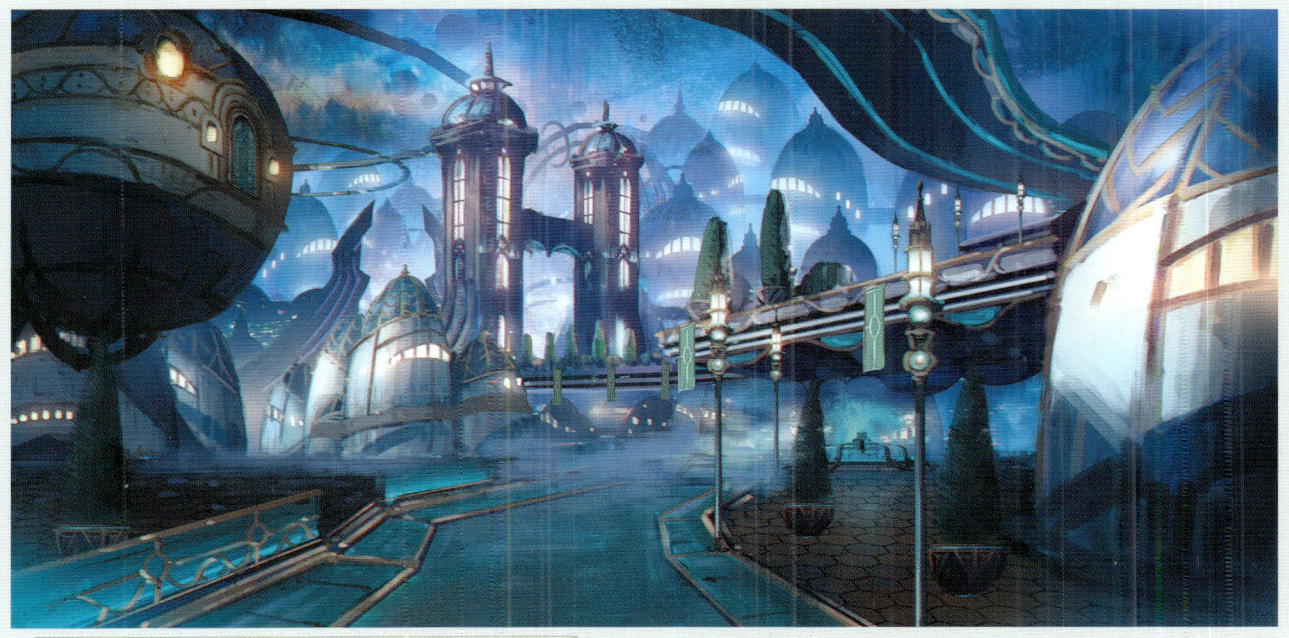

« Code of the Universe middle level, residential district »   « Code of the Universe middle level, workshop district »

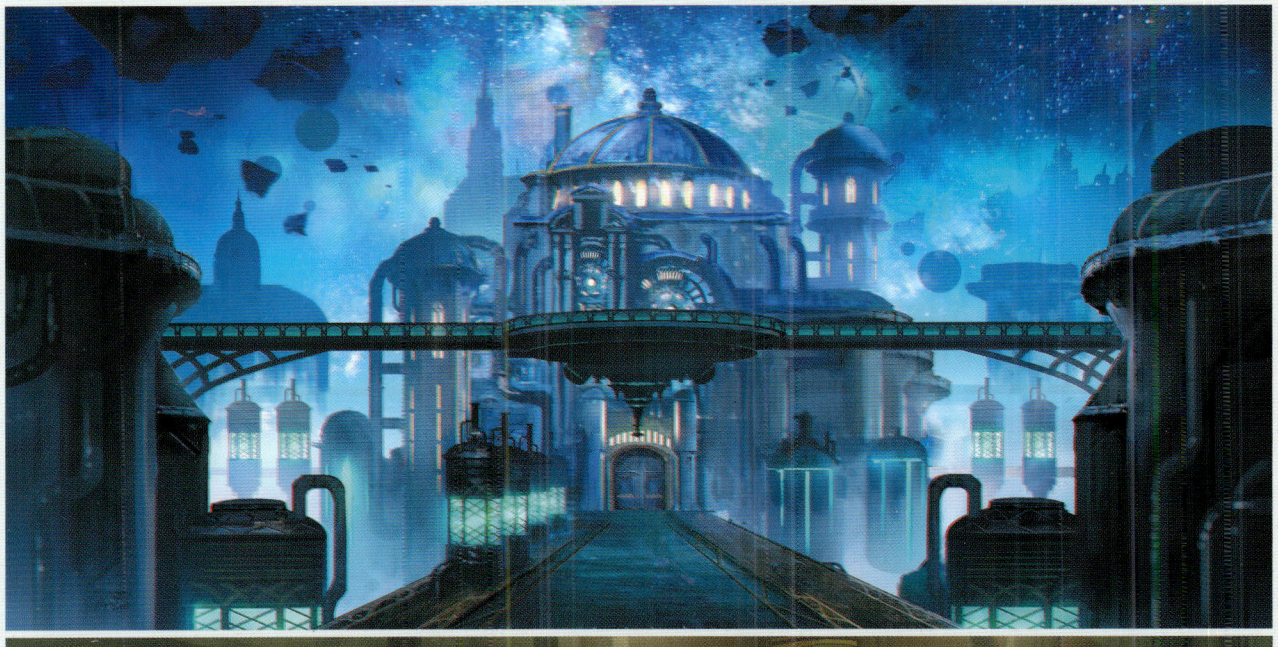

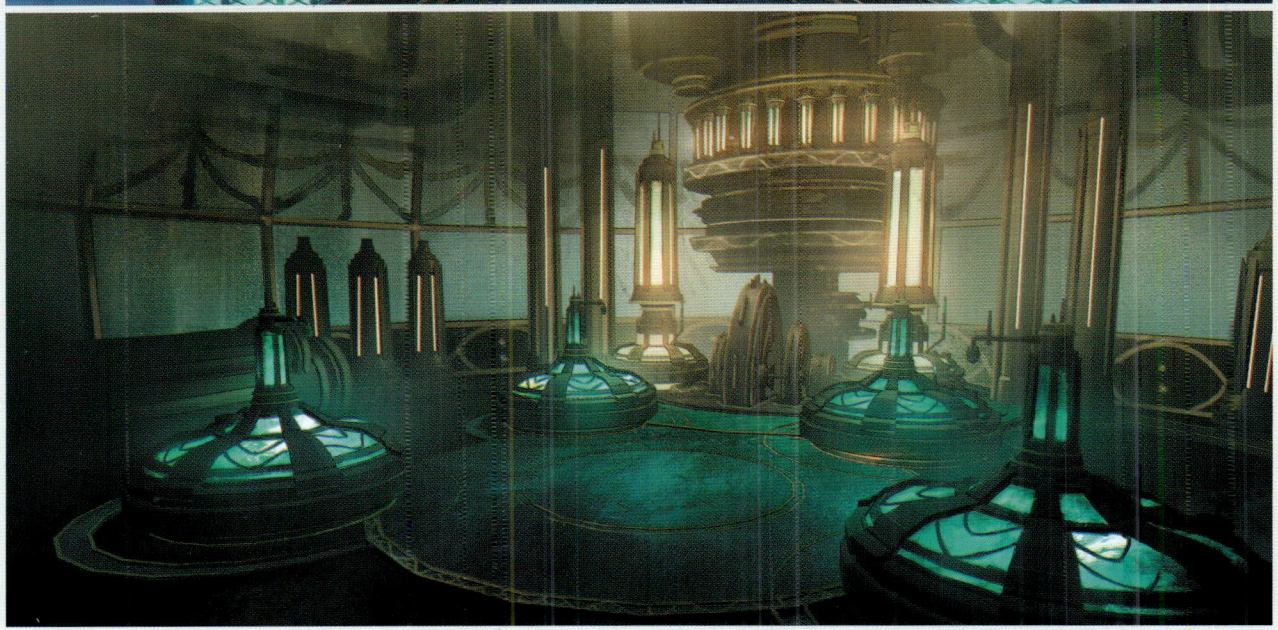

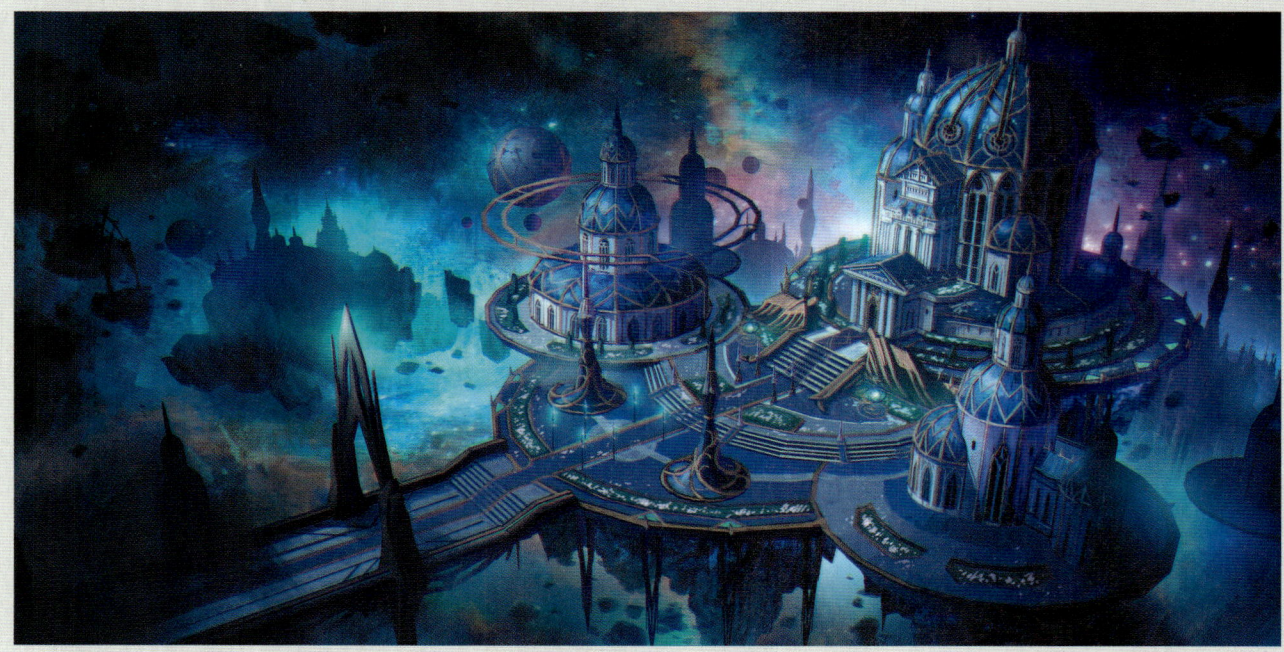
《 Code of the Universe top level, bird's eye view 》

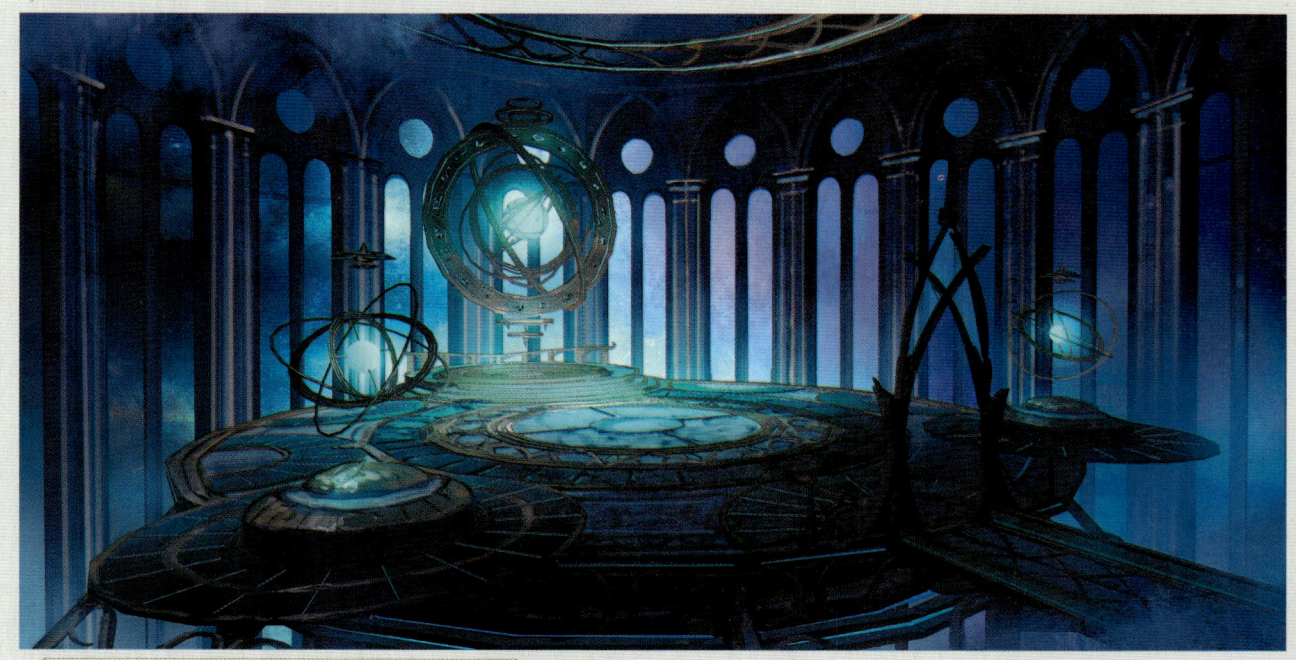
《 Code of the Universe top level, innermost part 》

Opening Storyboards

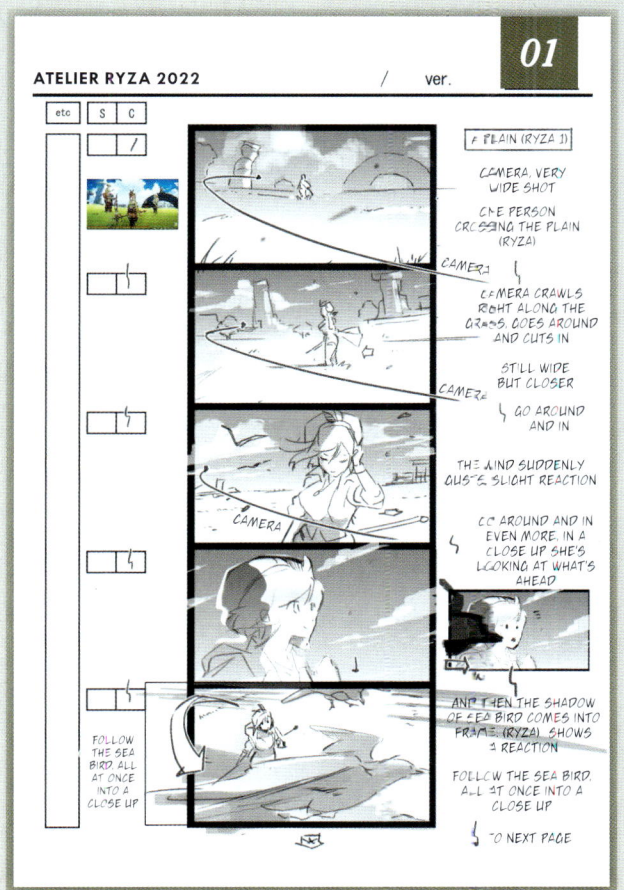
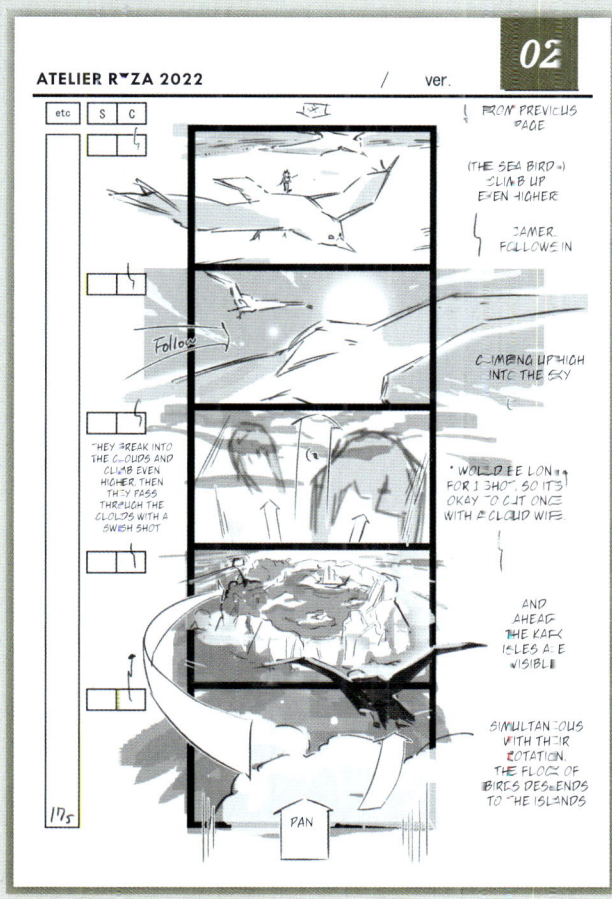
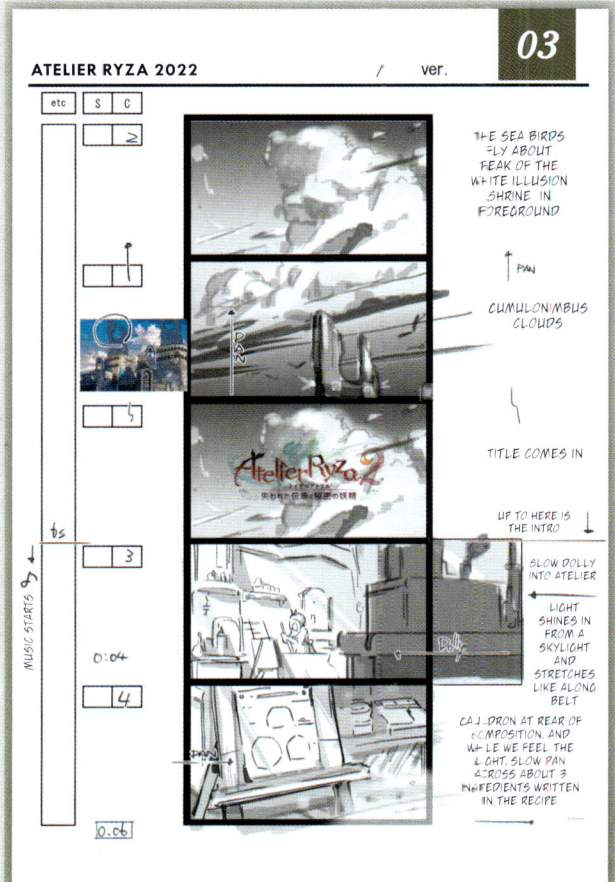
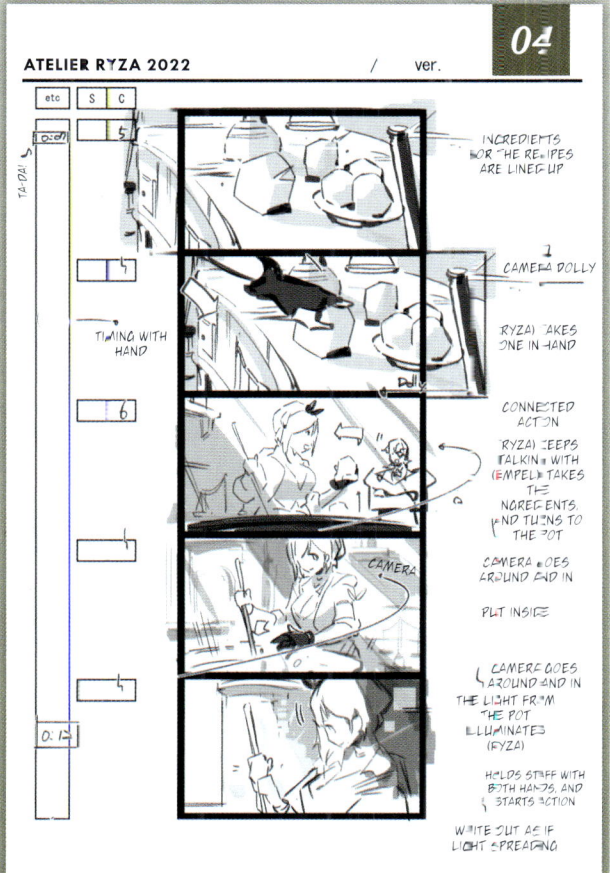

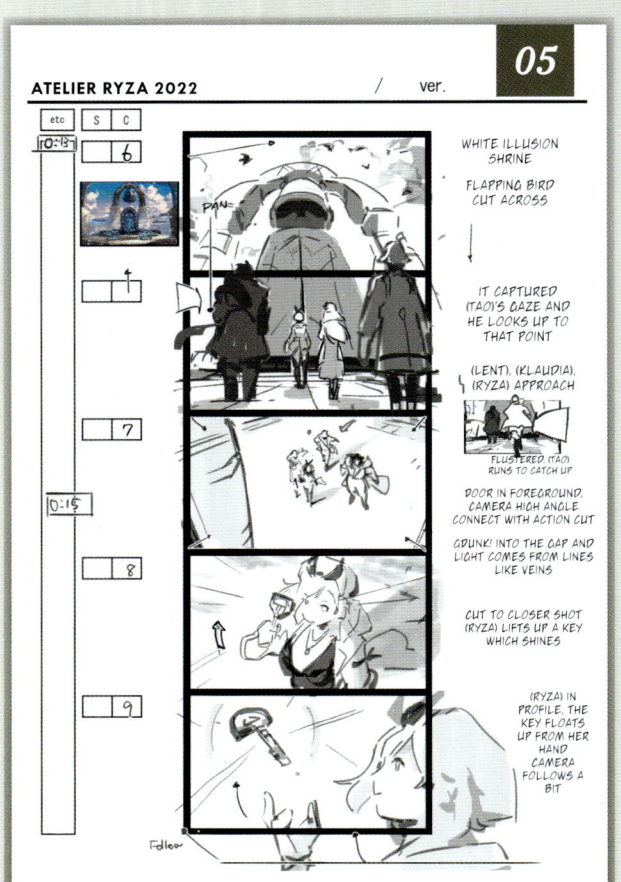
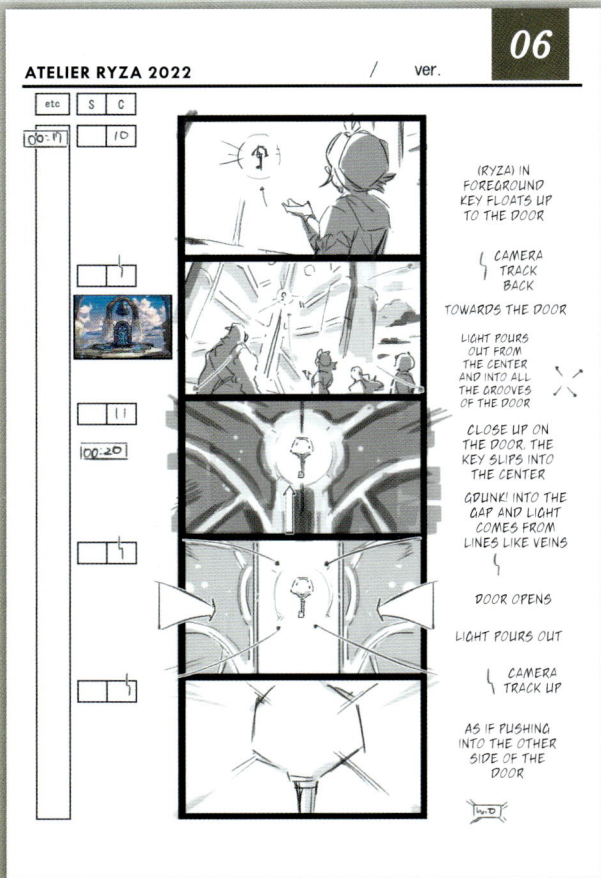
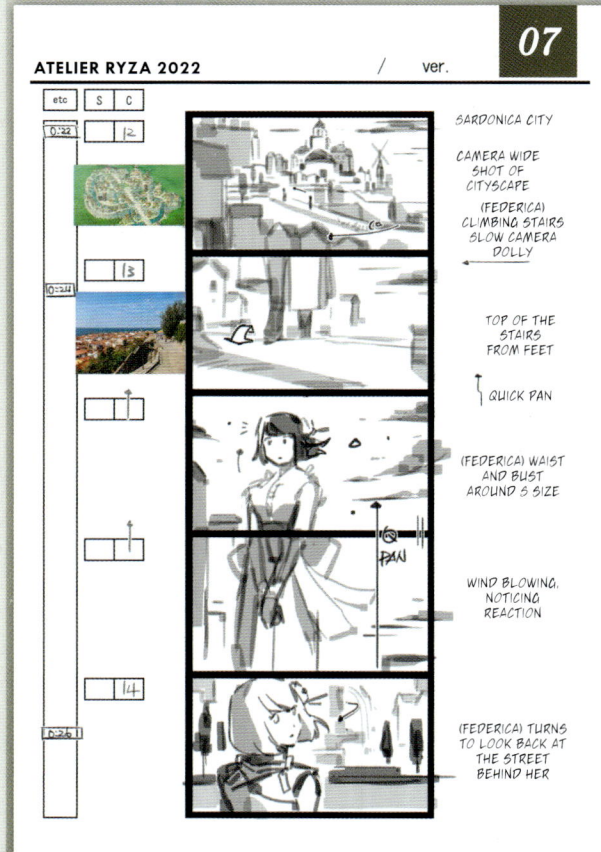
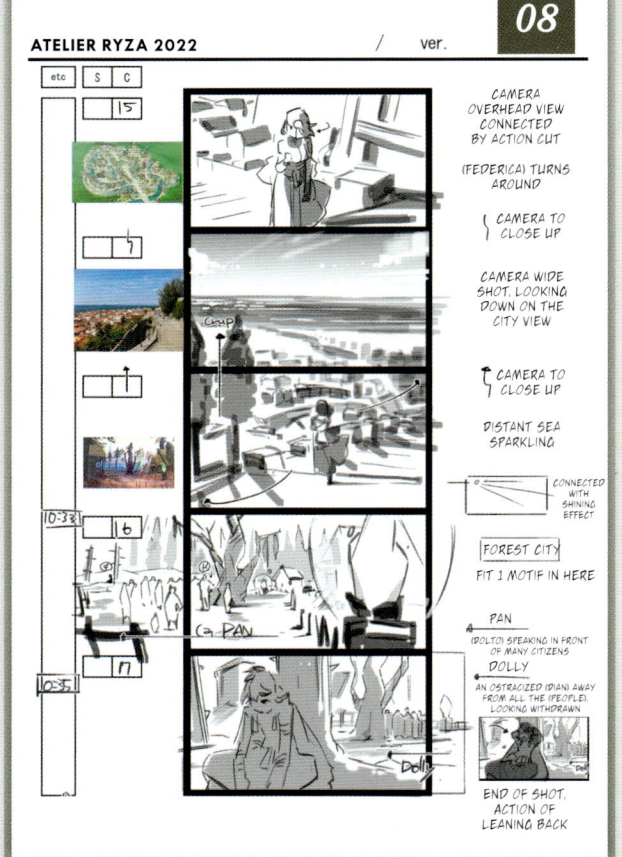

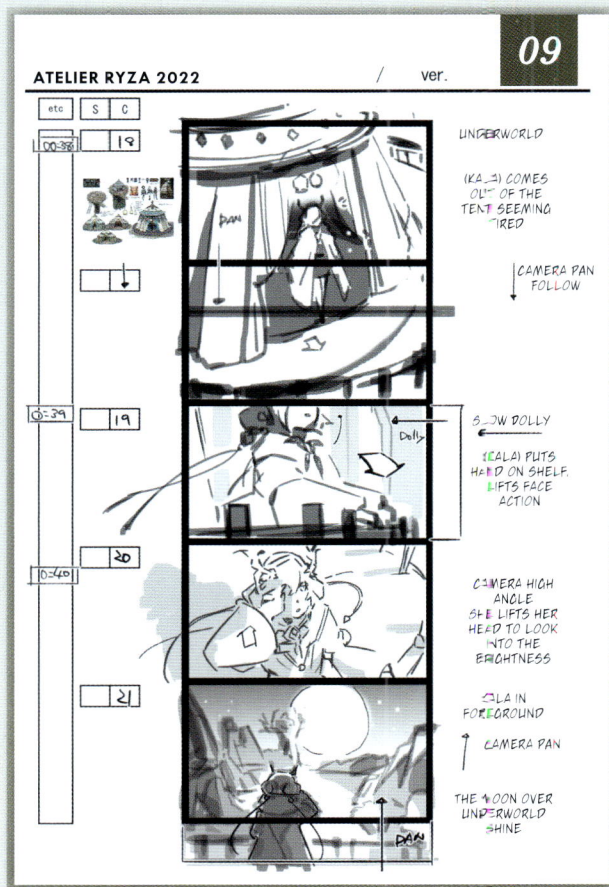
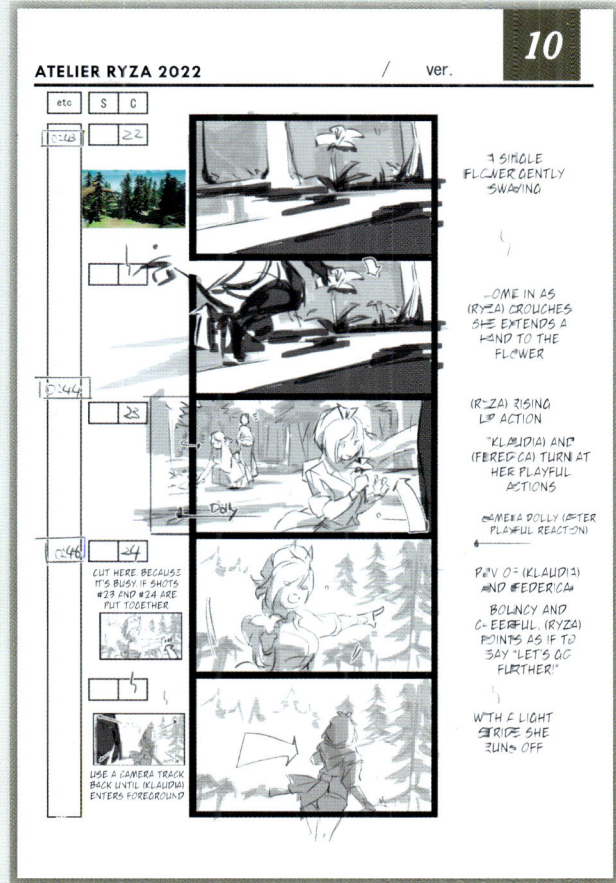
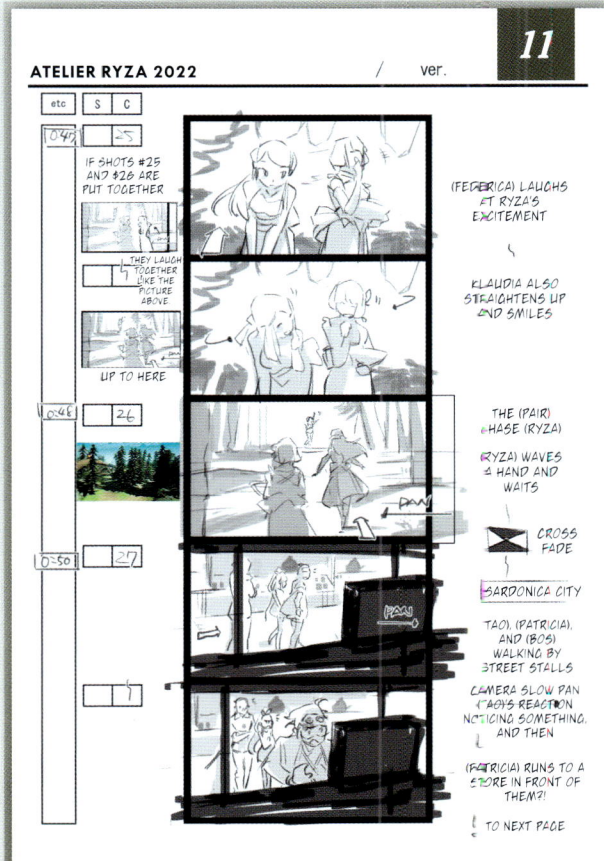
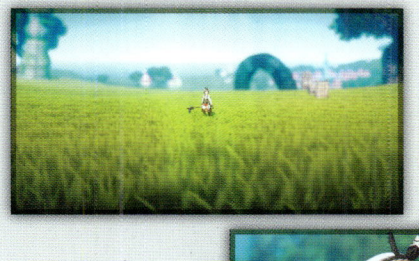
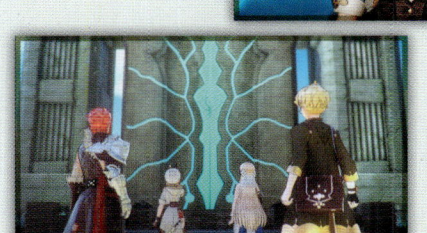
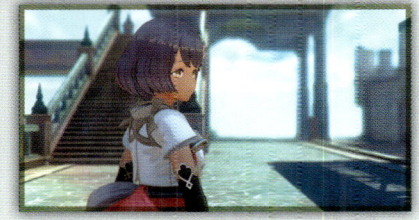

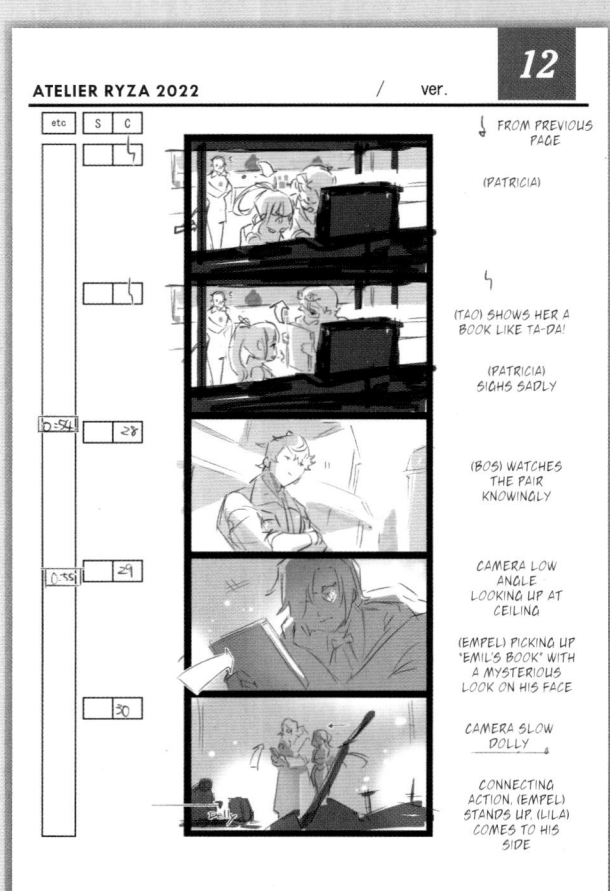
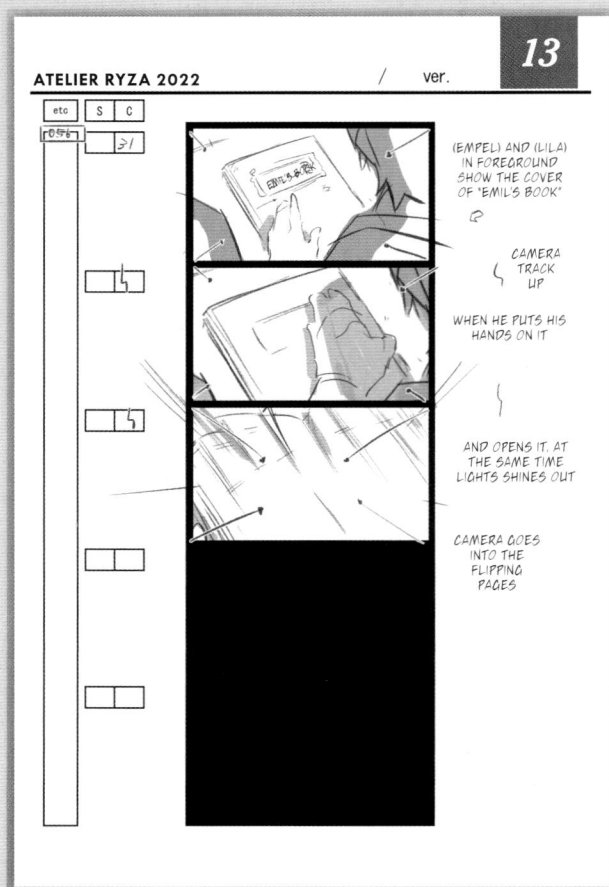
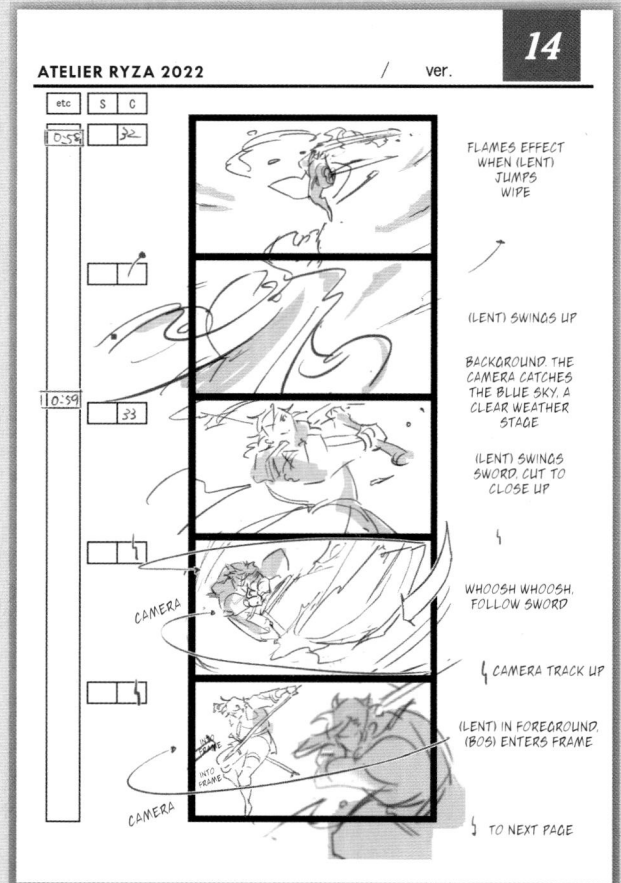
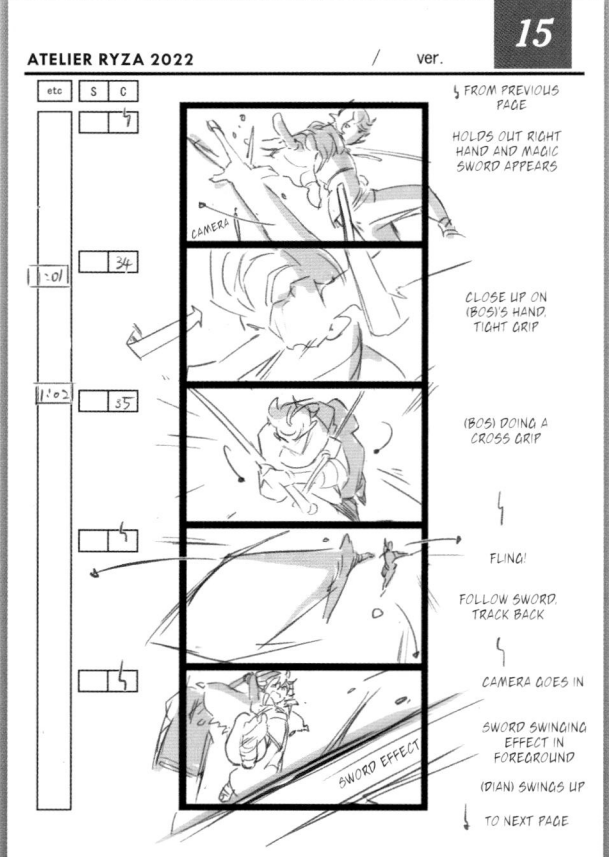

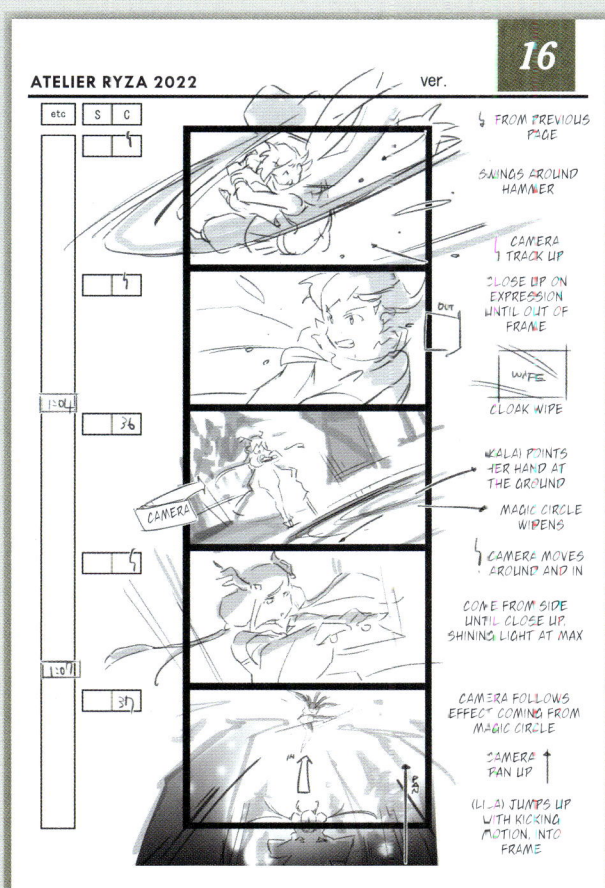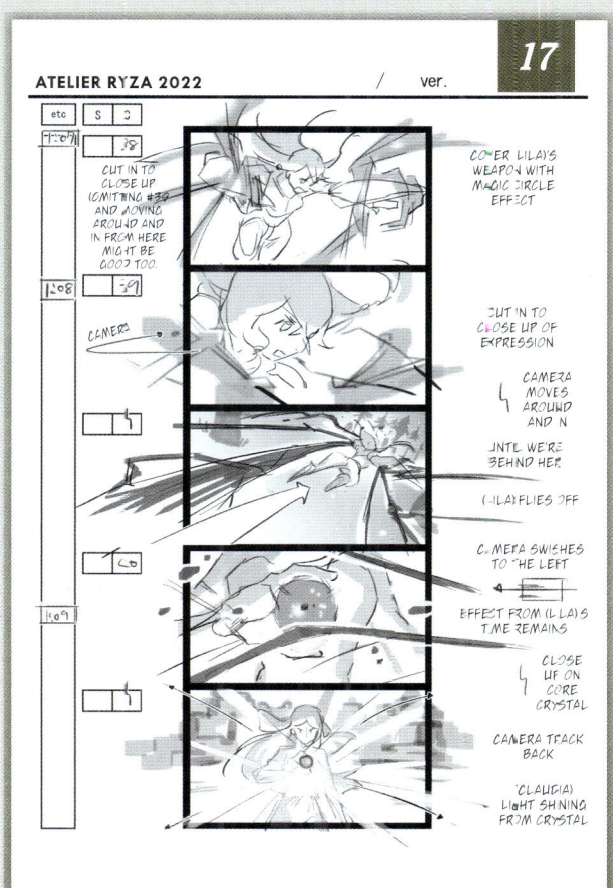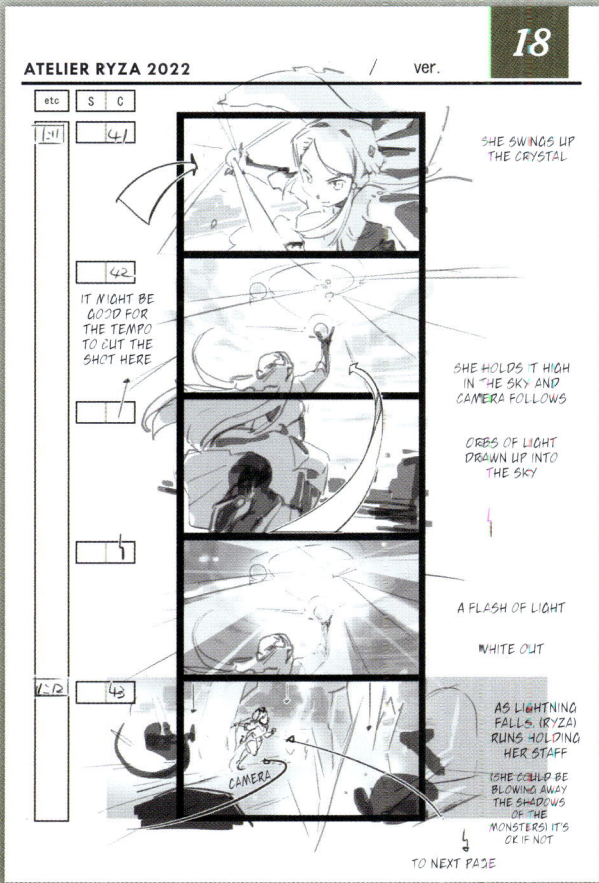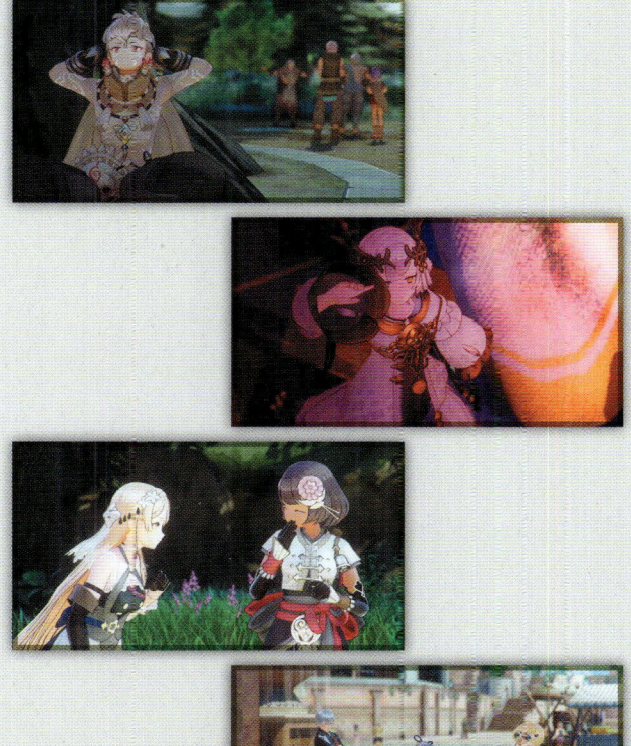

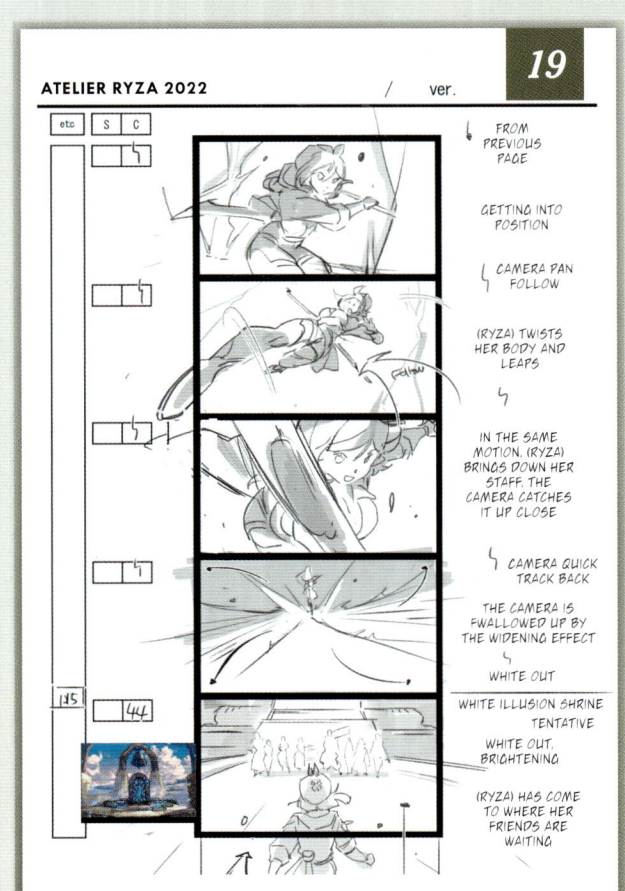
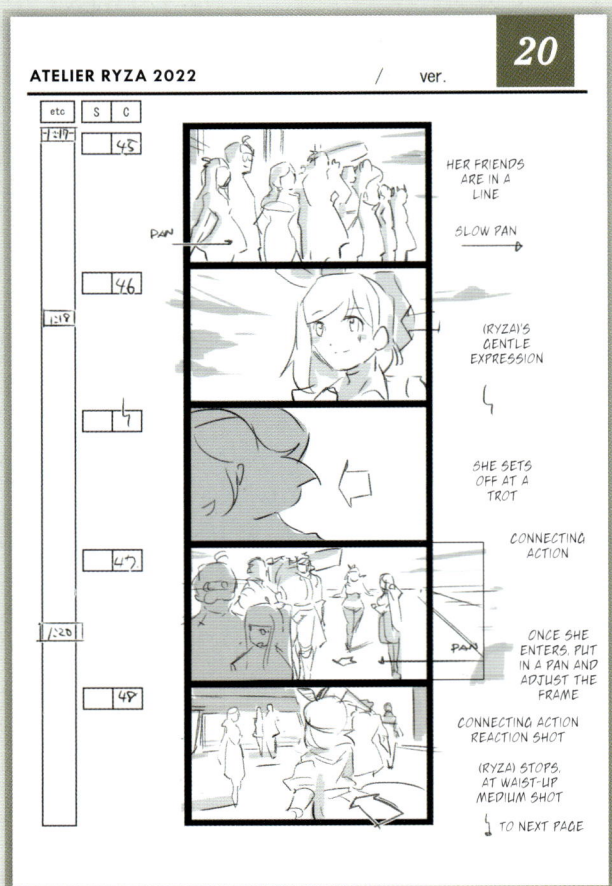
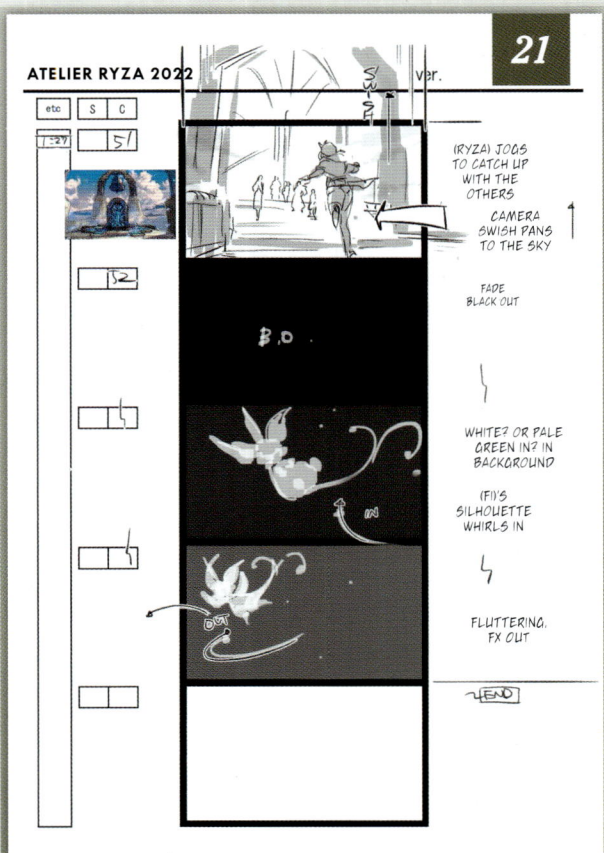
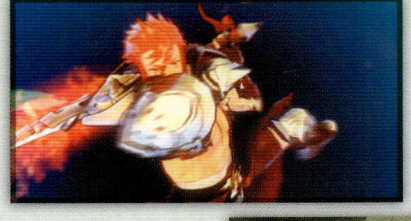
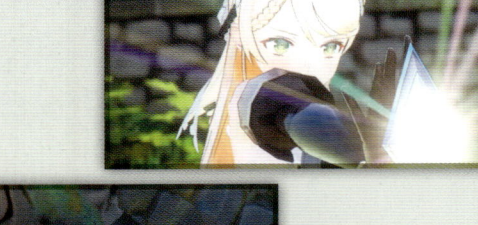
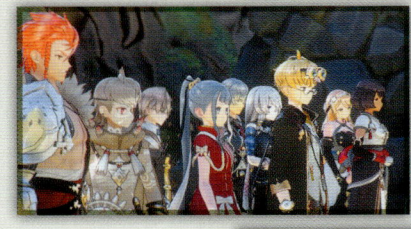
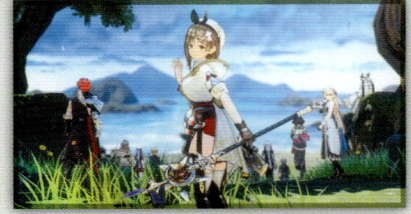

EXTRAS

Toridamono Bonus Illustrations

ROUGH SKETCH GALLERY

This is a presentation of the rough sketches of the official illustrations done by Toridamono, who handled the character designs. They include other alternate ideas for different poses and compositions, so readers can enjoy comparing them with the illustration gallery at the beginning of this book.

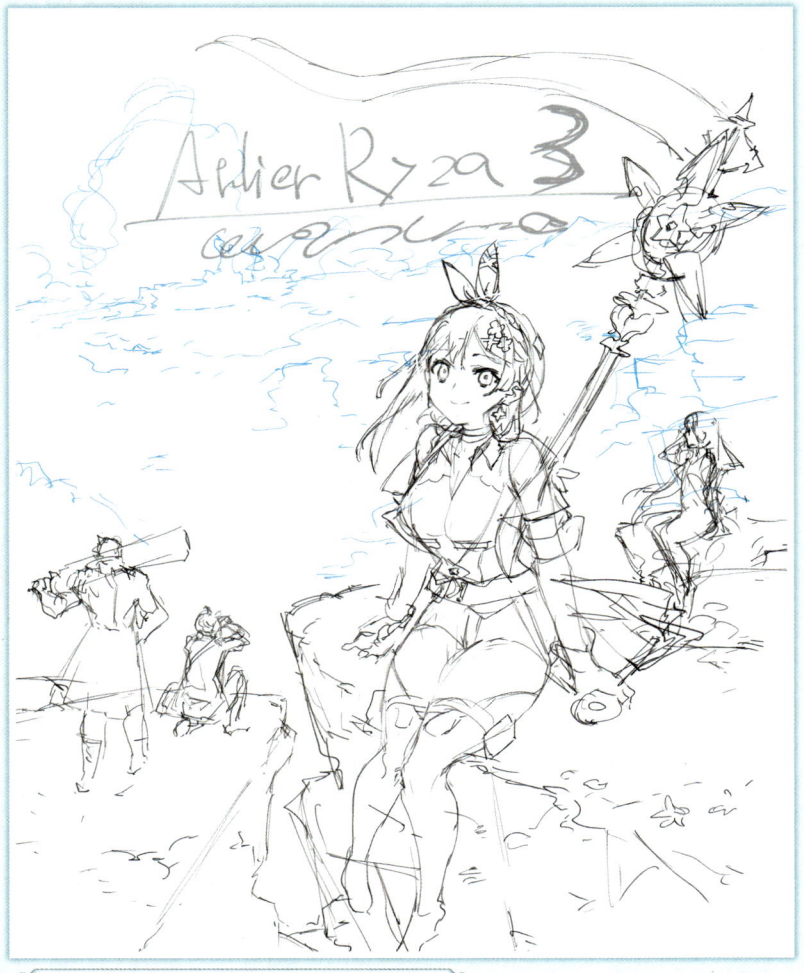

« Standard edition package visual (P. 002) »

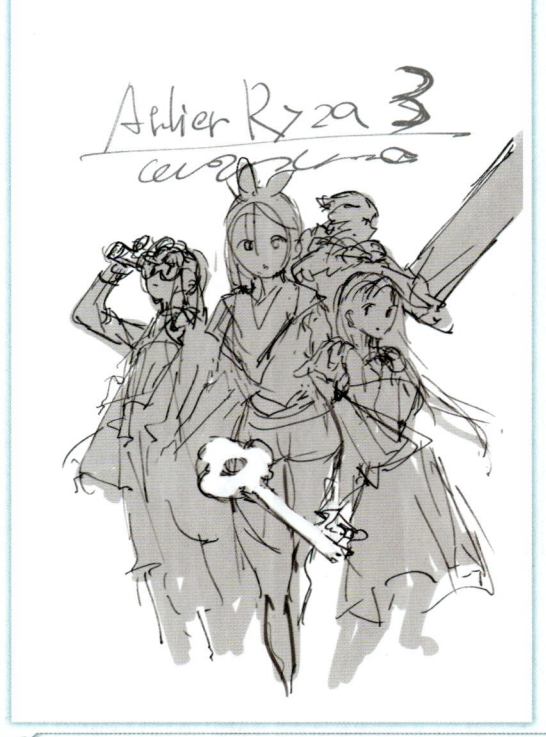

« Standard edition package visual, unused composition »

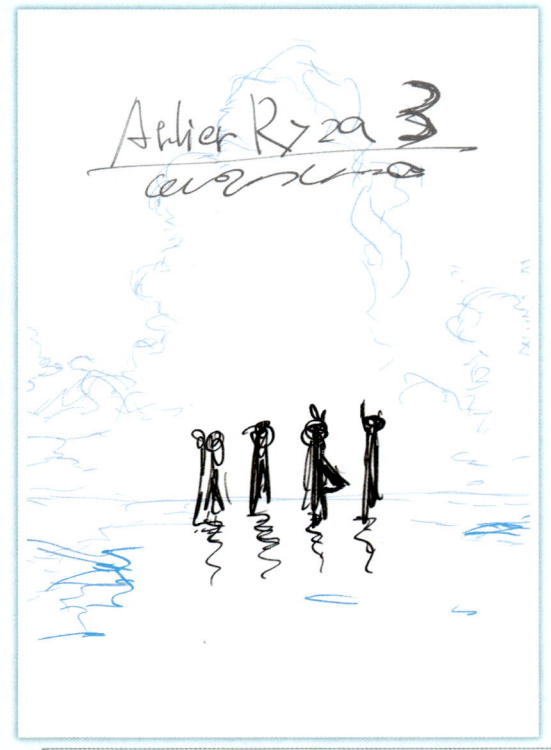

« Standard edition package visual, unused composition »

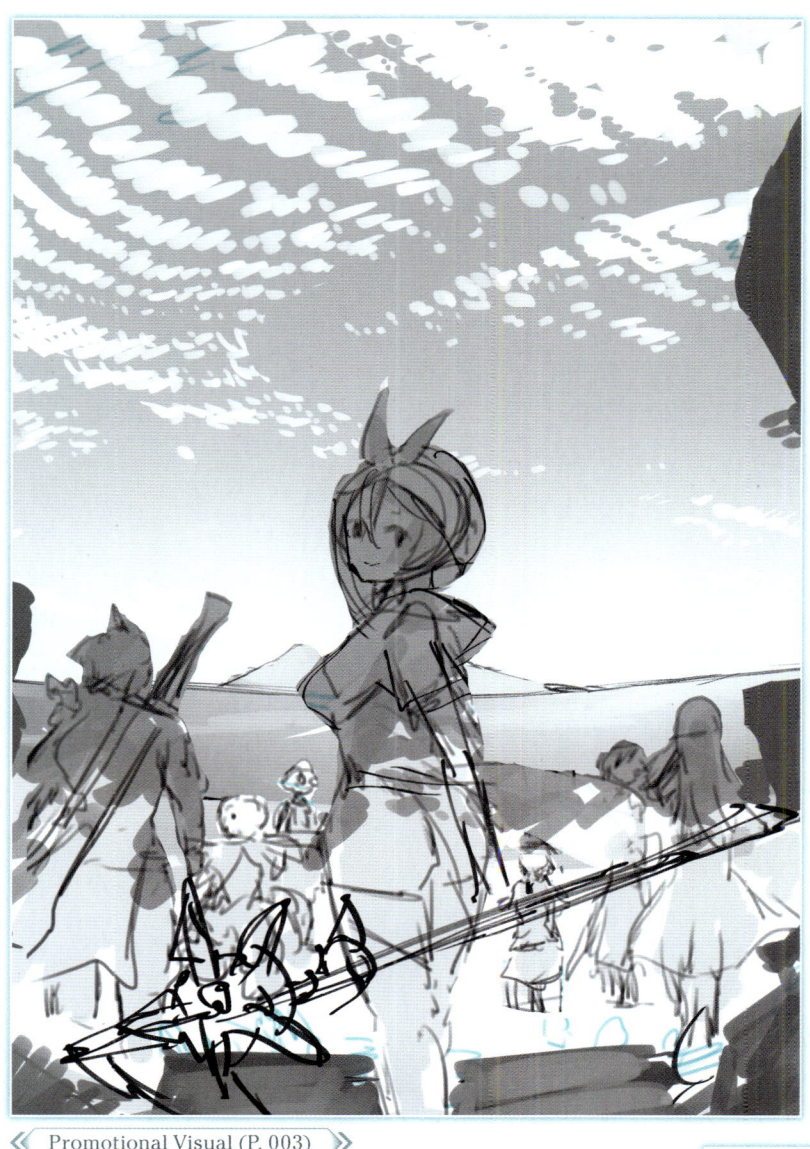
《 Promotional Visual (P. 003) 》

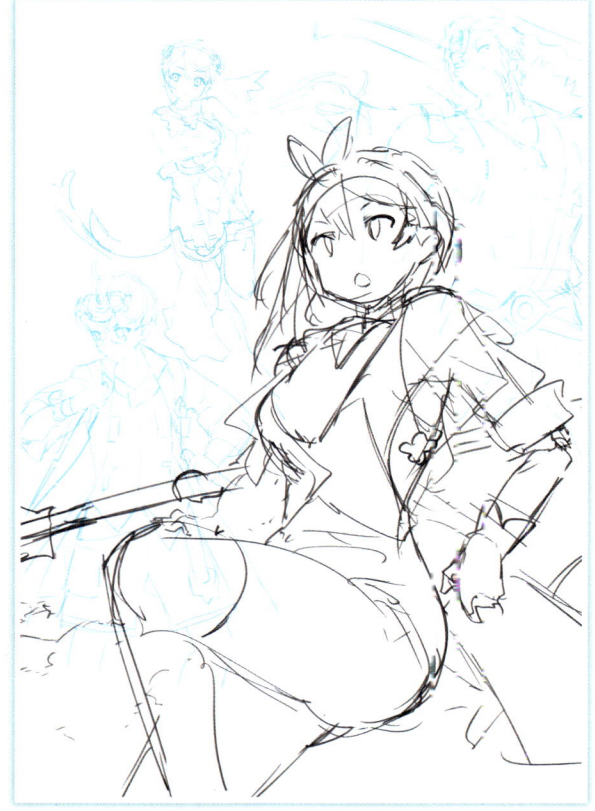
《 Promotional Visual (P. 004) 》

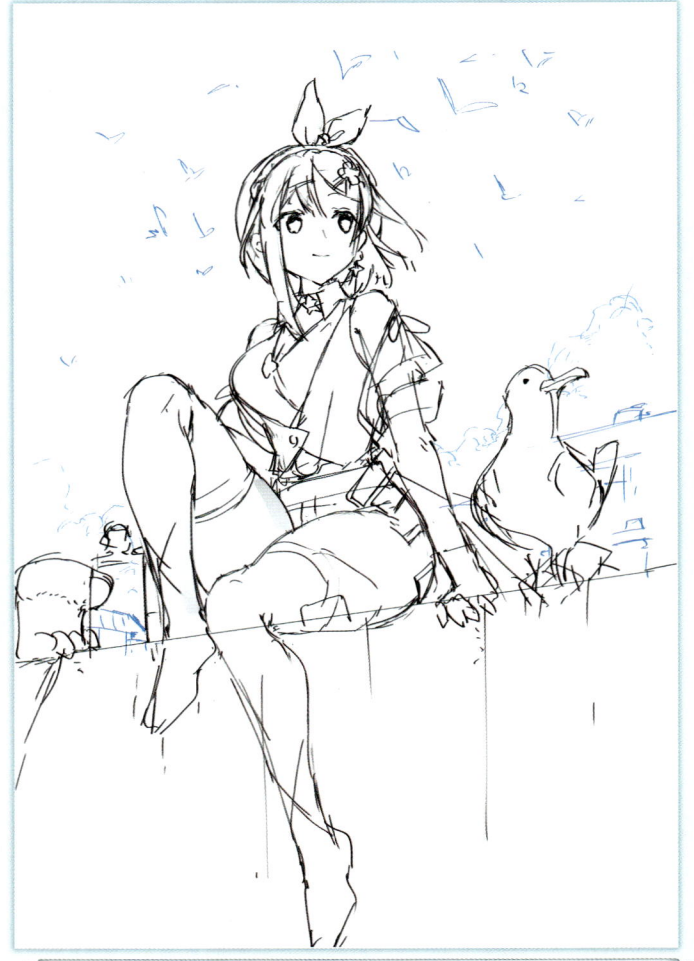

《 Premium Box special bonus B2 cloth poster illustration (P. 005) 》

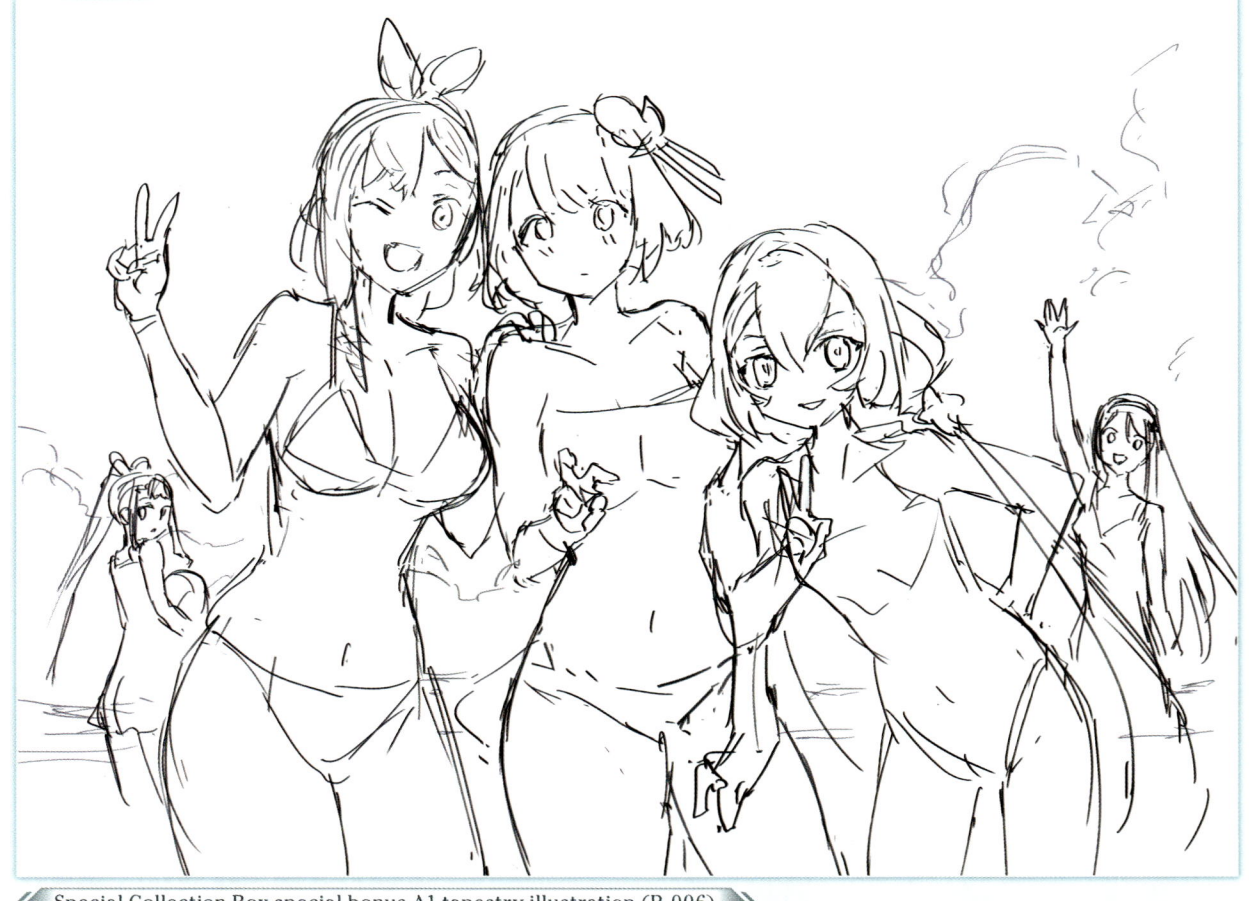

《 Special Collection Box special bonus A1 tapestry illustration (P. 006) 》

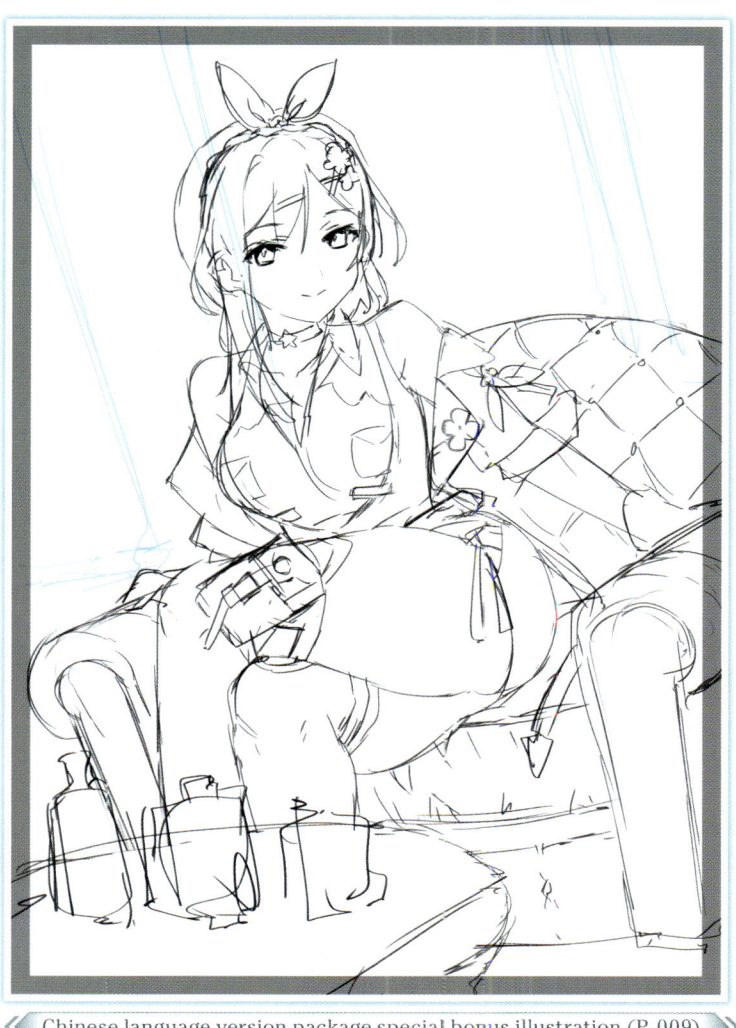

《 Chinese language version package special bonus illustration (P. 009) 》

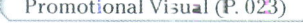

《 Promotional Visual (P. 023) 》

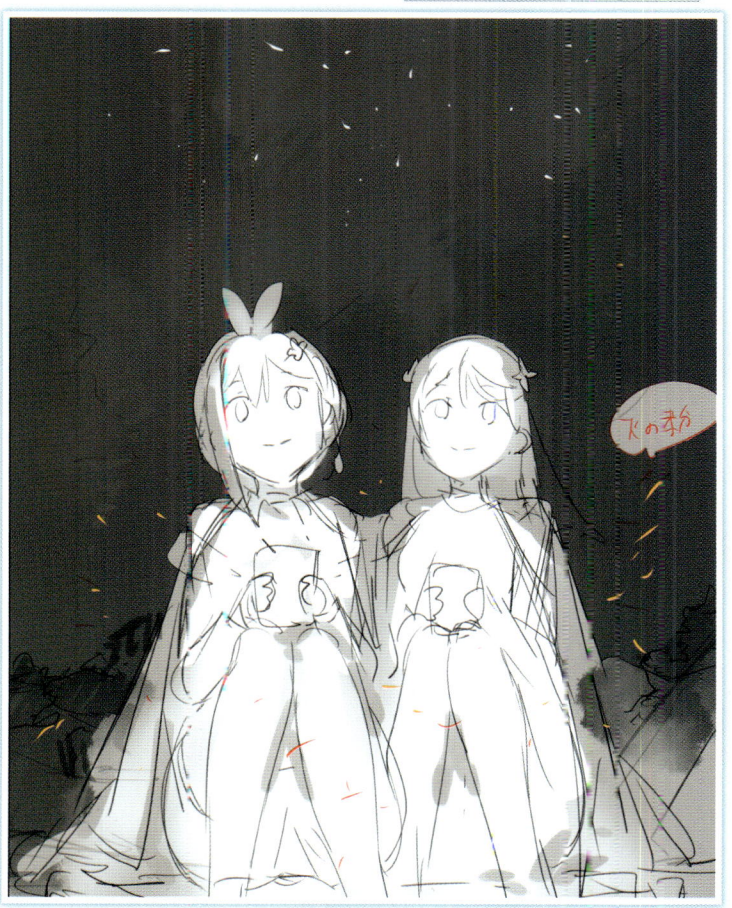

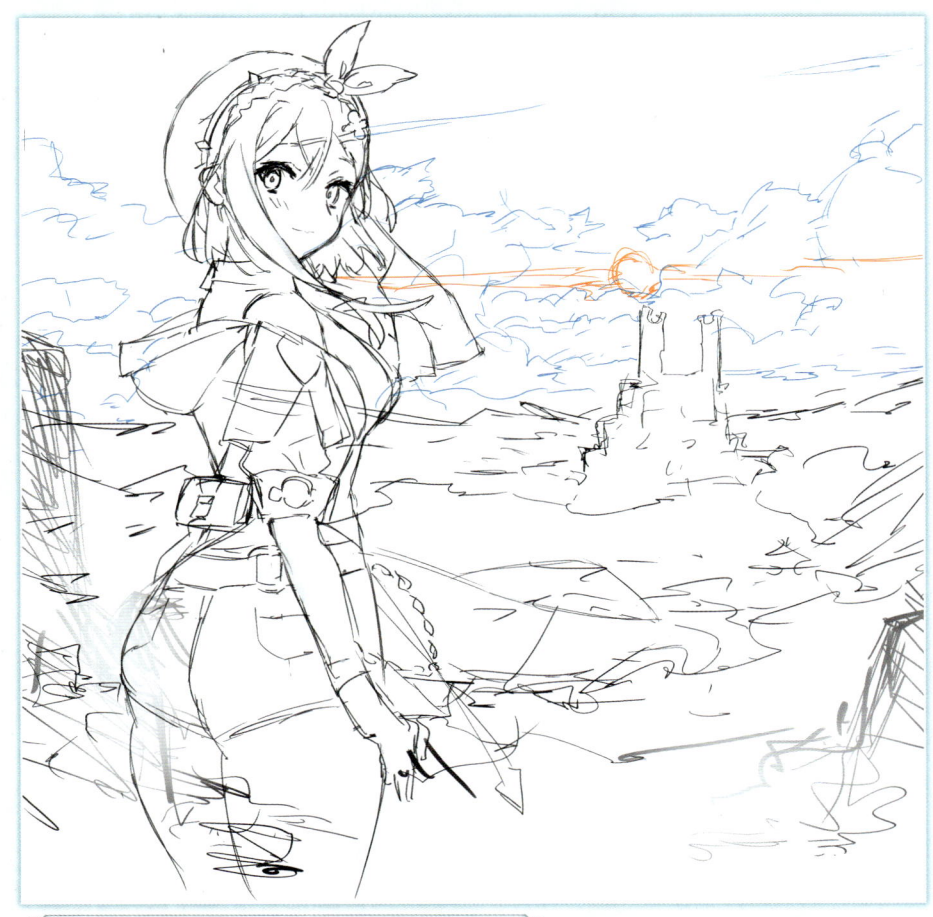

《 Original Soundtrack Jacket illustration (P. 024) 》

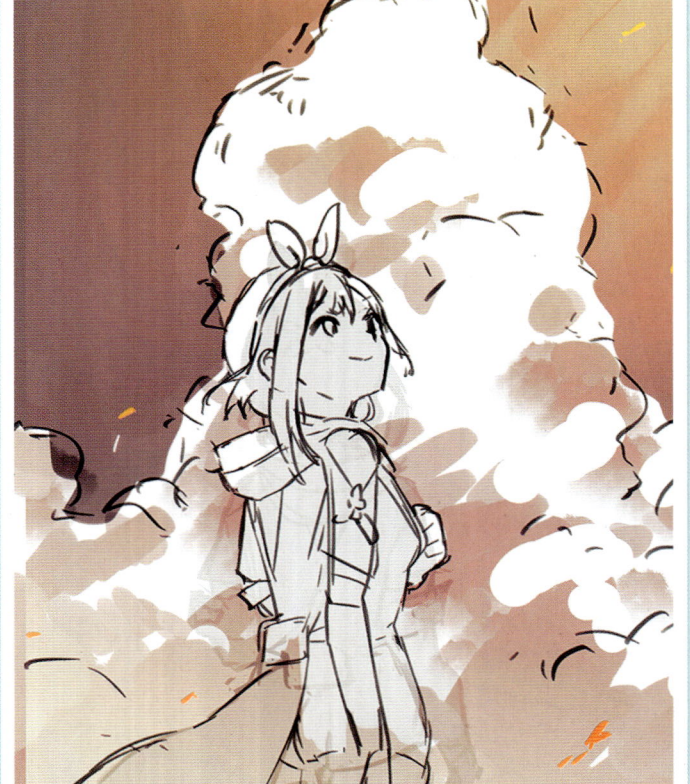

《 This book's cover illustration (P. 027) 》

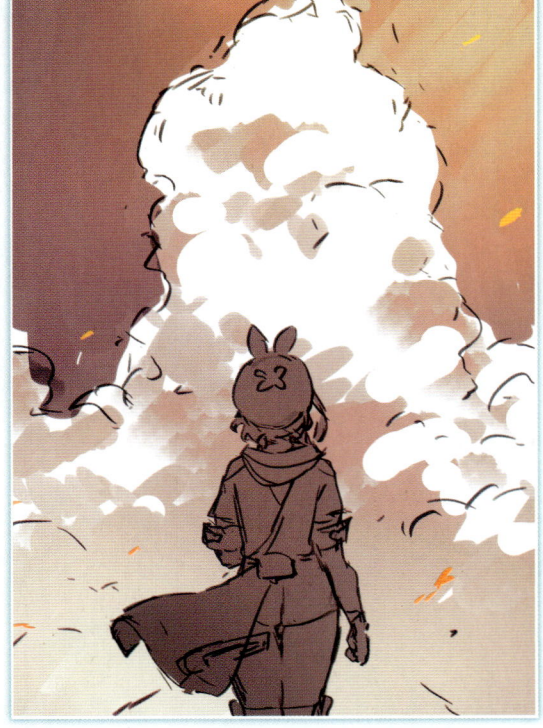

《 This book's cover illustration, unused composition 》

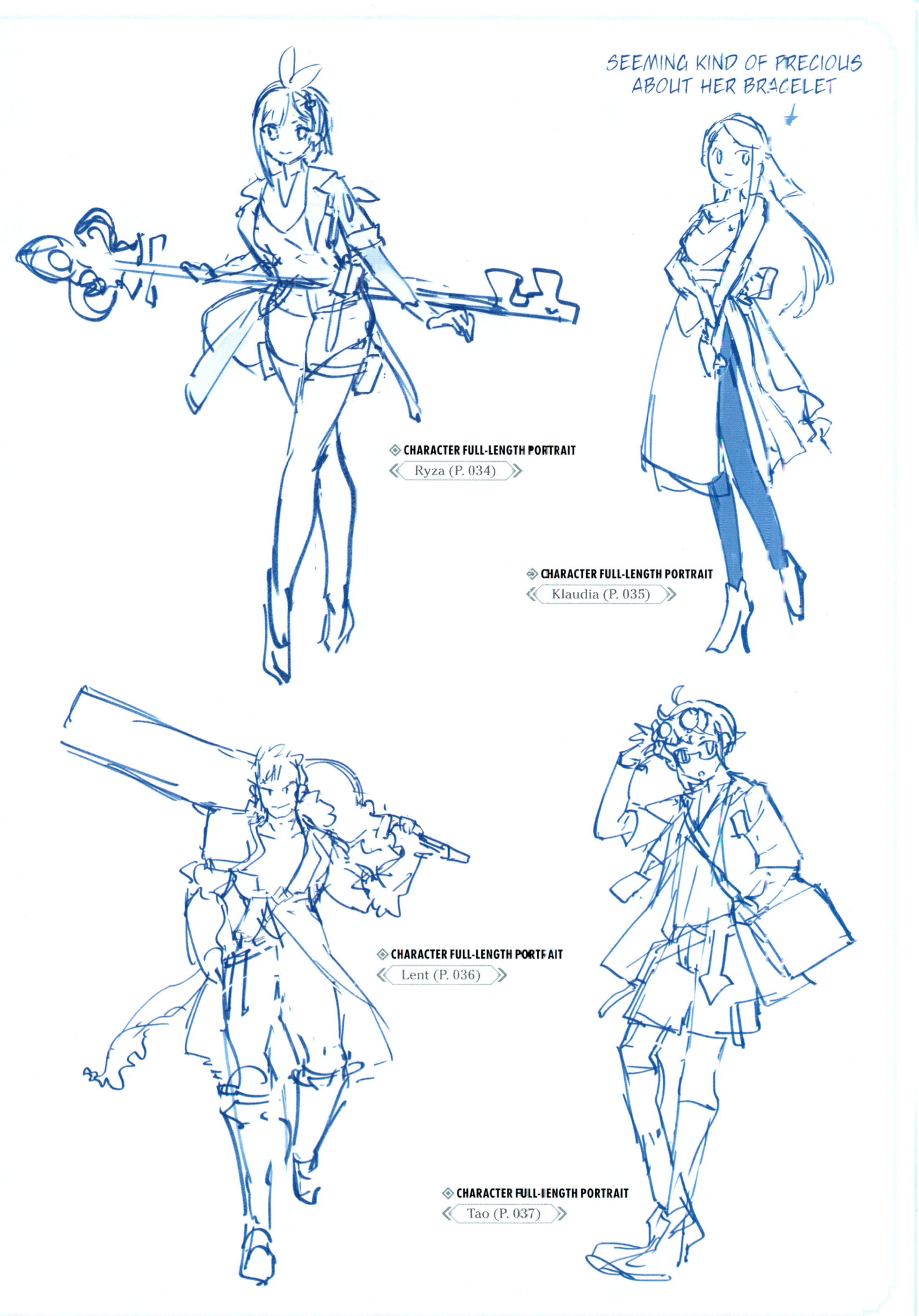

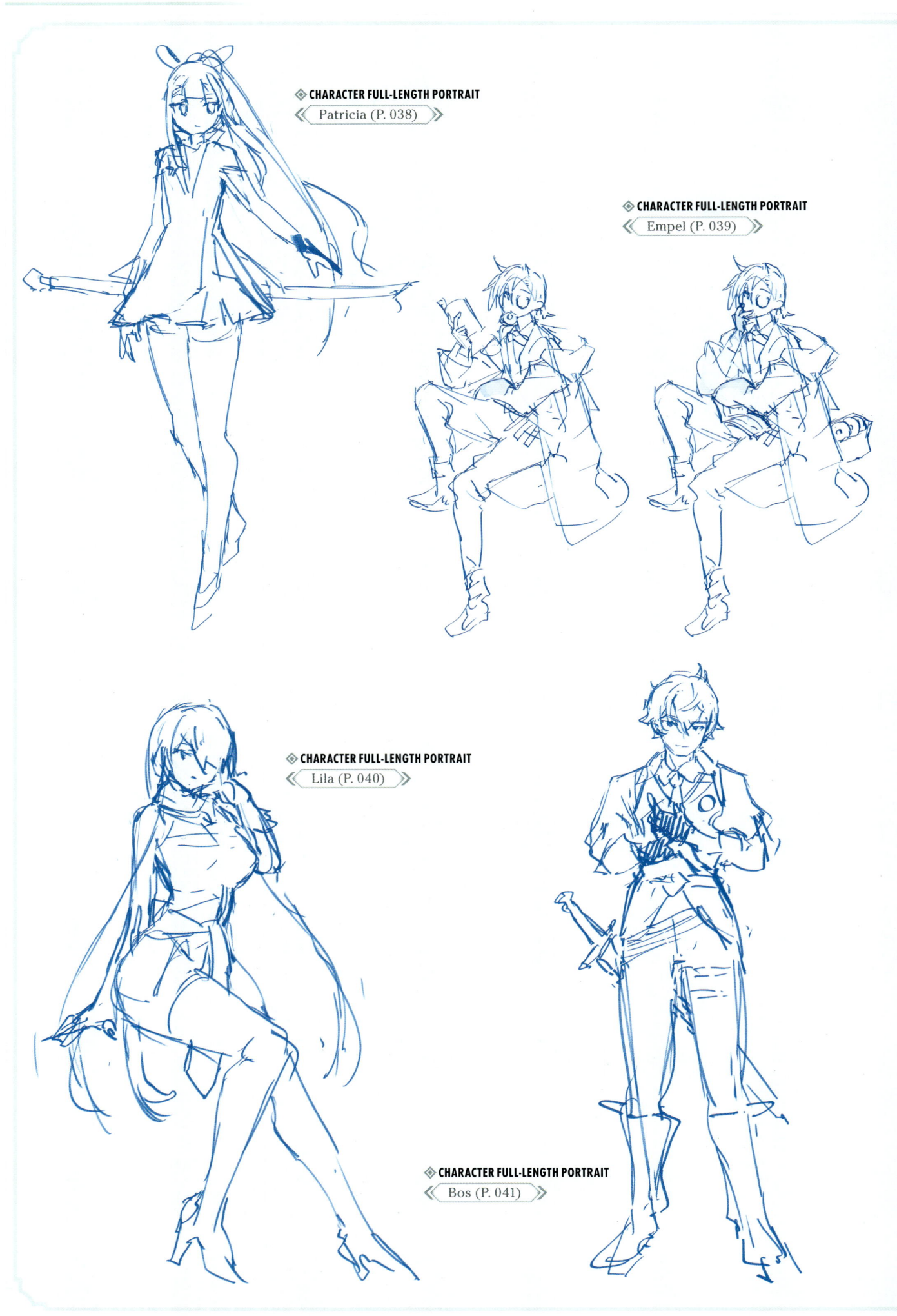

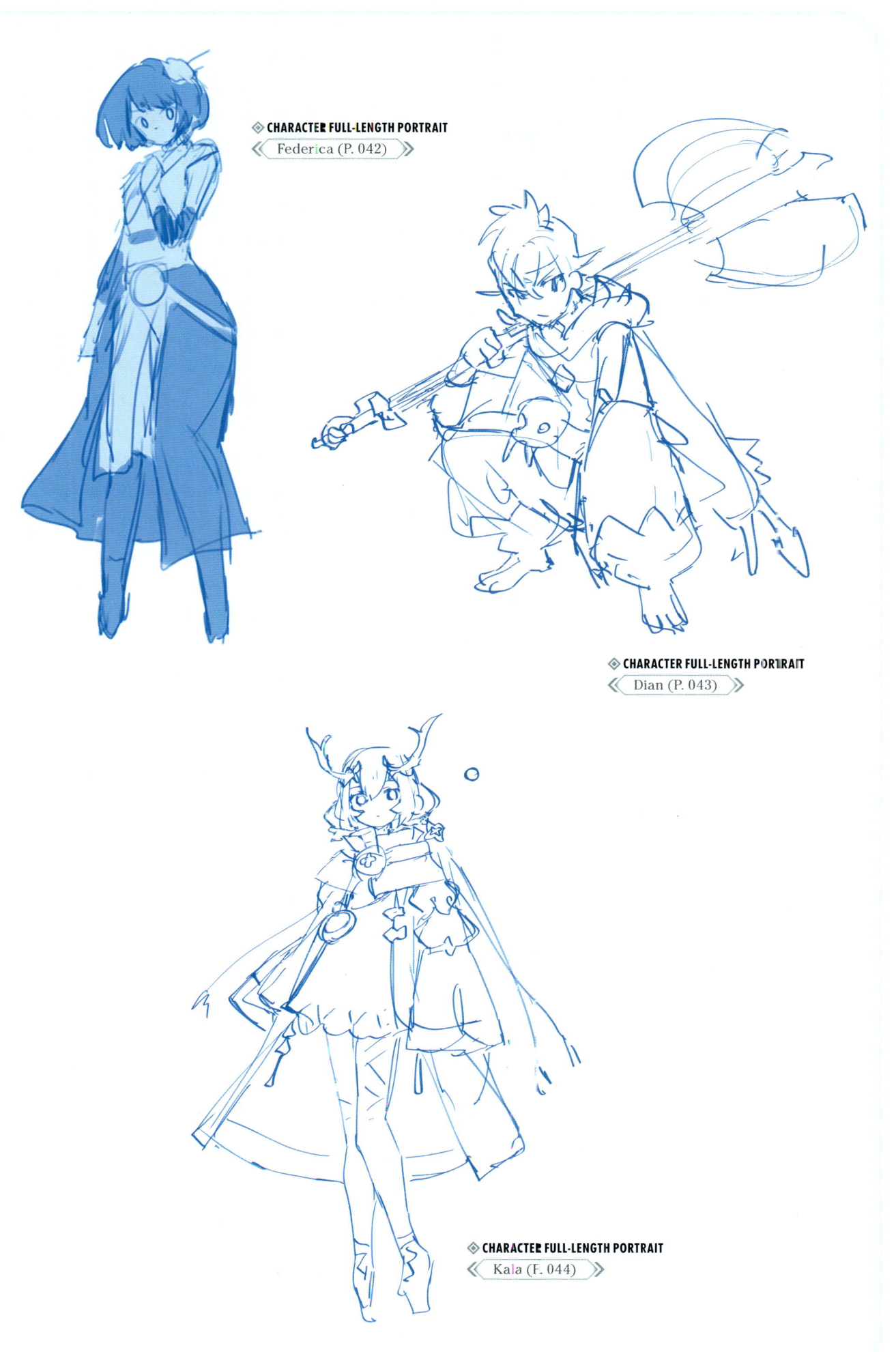

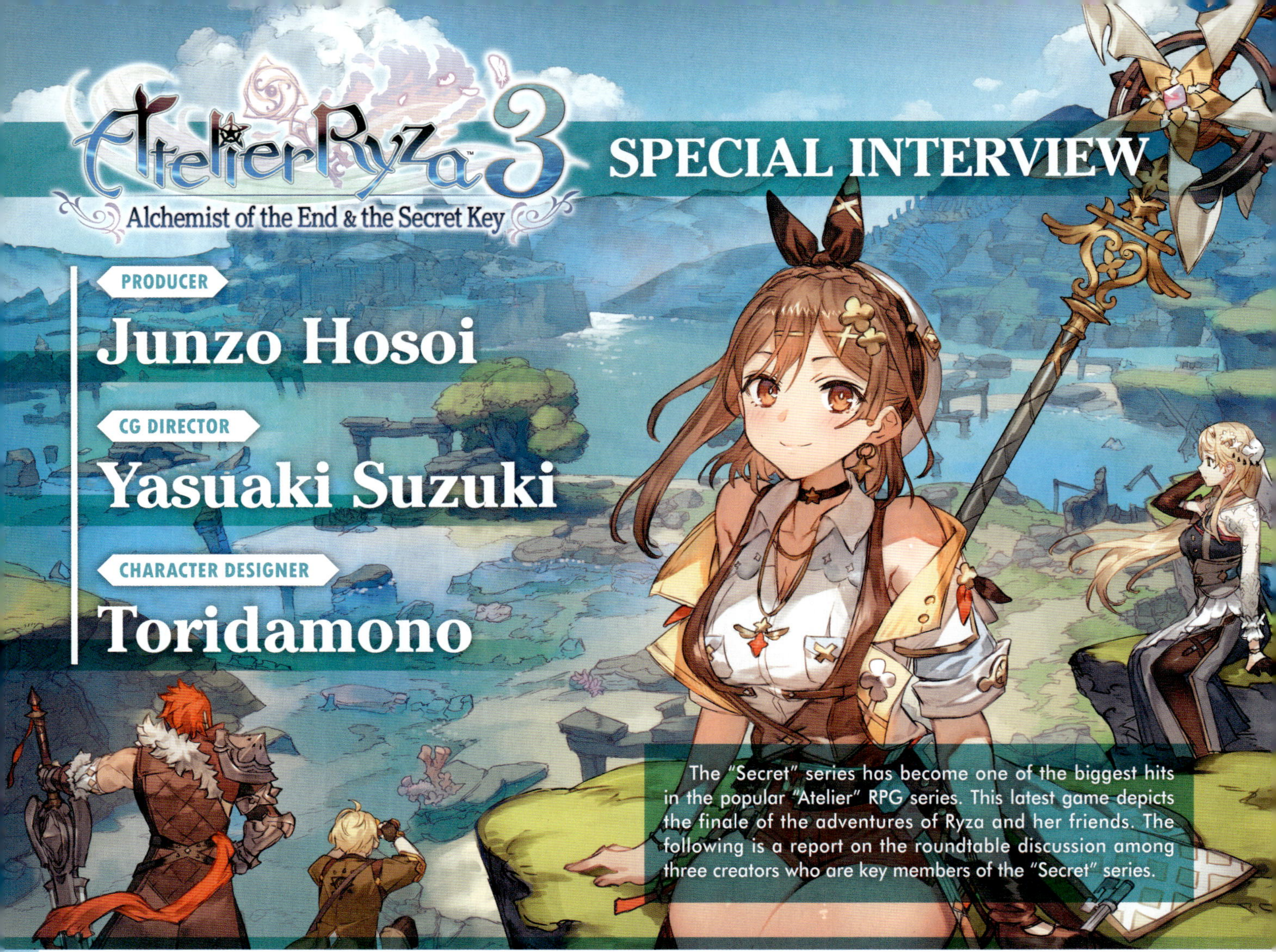

Atelier Ryza 3: Alchemist of the End & the Secret Key — SPECIAL INTERVIEW

PRODUCER Junzo Hosoi
CG DIRECTOR Yasuaki Suzuki
CHARACTER DESIGNER Toridamono

The "Secret" series has become one of the biggest hits in the popular "Atelier" RPG series. This latest game depicts the finale of the adventures of Ryza and her friends. The following is a report on the roundtable discussion among three creators who are key members of the "Secret" series.

What instructions were you given for the third of the "Secrets" series?

Thank you for taking time out of your busy schedule to join us today. First of all, congratulations on the release of "Atelier Ryza 3: Alchemist of the End & the Secret Key" (hereafter referred to as "3").

ALL: Thank you.

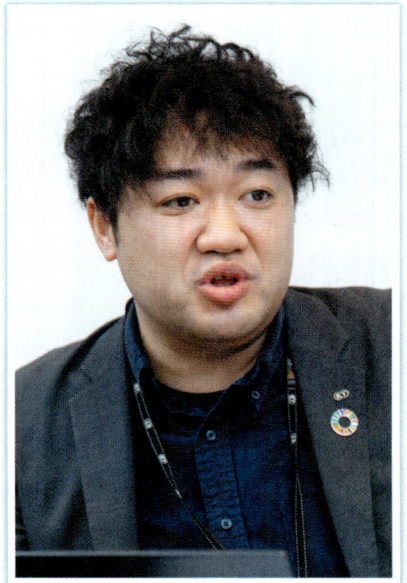

This is the last material we'll see related to Ryza, isn't it?

HOSOI: Yes, that's right. Largely, that's what it amounts to.

TORIDAMONO: The interview for the visual book always feels like the final job to be done.

Now that you're all able to catch your breath, we'd be pleased if you could tell us about all your thoughts and feelings up to this point.

ALL: Sure.

First of all, please tell us about this game, "3". The map is vaster than ever before this time around, and one can move around it seamlessly. What were your aims in this regard?

HOSOI: This game depicts the final adventures of Ryza and her companions, and it's also part of the 25th anniversary of the "Atelier" series. For those reasons, we wanted to present a new direction for the "Atelier" series.

What do you mean by a new direction?

HOSOI: The first game in the 25th anniversary series was "Atelier Sophie 2: The Alchemist of the Mysterious Dream", but the concept of this game was that we wanted to present a new progression in the "Atelier" series to players, and to update the turn-based RPG in a modern way.

I see.

HOSOI: With "3", we wanted to make it a "crossroads" in the future development of the series. In the "Atelier" series so far, we have continued to create turn-based RPGs as the basic system, but I felt that turn-based RPGs were becoming relatively rare as global game trends go nowadays.

That's true.

HOSOI: Therefore, our development concept was to create a new type of game, a type of gaming and quality... in other words, to seriously dig into its quality framework as a game to look towards the 30th and 40th anniversaries with this game as the "starting point". To that end, the title aimed to present a number of "evolutions", such as the introduction of seamless maps and improved graphics. However, being a crossroads does not mean we're abandoning the traditional "Ateliers". The "Secret" series is a branching off in one direction within the "Atelier" series.

Is the introduction of the "key" system also one of them?

HOSOI: This being the third title in a series, it was necessary to maintain the gameplay

---

This game was produced to be a "crossroads" in the "Atelier" series.

PROFILE
Junzo Hosoi 細井順三 氏
PRODUCER

Managing Executive Officer of Koei Tecmo Games. Since his time with Gust Co. Ltd., he has been involved in almost all of Gust's titles since "Mana Khemia 2: Fall of Alchemy" as a PR manager. Currently, he is also the Gust Brand Manager and oversees the Gust brand.

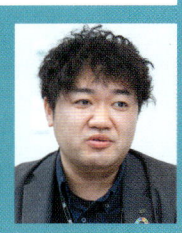

PROFILE
Yasuaki Suzuki 鈴木康昭 氏
CG DIRECTOR

Joined Koei Tecmo Games in 2006. He has been involved in CG design for various titles, and he has been active as the CG director for the "Secret" series since "Atelier Ryza: Ever Darkness & the Secret Hideout".

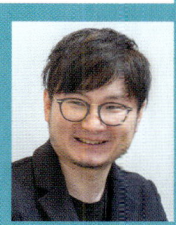

PROFILE
Toridamono トリダモノ 氏
CHARACTER DESIGNER

After graduating from art school, he worked for a video game company before becoming an independent freelance illustrator. He has been active in creating illustrations for various media. He was in charge of character design for all three parts of the "Secret" series.

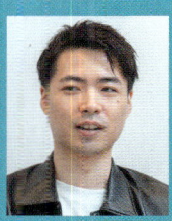

---

of the previous titles in parts, so we didn't have any intentions to drastically change the game system itself here. However, we believe it is necessary to pursue new game experiences.

What do you mean by those new game experiences?

HOSOI: One of them is the point that you can adventure in a vast world in an open field, but this must be well linked with the gathering and synthesizing. That's why we introduced the "key" system, which affects all activities such as adventuring, combat, gathering, and synthesizing... We wanted to create a system that would affect the entire sequence of actions.

I see.

HOSOI: But, strictly speaking, you can play the game without using the keys. However, the more you use them, the handier it is, and by proactively using the keys, you're able to have a new game experience.

It's not only the keys. There's also field exploration, searching for treasure chests, and the countless quests scattered around. But you can proceed through the story without forcing yourself to grind all of that.

HOSOI: Collecting and synthesizing ingredients are the basic gameplay components of the "Atelier" series, and I think it's been welcomed by so many players because of these systems. Meanwhile, in part, our minds on the development staff were filled with the idea that "Atelier" had to be "this certain way". I can talk about this now, but from the very beginning, our intention with the "Secret" series was to make it "Atelier" but not too "Atelier".

Is that so?

HOSOI: Yes. Our creative principle with the "Secret" series was: "Those who want to challenge themselves and play intuitively can play it and have a thorough challenge". The system is such that you can defeat enemies even with items that you have created without fully understanding them, and if you keep probing further into it you'll be able to defeat enemies easily. The same is true for this game.

You definitely get a strong sense of that.

HOSOI: Before the development of the first title, "Atelier Ryza: Ever Darkness & the Secret Hideout" (hereafter referred to as "1"), there was a period in which we felt a sense of panic. We felt that we had to increase the RPG qualities of the game in order to make a wider user base aware of the "Atelier" series. However, we were extremely troubled about whether that would be the appropriate evolution for the "Atelier" series. So, as I mentioned earlier, with regards to the "Secret" series, we developed it with an awareness that, although it is part of the "Atelier" series, it is not overly restricted to that. We also tried to make it playable with basic parts of the system like synthesizing as stress-free as possible.

That experiment was a great success, and it became one of the biggest hits of the "Atelier" series to date, didn't it?

HOSOI: I thought we might wind up ending the "Atelier" series, so that was a relief from the bottom of my heart. Really it was thanks to all the players.

A storyline scenario that concludes the adventures of Ryza and her friends, and foreshadowing

Did you make any major changes to the combat system in this title?

HOSOI: The combat system was well received by many people in "Atelier Ryza 2: Lost Legends & the Secret Fairy" (hereafter referred to as "2"), so we had no intention to forcibly make major changes. We polished it up and fine-tuned it to be more speedy and action-oriented.

Ryza's attack actions include a kick. Whose idea was that?

HOSOI: That was a suggestion from the motion team.

Mr. Takahashi Yashichiro returned to work on the storyline for this game. Did he accept that without issue?

HOSOI: Yes, that's right. He readily agreed.

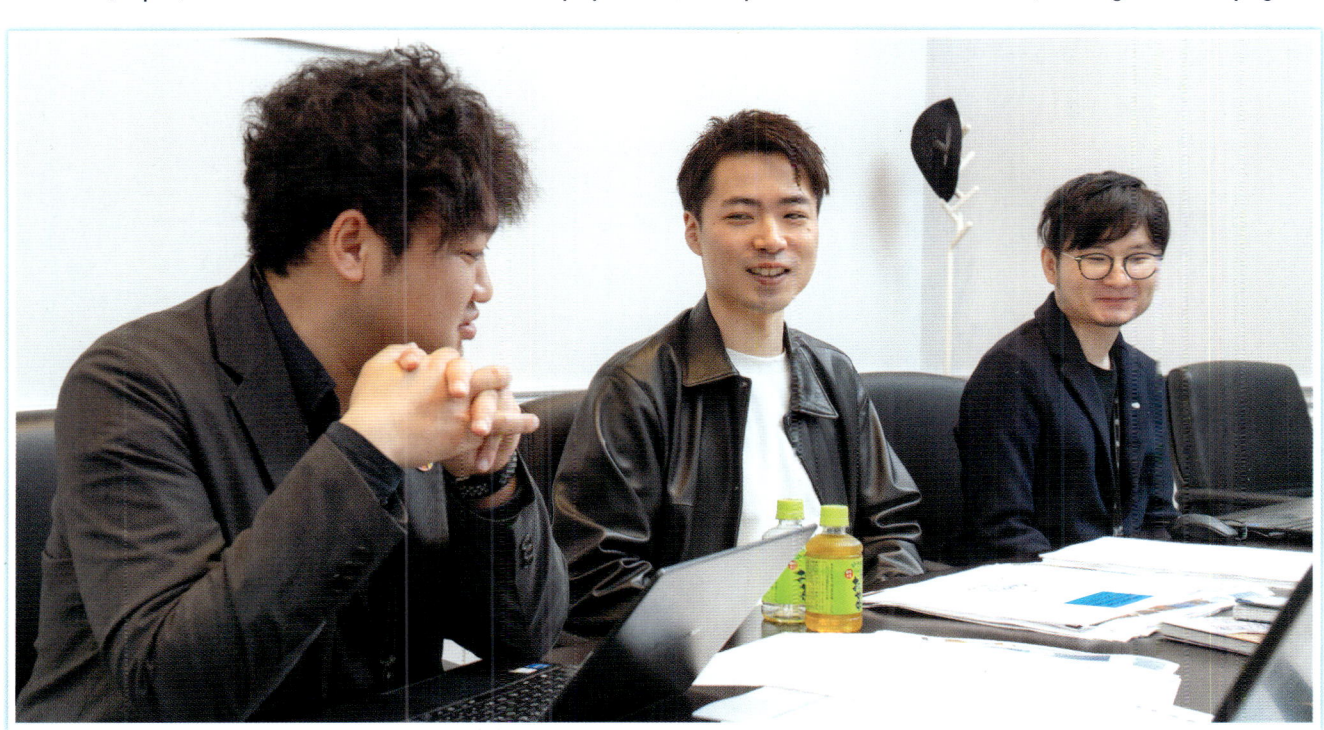

On "2", we were unable to work together due to scheduling conflicts.

HOSOI: We started the "Secret" series in part because we wanted to thoroughly depict the growth of one main character. In "1", the setting was the hometown of Kurken Island, and Ryza and her friends were one step short of adulthood, and on an adventure to find what's important to them. In the follow-up, "2", the setting moved to the royal capital, and it depicted Ryza's growth as a person as she experienced important encounters and partings. So if we were going to make a third game, we wanted to depict Ryza and her friends as they discover what they want to accomplish in their lives, and as they become adults. Ryza is an alchemist, so I had a kind of sense of duty that the story should close the curtain as the tale of one alchemist.

Regarding Bos, I heard that originally there was no plan for him to be a main character because of his particular history with Ryza and the others. How did he come to be so deeply involved in the story this time, and as a party member?

HOSOI: The main reason for this is, as you'd expect, that the players have grown to like the character of Bos. We felt that we had to be proactive in reflecting the voices of those players.

The production of "3" and new development technologies

"1" and "2" were released about a year apart, but what was the reason for the two-year interval this time?

HOSOI: We had decided on the schedule of a two-year gap quite a while ago. However, due to the postponement of the release, we ended up taking more time than originally planned. Once again, the character design and actual CG production were very difficult.

SUZUKI: Yes, that's true...

For the production staff, which was more difficult? "1" or this game?

SUZUKI: It has to be "3". Not only was there more volume of content in the main game, but there were also the plans for updates and downloadable content (DLC) even after the game's release.

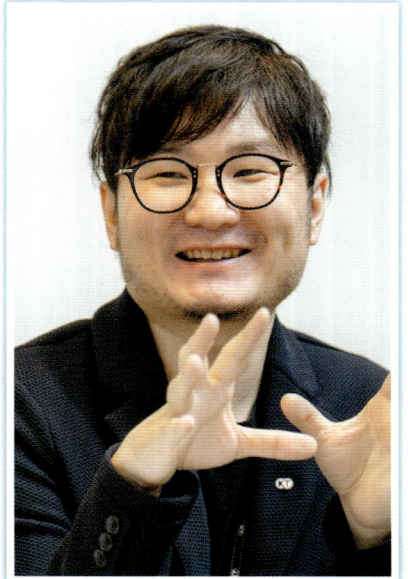

Mr. Suzuki, you've been involved in the "Secret" series consistently since "1", correct?

SUZUKI: Yes, I have.

Something I've felt from the beginning is that I think the process of reproducing Mr. Toridamono's detailed and elaborate designs in CG must be unbelievably difficult.

SUZUKI: Yes, it is. And since Mr. Toridamono was working so hard under a tight schedule, we knew that we couldn't cut corners in the modeling.

Did you receive any requests from the production side not to attach safety pins or other unusual items to Ryza this time as well?

SUZUKI: Our policy is to adhere to the design, so this did end up causing trouble in fine-tuning some of the models.

Mr. Toridamono, from your point of view, since this was the third time around, did you do your designs with the labors of the CG artists in mind?

TORIDAMONO: No, I didn't.

ALL: *laughter*

TORIDAMONO: What I mean is... I'm so focused on my own thing that I don't have the spare flexibility for that. *laughs* I realize in my head that it would be best if I could be conscious of them, but if I think about that too much while drawing, the design ends up shrinking in some ways.

Looking back now, I feel that Mr. Toridamono's character designs are a perfect fit for the new RPG system of the "Secret" series.

HOSOI: I am glad to hear you say so, but I wasn't very conscious of that. It was more important that Mr. Toridamono adjusted his design work to the theme of "summer".

Regarding that summer theme, one of the things that left an impression on me, when you first mentioned it in "1", was that you wanted to be able to better express the contrast between "shadow and light". The visual effects in this game have evolved even further, haven't they?

HOSOI: Yes, I'd say so. In "3," we vastly changed our development systems. For our part, I think we can now present the visuals with confidence.

I see.

HOSOI: When we were developing the first game, the scale wasn't actually that large, and finding ways to present new visual expressions within that scale was a difficult problem. We wanted to give a different impression from the previous "Atelier" games by creating strong expressions of shadows coming from the seasonal theme of "summer" despite it being a fantasy game.

So it was a decisive choice.

HOSOI: Yes. The first time we went in that direction was with "Blue Reflection" which was released in 2017, and we thought about trying to incorporate that into a fantasy game. Basically, we re-used the development engine from that game, but for "3" we rewrote around the shaders *(computer program that processes shadows)* into something completely new.

The difficulties of drawing characters a year later

It's time I asked about character designs. Mr. Toridamono, what kind of concrete character design instructions did you receive for this project at first?

TORIDAMONO: Eh, there was nothing.

HOSOI & SUZUKI: Of course not! *laughter*

TORIDAMONO: Well, there were none. I think the only thing was, "It's about a year after '2'". Wasn't that it?

Really?

TORIDAMONO: Also, I feel like there were more explanations about systems, like that it would be an open field, than about the setting and worldview.

And the new drawings you did were for three characters?

TORIDAMONO: Yes, that's right. Federica, Dian, and Kala... and Bos is basically new too.

It seems that there are quite a few design sketches for new characters, but are there any aspects that make them easier to design than existing characters?

TORIDAMONO: New characters are easier to design because they have no ties to the past. The settings we received were also unique, so it was easy to understand.

It seems like there aren't very many design sketches for the new characters. Are there things about them that make them easier to design than existing characters?

TORIDAMONO: New characters have no ties to the past, and in that respect they're easier to design. The backstories I was given for them were unique too, so it was easy to understand what was required.

SUZUKI: For "2", it was three years after "1", so we were focused on making major changes. But this time we had to have discussions around how much to change as we boiled things down.

Do you and Mr. Suzuki always think about the direction of the character design together?

TORIDAMONO: The three of us, including Mr. Hosoi, discuss it together.

Does Mr. Suzuki also make suggestions, like, "I'd like it to be this certain way"?

SUZUKI: Yes, that's right. In "1", when Mr. Toridamono seemed to be stuck, I made suggestions and made efforts to smooth things out. After all, Mr. Toridamono is the type of person who gets stuck in a quagmire if he stews over things by himself. *laughs*

TORIDAMONO: I'd often ask, "Don't you have anything for me?" *laughs* I was looking for some ideas, so if I was stuck, I would go to him to ask him for help.

Mr. Toridamono, which character did you have the most difficulty with this time?

TORIDAMONO: Hmm. Well, I'd have to say Ryza.

Mr. Hosoi, did you have any wishes regarding Ryza for this game?

Character design progressed with various ideas being put forward.

HOSOI: No, this time it was more like we had discussions and created it as we went along.

TORIDAMONO: This time, it was like we didn't have a clear concept in mind. We kept going back and forth as we progressed, so to be honest, I can't really remember the details of how she ended up the way she did.

HOSOI: I didn't think there would be any obvious changes in just one year after all. That was also part of our aim with her...

What do you mean by that?

HOSOI: If there had been any encounters or incidents that transformed Ryza's image in the one year gap between the previous game and this one, the players would be taken aback, and they'd feel left behind. Therefore, it was our intention to not make any extreme changes.

TORIDAMONO: It is difficult... to make changes when things haven't changed.

Did you ever change Ryza's body balance throughout the trilogy?

TORIDAMONO: We did somewhat. We've made her face sleeker and made her slightly taller. Just a little bit though.

When I asked you earlier, you said that Tao hadn't posed much difficulty before, but this time he seems to have been a real problem.

TORIDAMONO: He was hard work in his own way in "2" as well. This time, we gave the OK once, but then we decided that he wasn't quite right, so we went back to the drawing board. Surprisingly, he took some time.

HOSOI: I wouldn't say "surprisingly". We had already made the CG model. *laughs*

TORIDAMONO: I created trouble for the CG team... I apologize.

SUZUKI: No, no. *laughs*

TORIDAMONO: We wanted to keep an even balance among all the characters. As we made progress with the other characters, we ended up wanting to make slight adjustments to the ones we'd already approved.

Bos is a character that wasn't originally designed by you, Mr. Toridamono. You must have found it awkward to redesign him, didn't you?

TORIDAMONO: It wasn't awkward at all. Nothing of the kind. In fact I enjoyed it.

Don't you feel any difficulty in fiddling with something that was drawn by someone else?

TORIDAMONO: Originally, Bos was an NPC with a simple design. The instructions to attach more individuality to him as a playable character and make him seem like a swordsman were easily understood. It's fun to design a character when you're given a clear direction to aim towards.

Regarding the NPCs, were they designed by in-house staff this time as well?

SUZUKI: Yes. That said, they've been checked by Mr. Toridamono each time. He gives us detailed instructions for alterations, things like, "The hair style shouldn't be like this", etcetera.

It must be hard work for you, Mr. Suzuki, because you have to check not only Mr. Toridamono's characters, but also the NPCs and creatures, etcetera.

SUZUKI: I suppose so. Basically, I do look at them and give instructions for most of the characters.

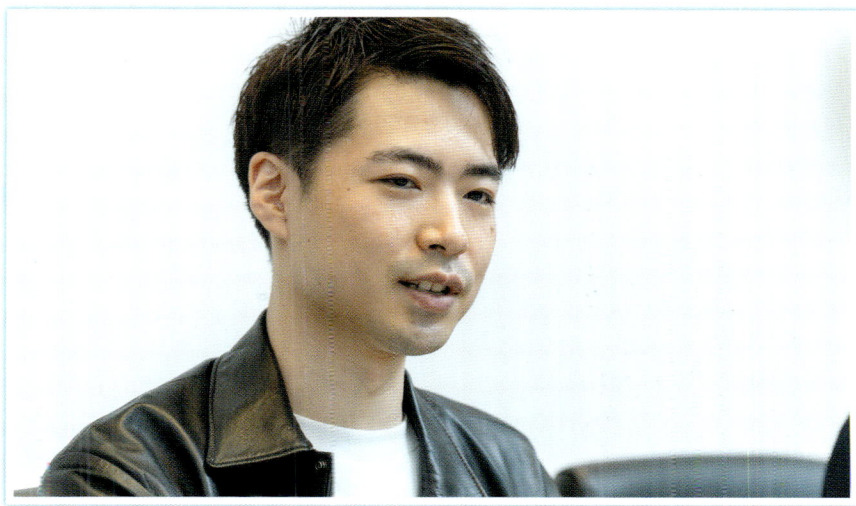

The process of redesigning Bos was enjoyable.

On the production side, were there any aspects of this game that you struggled with?

SUZUKI: I would have to say the field becoming wider. Since it was larger, we had to create more elements to fill it. With the characters, it wasn't that much of a struggle.

Were there any characters that were difficult to do CG modeling for this time?

SUZUKI: By a large margin, Kala.

HOSOI: Suzuki told me almost in tears, "I may have failed with this one". *laughs* The arms got lost and stuck in the clothes so much that it was hard to tell what was going on. The motion wasn't matching either...

TORIDAMONO: No. There were some minor adjustments, like they wanted some cuts and notches in the outfits, but I didn't realize how much you were suffering.

SUZUKI: I endeavored to maintain the original design as much as possible somehow. *laughs*

By the way, there's a design for a mysterious girl in the character design sketches (P.120). Who was this character?

HOSOI: We originally thought it would be interesting to have not only Ryza but also another main character to have double leads, so we had this character drawn

I see.

HOSOI: I thought it seemed interesting and had her designed, but Mr. Toridamono commented, "This seems a little wrong..." And he then added in no uncertain terms, "This is definitely not right. Don't you think it's off? I think something's wrong with it."

TORIDAMONO: But I did sort of start working on it. He said, "I want to include Ryza's cousin or something. What do you think? Give it a shot". To be honest, I had no enthusiasm at all when I drew it.

HOSOI: After a while, I asked him, "How do you feel about it?" and he said, "I really think we should drop it..." I agreed, and decided to give up on the idea.

In the titles of recent years, a lot of costumes have been included as perks or DLC. Are you involved in this, Mr. Toridamono?

SUZUKI: No. For perks and DLC, we receive various requests from the development side, for instance "Japanese style" or "swimsuit", so the CG team carries it out in each instance.

TORIDAMONO: I'm not involved at all. I would love to supervise at least, but I'm too busy working on other illustrations. *laughs*

You have done a great number of one-page illustrations this time as well, including illustrations as special bonuses. You said before that these are easy compared to character design.

TORIDAMONO: Well, they are still a pain. However, most of the illustrations are done with specific instructions, such as "in such and such a pose" or "such and such a scene", so that helps.

Will there be various other drawings for "3" after this?

TORIDAMONO: There are a few left to do, but they're mostly done. Every time around this time is a period when I feel an invigorating sense of accomplishment.

This will be the third time you've drawn for an "Official Visual Collection". What's your state of mind when working on these?

TORIDAMONO: I always enjoy drawing these because I can do them as I myself please. I sometimes cause trouble by proposing quite reckless compositions. *laughs*

Do you give him any instructions in this regard, Mr. Hosoi?

HOSOI: Not at all. As for the visual collection, I leave it all to him.

TORIDAMONO: Every time I do the illustrations, I strive to make them look like "the end of summer" or "after Ryza's adventure is over". This time too, the first rough sketch was not good enough *laughs*.

The other day it was announced that "Atelier Ryza: Ever Darkness & the Secret Hideout" will be adapted into an anime TV series. When did discussions about turning it into an anime begin?

HOSOI: Actually, I had the idea of making an anime adaptation from the time of the first game.

As I became more emotionally invested in the work, I began to state my own opinions.

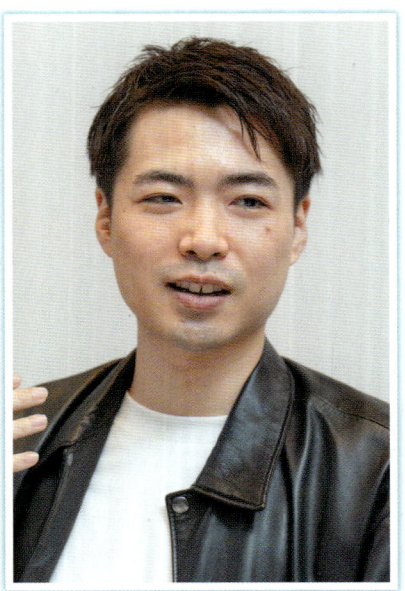

I think your character designs have the right look and would be suitable for animation. How do you feel about it?

TORIDAMONO: Well, I wonder about that. My designs have too many parts, and it would be difficult in animation... I think it would be too much work.

HOSOI: But for the actual animation designs, they didn't reduce the number of parts at all, did they?

TORIDAMONO: Yes, that's right. That's amazing, isn't it? I felt that must have been extremely difficult.

I can't wait. I'm looking forward to the broadcast.

On the passage of time and unforgettable memories made in the past five years

When you include the development period, the "Secret" series has been in production for more than five years. However, during this time the environment surrounding you, Mr. Hosoi and Mr. Toridamono, has also changed greatly, hasn't it?

HOSOI: Yes, that's true.

You in particular, Mr. Hosoi, became the head of the Gust brand and then the managing executive officer of Koei Tecmo Games... It must have been a very turbulent five years, wasn't it?

HOSOI: Actually, the turbulence started a little earlier, but it doesn't feel like it stopped there at all. We were thinking about what we should do towards the future, both as a brand and for the "Atelier" series... I'd have to say that it was during the production of "1" - which as I mentioned was a crossroads - which was the most difficult time.

In your case too, Mr. Toridamono, your participation in these projects must have been a great leap forward these past five years.

TORIDAMONO: Yes. I'm glad I did it. Meeting Mr. Hosoi, Mr. Suzuki, and the others has changed me, and I am very grateful for that.

Mr. Hosoi, how do you think Mr. Toridamono has changed from your point of view?

HOSOI: I think he's gained confidence. In the beginning, your stance was "As a professional, I'll do a proper job on the work I'm given, regardless of whether I like it or not". But gradually, what you wanted to do and what you didn't want to do became apparent in actuality, and you changed your approach so that you were considering these things within yourself as you did the work.

TORIDAMONO: Hm, I suppose so... At some stage that's how it became. As you'd expect, as I became more and more emotionally attached to the work, I began to say, "I'd like to do this and this", or "If I don't do it this way, it won't be right".

HOSOI: I have to say, I think that the contact and interaction with various people was good stimulation for Mr. Toridamono. I think that he came to consider not only design aspects, but also various other perspectives including business aspects.

Did being in charge on the "Secret" series trilogy change the overall reaction to your work from other sources?

TORIDAMONO: Yes, it did. Even people who don't know me well are like, "Oh, I see!" when they find out that I'm Ryza's character designer.

Do you ever get requests, like, "Please make us a Ryza-style character"?

TORIDAMONO: I haven't had anyone ask me directly yet, but I sometimes get the feeling that maybe they're expecting something like that. It's not that easy to produce a design like Ryza's, so I

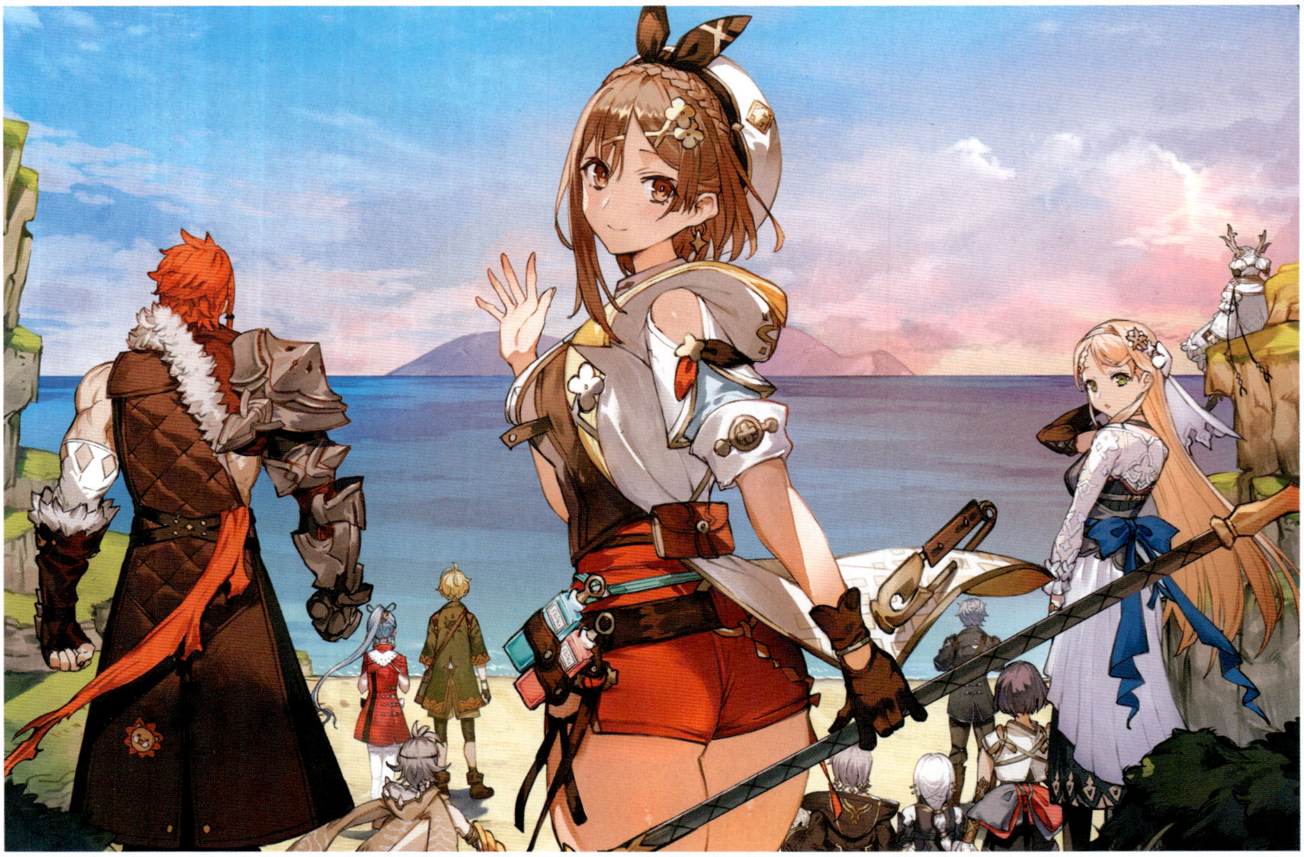

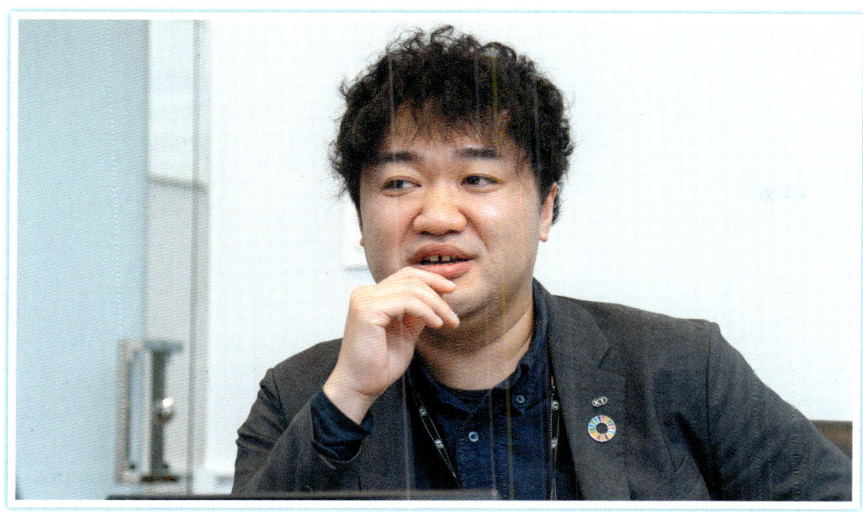

We want to create a new "Atelier" that fuses an even more engaging world view.

worry about whether or not I could fulfill such a request.

Are there any memories that have left a particularly strong impression on any of you over the past five years?

TORIDAMONO: Without a doubt, that would have to be my "quitting at the pork cutlet shop" incident *laughs*.

HOSOI: I talked about this in a previous interview, but in the early stages of "1" he seemed to be really struggling, so I said, "Let's have dinner" and took us to a rather pricy pork cutlet shop.

A pork cutlet shop. I see.

HOSOI: Where was it again? Was it at Tokyo Station or something like that maybe…?

SUZUKI: Yes, that's right.

HOSOI: At that pork cutlet shop, Mr. Toridamono kept saying such weak-kneed things, so I told him, "If you're finding it mentally tough, then you ought to decide whether or not you want to continue here." Then suddenly his chopsticks stopped, and he said, "Well, then, I'll stop." *laughs*

Of course, you meant that to get him fired up, didn't you? You were hoping for an answer like "I'll do my best"…

HOSOI: Yes, that's right. But then it had the opposite effect and he said, "I can't do this anymore…" *laughs*

TORIDAMONO: Well… but even so he was persistent and kept me in check and encouraged me, and that's why I'm here now. That was the biggest "turning point" for me, and that's why it's the most memorable single day for me.

Did you say "I want a break" before the production of this game?

TORIDAMONO: "I want a break" is something I say every time. *laughs* There are long periods of tension on these jobs, so it's impossible to do them without certain intervals. But I never said "I want to quit" again. *laughs*

Future "Atelier" games and new activity from each interviewee

With this game, "Ryza's story" is now complete and the curtain is closed, isn't it?

HOSOI: Yes, that's… where we've come to now.

So, what are your thoughts on future developments in the "Atelier" series?

HOSOI: We've built up a great amount of confidence working on the "Secret" series, and we'd like to create new titles in the future that fuse the "Atelier" series with even more engaging characters, storylines, and other aspects of the world building

Mr. Toridamono, I suppose this will be a parting of the ways for you, but what would you do if another Ryza-related job came your way?

TORIDAMONO: If the offer comes, I'd take it. However, I've been drawing this for a long time, and I feel strongly that I'd like a little bit of distance for now.

Mr. Toridamono, are you curious about "Atelier" games to come from new character designers?

TORIDAMONO: Naturally. I'm looking forward to it.

Do you have any feelings about what kind of thing you might like to do in the future?

TORIDAMONO: In working on Ryza I was given the opportunity to do figure-related design work. That was fun… I'm interested in three-dimensional objects to begin with, so if I have the chance again in the future I'd definitely like to do something like that.

So, lastly, do you have any messages for players who have enjoyed the "Secret" series trilogy?

SUZUKI: The "Secret" series is rare in that it was developed with Ryza as the main character for three games in a row. If this was the first game you played in the "Secret" series for the first time with this title, if you play the previous games as well I think you'll get different emotions from them.

HOSOI: I believe that the fact that we've been able to continue the "Atelier" series for 25 years is the result of the support of passionate players. Thank you truly. Also, for us on the development side, we believe that this is the result of the continued creativity with enthusiasm and hard work of the creators on each game. This is brings us to the end of "Ryza's story", but for our part we can feel pride that we have created the best game of them all at this point. We hope you enjoy it.

Well, then, let's go to you for the conclusion, Mr. Toridamono.

TORIDAMONO: I have nothing but gratitude for all the players who have supported us across these three games. I saw various opinions, but I was encouraged by everyone who continued to support us in a positive way.
Thank you very much.

Thank you very much! We hope to have the opportunity to talk with the three of you again some day.

24 March 2023
Recorded at Koei Tecmo Games Headquarters

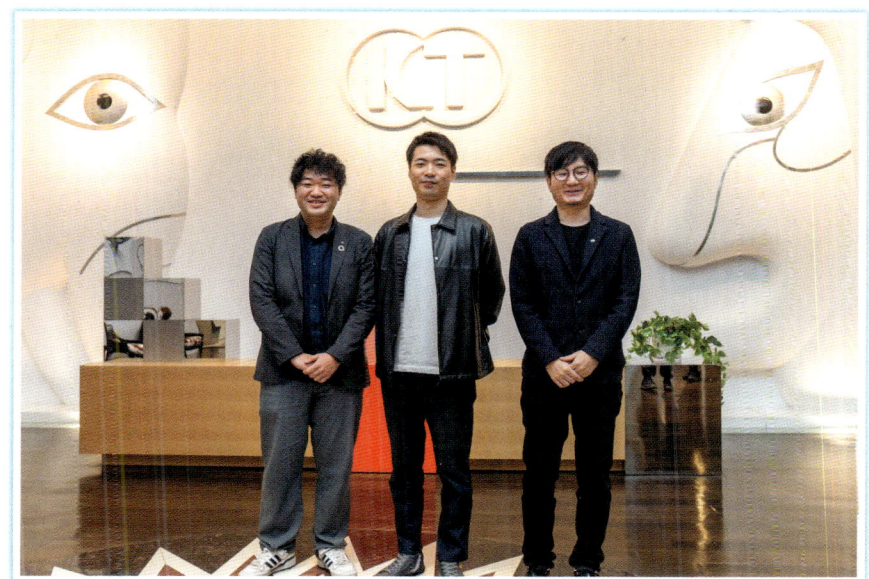

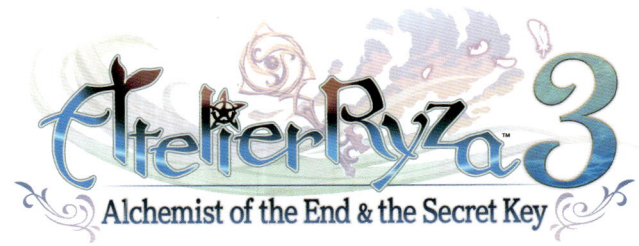

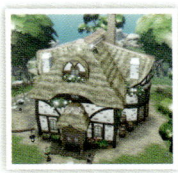

Atelier Ryza 3: Alchemist of the End & the Secret Key
OFFICIAL VISUAL COLLECTION

English Edition

Translation	Kumar Sivasubramanian
Layout & Design Adaptation	Matt Moylan
Associate Editor	M. Chandler

UDON STAFF
Chief of Operations	Erik Ko
Director of Publishing	Matt Moylan
Director of Operations	Marshall Dillon
VP of Business Development	Cory Casoni
Director of Marketing	Meg Maiden
Japanese Liaison	Megumi Cummings

Japanese Edition

Publisher	Shusuke Toyoshima
Editor	Noriyasu Suzuki
Director	Michiko Oishi/Mikio Katai
Editor & Writer	Hiroji Shibano/Michiaki Kataoka
Proofreader	Hiroshi Tokita
Cover Illustrator	Toridamono
Designer	Toshihisa Funaba
Coordinator	Yohei Tatara
Binding	Toshihisa Funaba
Special Thanks	Koei Tecmo Games

RYZA NO ATELIER 3 ~OWARI NO RENKINJUTSUSHI TO HIMITSU NO KAGI~
KOSHIKI VISUAL COLLECTION

©KOEI TECMO GAMES Co., Ltd. All rights reserved.
©2024 KADOKAWA Game Linkage Inc.
All Rights Reserved.

First published in Japan in 2023 by KADOKAWA CORPORATION, Tokyo.
English translation rights arranged with KADOKAWA Game Linkage Inc., Tokyo
through Tuttle-Mori Agency, Inc., Tokyo.

www.UDONentertainment.com

Published by UDON Entertainment Corp.
118 Tower Hill Road, C1, PO Box 20008
Richmond Hill, Ontario, L4K 0K0, Canada

Any similarities to persons living or dead is purely coincidental. No part of this publication may be reproduced, stored in retrieval systems, or transmitted in any form or by any means (electronic, mechanical photocopying, recording, or otherwise) without the prior written permission of the Publisher.

First Printing: November 2024
ISBN: 978-1-77294-366-5

Printed in China